D1713326

The Collected Speeches of Sagoyewatha, or Red Jacket

The Iroquois and Their Neighbors
Christopher Vecsey, *Series Editor*

The Trial of Red Jacket, by John Mix Stanley, 1868. This painting is an imaginative reconstruction of Red Jacket's trial for witchcraft in 1801. With permission from the Buffalo and Erie County Historical Society.

The Collected Speeches of

SAGOYEWATHA,

or

RED JACKET

Edited by Granville Ganter

SYRACUSE UNIVERSITY PRESS

Library of Congress Cataloging-in-Publication Data

Red Jacket (Seneca chief), ca. 1756–1830.
[Speeches]
The collected speeches of Sagoyewatha, or Red Jacket / edited by
Granville Ganter.—1st ed.
p. cm.—(Iroquois and their neighbors)
Includes bibliographical references and index.
ISBN 0-8156-3096-4 (cloth : alk. paper)
1. Red Jacket (Seneca chief), ca. 1756–1830—Oratory.   2. Speeches, addresses, etc.,
Iroquois.   I. Ganter, Granville.   II. Title.   III. Series.
E99.I7.R43 2006
974.7004'9755460092—dc22
2006006449

Contents

Maps

Granville Ganter is an associate professor of English at St. John's University in Queens, New York. His research specializes in early-nineteenth-century oratory. He has written essays on Ralph Waldo Emerson, Frederick Douglass, Daniel Webster, Sarah Josepha Hale, Red Jacket, and the Grateful Dead.

Acknowledgments

I WOULD LIKE TO THANK the American Antiquarian Society for a 2001 Peterson Fellowship that partially supported this research, and the New York Historical Society for a Delmas Fellowship in 2002. A Helaine Newstead Fellowship from the City University of New York Graduate Center funded part of the initial research for this project. The staff at the Buffalo and Erie County Historical Society has been extraordinarily generous and helpful. I am grateful also to the Massachusetts Historical Society, Vassar College Special Collections, the staff at special collections at Penfield Library at SUNY-Oswego, and the sponsors of the Werthheim study at the New York Public Library. I owe a great debt to Christopher Densmore, who shared some of his research with me and provided very useful suggestions. Barbara Mann invited me to write the essay that inaugurated this project, and I am grateful to her for her warm support and advice. I am greatly indebted to my professors at the CUNY Graduate Center: Morris Dickstein, William Kelly, and David Reynolds. Pauline Dowell acted as spiritual advisor with Adobe Illustrator. Marc Bousquet and Maria Farland helped support me with great enthusiasm throughout this project. Most importantly, this book is dedicated to Joseph Wittreich, whose magnanimous friendship and vision have been an inspiration.

Abbreviations

ASPIA	*American State Papers, Indian Affairs*
BECHS	Buffalo and Erie County Historical Society. Buffalo, New York
CNA	Canadian National Archives. Ottawa, Canada
DNA	National Archives. Washington, D.C.
GP	Erastus Granger Papers, Special Collections of Penfield Library, SUNY at Oswego. Oswego, New York
IIDH	*Iroquois Indians: A Documentary History of the Diplomacy of the Six Nations and Their League*
LC	Library of Congress. Washington, D.C.
MHS	Massachusetts Historical Society. Boston, Massachusetts
NYHS	New York Historical Society. New York, New York
NYSA	New York State Archives. Albany, New York
OP	Ogden Family Papers, William Clement Library, University of Michigan. Ann Arbor, Michigan
ORWM	O'Reilly Collection of Western Mementos, New York Historical Society. New York, New York
PP	Pickering Papers, Massachusetts Historical Society. Boston, Massachusetts
WRHS	Western Reserve Historical Society. Cleveland, Ohio

Editorial Method and Sources

THIS EDITION is a complete collection of Red Jacket's political and ceremonial speeches with the exception of council records where he only introduces the main speaker, or affirms the words of a preceding speaker. I have also chosen not to reprint several paragraph-long personal expressions from William Leete Stone's biography, generally rendered as second- or thirdhand information. These records could be called speeches, but they tend to be anecdotal in character and concern personal rather than public business. Several speeches attributed to Red Jacket in the 1770s appear in Governor Blacksnake's memoir, dictated more than seventy years after they occurred (Abler 2005, 50, 55, 163). Although Blacksnake is an important historical authority, his dating of events is sometimes unreliable, and his memory of the wording makes it a problematic source.

Readers need to be aware that these documents are historical artifacts subject to a variety of honest transcription and transmission errors, not the carefully polished texts of a single author who monitored their publication history. Most of the texts from early treaty negotiations were scribbled short-hand in the lap of the interpreter, or hastily copied by the Indian agent as the interpreter spoke.

Because condolences and recapitulations are often left out of council records, the definition of a *speech* in this volume is used broadly. Some of the speeches in this volume are obviously summarized in the words of the recorder who preserved them. Hence, an account of what Sagoyewatha said varies from situation to situation. Some treaty records are explicit attempts to quote exactly. Others begin "Red Jacket spoke in substance the following" or "Red Jacket said that. . . ." In some cases, manuscript documents do not always signal the transition between explicit translation and authorial summary. Some of Sagoyewatha's most dramatic performances, such as his speech at Brownstown in 1810 or his July 1828 speeches during Livingston's inquiry, exist only in chimerical form, part summary, part literal translation. These documents have been formatted as speeches, even though readers are encouraged to be wary. Frequently, a pronoun shift to "I" in the middle of a speech summary indicates that the transcriber is trying to convey an actual speech.

Furthermore, given that translation is implicitly a type of redaction, the question of the length of a speech is also a difficult issue. The speeches presented here are either political or ceremonial remarks of a paragraph or more.

Sagoyewatha's letters and petitions to the state and federal authorities are presented as speeches. Although he was most efficacious as a public speaker, Sagoyewatha was very aware of the power of written text. In the 1810s and 1820s, he often sent effective political petitions, or "memorials," to the state governor and legislature.

The purpose of this text is to provide a readable typescript that also conveys a sense of the manuscript source from which it was taken. To aid readability, extensive technical apparatuses have been minimized. Except for the long eighteenth-century "s," which has been transcribed as a modern "s," original spelling, punctuation, superscription, capitalization, and emphasis from sources have been maintained, but missing letters of contractions have often been supplied in square brackets, at least the first time they appear in a document. Many of the early manuscripts are filled with contractions like "Btn Cn of F," which means "brighten the chain of friendship," making for difficult reading at times. With the exception of footnote numerals, all editorial additions appear in square brackets. Cancellations—which are rarely important in these types of manuscripts—are not included unless they provide significant additional information. Similarly, all insertions are silently included without apparatus (that is, no insertion carets). Editorial comments in italics have occasionally been used to provide supplementary information not contained in the preface to the speech. Page numbers and end-line hyphens in the source documents have been silently deleted, as are manuscript collation keys where the first word of a page is repeated at the end of the previous page.

Consistent spelling was not a great concern of writers of the early republic, especially with Indian names. I have not regularized spelling. The word Allegany appears in many different forms: Alleghany, Allegheny, Allegeny, and so forth. An ear for the general sound of words is helpful: Gs and Ks and Cs are frequently confused (the difference between voiced and unvoiced velar stops), among others. Alternative spellings are cross-indexed in the index.

The transcriptions are roughly formatted as they appear in the source documents. Interpreters and transcribers did not employ standard styles of spacing and paragraphing. Generally, Sagoyewatha spoke in paragraph form, beginning each significant new idea with "Brother." Most transcriptions of Native oratory adopt this paragraphing format. However, this general principle was not always followed by Native speakers, nor was it always followed by interpreters and transcribers. As a result, little significance should be attributed to paragraphs without the word "Brother" in front of them.

Many of the speeches are available in slightly different versions. Although each text poses different editorial questions (is a copied manuscript version more authoritative than an early newsprint document? For what purpose?), I have generally chosen to print the longest variant from the earliest, most trustworthy source extant. In some cases, I am persuaded that government records, pamphlets, or newspapers are more valuable for the purposes of most readers than shorthand council notes, provided that the shorthand versions do not add (or lack) significant information. In any case, alternative sources have been noted.

Of the more than 100 speeches presented here, most come from sources surrounded by corroborated information or from sources about whom something is known. Only very few speeches seem of dubious authenticity. Two speeches are from completely unknown origins: Thomas McKenney's "Sagoyewatha's Death," and "On Separate Races and Religions, ca. 1822." Two others show signs of literary colorization beyond the habits of Sagoyewatha's typical interpreters, even though they may have once been founded on an actual text: "A Variant Text of the Reply to Cram" and "Variant Texts of the Reply to Ogden, 1819." Only two, "In Hartford, c. 1795" and "Insulting the Wyandots and Delawares" seem like they came from James Fenimore Cooper novels.

Two fires have destroyed official records of Sagoyewatha's diplomatic career: a fire in Albany in 1911 burned almost all the records of intercourse with the Six Nations from the early nineteenth century. The majority of documentation of New York State interaction with the Senecas thus comes from books, newspapers, and private collections. Similarly, a fire consumed almost all the records of the secretary of war in November 1800, which destroyed most of the Indian relations archives of 1783–1800.

There are conspicuous absences in the federal records held at the National Archives (DNA). Many of the letters no longer contain their enclosures (which contained speeches and council notes), and many important petitions from the Six Nations were never saved, particularly in the period 1816–30. As Secretary of War Calhoun's letters from the mid-1810s show, he wanted to push the Indians west of the Mississippi, and keeping extensive records of their protests did not serve the government's interests. Thomas McKenney, who was appointed head of the new Office of Indian Affairs in 1824, also kept very few enclosures in his correspondence.

The result is that the lion's share of documents come from newspapers, missionary notes, private collections, and British documents, rather than from U.S. government archives: the Timothy Pickering Papers (MHS, Boston, Massachusetts); the Henry O'Reilly Collection of Western Mementos (NYHS, New York City); Buffalo and Erie County Historical Society (BECHS, Buffalo, New York); the Erastus Granger Papers (SUNY-Oswego, New York). Official British records, which are useful for the period of 1792–1805, include the John G. Simcoe Papers (copies of originals held in London at the University of Toronto, and the Ontario Archives, Toronto); and the William Claus papers (Canadian National Archives, Ottawa). Simcoe was British lieutenant governor of Upper Canada, and Claus rose from Indian agent to British deputy superintendent of Indian affairs.

Because of its length, this book is intended as a reference tool rather than a text to be read from beginning to end. Some of the earliest records may be of limited interest to lay readers. Those looking for literary pyrotechnics can page to the sections after 1815. Some remarkable earlier speeches include "Diplomacy in Philadelphia, 1792," "Council at Fort Niagara, 1796," "To Rev. Elkanah Holmes," in 1800 and 1803, "In Washington, 1801," "To Chapin, 1801," and "Defense of Stiff-Armed George, 1802." Sagoyewatha's most famous speeches, reprinted many times over during the nineteenth century, are the "Reply to Rev. Jacob Cram, 1805," and the replies to Alexander and Richardson in 1811.

Supplementary material for these speeches, which have been summarized in this volume to conserve space, can be obtained at a website maintained by the editor: http://facpub.stjohns.edu/~ganterg/redjacket/home.htm. These texts include speeches of Red Jacket's interlocutors in council, as well as a November 15, 1822, speech of Sagoyewatha. In it he defends his alcohol use as a "private" matter; the text was located as this manuscript went to press.

Introduction

IN JULY OF 1819, the Ogden Land Company found that its latest attempt to buy more Seneca land had been thwarted by an old opponent, the Seneca orator, Shay-gó-ye-wátha, or as he was also known, Red Jacket (ca. 1758–1830).[1] As he described the reasons why the Senecas would not sell their lands, Sagoyewatha pointed to a white man present who had become wealthy and enormously fat working for the Holland Land Company, Joseph Ellicott. He told his audience, "Look at that man . . . he has plenty of land: if you want to buy, apply to him." Responding to the Ogden Company's claim that it had spent large amounts of money trying to buy Indian lands, the orator admitted that the land company's financial decisions had been "unfortunate." Criticizing David Ogden's claim of jurisdiction over Indian lands, Sagoyewatha contemptuously noted that perhaps if the owner of their company "had come down from heaven with the flesh on his bones, as he now is, and . . . the Heavenly Father had given him a title, we might believe him." Sagoyewatha also declared that President Monroe must have been "disordered in his mind" when he proposed that the Senecas would sell all their reservations and move to Allegany. As he concluded his speech, Red Jacket reminded Ogden that when he had been approached by land buyers earlier, he told them that the Senecas would never sell their lands while he lived. Drawing himself up before the Americans, Sagoyewatha said, "You have come, but I am living. See me before you."

Red Jacket's performance at this council illustrates many of the techniques that made him one the most famous Native orators of the nineteenth

1. Because Sagoyewatha was most commonly known in English as Red Jacket, and his family was comfortable enough with the English name that his children took "Jacket" as their surname, this text will refer to Sagoyewatha by both names interchangeably. Other Native names will appear primarily in their English forms, but I have also provided phonetic renderings of their Native names both in the index and glossary. See Densmore for questions over the pronunciation and meaning of Sagoyewatha's name (1999, 18). Wallace Chafe (1963, 1967) has produced an orthographic system for Seneca that compensates for the shortcomings of English transcriptions. I will also refer to the confederacy of the Longhouse, or the Iroquois, as the Haudenosaunee (roughly pronounced, Oh-Den-o-Show-Nee) or Six Nations.

century. He was confrontational, sarcastic, and knew how to tell a joke. A leading spokesman for the Senecas from 1790 to his death in 1830, Sagoyewatha was best known for his opposition to Christian missionaries and Native land sales. In addition to his wit, he was also known for his compelling accounts of North American history from a Native point of view (Konkle 2004).

There are many speeches that purport to be translations of Sagoyewatha's words, but literary critics have been rightly skeptical of such texts. Like Logan's famous speech, whose transmission history appears as unlikely as it is unverifiable (Seeber 1947), other well-known eighteenth- and nineteenth-century Native American speeches, such as those of Tecumseh, pose difficult questions about the reliability of their origins and transmission (Klinck 1961). As Albert Furtwangler has demonstrated in his study of Chief Seattle's famous speech of the mid-1850s, the provenance and reliability of Seattle's speech disintegrates under scholarly investigation. Furthermore, as literary scholars such as David Murray and Eric Cheyfitz have pointed out, the act of translation intrinsically changes Indian texts, tending to illustrate the translator's ideas more than the original speaker's.

Of similar anthropological concern is the attempt to *translate* texts from an oral culture to a literate one (Todorov 1984; Krupat 1992, esp. 6, 176–99). As scholars such as Walter Ong have noted, the methods of preserving meaning in an oral culture are profoundly different from those of a literate culture. For example, the printed text of a ritual song does not carry with it the performance practices, specific circumstances, and interpersonal relationships that give ritual songs and folk stories their cultural value.

Fortunately, Red Jacket's treaty and council speeches—the contents of this volume—are very different from ritual oratory. Sagoyewatha usually had well-known and highly skilled interpreters; the occasions of most of his speeches were well documented; and finally, there are a large number of his speech texts whose tone and content compare favorably with each other when collated. His job as an ambassador also minimizes the interpretive problems posed by such culturally embedded oral literatures as myths and songs—those literatures framed by ancient and textually unavailable social practices. One of the reasons Red Jacket was such a formidable political orator was because he knew how to vocalize his nation's views in ways that his Euro-American auditors would understand.

Furthermore, despite philosophical anxiety about the justice of translation, translation was a common part of pan-Indian political life. Interpreters were always used to allow distant Indian nations to speak to each other. Native representatives developed a number of techniques to minimize misunderstandings, such as repeating the ideas of previous speakers before responding to them. Extensive contact with the various European nations in North America had occurred for several hundred years before Red Jacket was born. Trained as a Seneca orator and Anglo-Native message runner from his youth, Sagoyewatha grew up expecting that his words would be translated into English.

Translation worked according to the unique demands of the speech and the event. During long speeches, interpreters would alternate paragraphs or sentences with the speaker, or sometimes wait for the speaker's permission (Simcoe 1923, 260; Phillips 1966, 189). Some speeches would be translated all at once, with the interpreter referring to shorthand notes. Using the alternation method at Canandaigua in 1794, for instance, Sagoyewatha became angry that the U.S. commissioner Timothy Pickering was busy copying the speech from the words of the interpreter. Sagoyewatha would not continue until Pickering put down his pen to look at him as he spoke.

The repetition of the previous speaker's ideas generally composed the beginning of council speeches, a confirmation process that is usually deleted from the Anglo records of council proceedings. Also, most political councils were prefaced by condolence ceremonies, which acknowledged the difficulties of travel, circumstance, or death that may have occurred prior to the council. Many speech records begin with the phrase "after the usual ceremonies &c . . ."[2]

Sagoyewatha's speeches are even more interesting in consideration of the fact that most of his interpreters lived with the Senecas. Two of Sagoyewatha's principal translators, Jasper Parrish and Horatio Jones, were fluent in English and Seneca. They had both been captured in their teens by the Senecas and chose to live close to them after they had the opportunity to leave (for their biographies and references, see glossary). Although Jones and Parrish were both corrupted by the Holland and Ogden land companies, and they eventually became Sagoyewatha's political opponents, their translations were seldom faulted by the Senecas.

---

2. Another element of the speech context sometimes left out of council records is reference to wampum exchange. Wampum is usually composed of shell fragments threaded onto strings and woven into ornate belts. In a political context, the presentation of white wampum belts accompanying a speech generally signifies peace; black refers to hostility; belts of mixed color and pattern mean what they did when presented—their pattern simply identifies them for future reference. Strings are thinner than belts and used for occasions of less importance, or when belts are scarce (for an eighteenth-century English understanding of wampum, see Colden 1994; for a more comprehensive view of New York Native practices and wampum, see Beauchamp 1978; Snyderman 1954).

A few historians of Red Jacket's day complained that his interpreters were illiterate and their translations were only faint copies of the originals (Stone 1841, 39–40; McKenney and Hall 1836, 1:2–12). Some of the early council notes written by Jasper Parrish are poorly spelled and ungrammatical (see, for example, in this volume the speeches of April 28–29, 1795). These historians, however, were also voicing their dismay that Jones and Parrish did not try to dress up Native expression to fit the romanticized expectations that literary audiences had for Indian speech. By the late 1810s, Sagoyewatha himself knew English well enough to joke in the language (Bryant 1879, 353–54; Stone 1841, 336–51). He knew if he was being mistranslated, and he chose his interpreters according to his taste (Bryant 1879, 371). He continued to speak publically in Seneca, however, to affirm his nation's independence from the United States (Stone 1841, 358–59).

In addition to his political responsibilities, Sagoyewatha clearly enjoyed working with language. His is well known to have said about himself: "I am an orator!—I was born an Orator!" (Stone 1841, 1). The aesthetic elements of his speeches were an important part of his reputation among his Native peers as well as with Euro-Americans. Although it is difficult to make claims about Sagoyewatha's literary style based upon translations of his words, he was clearly a gifted ironist. A comprehensive review of his speeches shows that Sagoyewatha tended to use language in complex ways that most people—of European origin or Native—do not. Sometimes Red Jacket would adopt the humble tones of a subjugated people or alternatively the defiant voice of a sovereign nation. These passages from his speeches show a speaker in full command of his subject and sensitive to the nuances of the ideas he presents. At the same time, he would often take unexpected turns in the middle of such performances, abruptly juxtaposing one role against another. The effect is riveting. These ironized moments seem to be the reason why his speeches were heralded with such respect among his contemporaries. Although John Heckewelder pointed out early in the nineteenth century that the Haudenosaunees enjoyed a long tradition of literary wit in their diplomacy, Sagoyewatha was a poet among politicians (1819, 138–42).

A representative anecdote of the disorienting effects of Sagoyewatha's rhetoric is evident in a letter from David Ogden (principal owner of the Ogden Land Company) to Secretary of War John Calhoun in 1822. Complaining of Sagoyewatha's increasingly successful opposition to the missionary presence on Indian land, Ogden wrote that Red Jacket "lays it down as a principle, that no Indian Nation has ever adopted Civilization, without becoming merged, in the White population, & losing their national Character and respectability. He asserts that an Indian is incapable individually of providing for himself, or of taking care of his Property, & he Cites himself as an Instance of this" (Calhoun 1969–74, 7:104). Red Jacket enjoyed this unorthodox manipulation of point of view, at first presenting himself as an exotic foreigner and then deftly reframing that pose from a different perspective (see, for example, similar comments to Moses Cleaveland in 1796; at Big Tree in 1797; to Alexander and Richardson in 1811; to David Ogden in 1819). Like explanations of Mark Twain's wit, however, the semantic complexity of such a remark might take several paragraphs to explain and yet not do justice to its striking economy.

Because council speeches are typically understood in the context of the council, this edition features several significant differences from previous anthologies of Indian oratory. In addition to providing information about the provenances of speeches from a single Native American orator's career, this edition includes as many before-and-after speeches by Natives and whites in dialogue with Red Jacket, particularly where these interactions have been previously available only in manuscript form (for example, see "Reply to David Ogden, 1819").[3] To save space, summaries of council speeches and references to easily obtained texts are also employed.

Life in Brief

Red Jacket's birth name was Otetiani ("Always Ready"). According to Seneca anthropologist Arthur C. Parker, he was born to a Seneca mother of the Wolf clan named Ah-wey-ne-yonh ("Drooping Flower" or "Blue Flower") (Parker 1943, 528). His father was Thadahwahnyeh, a Cayuga of the Turtle clan (Parker 1998, 3). There are a number of rival stories about the date and location of his birth, but Christopher Densmore argues that he was probably born in 1758 on the west side of Cayuga lake, near either Geneva or Canoga. He was drawn to public speaking as a child and was rumored to practice the art by himself in the woods (Parker 1998, 43), although this story seems fanciful. As was customary, upon his maturity he was given a new name, Sagoyewatha (roughly pronounced, Shay-gó-ye-wátha or Say-go-ye-wat-ha), which has been variously translated as "disturber of dreams," "keeper awake," "he keeps

---

3. Most popular collections of Native oratory, such as Verderwerth's 1971 *Indian Oratory*, provide little discussion of speech provenance and translation. Scholarly collections of a single Native American orator's speeches are rare. See, for example, Carl Klinck's valuable *Tecumseh: Fact and Fiction in Early Records* (1961). Klinck surveys a number of Tecumseh speeches, sorting documented speeches from folklore but supplies little information about Tecumseh's interpreters.

us awake," or "he wakes them up early" (Morgan 1990, 70–71, 90; Morris 1844, 12; Abler 2005, 19; Densmore 1999, 18).

Red Jacket served as a message runner for the British during the Revolutionary War. For this work, he was awarded a red jacket, from which his English name derived. By the 1790s, he was as well known by his English name as by his Seneca name. Shortly after the war, Sagoyewatha was appointed as a chief, but what kind of chief has never been clear.[4] In the early years of his political work among the Senecas, he primarily convened councils with condolence speeches and introduced senior chiefs. He also acted as a speaker for the clan mothers, charged with conveying their deliberations to councils of sachems and warriors. When he dictated his memoirs at the end of his life, Governor Blacksnake reported that Red Jacket spoke in the mid-1770s at several councils with the United States alongside Cornplanter, a leading Seneca chief. However, as with his report of Sagoyewatha's attendance at Fort Stanwix in 1784, Blacksnake's memory of these events has been drawn into question (Manley 1932; Abler 2005, 37–55, 74, 163; Densmore 1999, 11–18).

Although distinguished for his verbal abilities during and after the Revolution, he also earned a reputation for cowardice that followed him for many years afterward. Cornplanter claimed that Red Jacket fled from the Battle of Newtown in 1779. Joseph Brant was fond of retelling a story that Red Jacket and a friend smeared the blood of slaughtered cattle on their swords to claim that they had been in battle (Stone 1841, 20n; Abler 2005, 109; Blacksnake n.d., 36). As a result, Brant named him Cowkiller, an unflattering name by which he was designated in most British council records of the 1790s and 1800s. Fighting on the American side during the War of 1812, however, Red Jacket redeemed his martial reputation with his conduct at the battle of Chippewa.

Sagoyewatha was an active participant at the well-publicized U.S.–Six Nations councils of Tioga Point and Newtown in 1790 and 1791. He served

---

4. Seneca government is divided into three parts: the clan mothers, who appoint sachems and decide issues of land possession; the warrior chiefs who hunt and supervise martial affairs; and the sachems who deliberate over civil issues (see Morgan 1990, 90). The warriors typically hold the least authority in civil affairs. In 1844, Thomas Morris, who knew Sagoyewatha, wrote that because of his family pedigree, Sagoyewatha was not entitled to a sachemship (one of forty-nine male leaders of the Six Nations, generally appointed on a hereditary basis (Morris 1844, 9). Nor, apparently, was he ever designated as a "pine tree chief," a lesser order of chiefs or warriors appointed by the Senecas according to their merit. Densmore suggests that he may have been a sub-sachem, an assistant sachem (1999, 21). Whatever his actual rank, Sagoyewatha is usually described as a sachem in council records from the 1790s onwards.

among the leading spokesmen of a Seneca deputation meeting George Washington in Philadelphia in 1792. While in Philadelphia, Red Jacket was given a large chest medal by the president that he wore proudly for the rest of his life (several other chiefs were also given medals). Governor Blacksnake reports that he and Sagoyewatha went rifle shopping with President Washington later that year at Fort Pitt prior to the council of the Glaize (Abler 2005, 192). Sagoyewatha was a principal negotiator at the 1794 Treaty of Canandaigua, where the Seneca secured nearly four million acres of land for perpetuity.

The Six Nations found themselves in great economic poverty in the late 1790s, and they sold land to secure annuities. In 1797, Sagoyewatha was a principal speaker at the Treaty of Big Tree, where the Senecas sold much of the land guaranteed to them by the Treaty of Canandaigua. At this famous council, Red Jacket was among a group of sachems who opposed the sale, but once the warriors and clan mothers overruled the decision of the sachems, Red Jacket successfully argued to double the proposed size of the Buffalo Creek reservation. Because of this apparent change in attitude, the historian William Leete Stone charged him with duplicitous behavior. The allegation of demagoguery was supported by his Indian political rivals, such as Joseph Brant, but it has little evidence behind it (see Densmore 1999, 53; Ganter 2000).

Sagoyewatha also became famous for two oratorical performances around 1800. The first was his courtroom defense of Stiff-Armed George, who was accused of murdering a white man. Sagoyewatha's catalogue of injustices recently committed by the whites was so compelling that George was pardoned after he was convicted. This speech was reprinted nationally, in part because Sagoyewatha criticized the new Jefferson administration for not reappointing their Indian agent. The second event is poorly documented, but it is possible that the Seneca prophet Handsome Lake accused Sagoyewatha of witchcraft in 1801.[5] The story, as told by DeWitt Clinton in 1811, is that Red Jacket spoke for three hours and successfully acquitted himself of the charges (Densmore 1999, 57–59).

During the first decade of 1800, Sagoyewatha gained his reputation as an opponent of Christianity. The Buffalo Creek Senecas were subject to the visits of several missionaries who came ostensibly to open a school for Indian children, but who also came as religious evangelists. The Senecas initially put up with the visitors in compliance with the assimilationist policies of the United States. Many of the Senecas also genuinely wanted their children to

---

5. See glossary for a brief biography of Handsome Lake.

learn how to write and farm. Greatly influenced by Quaker agricultural education at his home on the Allegany reservation, Handsome Lake exhorted his
peers to learn better agricultural skills (Wallace 1971, 1972; Jackson 1952,
1957; Philips 1956). Observing that the consequence of missionary company
on Indian lands resulted in land sales, Sagoyewatha began to denounce the
missionaries' presence. His public rebukes of Christian missionaries in 1805
and 1811 are among his most famous speeches. The private journals of the
missionaries who lived with the Senecas report that even when Sagoyewatha
met them on the road with a smile, he was often working behind their backs to
remove them from the reservation (Cumming 1979; T. Harris 1903, 342–45).

By the end of the War of 1812, the Senecas lived on ten reservations to-
taling about 200,000 acres. They were beset by land companies, the threat of
government removal, and increased Christian conversion on the reservations.
By 1819, the principal Seneca chiefs, Young King and Captain Pollard, had
become Christian. After the conversion of two of his sons in 1818 (*Niagara
Patriot*, December 29, 1818), Sagoyewatha allied with the so-called Pagan
party and he began to stridently condemn missionary presence and land sales
(Densmore 1999, 103; Howland 1903, 136). Every year, he and other traditionalist chiefs lobbied the state legislature and federal government on behalf
of the Senecas. He succeeded in passing a law which prohibited missionaries
living on native lands from 1821 to 1824.

Red Jacket spent the 1820s denouncing the corrupt practices of the
Ogden Land Company and opposing a proposed removal to Green Bay (Horsman 1999). Unfortunately, the Ogden Company succeeded in buying large
portions of the Seneca lands in August 1826. Red Jacket traveled to Washington to overturn the sale without success. Rumors circulated that he was becoming discouraged and drinking too much (see the narrative of John
Breckenridge in Stone 1841, 336–51). Following the conversion of his wife to
Christianity in 1827, he left her for six months, but finding himself still unhappy, he came back to her promising not to complain about her religion. At
the same time, the secretary of Indian affairs, Thomas McKenney, convinced
the Christian chiefs to depose Red Jacket as a troublemaker, which they did in
1827. A year later, after having finally achieved federal acknowledgment of
Ogden's fraudulent purchase, Red Jacket was reinstated as a chief in July 1828.
Unfortunately, however, even though Sagoyewatha's remonstrances were successful in keeping the federal legislature from ratifying the Ogden purchase, it
stood until the Seneca land sale of 1838 rendered it a dead issue.

During his political battles with the Christian Senecas, in both 1828
and 1829, Red Jacket financed costly trips to Washington by giving public

speeches and performances (Bryant 1879, 353–54). In the spring of 1829, Red Jacket spoke from Boston to Philadelphia. Assisted by interpreters James and Henry Johnson, he usually spoke at atheneums and museums for about twenty-five cents admission, sometimes accompanied by Indian dancers.[6]

Just before he died of cholera morbus on January 20, 1830, Sagoyewatha was brokering a council of reconciliation between the Pagan and Christian parties (Stone 1841, 392). Concerning his final wishes, there are conflicting stories about whether he wanted to be buried according to Indian tradition (McKenney and Hall 1836, 1:12) or with a missionary present (*Red Jacket* 1885, 65; Stone 1841, 393). It is possible that he said both things. According to Anna Johnson Miller, who knew Red Jacket's favorite step-child, Ruth Stevenson, all of Red Jacket's blood children died without issue (*Red Jacket* 1885, 65; Miller 1855, 189–90). However, one direct descendant, John Jacket, may have been alive when Sagoyewatha's bones were reinterred at Buffalo's Forest Lawn Cemetery in 1884 (Densmore 1999, 123).

Historical Context

There are four principal biographies of Sagoyewatha. The first, by William Leete Stone, was published in 1841. It contains a wealth of primary and anecdotal information because Stone was able to interview and correspond with many people who knew Red Jacket. More importantly, Stone collected and reprinted as many of Red Jacket's speeches as he could obtain, thinking that

---

6. Sagoyewatha had experimented with giving public speeches for money in New York City and Albany on his return from Washington, D.C., in April 1828 (*Albany Argus*, April 15, 1828). Orlando Allen remarked that Red Jacket was broke and performed these political treks on sheer willpower. Allen recalled meeting Sagoyewatha and his interpreter as they walked home in the mud from Albany in 1828 because they had no money for the horse-stage (Bryant 1879, 353–54). Red Jacket's January–April 1829 tour shocked his Christian peers at Buffalo Creek, who disowned his conduct in a letter to President Jackson on January 15, 1829: "We thought it proper to inform you that one of our old men by the name of Red Jacket has left us recently and proceeded east and probably will go to Washington as usual before he returns. He and his interpreter, we are grieved to say, left us with an impression that they had attached themselves to a company of your theater people: calculating as we understand to exhibit themselves, to gratify the curious among our brethren the Whites. Father, we are grieved to think that any of our old men should stoop so *low* as this. Bad and disgraceful to us, as this appears, we sincerely hope that while absent he may not be engaged in anything worse. We sincerely desire that you be informed that he is altogether unauthorized by us—and that whatever he shall either do or say at the seat of government is altogether without *our* sanction" ("Letters Received by the Office of Indian Affairs, 1824–1881," M-234, DNA microfilm, roll 808, 208–9). Newspaper notices of his tour include *Albany Argus*, January 5 and February 19, 1829; *New York Commercial Advertiser*, January 21 and March 6, 1829.

future generations of historians would benefit more from original documents than historians' glosses of them (1866, vii). Stone's versions compare very well with document sources. He occasionally changed a preposition or inserted periods for clarity, but he did not dress up the vocabulary. The major drawback of Stone's biography is that he accepted the opinions of Red Jacket's opponents, Thomas Morris and Joseph Brant, both of whom were invested in protecting their own reputations. Niles Hubbard's 1886 biography largely reprints Stone's material without Stone's allegations of demagoguery and alcoholism. There were several other books published on Red Jacket at the end of the nineteenth century, based on the memories of a passing generation of witnesses. They contain many interesting anecdotes about Red Jacket, but their basis in fact is difficult to assess (Miller 1855; Conover 1884; Seelye and Eggleston 1879; *Red Jacket* 1885; Pollard 1903). Arthur C. Parker's 1952 biography is important for its sources in Seneca oral tradition, but it seems to be written as a children's book, not an academic history. The best biography is Christopher Densmore's, which avoids the demonization and hagiography of the earlier works, and which puts dates and places to some of the events Stone did not document.

Readers interested in the general historical situation of the Senecas during Sagoyewatha's life may want to consult Thomas Abler's concise introduction to *Chainbreaker: The Revolutionary War Memoirs of Governor Blacksnake* (an excellent overview of Seneca politics in the early national period); Anthony Wallace's *Death and Rebirth of the Seneca* (very good on Handsome Lake's religion and Seneca culture); Laurence Hauptman's *Conspiracy of Interests* (a study of land sales of the 1810s and 1820s) and Isabel Kelsay's biography *Joseph Brant, 1743–1807: Man of Two Worlds* (detailed discussion of British-U.S. affairs during the 1790s). Background histories of the Haudenosaunee during the seventeenth and eighteenth centuries include Francis Jennings's *Ambiguous Iroquois Empire* and David Richter's *Ordeal of the Longhouse*. For the Senecas in the Revolution and the War of 1812, see Barbara Graymont's *The Iroquois in the American Revolution* and Carl Benn's *The Iroquois in the War of 1812*.

One final word about historiography. Even sympathetic historians, such as Arthur C. Parker, have characterized Red Jacket as the "Last of the Senecas," an old soldier fighting for a lost cause (1998; for lost-cause rhetoric, see Dippie 1984; Gallagher and Nolan 2000). As the field of ethnohistory has taught us, this retrospective, winner-takes-all view can block an appreciation for Red Jacket's formidable record of diplomatic victories with the United States (see Axtell 1985; White 1991). Sagoyewatha's faith in his ability to persuade people at a public council was not quixotic nor in vain. Given the economic and political forces against the Senecas in the early national period, their efficacy with councils, petitions, and lobbying was impressive. The 1794 Treaty of Canandaigua has been used as a legal landmark for two hundred years after its signing. Using words as his primary tools, it is a wonder Sagoyewatha was able to accomplish so much.

Map 1. Six Nations regional geography.

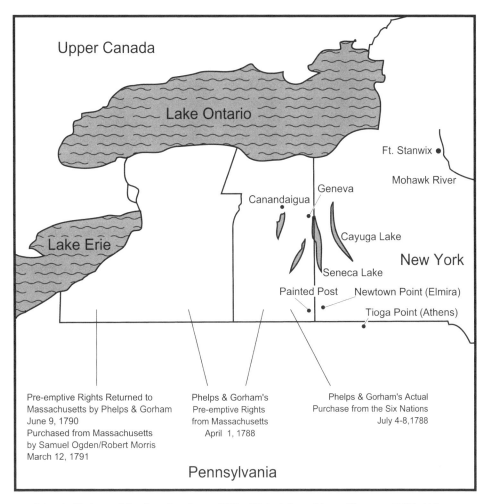

Upper Canada

Lake Ontario

Ft. Stanwix ●

Mohawk River

Geneva

Canandaigua

Cayuga Lake

Lake Erie

New York

Seneca Lake

Painted Post   Newtown Point (Elmira)

Tioga Point (Athens)

Pre-emptive Rights Returned to
Massachusetts by Phelps & Gorham
June 9, 1790
Purchased from Massachusetts
by Samuel Ogden/Robert Morris
March 12, 1791

Phelps & Gorham's
Pre-emptive Rights
from Massachusetts
April 1, 1788

Phelps & Gorham's Actual
Purchase from the Six Nations
July 4-8,1788

Pennsylvania

Map 2. Phelps and Gorham Purchase, 1788–1791. Adapted from Chernow 1977, 198.

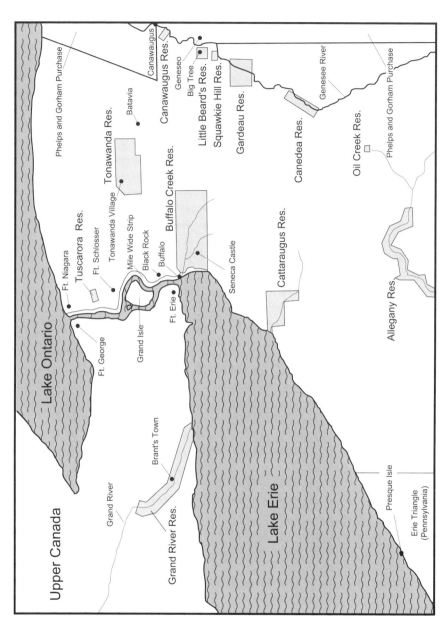

Map 3. Big Tree Purchase, 1797. Includes Tuscarora reservation (1798) and Grand River (1784). Adapted from Holland Land Company Map, 1804. Archives of the Holland Land Company, microfilm, reel 28 of 202.

Map 4. Connecticut Western Reserve, Ohio, 1798. Adapted from map by Seth Pease, surveyor for the Connecticut Company, 1798, in Rose 1950, 24.

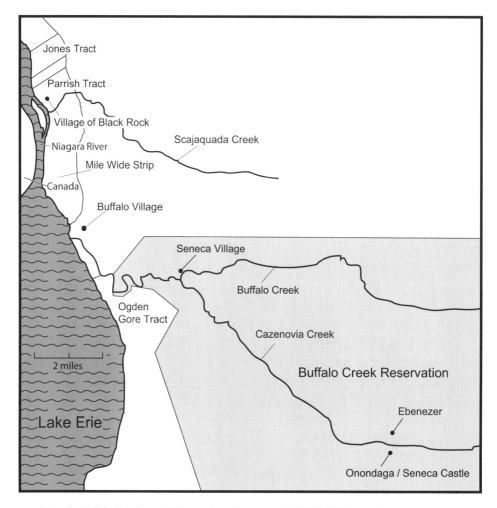

Map 5. Buffalo Creek, ca. 1801. Adapted from map in Hill 1923, 1:84–89.
(Ebenezer and Black Rock were not incorporated until the 1830s.)

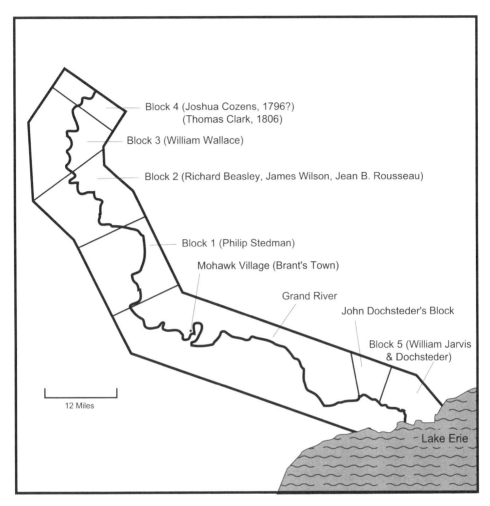

Map 6. Grand River, ca. 1798. Adapted from maps in Johnson 1964, figs. 2 and 3.

The Collected Speeches of Sagoyewatha, or Red Jacket

The Council of Tioga Point

NOVEMBER 15–24, 1790

THE COUNCIL OF TIOGA POINT, held at the confluence of the Chemung and Susquehanna rivers (present-day Athens, Pennsylvania; see map 2), was an attempt to improve deteriorating relations with the western Indians, particularly the Miamis, who were urging a pan-Indian confederacy to resist U.S. expansion (Phillips 1966; Downes 1940). Following the murder of two Seneca traders near Pine Creek, Pennsylvania, on June 27, 1790, by whites, the Senecas requested a council, complaining that the "chain of friendship" was growing rusty.[1] The federal government appointed Timothy Pickering, a Revolutionary supply officer who was seeking political advancement, to call a council immediately (Phillips 1966, 164).

With a few significant exceptions, it was primarily Senecas who attended Tioga. The leading chiefs were Farmer's Brother, Young King, Little Billy, Little Beard, Big Tree, and Sagoyewatha. Other important chiefs were Good Peter (Oneida) and Hendrick Aupaumut (Stockbridge). Fish Carrier, a senior Cayuga chief, was supposed to attend but never arrived.

Among the whites present at Tioga were Colonel William Wilson, appointed to represent the governor of Pennsylvania, and Samuel Street, a Buffalo trader who the Indians trusted. Other observers included John Parrish, a Quaker, and General Israel Chapin Sr., a Revolutionary War officer who shortly afterward became superintendent to the Six Nations. Pickering's interpreters were Joseph Smith and Jasper Parrish. As the Senecas themselves declare, they were both able translators. During negotiations, the Indians bestowed the name Con-ne-sauty ("Sunny-side-of-a-hill") on Pickering, a term with which he occasionally identifies himself in his own treaty notes.

After discussion of the murders, the council moved to Haudenosaunee complaints about the Phelps-Gorham Purchase (see map 2). In July 1788,

---

1. See Jennings (1984) for the significance of the term "chain of friendship" and its relationship to the Haudenosaunee "covenant chain," esp. 34–46, 145–71, 373–74.

Oliver Phelps and Nathaniel Gorham met the Six Nations at Buffalo Creek and bought the central third of western New York state, roughly between Geneva and Geneseo, for $5,000 and a $500 annuity. As Red Jacket notes below, the Indians thought the agreed selling price was $10,000, and they felt cheated the following spring when the rest of the money was not forthcoming. They also disputed the northwestern boundaries. At Tioga, the Haudenosaunees managed to convince Pickering that their complaints merited investigation, but Pickering was later unable to find any proof to support their claim (Simcoe 1923, 5:4–5).

For good backgrounds on Tioga, see Campisi (1988), Campisi and Starna (1995), and especially Phillips (1966). For the complex history of the Phelps-Gorham Purchase, see Turner (1850), Osgood (1892), Hauptman (1999), Chernow (1977), Wandell (1942), Humphrey (1927).

With a few exceptions, these transcriptions are from the Pickering Papers, most of which are copies of his rough notes taken during the councils. In these texts, Pickering frequently uses a typographical symbol for a new paragraph (¶), which is reproduced here. Sagoyewatha's well-known speech on November 23 appears in the official government version (based on a clean version supplied by Pickering) published in the *American State Papers, Indian Affairs* (*ASPIA*). The first document, the Senecas's reply to the governor of Pennsylvania, held at the New York Historical Society, was chosen because it is slightly longer than the version in the Pickering Papers.

The following is the Six Nations' letter of response to Timothy Pickering's invitation to the council. It was signed by three major war chiefs, two of whom sometimes spoke at treaties during this period (Little Billy and Little Beard). Sagoyewatha's signature among them, however, suggests his role as a speaker of the message on behalf of the other chiefs. Otherwise, there is little reason he would have signed.

To the Governor and Council of Pennsylvania.

Brothers,

We received your letter and verbal message on the 7th of this Ins[tan]ᵗ.— Brothers we are very sorry to hear of the Murder of Two of our people committed on pine creek which you say you are much concerned for—Brothers you say you have offer'd a Reward of Eight hundred Dollars for the murderers, which we are very glad to hear & hope they may be taken, and that we may See them Executed, as it is natural to look for revenge of Innocent blood— Brothers, the two men you have killed were very great men & were of the great

Turtle Tribe, one of them was a Chief, & in one year the other was to be put in the great King Garoughtas place, who is Dead also—

Brothers, you must not think hard if we speak rash, as it comes from a wounded heart, as you have stuck the hatchet in our head, and we can't be reconciled until you come & pull it out; We are Sorry to tell you, you have Killed Eleven of us Since peace, and we never said any thing until the other day, when in liquor we got a fighting with one of our brothers, and hurt him a good deal, and our Brother Gen[era]¹ Chapin insisted upon having a number of us taken though the man was in no danger, and is now well; this is what makes us tell you how many of us have been killed by you, and now we take you by the hand and lead you to the painted Post, or as far as your Cannoes can come up the creek, where you will meet the whole of the Tribe of the deceased, and all the Chiefs, and a number of Warriors of our nation, where we expect you will wash away the Blood of your Brothers, and Bury the Hatchet, and put it out of memory, as it is yet sticking in our Head—

Brothers, it is our great brother, your Governor, who must come to See us, as we will never bury the hatchet until our great brother himself comes & brightens the chain of friendship, as it is very rusty—Brothers, you must bring the property of your brothers you have murdered, and all the property of the murderers, as it will be great satisfaction to the families of the deceased— Brothers, the Sooner you meet us the better, for our young warriors are very uneasy, and it may prevent great trouble. Brothers, as Soon as you get on your feet to meet us, and turn your face this way you may walk all day, and lay down & Sleep at night in Safety and peace until you come to the place we have mentioned—

Brothers, this is from your brothers, Sachems, Chiefs and Warriors of the Senecca Nation, dated at Geneseo River & Flats. August 12th, 1790.

      Little Beard   **X**   his mark   Beaver tribe [drawing of a beaver]

      Saugoyeawatau [Sagoyewatha]

      Gissehhacke [Little Billy]   **X**   his mark   Wolf Tribe [drawing of a wolf]

      Caunhesongo [Capt. Shongo]   **X**   his mark

[Source: ORWM, vol. 6, item 18. Shorter versions in PP, 61:1–2; Turner 1851, 289; Ketchum 1864–65, 1:333.]

Pickering had invited the chiefs to arrive on October 25, but the Indians did not arrive until in late in the afternoon of November 14, a twenty-day delay that annoyed him. Addressing them on November 15, he hoped he could "pull the hatchet" from their heads. Farmer's Brother responded that they were not yet ready to hear him be-cause Fish Carrier had not arrived (PP, 61:60–66). Red Jacket then spoke:

Brother, We are happy to see you here; for which we thank the Great Spirit.

Brother, you say you are not acquainted with our customs. Brother, We are young: but we will describe the ancient practices of our fathers. The roads we now travel were cleared by them. When they used to meet our brothers of Pennsylvania, at Philadelphia, our brothers not only pulled the hatchet out of their heads, but buried it. You say you have now pulled the hatchet out of our heads: but you have only cast it behind you; and you may take it up again. Brother, while the hatchet lies unburied, we cannot sit easy on our seats.

Brother, From the time we made peace with the United States, we have experienced troubles, even more than before. The United States have also had their troubles. Brother, we now hear General Washington, the Great Chief of the United States, speaking to us by you; and hope our troubles will now have an end.—But our eyes are not yet washed that we may see, nor our throats cleared that we may speak. [Source: PP, 61:62–63]

After Red Jacket finished, Pickering declared that he now was burying the hatchet and passed around glasses of rum. Afterward, Farmer's Brother declared that the women, too, wished to be recognized by Pickering, and he shook hands with all the women present. The council was delayed for another three days waiting for Fish Carrier. On November 19, Farmer's Brother reiterated the principal points ("heads") of Pickering's statements to date, and Red Jacket followed him, speaking with a belt in his hand.

B.[rother] Now you will begin to hear a few words which y[ou]r. brothers have to say to you. ¶ B.[rother] You told us we must follow our own anc[ien]t customs, in using belts. B.[rother] This was the mind of our forefathers. These were their rules & they told their sons to observe them as long as the world should last. Our for[efathe]rs used to tell us that when peace was made war might break out & directed us to use such belts as this to preserve friendship that it might never be broken.*[2] ¶ B.[rother] our for[efather]s used to tell us that the heads or chiefs us[e]d [to] have the most trouble to keep the minds of our nation quiet. ¶ B.[rother] our forefathers used to tell us, That we sh[oul]d

2. Pickering's note in the margin: "Our for[efathers] used to tell us that when a treaty was finished, by preserving the letter, we sh[oul]d know & could tell our children what had been done."

meet with troubles, & we now find what they said has come to pass. B.[rother] You have been troubled how to settle the present difficulty. We shall now tell you how to do it. B.[rother] Our forefa[thers] used to tell us, that when we had concluded any business with our brother we sh[oul]^d thrust a stake in the ground & make a hole, then pull it up, & in the hole bury all the troubles. It is now time to do it in the present case. The business is almost completed. It is now time to stick in the stake—that all may see it. ¶ Now B.[rother] you must caution y[ou]r people of P.[ennsylvania] that your brothers may pass and repass unmolested. You may expect that we will do the like. We will give the same caution to our people, that the white people may pass & repass freely. We sit side by side; & it ought to be done.B.[rother] ¶ Now this business is finished, according to our ancient customs.

(Then he delivered me[3] the belt.)

B.[rother of] the 13 States & Pen.[nsylvani]^a You told us you had something more to say to us in behalf of the State of Pen[nsylvani]^a. But it is time to wash the tobacco out of our throats—for we can hardly speak. [Source: PP, 61:71A–72]

After Red Jacket's speech, Pickering ordered a glass of alcohol to be passed, declaring his pleasure with the council proceedings. He also summarized a speech by Colonel Wilson, apologizing to the Indians on behalf of the governor of Pennsylvania for not attending the council and declaring Wilson's intention to go home the following day. In response, Sagoyewatha said:

Brother of Pennsylvania,

You have now set out all you had to say to us from The Gov[ernor] of Pen[nsylvani].^a & y[ou]^r brothers have heard it. B.[rother] you have [hurried?] in your speech at this time, because you were going off tomorrow. But it is not customary to [illegible word] [wash?] away things that [were?] brought to a treaty. What you said y[ou]^r broth[ers] [heard?] in good part & their minds are easy. But it is not the custom to turn ones back the moment what is to be said is spoken. Now B.[rother] we are going to speak. B.[rother] You must stay till the business is over & then you can tell y[ou]^r great men all that has been done. B.[rother] you must be easy & keep y[ou]^r seat till the business is done; otherwise y[ou]^r brothers minds will be in danger of being disturbed. When the business is finished, you can take your brothers by the hand & part in friendship. [Source: PP, 61:75–75A]

3. "Me": Pickering.

Pickering then concluded the council with a long speech describing the Indian Trade and Intercourse Act of 1790.[4] *He concluded by saying, "The act which I have now read cannot fail to give you satisfaction: for it must convince you of the friendly disposition of the federal government towards you" (PP, 61:76–79).*

The following day, on Saturday, November 20, Red Jacket responded:

Brother. The Great Spi[rit] has appoin[te]^{d.} this day that we sh[oul]^{d.} meet our bro.[ther] at the Council Fire, & that you sh[oul]^d deliver what you had to say to us. Y[ou]^{r.} bro[the]^{rs,} the whole, men & children, are well pleased with what you have s[ai]^{d.} as it will preserve us in friendship. You must keep y[ou]^{r.} mind easy. This is the mind of y[ou]^{r.} brothers here & tomorrow we will give you an answer to what you have said. You must not think hard of us, when to-moro[w] we lay before you all we have to say & the Interpreters who know the ways of Indians must not take it amiss. We look at the Fire & see there is not time to day to relate all we have to say. [Source: PP, 61:82]

Farmer's Brother asked that drinks be passed around. Pickering agreed, but he complained that he was growing impatient with the delays, and he hoped they would finish business the following day. That night, in private council, Farmer's Brother began by noting that Pickering had expressed a desire to learn Indian customs. Red Jacket continued:

B.[rother of the] 13 States. We have met this evening; and this is the first time that it looked like brightening the chain of friendship. That was the rule of our forefathers in old times in treating with our brothers of N[ew]York, who used to [attend?] in the manner you are now doing. That was the way in the time of Sir W[illia]^m Johnson.—That when the chain had been brightened goods were to be delivered, they were put on the side, whether they were more or fewer. At that time, belts were used; & if a person was killed a belt was del[ivere]^{d.} to one of the relatives of the deceased to comfort their minds, & we supposed you meant to observe the same custom. You have a small parcel of goods to deliver, some papers & packages, no belt, supposing the goods were sufficient. It is the minds of us who are here, that the rule of our forefathers sh[oul]^{d.} now be observed. As you desired to know our rules, we have now told you what they are.

---

4. The Trade and Intercourse Act, modified several times over the next several decades, specified that all Indian land sales had to be performed in the presence of a federally appointed commissioner. It also stipulated a supervisory system of Indian agents, and regulated trade with the Indians. See Prucha (1994, 145); also Hauptman's response (1999, 159).

You now see the burden which lies upon the Chiefs. They take pains to keep the Chain of Friendship bright.

We few have all the trouble & do all the business of our nation; & you thought you w[oul]ᵈ take an opportunity of discoursing with them on the subject. You see these are the Chiefs who do the business, & hear all the trouble of the nation. The person who kindles the Council Fire uses his pleasure in giving them something [so?] particular or not, as He thinks fit, for their trouble, for it is not for the chiefs to say what they will have.

Now you know our method of proceeding & what has been the practice at other treaties.

We have young warriors who are light & can move quick, who are often first with messages; and it is common to reserve something for them over the common proportion to recompense them for their trouble; because they cannot at their pleasure go a hunting, but must wait the determination of the Chiefs and move when they desire it. [Source: PP, 61:80–81]

The next day, Sunday, November 21, Red Jacket spoke while holding a copy of the Intercourse Act from the previous day:

B.[rother] Yesterday you kindled the council fire, & told y[ou]ʳ brothers that if they were ready you had something more to say to them. Then y.[ou] told us that you had built the council fire at Ti[oga] by direction of the Great Ch.[ief] Then you told us that the paper in your hand contained what you were directed to deliver to us by the Gr[eat] Ch.[ief] of the 13 States. Br.[other] You told us that at this cou[ncil] fire the chain of friendsh.[ip] was to be brightened & you began to brighten it & told us the only business you had to proceed upon was to brighten the chain of friendsh.[ip] between the U. S. & the 6 nations, & told us to give great attention to what you had to relate. ¶ Then B[rother] you told us you were going to relate to us, the good will of the 13 States towards the 6 Nations.—Then you told us that the Gr[eat] Ch.[ief] Gen[era]ˡ W[ashington] was the great Ch.[ief] of the 13 States, & that he was taking regular methods to settle affairs with the Indians. Then y[ou] t[ol]ᵈ us that the good will of the 13 States was very great towards us & that we might pass and repass freely & safely—& that we sh[oul]ᵈ keep this paper in remembrance of what was done at this council fire. ¶ B.[rother] Then you told us to give great attention to what you were going to say as this paper contained the law of the 13 States by which the whole Island was to be regulated. You then t[ol]ᵈ us how this manner of proceeding with Indians fell under the direction of Congress who were now to regulate the whole, from the rising to the setting sun. Then you t[ol]ᵈ us, that after those 13 Fires had made 1 big fire, they began to brighten the ch.[ain] of fr[iendshi]ᵖ with the Indians. that this was the law which was going to be put in force thro' the 13 States, that those who hurt the Indians were punished as if they had hurt White men. That this was con[taine]ᵈ· in this paper, and wh.[ich] we could look at any time. Then you said you told us that when that fire began to burn—a man was to be sent to have the charge of Indian affairs and if any thing amiss was done then we were to [report the same?] to him who w[oul]ᵈ· report it to the Congress. Then you t[ol]ᵈ us you would show us the ways of the white people—the laws in use among them & that you supposed we had some such among us. Then you told us that G[eorge] W[ashington] the Ch.[ief] of the 13 States, that he sent you here, & that he w[oul]ᵈ· put the law in [two illegible words] all the bad men. Then yo[u] t[ol]ᵈ· us that [some in the?] Congress took this [power?] upon them, they began to [renew?] peace among the [nations?] & to brighten the ch.[ain] of fr.[iendshi]ᵖ· Then you t[ol]ᵈ· us that when the big fire was kindled a law was made to regulate traders among the Indians to prevent their being cheated by those who went among them. Then y.[ou] told us that this law w[oul]ᵈ· be put in place, & a person appointed by the President to regulate the traders. Then y[ou] t[ol]ᵈ· us of the consequences of a person going to trade with us without [a] license, & how he was to be punished & the forfeiture. You told us if we looked into this paper we could see when the forfeiture was & that we c[oul]ᵈ· carry this paper to any council fire & see what you had spoken. Then you told us that if a trader came into our country without license, by looking into the paper we could find what [was?] the forfeiture, and that half was to go to the prosecutor & half to the 13 States. Y.[ou] t[ol]ᵈ· us that after the Ch.[ain] of F.[riendshi]ᵖ was brightened between the 13 States & the 6 Nations, a person w[oul]ᵈ· be ap[pointe]ᵈ· to regulate Indian affairs in whom we could confide, & that the President w[oul]ᵈ· appoint only such. Then you told us that the reason we had been cheated selling our lands was that we had treated with all the little council fires. Then you t[ol]ᵈ· us that now no other fire was to be kindled than that of the 13 S.[tates] & that we must not believe any one who came to kindle a fire unless he came in the name of the 13 S.[tates] Then you told us that the directions in this paper were by order of the 13 S.[tates] & that if any person went among the Indians & acted contrary to these directions & cheated them then we must complain to the 13 S.[tates]

Then you told us we must keep this paper. That the law w[oul]ᵈ· continue but 2 years. then if the ch.[ain] of F.[riendship]ᵈˢʰ should want brightening, it would be brightened & that this paper c[oul]ᵈ· be produced to show what was now done.

(Then laying by the copies he added)

Brother The reason why I went over the heads of y[ou]^r. speech was that you might know whether it had been rightly interpreted. This is the first time since the peace that it has been proposed to brighten the Ch.[ain] of Fr.[iendship] And y[ou]^r. brothers of the 6 nations who are looking on are very happy to see you come to brighten the chain of friendship & heartily thank you for it. [Source: PP, 61:83–84]

Farmer's Brother continued, protesting that they were asked to go to too many differ-ent places for federal councils. He said their lands were unfairly taken at Fort Stan-wix in 1789 and again at the Phelps-Gorham Purchase, but the United States was slow to respond to their complaints (PP, 61:84–85). Red Jacket then spoke:

BROTHER:

Now you begin to hear of the situation of our lands. Mr. [Oliver] Phelps and Doctor [Caleb] Benton came on to rake open the fire again at Canedesago. After they were come there, Mr. Phelps passed on to Niagara, and went to our old friend Colonel [John] Butler, whom he met at a tavern. Colonel Butler asked him of his business. He answered that he came to kindle a fire at Canedesago. Then Colonel Butler told him that Canedesago was not a fit place at which to kindle a fire; and that our old custom was to kindle a fire at our own castle. Colonel Butler told him that he thought he might build a fire at Buffalo Creek; and if he did that he believed that he should attend the treaty. Mr. Phelps expressed his fears, that if he held the treaty there, he should meet some difficulty. Then I, Billy, and Cajeagayonh, (Heap of Dogs) went to Canedesago, took Mr. Phelps by the hand, and led him to our council fire at Buffaloe Creek. All these people here know what speech Mr. Phelps sent us— (then pointing to the Farmer's Brother, Billy, and others, said)—these went to Canedesago, to see what the business was. These all know, and Mr. [Samuel] Street knows, that Mr. Phelps held up a long paper, with a seal as big as my hand. When he opened his mind to us, we took it hard. We wanted to keep a large piece of land, but it was not in our power. Mr. Street, (pointing to him on the bench) you know very well, a treaty was held all night, to fix the boundary, and the price of the land. These men (Mr. [Joseph] Smith, Farmer's Brother, O'Beel [Cornplanter], Little Billy, Heap of Dogs, China Breast-plate, and I, were there) know very well, the proposal was, that Mr. Phelps should give us ten thousand dollars for the purchase, and five hundred dollars annual rent. That was the agreement made that night. The bargain was not finished till morning, and just as we went out of the house, the sun arose. Then we sought for persons to draw the writings. The persons chosen were Mr. [Rev. Samuel] Kirkland, Colonel Butler, and Captain Brant. Mr. Street was not then present.

After this, the bargain being completed, Mr. Street took our papers with him to Niagara. And, last summer a year ago, we came out to Canandaigua, expecting to receive ten thousand dollars; but then we found that we had but five thousand to receive. When we discovered the fraud, we had a mind to apply to Congress, to see if the matter could not be rectified: for, when we took the money and shared it, every one here knows, that we had but about a dollar a piece, for all that country. Mr. Street! you very well know, that all that our lands came to, was but the price of a few hogsheads of tobacco. Gentleman who stand by, (looking around, and addressing himself to the white people who were present,) do not think hard of what has been said. At the time of the treaty, twenty broaches would not buy half a loaf of bread, so that when we returned home, there was not a bright spot of silver about us. The last spring again, again, General Chapin stretched out his hand to us to open a little fire at Big Tree flats; and then I had a little talk with him; and finding we had but a shilling a piece to receive, we desired him to shut up his hand again. This is all we have to say of that time. Mr. Street knows how hard it was for us to part with our land. And this we have said, because we wish the President to know how we have been treated.

NOW, B[R]OTHER—the Thirteen States: you must open your ears. You know what has happened respecting our lands. You told us, from this time the chain of friendship should be brightened. Now, brother, we have begun to brighten the chain of friendship, and we will follow the steps of our forefathers. We will take those steps, that we may sit easy, and choose where and how large our seats should be. The reason we send this message, is, that the President, who is over all the thirteen States, may make our seats easy. We do it that the chain of friendship may be brightened with the thirteen States, as well as with the British; that we may pass from one to the other unmolested. Brother, this is what your brothers, chiefs, and warriors, have to say to you, relative to brightening the chain of friendship. We wish to be under the protection of the thirteen States as well as of the British.

(Then he delivered me the belt, after which, taking up a parcel of papers, he proceeded thus:)

BROTHER: You know all relating to our lands; You know the whole affair. We have just told you how it was two years that we have wanted to have a conference with Congress. Mr. Phelps did not purchase, but he leased the land. We opened our ears, and understood that the land was leased. This happened to us for our not knowing the papers. Here they are, and you may see what they contain.

(He then handed me the papers. They were Mr. Phelps's bond for the 500 dollars annual rent of the land he bought of them, some copies of it, and a copy of their deed to him. He then proceeded.)

BROTHER: We have a little more to say to you. Here are Billy, and some others, who were at the treaty at the Ohio.[5] They brought with them these papers, which we wish you to see. It is the mind of the Six Nations to keep these papers, that we may show them at treaties held by the thirteen States. It is our mind that you should know it. This belt came with these papers, and on the parchment annexed to it is mentioned the price of the land.

(He then handed to me the papers. One contained articles entered into between them and General St. Clair describing certain boundaries between their lands and those of the United States. The subject of the other I do not recollect. The parchment label annexed to the belt, showed that it had been delivered by Richard Butler and John Gibson, whose names were written upon it; but nothing about the price of any land. The Indians desired of me information of the nature of these papers, which I gave them in general terms.) [Source: *ASPIA*, 1:214–15. Shorthand versions in PP, 61:84–86; ORWM, vol. 15, item 12]

The next day, on Monday, November 22, Pickering formally closed the council with two speeches (although discussion went on for another two days). In his first speech, he expressed his satisfaction with the council, and his hope that in the future, the Indians would speed time and expense by bringing fewer people. Pickering's second speech was a short farewell address and a formal obsequy on the two murdered Senecas, during which he presented mourning belts to the relatives of the deceased (PP, 61:89–92A). Although the council had thus officially ended, two days later, on Tuesday, November 23, Sagoyewatha addressed Pickering with a bundle of papers in his hand:

B.[rother] Here are but a few of us together who have met at y[ou]ʳ Council fire to-day. Yesterday, you kindled the fire, in order to deliver all you had to say to us. I have in my head all that you have del[ivere]ᵈ to us. You told us that all you had to say was to brighten the ch.[ain] of Fr[iendship]ᵈ between you and the Indians; and that you were going to show us y[ou]ʳ speech what was the way of the White people. Bro.[ther] We thank you for the speech you del[ivere]ᵈ yesterday & we listened to it with attention. This you said was the wish of the white people that the tomahawks would be made into hoes & the guns into Plowshares. We thank you for all y[ou]ʳ advice; & for the declaration of your wish that the tom.[ahawks] be maid into hoes & the guns into

5. Fort Harmar/Muskingum, 1789.

plowshares. Now you shall hear our method of brightening the ch.[ain] of Fr.[iendship]ᵈ

(Laid by the papers, & took up a belt & strings)

Now Brother of the Thirteen States & Pres[iden]ᵗ Gen[era]ˡ W.[ashington] open y[ou]ʳ ears. Now we proceed to make the ch.[ain] bright. These were the ways of our f[ore]fathers wh.[ich] I am going to relate. It was the case in our f[ore]f[athe]ʳˢ days that peace was made at Canestogoe [Canadesago]—not long after wh.[ich] they met with troubles. It was the case of the Tuscaroras in those days to do the same & yes they were soon swept away. The reason was the same wh.[ich] we begin to experience, the taking away [of] their lands. So also it was with the Oneidas. The white people took them by the hand & led them from their council house. That has been the case with the Stockbridge Indians who lived among you: Their lands are all gone, & they are almost reduced to nothing. ¶ Now B.[rother] you begin to hear a few words from y[ou]ʳ bro[the]ʳˢ of their ancient ways. You told us yesterday you began to brighten the ch.[ain] of f[riendship]ᵈ to clear the path between us, now that you found out our troubles respecting our lands. Now you begin to find the situation we are in. it is the mind of all your brothers here that the President sh[oul]ᵈ know it.—for if he is so great a man that he can look from the rising to the setting sun, he can justify what is wrong in past proceedings. Now you know all the misfortunes which have befallen us. They came from the white people, & we should be glad if he would remedy them. We shall thank him if he will follow the steps of his f[ore]f[athe]ʳˢ & clear the paths that we may walk straight & not stumble. Here you see the belt with wh.[ich] the 13 States took your bro[the]ʳˢ by the hand. This is the belt with which⁶ Tis a long time since it was del[ivere]ᵈ We supposed it had been forgotten. We have had no conference with them since it was del[ivere]ᵈ & this was given when the ch[ain] of fr[iendship]ᵈ was bright[ene]ᵈ between us and the US. Now we thank the Gr.[eat] Spirit that we are going again to brighten it & make the way clear. ¶ The old rules came from this Island: they were the rules of our forefathers— Other practices came from people of y[ou]ʳ colour. The first time we saw people of y[ou]ʳ color, they were in a vessel on the water. When we came to see the vessel, we thought not to let the people of the other color come ashore, for fear we sh[oul]ᵈ have trouble. From that time, the trouble began: from your glass of grog—as is the case with me now⁷ We did not like to have them hang

6. The preceding fragment, "This is the best with which," is a copyist's error.
7. Pickering's note in the margin: "Red Jacket had been very active at the public dance the evening preceding & drank liberally."

on their kettles.[8] (Now those troubles of our forefathers, came from the [illegible word] & they have travelled on to this place.) Then the people of that vessel asked if they might come ashore to dig up some [foods?]. Our old people then consented that y.[ou] might come ashore for that purpose—& then they began to hang their kettles on this Island. This was the origin of these old practices. After they came ashore & hung on their kettles, they asked leave to take a peice of land & draw a boundary line. The Oneidas & Onondagas agreed that they sh[oul]^d. come to a certain hill & there fasten their vessels & come no farther but they soon ran thro' the country. Then they pretended to make peace & invited the chiefs but the Chiefs in that day were ignorant & did not know what trouble was; it being the first time they has seen any other people but themselves. All that time our fathers councilled with y[ou]r people who had landed on this Island but did not make peace: for all they wanted was to get their land from them. ¶ Now B.[rother] you must not be offended that at this time we have mentioned some of our ancient ways. But now you have come to make peace among us. Now our troubles begin to cease. Brothers, now you know the ways of the Indians in treating. all this land belonged to them & we gave it to you. This Island and the game upon it, were made by the Gr.[eat] Spi.[rit] for the Indians. He gave it to them for their support. This was their money & he so ordered it that they sh[oul]^d. suffer a great deal in hunting for their money. From that time our warriors found trouble in hunting for their money. Our fathers told us in those days that [those? white?] traders came among us we sh[oul]^d consider it as a token of fr[iendship]^d. We thank you that you told us yesterday that the traders were regulated—for they have cheated us out of all our money. Since the traders have been in this country we have been cheated out of our furs, for they have taken them at a low price, & then carried them across the water, & get theirs at 3 prices. But it is not fair for them to set the prices on both sides—The goods [we have?] made [use by them &?] wh.[ich] they set their own prices & then come & set the prices upon our skins. Now Bro.[ther] it will be right if both sides will behave alike & do not cheat one another. This will keep the ch.[ain] bright: This we hope will be done since Gen[era]^l. W.[ashington] has taken it in hand. ¶ Brothers It is not the mind of the Indians like yours, that the tom^ha [tomahawk] sh[oul]^d. be beat into hoes & their guns into plowshares since by them they get their living. It will be very hard to take away all the warriors guns, for they have no other way of cloathing themselves—But you can make your own cloaths. Brother It is the mind of y[ou]^r bro[the]^rs of the Six Nations that since Gen[era]^l. W.[ash-

8. That is, set up camp.

ington] has taken the business in hand to brighten the ch[ain] of fr[iendship]ᵈ·
we sh[oul]ᵈ· be suffered to follow our ancient rules. We must hang upon our ancient rules—& the wh.[ite] people upon theirs. We can then as well agree together as if we followed one rule. ¶ Now you hear the minds of y[ou]ʳ
bro.[the]ʳˢ. You know very well the Ch.[ain] of fr[iendship]ᵈ· is between us &
now you have begun to brighten it. At treaties of peace in old times, both parties took hold of the Ch.[ain] and there was nothing to part them. After that,
something happened among us that was not good. Now G.[eneral] W.[ashing-
ton] must keep the path straight on both sides & if any accident happens we
both sides must complain to him.

If some of G[enera]ˡ· W[ashington's] people sh[oul]ᵈ come to an Indian to
buy land—suppose to myself—& give me a glass of rum & I sh[oul]ᵈ say here
my fr[ien]ᵈ· I will sell you a piece of land: an act must be made to render such
sales good for nothing. ¶ Now we must follow the steps of our f[ore]f[athe]ʳˢ &
keep peace that our children may grow up in peace & quietness. ¶ This is what
y[ou]ʳ· brothers had to say to you. This belt was once before given to us to
brighten the ch.[ain] of fr[iendship]ᵈ· You may think that we lie: but here it
is—you can look at it (handing me a belt with 13 spots and 12 strings). I give
you this to hang upon the ch.[ain] where it has been hung once before.
[Source: PP, 61:93–94A]

*Farmer's Brother then spoke, explaining that the Six Nations had recently attempted
to counsel the Shawnees toward peace. Little Billy then spoke on behalf of the warriors, indicating their frustration with the sachems for recent land sales and their satisfaction that the United States seemed to be genuinely brightening the chain of
friendship. He also spoke for the women, who reminded the president that they were
"the principal support of the nation." They said that they would attend future treaties
and that they hoped that the president would let them remain undisturbed on their
lands (PP, 61:97–97A). Pickering repeated briefly the main points of their speeches.
He noted that the burden of their complaint toward the end of the council was about
land sales. He informed them that the losses they suffered in the past may be irre-
trievable but that the new laws were to prevent such mischief from happening in the
future. That day he also delivered to them goods he had brought. On Wednesday,
November 24, just before the Senecas were to depart, they held a brief private council with Pickering. Red Jacket said:*

Brother, You have now begun to settle the affairs of the nation & brighten
the Ch.[ain] of Fr[iendship]ᵈ· This has been the case since so many small council fires were kindled, that there were different ((ears)—interpreters) and they
did not know at one Council what had been done at another. Now we have

brightened the Ch.[ain] of Fr[iendship]ᵈ· & the business is begun upon a large scale; It is the mind of the Six Nations here that they should have the same interpreters (pointing to Joseph Smith and Jasper Parrish) at another treaty (if another should be held) as of this—for these know what has now been done here. It is our mind (& it was always the mind of our forefathers) when we find men who have faithful ears, & know the ways of Indians that they should attend to all our business in treaties with the U.[nited] States & the citizens thereof.—As the business done at the present treaty has been publically done, we wish the account thereof may be spread far & near: for everything has been done openly. We meant not to do any thing in the dark, but in the light that every one might see. We wish Mr. Street (pointing to him) may attend future treaties, as he has been present & knows what has been done at this time. These are the few words we had to say, that the President of the U.[nited] States after he has heard what is our mind, may soon let us hear from him. [Source: PP, 61:107]

Pickering responded by saying that he would report back all the speeches to the president. He noted that they requested a copy of the Trade and Intercourse Act, as well as the appointment of a superintendent. Farmer's Brother concluded the council by giving Parrish the name of Soneaúhtawau, "Big-Throat," and Smith the name of Nhowetau[?], "Rising-Sun" (PP, 61:107).

Colonel Thomas Proctor's Embassy West

APRIL 27–JUNE 7, 1791

IN OCTOBER OF 1790, at the same time the federal government commissioned Pickering's peace council with the Senecas at Tioga, an army of General Harmar's was sent into Ohio to build forts and make a show of strength to quiet the Miamis, who were organizing for war. Unfortunately for the United States, the Miamis killed an expedition of 182 of Harmar's men (Phillips 1966; Downes 1940). In March 1791, just after Harmar's defeat, Colonel Thomas Proctor was sent west by Washington to attempt to broker peace with the Wabash and Miami Indians. Proctor's mission was to stop at Buffalo Creek and recruit Senecas to sway the Ohio Indians' minds toward peace. The entirety of Proctor's narrative can be read in the *ASPIA*, 1:149–65. Accompanied by Cornplanter, who had agreed to go with him on his peace mission, Proctor arrived at a council in Buffalo Creek on April 27, 1791. Young King, Farmer's Brother, and Red Jacket were present.

Proctor hired Horatio Jones as his interpreter, regarded as one of the best Seneca interpreters of the area (*ASPIA*, 1:151, 161). The majority of the transcriptions come from Proctor's journal, but some texts can be found only in other sources.

On April 27, Red Jacket welcomed Proctor and Cornplanter to Buffalo Creek with these words:

"BROTHER: Listen! It is usual for us to speak; and to you we do it as to a brother that has been absent a long time. Now we all speak to you, and to our Head Warrior that left us last fall:—and we thank the Great Spirit for his and your safe arrival here, as you are together, hand in hand, from Honandaganius,[1] upon great business.

---

1. This is the Seneca name for George Washington and it means "Town Destroyer." Washington was given the name after General Sullivan's punitive raid into central New York State in 1779, which burned and leveled many Indian towns.

"You have travelled long, with tears in your eyes, upon account of bad roads, and bad season of the year. Besides the disturbances between the bad Indians and our brothers the white people, every thing has been trying to prevent your coming, and to stop your business, and make you lose your way.

"Thus the big waters might have stopped your coming; and the wars might have stopped you; and sickness might have stopped you; for we cannot know what is to happen until it comes upon us. So, therefore, we thank the Great Spirit who has preserved you from such dangers that might have hindered us from hearing of the good news which you and our head warrior have opened to us. But how could it be that any thing bad could have happened to you, while you have such important business to transact, as we understand you have come on?

"You must now wipe away those tears occasioned by all the great dangers you have come through. And now we set you upon a seat where you can sit up straight,—and a seat where you are secure from the fears of your enemies;— where you can look round and see all your friends and brothers in peace. Besides, you have come along with your heart and your throat stopped up, to secure all that you had to say in your body. But now we open your heart with your brothers' hands, and we run our fingers through to open your mouth, that you may speak clear, and not be molested. Your ears also have been stopped by Honandaganius until you should see your brothers at this place, being spared by the Great Spirit to arrive safe.

"Now, open your ears to hear what your brothers may say after you have made your speech. This is, therefore, the compliment of the chiefs and head men at Buffalo Creek, to you and our great warrior, the Cornplanter, and you may each of you go on safely with your business." [Source: Stone 1841, 49–50]

The following day, Proctor proposed that several Seneca chiefs accompany him and Cornplanter to Ohio. The Senecas, well aware of their difficult position between the British, United States, and western Indians, deferred on the issue and kept Proctor waiting for nearly two weeks before they would answer. Proctor wrote in his journal that the Senecas seemed very suspicious of his motives. He noted that after Red Jacket's condolence speech, Red Jacket challenged him with the statement that many people came into Indian country claiming the authority of the Thirteen Fires but the Indians were not often convinced of their truth (ASPIA, 1:155).

The day before Proctor arrived, William Ewing, a businessman, arrived to notify the Senecas of the recent sale of the preemptive rights to their land to Robert Morris (ASPIA, 1:156; see also maps 2 and 3). Ewing gave the Indians a letter of friendship from Morris and his Philadelphia agent, Samuel Ogden. Morris noti-

fied them that he wanted to run surveys of the land as a means of protecting the Indians.

In the following speech, also on April 27, Sagoyewatha responded to Ewing about the sale of the preemptive rights. Ewing's interpreter was Jack Berry, a Seneca chief with a reputation of being a very good translator (ASPIA, 1:160).

I am Now agoing to speak to You, for You came first here & kindled a fire with us at a time, when it was very agreeable, to us, it was to let us know, where you have been & what news you have heard. & You have told us a great deal, now friendly the Thirteen Fires, which is very good; You have handed us a Belt of Friendship from two Great Men of Pennsylvania, which You desire us to Hold fast; They will hold fast also, and You will hold fast, there Hands & our Hands untill You bring us face to face, and You have also handed us a letter of Information, informing us that these great Men have purchased our Lands out of the Hands of the New England People which we are very glad to hear & that it is their determination to do their Brothers of the Six Nations Justice, and also that it is the desire of these Great Men, that the Lines which divided our Land, which We own, from the Lands, which we have sold, acqurately Run & well marked, & that a survey, of all our Lands be taken, so that we may have Justice done us, hereafter[.] and You have asked, for one Chief to send down to these Great Men, your Brothers the Pennsylvanians, to return up with them, & now we have, listened to all you have to say at this time & we think it very good & we desire before we give You any answer that You will set down & make Your Mind easy & listen with us to what Colonel Proctor has to say, for he [illegible word] the Fire, & we shall make Your Seat easy to set On— [Source: ORWM, vol. 15, item 22]

The following day, Ewing continued to press Morris's affairs with the Indians. Proctor complained that he was interfering with important government business and eventually threatened him with imprisonment. Proctor spent April 28 and 29 reading to the Senecas from the letters and speeches from the president, the secretary of war, and from Cornplanter. He also read to them what he planned to say to the western Indians, statements that emphasized the military power of the United States.

On April 29, Sagoyewatha gave Proctor the Senecas' formal response to his offer. Proctor noted that Red Jacket was flanked by Farmer's Brother and Fish Carrier and seemed to speak at their behest. The Senecas asked for more time to consider Proctor's plan, insisting that they be allowed to counsel first with the British at Fort Niagara.

BROTHER FROM PENNSYLVANIA:

"We have heard all that you have said to us, and by which you have informed that you are going to the bad Indians to make peace with them, and that you are sent to us to receive our assistance. Now we must consider the matter thoroughly, and to choose which way we must go, whether by land or by water. You likewise tell us, that you have messages to the Wyandots, and to Captain Snake, of the Delawares; and that they are to take hold of you and us by the hands, and go to the bad Indian nations with us; and this, also, we must consider of thoroughly: for we find that all our Six Nations are not present; and, as our brother, Captain Powell, of the British, is here, and true to us, for he is with us at every treaty, we must let you know that we shall move our council-fire to Niagara with him, and that you must go with us to-morrow, as far as Captain Powell's house.[2] And, as soon as we can know what time we can reach Niagara, we will send runners off to the fort, to acquaint the commanding officer of the garrison. And now the council want to have your answer."
[Source: *ASPIA*, 1:156]

Proctor refused the Senecas' proposal to go to the British at Fort Niagara, and the Senecas responded by asking that Colonel Butler, their British ally, come to them. On May 3, 1791, Sagoyewatha told Proctor that his words were likely to threaten the Miamis and endanger any Seneca ambassadors who went with him:

"Tell him [Proctor], said he, (speaking to the interpreter) that some of his language is soft, but that other parts of it are too strong; for the danger that is before us is great, and our enemies are drunk; and they will not hear what we say, like a man that is sober, and we consider that, whatever number of the Six Nations accompany him, will be in the same danger with himself, and it is likely that we shall not live long, when the bad Indians shall see us. Therefore as it is a business of such great weight to us, we must take counsel, in order to save ourselves, and him, from falling by their hands. Moreover, the Indians are not like white men: for they must think a great while. He must therefore attend our councils, and look and hear till we shall speak on his business; and to-morrow our head-men will meet together, and try what can be done."
[Source: *ASPIA*, 1:157]

Eventually, Colonel Butler and Joseph Brant decided that it was not a good idea for the Senecas to go west with Proctor. The Senecas told Proctor they would not go.

2. Powell was a British officer who lived several miles from Fort Erie, across the Niagara River from Buffalo Creek (see Ketchum 1864–65; Hill 1923).

Proctor responded that he regretted taking a negative report back to Washington. This threat caused concern among the Clan Mothers, who sent word to Proctor on May 15 that they had something to say. Proctor identifies Red Jacket as "the women's speaker" later that day, so it is likely Red Jacket also delivered this speech, but Proctor does not here specify who the speaker was.

"BROTHER: The Lord has spared us until a new day to talk together: for, since you came here from General Washington, you, and our uncles, the sachems, have been counselling together. Moreover, your sisters, the women, have taken the same into great consideration, because that you and our sachems have said so much upon it. Now, that is the reason why we have come to say something to you, and to tell you, that the Great Spirit hath preserved you, and you ought to hear and listen to what we women shall speak, as well as to the sachems; for we are *the owners of this land*—and it is ours; for it is we that plant it, for our and their use. Hear us, therefore, for we speak of things that concern us and our children, and you must not think hard of us, while our men shall say more to you; for we have told them." [Source: *ASPIA*, 1:159–60]

The Senecas met with Proctor later that day, with the women sitting next to the sachems. Sagoyewatha delivered the women's decision to Proctor.

"BROTHER FROM PENNSYLVANIA:

You that are sent from General Washington, and by the Thirteen Fires; you have been sitting side by side with us every day, and the Lord has appointed us another pleasant day to meet again.

Now, listen, Brother: You know what we have been doing so long, and what trouble we have been at; and you know that it has been the request of our head warrior (O'Beel[3]) that we are left to answer for our women, who are to conclude what ought to be done by both sachems and warriors. So hear what is their conclusion. Brother, the business you have come on is very troublesome, and we have been a long time considering on it, ever since you came here; and now the elders of our women, considering the greatness of your business, have said that our sachems and warriors must help you over your difficulties, for the good of them and their children. Moreover, you tell us, since the treaty at Tioga with us, the Americans are strong for peace.

Now, all that has been done for you has been done by our women, and the rest will be a hard task for us: for the people at the setting sun are bad people, and you have come on us in *too much haste* for such great matters of importance. And now, brother, you must look when it is light in the morning until

3. Cornplanter.

the setting sun, and you must reach your neck over the land, and take all the light you can, to show the danger. And this is the words of our women to you, and the sachems and warriors who shall go with you. And now we shall name them, as they have first presented themselves in this full council, viz: Our first great sachem Kuyascetta, Red Jacket, the young prince of the Turtle tribe,[4] Captain John, of the Onandagoes, the Grand Carrier, Awangogathe.[5] And now we will name our chief warriors, viz: Sawishua, Cuyanddoas, Unundatheuous, Thenachqua, Conneague, Tenanquachqua, Othanjohngottang, Hottendeyoucke, and Attwanikea.

Now, brother from Pennsylvania and from General Washington, I have told you what has been directed. Let us, therefore, throw all care on the mercy of our Great Keeper, in hopes that he will assist us. You now know that Col. Butler, of the British, told us that he must take our writings down to Col. Gordon, as he is a very wise man, and perhaps he may have something to say to us that is for our good. And we also want his assistance, as he is the man that keeps all the vessels that is on the lake.

Therefore, my brother, make your mind easy, for your request is granted, and when we hear from our brothers the British, then we shall know what time we can start. And you must not be uneasy that our brother O'Beel does not go with you, for he is *very tired*, and he must rest awhile, and take charge of our young warriors while they *are playing*, (hunting) to keep them *in peace*, for fear of danger. And now, while we are speaking, more of our young warriors have given their names to go with you." [Source: *ASPIA*, 1:160]

When Proctor went to the British at Fort Niagara to charter a boat to take him to Ohio, however, the British commander disputed the validity of his credentials and denied him passage. The failed expedition was fortunate for Proctor—the word was spread that Simon Girty, a white frontiersman living with the Indians in Ohio, claimed he would have killed Proctor even if he came with a hundred Senecas (ASPIA, 1:197).

4. Apparently an error: Red Jacket was Wolf.

5. Proctor's note: "The foregoing are four chiefs of six, who were appointed to conduct me into the country of the unfriendly Indians. The names of the two other grand chiefs were at the same time given, but, by some accident, not inserted."

Council of Newtown Point/Painted Post

JULY 4–17, 1791

THE COUNCIL OF NEWTOWN POINT was called to build working relations with the Indians following General Harmar's defeat. Timothy Pickering was commissioned to hold the council to air any grievances of the Six Nations and to convince them to undertake steps toward civilization. Initially proposed to be held at the trading depot known as Painted Post, the council was moved twenty miles east to the more developed area of Newtown Point (Elmira, New York) (PP, 60:74; Phillips 1966, 173; map 2). It was a large council, with a thousand Indians eventually attending and many U.S. observers, such as New Jersey senator John Rutherford; John Parish, who led a small Quaker delegation; Oliver Phelps, a Connecticut businessman beginning to invest heavily in western lands; and Thomas Morris, who was being trained by his father (Robert Morris) to run his land investments with the Indians. With the significant exception of the Mohawks, whose absence was prompted by Joseph Brant's disapproval of the council, all other members of the Six Nations were represented. Although Pickering and Sagoyewatha sometimes clashed, Pickering managed to convince the Six Nations that the United States wanted to teach them better means of agriculture, and he invited several of their chiefs to visit Philadelphia in the spring to discuss it more. Because of his successes at the councils of Newtown and Tioga, Pickering was awarded the position of postmaster general of the United States in August 1791. For more details about the proceedings of this council, see Phillips (1966).

Joseph Smith and Jasper Parrish served as Pickering's interpreters (PP, 60:66). Unless noted, the following texts are from the Pickering Papers.

On July 4, Pickering opened the council with a long speech that acknowledged the Indians' fear that their lands might be taken, and he assured them that the United States wished to live in peace. On July 6, he spoke of Cornplanter's recent trip to Philadelphia,[1] and the need for Indians to lay aside their old customs of hunting and warfare

1. Cornplanter's speeches in Philadelphia can be read in *ASPIA*, 1:140–45.

to learn writing and husbandry, as the English had done hundreds of years ago (PP, 60:82–87). On July 10, Good Peter responded to Pickering's comments. He defended the Indians' methods of warfare and complained that relations with the Indians were bad because whites often cheated them. Red Jacket then spoke:

Brother Con-nés-au-ty,[2] we are now going to speak, and we wish you to hear. We raise our voices only that you may hear a few words. Put a favorable construction on what we say.

You told us that the white people were once in the same condition with us, and loved hunting as well as we; & that some of the white people loved to paint as the Indians do now. The white people, you say, are now entirely different, having put the old rules aside. You described to us the ways of the white people in those days, how the white people in America increased—how they got along in the world.

I will repeat a few words which you said O'Beil[3] spoke to Congress, asking for some things as the wish and for the advantage of the Six Nations: That you should give us saw-mills—establish schools, teach our children trades, farming, &c, because the game was leaving us. After Obeil made these requests to Congress they were pleased, and appointed you to call us to this treaty that you might lay these matters before the Six Nations, to learn if they were acceptable. Congress having considered of this request, thought it was right. Was this their mind?—You then (we suppose) thought the Indians in a good disposition; as he spoke in behalf of the Six Nations. When *we* had heard what Obeil had said, *Col Butler* & the *British* heard it: and we all liked what he had done.—I have only repeated a few words of what you said had passed with Obeil.

Connesauty, Now I am going to speak, and I wish you to hear,—that the President may hear the voice of the Six Nations.

When you delivered your speech to us, you spoke in the ears of all the Six Nations. You told us you would speak plain words from your heart. Now we are going to speak. You said you would speak with an open heart. You requested the same of us. You advised us not to speak with our lips only, but to speak in sincerity. We will do it: What we are going to say we shall take out of our hearts.

When you delivered us your speech, you told us of all the advantages which the white people reaped from their labour, since they left off the old rules. When you laid the whole speech before us, we took it into considera-

2. Pickering's Seneca name.
3. Cornplanter's English name was Henry O'Bail or O'Beil.

tion: We saw it was good: and were willing to accept of it. But we were not willing to throw away all our old rules: but were willing that both should live. Tis the opinion of all the Six Nations here, that we cannot take all the ways of the white people at once, but by degrees. And in the same manner we must lay aside our old rules—by degrees. Now to this day we have the rules of our fore-fathers in old times. We cannot transact business but in that way. I have their method in my hand (referring to a belt).—Now we have agreed to accept the new rules you proposed, that they may live alongside our old rules. We have accepted your advice and your rules, which we think are good, and put them by the side of ours: for we would have our rules live with yours.

Connesauty, now listen; you will hear the voice of the Six Nations.— They sit on one side—your people on the other. There are among us many bad people, who will not listen to the voice of the Chiefs: I suppose it is the same among the white people. We must use our old methods with our people, to teach them to be civil. You said that at this council fire, the bad acts of your people and ours must be buried. Our mind is the same.

Now set your mind at ease: have no hard thoughts—You engaged in the last war with your old father the British: because they intended, if they beat you, to make you their servants. You took up arms to prevent your being en-slaved, and in order to be independent. Now when this war happened, it raised a strong wind which blew over us, and brought us into the same trouble. Now we are for taking hold of the chain of friendship, and becoming an indepen-dent people.—Last fall, at the treaty, you talked of peace and brightened the chain of friendship. In such cases we are always willing to take hold of the chain. One thing I told you last fall—That when Sir William Johnson had the care of us, every time he talked of peace, we considered it, we accepted it. We do the same with the British to this day: but do not give ourselves entirely up to them; nor lean altogether upon you. We mean to stand upright—as we live between both.

At the treaty of Tioga, we told you we were willing to accept the offers you made us. Then you spoke what you thought fit. We will now do the same; and you must not think hard of it. What we said at that treaty, you have it all down. Neither you nor the United States must have any hard thoughts of what was then said.—Now the Six Nations are going to speak; and they will speak from the heart.

When you laid your speech before us, you told us to consider it deeply; and you would not hurry us. We did so. Now if we say any thing not agreeable, have no hard thoughts of it. Keep your mind easy; listen to what we say.

Now we would wish you not to hurry us. What you laid before us, showed the ways of the United States.—You must not hurry us, lest we take hold of something wrong.—When peace was first made, we strove to make peace with other nations. Now our minds are still strong for peace. Just before we came from home, we sent off Brant to continue the peace with the Western Indians. You say you desire to make peace with them: Now you listen to our speech we will show you that we are equally strong for peace. We hope the Great Spirit will assist Brant to make the Shawanoes & Delawares, the strongest bad nations in that country, take hold of the speeches he was to deliver to them, and on his return, enable him to bring back the pipe of peace. Now I suppose some of our friends have, our nephews,*[4] in council, are going on the same business with Brant. We hope they also will succeed, and that those nations may be brought to take hold of the chain of friendship with the U.[nited] States. When they return, so many as they bring with them, we will lay before them your speeches; and we doubt not they will accept of them.

When the white people have a fancy to go to another part of the country, they go; and your people are scattered over all the country. Our people do the like. Now if you happen to take one of our people prisoner, we hope you will not use him ill: remember the speeches you have made.

You have now heard us speak in council. We wish Congress to be very careful how they speak; and to speak to us of nothing but peace; and we desire they would do the same among their own people.

Now we have made our speech as short & straight as we could: for all you said was right and straight; we could find no fault with it.—When we speak, we confirm what we say with a belt. (He then delivered me a White belt of 10 rows, with sloping rows across of purple wampum as marked on this draft. Length 2 feet 2½ inches. Breadth of 2½ inches)[5] [Source: PP, 60:92–93]

4. Pickering's note: "Capt. Hendrick & three companions of his nation." In discussions at Newtown just prior to the opening of the council, Pickering had convinced Hendrick Aupaumut, a Stockbridge warrior who had fought for the Americans during the Revolution, to go on a peace mission westward to the Shawnees with specific answers to Indian "queries" concerning the disposition of the United States (PP, 60:89–90A). For more on Aupaumut, see Ronda and Ronda (1979).

5. Pickering elsewhere summarized the content of Red Jacket's speech in an attachment to this belt in a note: "The Sachem Soc-we-ya-waun-tau (usually called Red Jacket) in behalf of the Six Nations, on the 10th of July, delivered their answer. After descanting for some time on my speech, he declared their acceptance of the offered assistance, & their willingness to adopt the proposed improvements. He closed his speech with these words—'Now we have made our speech as short & straight as we could: for all you said was right and straight; we could find no fault with it.—When we speak, we confirm what we say with a belt.' He then delivered me the belt to which this parchment is attached" (PP, 60:119).

In Pickering's extemporary response, he reacted strongly to Red Jacket's assertion that the Six Nations would stand independent of both the British and the United States. He said that the Six Nations obviously leaned more toward the British side because they showed the British U.S. documents but never consulted with the United States on communications from the British. He said this policy might "produce mischief." Concerning the respectful treatment of prisoners of war, Pickering said that should members of the Six Nations become captured when warring with the western Indians, "they should expect no better treatment" than the captured "hostile" Indians, as it was hard for Americans to readily distinguish between the two. Pickering agreed with Red Jacket that Indians should adopt white customs only "by degrees" (PP, 60:94A–95). Three days later, on Wednesday, July 13, Sagoyewatha addressed Pickering:

Brother Connésauty, You are sent here once more by the U.[nited] States, to call your brothers, the Six Nations, to a council. What you heard back from the Oneidas*[6] was only the heads of your speech, which they had considered; and you thanked them for it. Then you heard a speech from your brothers the whole Six Nations. We told you of a great wind which blew over them in the last war, and which carried some of them one way & some another, just as it happened. The same may happen again in the present war—some may be blown to one side, some to the other.

Brother, The other day when we came together, we thought that all the transactions of the late war were buried—till we heard your speech; when you mentioned our leaning over to the British:—But we lived nearest to them, and that is the reason that we leaned most that way.

We were surprised—the whole nations round were surprised to hear you mention what you did about our showing your speeches to the British, & not showing theirs to you:—For we had told you of the wind which had blown; and when it had done blowing, we looked round and saw our women and children in distress. Then we turned our faces the other way, to make peace.

Then you asked us, Why, as we meant to be our own masters, we leaned to one side more than to the other?—We have told you we were surprised that you asked us that question: because we had told you that our old way was to use wampum and not writing. You are trying to put our old rules aside: but you know there is not one in our nation who knows writing. Therefore we are obliged to turn our faces to the British to know what the writings are when we receive them.

Now we give you to understand the reason why we were not our own mas-

6. Pickering's note: "referring to the speech of Good Peter, the Oneida Chief, July 10."

ters; as you have supposed we were not. The reason is, that we do not understand writing. So whenever we receive any writings, we are obliged to go to our brothers the British. Because they always advise us what is good, what makes for peace; and to listen to what the Americans say when they speak of peace. And whenever they hear any thing in our favour they let us know it, and advise us to pay attention.

Now you are hearing the reasons of our paying so much attention to the British, and of their hearing the news with us: it is because they give us such good advice that we can depend upon them. They advise us, if a treaty is called for peace alone, to attend it; and if presents are given for that purpose, to receive them.

Now as you were so much surprised to hear we were so much attached to our brothers the British, we are giving our reasons for it. Always when we counsel with the British, they advise us to take the counsel of the King, when he advises us for peace; and likewise to take the advice of the U.[nited] States when they advise us to peace.

Now brother you are hearing our reasons. The British always tell us we must be independent, and take advice from nobody, unless it pleases us. That is the reason we tell you we are independent nations, ruled by nobody.

Another thing you mentioned: You told us we never made any thing known to you which we got from the British; tho' we ran directly to them with what we got from you. We were greatly surprised when you told us that. You make use of writing: therefore we go to the British, to know what it means. And whenever there is a message sent from the British to us, it is done by wampum, and they have wampum laid up for that purpose. For another reason we were so surprised—because you know we had no agent appointed to unfold any thing to the United States. As for our parts, we are not able to go down to the Thirteen Fires: if we should set out, we should fall by the way: for we have no money.

Well, do you begin to understand why we unfold our affairs to the British?

Another thing you mentioned: You thanked us for accepting the speech you laid before us—that we found no fault—that there was not one article wrong in it; and you heartily thanked the Six Nations for accepting of it.

Now you must not think hard, nor suppose we are disturbed in our own minds, because we have given you the reasons of our surprise. You know that the day before yesterday we buried every thing that was bad; and that we were not to listen to any birds which told ugly stories.

Now we are telling you that the British use wampum instead of writing. If you had told us to fetch the British speeches to you, we would have passed up our wampum, and thrown the pack down before you, then you could have read the whole.

Now you have heard all the reasons for that part of our conduct with which you found fault. And you must not think hard of it. We have joined hands with the Thirteen States, and mean to do nothing but what is for peace.

I said before, that if you had told us to bring down what the British said to us, we would have made you up a pack & laid it before you: but as you did not do it, we have only brought a few of their speeches, which were of most importance, that our brother might hear them at this Council Fire.

Now you are hearing us. Now you are going to see a few of the principal speeches of the British, which have been delivered to us: as you think you ought to see the whole of them.*[7]

Now we are just beginning to do our business at this council, and by and by we shall pick a man who will be our agent. For in old times there used to be an agent. To him all the news came and from him it all went out, on whichever side it was. When we get an agent, you will hear the whole on both sides.

Now you have heard the reasons of that conduct for which you found fault with us. They come very light from us; because we know we are both alike, both concerned for peace: and now our true friendship is beginning; and we mean to give the reason of every thing concerning which you found fault with us.

Now you have heard the reasons of *these* things—where will you find the next fault? But let this be buried; as we have buried every thing that is bad. Let us not listen to birds, and suffer our minds to be wavering. (A Belt.) [Source: PP, 60:97A–98; versions of similar content but different phrasing appear in the *New Jersey Journal*, August 10, 1791; *Carlisle Gazette*, August 10, 1791; *Connecticut Courant*, August 15, 1791.]

Pickering responded on the same day with a long speech that asserted the growing military power of the United States and the foolishness of the western Indians who thought they could oppose it. He observed that those "birds" (the British) who counseled the Indians were liars. Addressing himself to the warriors in particular, Pickering advised them to pay attention to their sachems and old warriors who knew the

---

7. Pickering's note: "either the speaker or the interpreters have committed blunders: For instead of British speeches, he handed to me the President's speeches to Obeil [in December 1790], the speech of the Secretary of War to Obeil [December 1790], my speeches to the Senecas last fall at Tioga, a speech to the Senecas from Mssrs [Robert] Morris & [Samuel] Ogden, & some other papers; all of which they expected & listened to hear me give, an account; and which in a few words I accordingly described: But there was not one word from the British."

blessings of peace. He commented privately in his journal that he could tell that the Indians did not like what he said (PP, 60:98A–102A). The following day, July 14, Good Peter again defended the Indians' mode of warfare as humane and asserted that the British had always counseled them to peace (PP, 60:102A–105). Sagoye-watha then spoke:

Hear, Brother Connésauty, and the Thirteen United States, who built this council fire, for the Six Nations to meet around it.

Now set your mind at ease: you are going to hear the minds of our warriors, children, and brothers of the Six Nations.

When we heard your voice yesterday, it made the minds of the warriors of the Six Nations uneasy. Both you and we have opened here the business of peace: 'tis all of peace—the business you have opened in behalf of the United States.—Now you are going to hear the minds of the warriors, brothers children & sachems of the Six Nations—what few are left of us—Some few little ones are now growing up. Now the Six Nations & the United States are laying their minds together for peace.

Now, Brother, I wish you would give attention & hear what us brothers & brothers children of the Six Nations are going to say.—When you are talking to us of friendship and peace, you bring in past misfortunes; and your discourse is intermixed with friendship and trouble. When we speak to you, we speak of friendship unmixed.—You must excuse what we are going to repeat.—Now I also must look back to some things that are past.

In ancient times, when we were called to a treaty of peace, our discourse was of nothing but peace. We did not repeat misfortunes, when brightening the chain: because we put our minds of peace & friendship all in a heap. Now this was in old times. We not only made the chain of friendship very bright; but we locked arms, and took fast hold of each other's hands, and left the token of friendship.—Now as for this matter, you ought to know how your end of the chain of friendship should be brightened.

Now, brother, I must tell you of some of our ancient rules: I believe you do not know our old customs: therefore make your mind easy.—In ancient times, when we made peace, we cleared the path, and made it open both ways.— Now I wish you would keep your mind easy & have no hard thoughts. You do not know our ancient ways, tho' you know the ways of the white people in doing business.—When the two parties met together to make peace, we used to make it so bright that it was seen from the rising to the setting sun.—Now you begin to see our way of doing business in the times of our forefathers. What we did, we did well. If any thing was bad, we did it afterwards.

Now you begin to see our old methods, when we were yet numerous & the white people lived in the east & the Indians in the west. These matters you are unacquainted with. Now, Brother, keep your mind easy. You told us you did not understand the customs of Indians. Now you begin to get acquainted with our way of doing business. But what shall we say? Shall the way of doing business all be on one side? in one way? And we not follow any of our ancient customs?—As you hear us speak, brother, we are doing what you before told us—that we should speak whatever we thought.—You said just now you had told us all you had to say; and we were very much surprised at it. We are all as one: both our methods of living are joined together.

Now you have heard all we have to say. You have heard all our old rules of ancient times. Now we join both our methods of living together: we do not choose one before the other. All the methods you have proposed, we have accepted, and joined them with our own.—Now if you speak to us again, do not have any thing joined with it out of the way, nor find fault with us: for then it will take a good deal of time to set all right again. Let us keep the road of friendship between you and us open.

Now you have heard us; and we have told you the end of that speech: and we are going to begin another—which will be to choose an agent to settle every thing.

Now you have heard all we had concluded on to tell you.—Now we have been all day in council; and the tobacco does not smoke well; and as you have always used to wash our mouths, we expect you will do it again. (A Belt) [Source: PP, 60:105–7]

The next day, Friday, July 15, Pickering thanked Red Jacket for showing him how his words had caused pain, and he apologized to the warriors for making them uneasy. He also apologized that the United States had not yet appointed an Indian agent to serve them (107–108A). Good Peter responded, reemphasizing that peace had been made between the United States and the Six Nations. He told the warriors to stand easy. He said that although it was rumored the Joseph Brant was preparing for war, they would do their best to dissuade him (60:109–10). Sagoyewatha then said:

Listen, Brother Connésauty, The Thirteen States, and General Washington, and all the spectators, let them listen.

Now we have confirmed our friendship, and every thing is done: and we have concluded upon what we would say after we had confirmed our chain of friendship.

You know we said we were to appoint an agent, to see justice done on each side. We are tired of waiting; and now we are going to appoint an agent. We may happen to get a good one; and every thing will fall into his hands. Then let us go on very easy with our business, and consider what we are about; and if we happen to do wrong, let us put the wrong on our side, and try to do better. So this man (calling to him Thomas Reese, and putting his hand on his shoulder) we will choose. We will try him for a few days first, to see whether he is capable of doing our business or not; and if he does not do right, we will go on easy with our business.—Now our friendship is going on. You must consider this the voice of the whole; and we are going to try him forthwith. For he is the man who must go to take care of the money coming from Judge Phelps to the Seneka Nation, and see that justice is done in the division of it. Now you must be very careful to inform General Washington of this appointment: and if we have done wrong, let the matter be considered easily, as we told you before; and that is the way to keep friendship. Directly, when General Washington comes to hear this—if we have done wrong, do not let much be said about it. Let us try to make the matter easy, and mend it as quick as we can.

Now you are hearing a few words. We are going to try this man; and if he does us justice now, next spring he is to begin and receive the yearly pay for us the Seneka, the Onondaga, & Cayuga nations. He must receive it; and it must all go to Buffaloe Creek, where all the chiefs reside; that our minds may be at ease.

This is the whole of this matter: we have said enough about it.

You said we should have a gunsmith among us to mend our guns if they got broke: *and you said we might choose him*—(Here he [displayed?] a William Harris, but I interrupted the speaker, No: (said I) I said no such thing. Red Jacket sat down—but presently started up again & spoke these words) *"It won't do to talk much more—for perhaps we have been deceived in the whole!"* [Source: PP, 60:110A–111]

Pickering appended to the speech the following words: "It was now near sunset; and the executing of a deed by the Seneka Chiefs to Ebenezer Allan's two Indian daughters[8] *took up the rest of the day. The rain on Saturday July 16th having prevented the distribution of the goods intended as a present to the Six Nations, I called no council that day."*

On Sunday, July 17, Pickering gave out the customary council gifts, and he warned them that although they were free to make Harris their agent, he was not the agent of the United States, which required sober deliberation. He invited no more

8. The Senecas asked Pickering to validate a gift of land four miles square in the area known as Mt. Morris to Mary and Chloe Allan, the two Seneca daughters of a white frontiersman named Ebenezer Allan (Turpin 1932, 331).

than six to visit Philadelphia to discuss the introduction of people to teach farming and smithing among the Six Nations. He acknowledged that all the speeches made to him over the previous days represented the united voice of the Six nations, except for Red Jacket's remark that "that all the proposals of useful improvements which I had made to you, were a deception." *Defending his remark, Red Jacket* "said that when he was speaking to declare their choice of gunsmith, I [Pickering] had stopped his mouth, striking his mouth with his hand with a vehement motion. He continued to interrupt me, and behaved so rudely that for some time I could not proceed."

Shortly afterward, Pickering dispensed the gifts, and he writes that the council broke up in good humor. In his later notes, Pickering lists the gifts he gave to other chiefs and says the following about Red Jacket: "I should have compensated Red Jacket for a neck belt of wampum which he had left in a drunken frolic, and have given him eight or ten dollars to complete payment for a mare he had purchased and brought to the treaty. his wishes with respect to both were communicated to me: but after his public insults and rude behavior in council (of which he was sensible, but of which he was too proud, to make an acknowledgment.) I felt no disposition to make advances to him; and he did not think fit personally to apply to me. Finally, however, we parted as friends; he, his wife & children came to my quarters and shook hands before they set off for home" (PP, 60:117).

At a banquet at the end of negotiations, Sagoyewatha commented on the taste white men had for Native women. The translation is clearly embellished but Sagoyewatha made this remark more than once (Stone 1841, 346–47).

"BROTHER: You have during this negotiation said a good deal on civilization. No chief present can forget what you have told us. They will bear it in mind if they should not follow your advice.

"BROTHER: We thank you for your good counsel;—and, as an additional inducement to its adoption, I am happy to perceive,"—(casting his piercing eye around the table with an emphasis, look, and tone, peculiarly but insidiously significant,) "that you have introduced to our notice several young men who will doubtless feel that patriotism which your oratory is calculated to inspire,—proud that they can give a practical illustration of its sincerity by intermarrying with our women." [Stone 1841, 64–65, from manuscript collection of Joseph W. Moulton]

Diplomacy in Philadelphia

MARCH 14–APRIL 25, 1792

PICKERING'S INVITATION for six chiefs to visit the seat of the United States government in Philadelphia at the close of the council of Newtown Point acquired urgent importance by the spring of 1792. In the late fall of 1791, the Miami Indians under the command of Little Turtle killed nearly half of General St. Clair's army—630 men—in a single battle (Campisi and Starna 1995, 474). The victorious Ohio Indian nations then called a general Indian council for the summer 1792 at the confluence of the Auglaize and Maumee rivers to decide their next move (Phillips 1966, 178). Desperate to minimize trouble out west and in New York, Secretary Knox wrote to the Oneida missionary, Samuel Kirkland, to encourage Haudenosaunee chiefs to come to Philadelphia in the spring of 1792 to try to head off the success of the pan-Indian council. In the end, fifty chiefs began arriving on March 13. The Indians' visit was a great spectacle because the Indians held public mourning rituals for two chiefs who died during the trip, Peter Jaquette and Big Tree.[1] Among the presents President Washington gave to several of the chiefs of the Six Nations was a large chest medal for Sagoyewatha, which featured an emblem of Washington and an Indian chief sharing a peace pipe (see da Costa Nunez 1980).

Although the interpreters are not specifically mentioned, Pickering likely used Jasper Parrish, who he had employed for two years previously.

When available, the transcriptions below are taken from federal records at the National Archives. Copies of several of these speeches are held at the Buffalo and Erie Country Historical Society. The rest are from newspaper accounts of the Indians' visit.

---

1. Jaquette's funeral in mid-March was an impressive Anglo-Indian parade attended by 10,000 people. Extensive coverage of their deaths can be found in the *Pennsylvania Gazette*, March 19, 1792; *Gazette of the United States*, March 28, 1792; *Federal Gazette*, March 24, 1792; *Independent Gazetteer and Agricultural Repository*, April 28, 1792; and also the *Ontario Repository*, August 22, 1822.

Upon the Indians' arrival, Washington requested a $1,500 annuity from Congress for the Six Nations, and greeted the Haudenosaunee deputation. During later decades of treaty and land-sale negotiations, Sagoyewatha often recalled Washington's welcome speech, in which he refers to a lasting peace with the Senecas that would be "founded on the principles of justice and humanity as upon an immovable rock" (see Washington 2002, 148–49; Stone 1841, 72–73). After Washington's speech, Red Jacket addressed Washington through Pickering on March 31, 1792.

"I now request the attention of the President of the United States, by his agent Colonel Pickering here present

A few days since when the American chief had spoken to us, he gave us to understand that General Knox and Colonel Pickering should be the agents to negotiate with us on things which concern our welfare

"Let me call for Your compassion, as you can put all down upon paper, while we have to labour with our minds, to retain and digest what is Spoken, to enable us to make an Answer

Brother, whose attention I have called as the Representative of the great chief of this Island, when, the other day, he welcomed us to the great council fire of the thirteen United States, he said it was from his very heart. He said it gave him pleasure to look round and see such numerous representation of the five Nations of Indians and that it was at his Special request we had been invited to the Seat of the general Government to promote the happiness of our nation, in a friendly connection with the United States.

He then told us that his love of peace did not terminate with the five Nations but extended to all the nations at the Setting Sun; and that it was his desire that Universal peace might prevail in this Island

Brother Conneh-Sau-ty, (The Indian name of Col. Pickering) I requested your compassion; on account of our different Situations, that I should notice only a few of the principle things in the presidents Speech delivered to us the other day, Three things I have mentioned of the introductory part of his Speech. What other reply can we, Your brothers of the five nations Make to that introductory part of the Speech than to thank him, and Say, that it has given a Spring to every passion of our Souls?

Brother The President again observed to us, that he wished our minds might all be disposed to peace, that a happy peace might be established between Your brothers of the five nations, So firmly that nothing might move it: that it might be founded as upon a rock. this Sentiment of your Chief has given joy to our hearts—to compare that peace to a *rock*, which is *immoveable*.

The President further observed to us, that by our continuing [contriving?] to walk in the path of peace, and hearkening to his council, we might Share with you in all the blessings of civilized life: This also meets the Approbation of our Minds and has the thanks of all your brothers of the five nations.

He again observed to us, that if we attended to his council in this matter, our children and childrens children might partake in all the blessings which should rise out of this earth. This has taken hold of our Minds, and even we who are grown up look forward, and anticipate its fulfilment.

The President again observed to us, that what he had Spoken was in the Sincerity of his heart and that time and opportunities would give further evidence, that what he said was true. And we believed it, because we saw the words come from his own lips: and therefore they were lodged deep in our minds

The President of the thirteen fires, while continuing his Speech made also this remark, That in order to establish all his words for the best good of Your nation & ours—we must forget all the evils that were past, and attend to what lies before us, and take such a course as Shall cement our peace, that we may be as one

The President again observed, That it had come to his ears, that the cause of the hostilities now prevailing with the Western Indians, was their persuasion that the United States had unjustly taken away their lands. But he assured us this was not the case. That it was not the mind of any of his Chiefs to take any land on the whole Island without agreeing for it. He then mentioned a treaty at Muskingum,[2] and he concluded that what land was given up at that treaty was fairly obtained.

He also observed to us that it was his opinion that the hostile Indians were in an error, that they had missed the true path, whatever evil Spirit or whatever lies had turned them aside—he wished they could be discovered, that they might be removed. He expressed a Strong wish that those obstacles to the extending of peace to the Westward, might be discovered; and he would use all his exertions to remove them; that peace might be extended to the whole Island.

Towards the close of the Speech the President informed us that there were many things which concerned the future happiness of the five Nations the concerting of which he should refer to you (pointing to Colonel Pickering) here present, and the Chief Warrior of the United States.[3]

2. Fort Harmar/Muskingum 1789.
3. General Knox, secretary of war.

And at the close he observed, that our professions of friendship and regard were commonly witnessed by some token: therefore in the name of the United States, he presented us with this white belt, which was to be handed down from one generation to another, as a confirmation of his words, and a witness of the friendly disposition of the United States towards the peace and happiness of the five confederated Nations.

(Red Jacket here laid aside the white belt received from the President; and taking up a belt of their own (which is annexed) proceeded as follows)

Now let the President of the United States, possess his mind in peace, that we have made but a short reply to his address to us the other day, for the belt he gave us is deposited with us; and we have taken fast hold of it. What more can we say, than but to return our United thanks for his address in welcoming us to the seat of the great Council and for the advise he gave us, and our pleasure is increased that You, Conneh-sau-ty [Timothy Pickering], are appointed to assist us in devising the means to promote and secure the happiness of the five Nations

Brother! Now open Your ears, as the Representative of the great Council of the Thirteen United States in our present council—hear the words we may Speak. And all here present, of the great Council (some members of Congress were present—of which the Indians had been informed) and our Brethren of the five nations, hear!—We consider ourselves in the presence of the great Spirit, the Proprietor of us all.

The President, in effect, observed to us that we of the five nations were our own proprietors; were freemen and might speak with freedom, This has gladdened our hearts, and removed a weight that was upon them. And therefore You will hear us patiently while we speak.

The President has in effect told us that we were freemen; the sole proprietors of the soil on which we live. This is the Source of the joy; which we feel—How can two brothers speak freely together, unless they feel that they are on equal ground

I observed to you Brother that our considering ourselves by Your own acknowledgment as freemen has given this joy to our hearts, that we might Speak in Character. Therefore we join with the president in his wish that all the evils which have hitherto disturbed our peace, may be buried in oblivion. And this wish proceeds from our heart Now we can Speak our minds freely as they are free from pressure.

Now Brother, while you continue to hear in behalf of the United States let all here present also open their ears, while those of the five nations, here present Speak with one voice. We wish to see Your words verified to our

Children & children's children. You enjoy all the blessings of this life: to you therefore we look to make provision that the same may be enjoyed by our Children. This wish comes from our hearts. but we add, that our happiness cannot be great if in the introduction of your ways, we are put under too much constraint

Brother! Appointed agent to converse with us upon the affairs of our peace, continue to hear—we Your brothers of the five nations believe that the Great Spirit let this Island drop down from above—we also believe in his Superintendancy over this whole Island. Tis he who gives peace and prosperity, and he also sends evil[.] But prosperity has been Yours—American Brethren— All the good which can spring out of this Island You enjoy. We therefore wish that we and our Children and our Children's children may partake with you in that enjoyment

Brother! I observed that the great Spirit might Smile upon one people and turn & frown upon another. This you have Seen who are of one colour and one blood. The King of England and you Americans Strove to advance your happiness by extending your possessions upon this Island, which produces so many good things. And while you two great powers were thus contending for those good things, by which the whole Island was shaken and violently agitated, is it Strange that the peace of us the five nations was Shaken and overturned? But let me say no more of the trembling of our Island[.] All is in a measure now quieted. Peace is now restored. The peace of us the five nations is now budding. But still there is some Shaking among the original Americans, at the setting sun—and you the thirteen fires, and the King of England: Know what is our situation, and the causes of this disturbance now here[.] You have an Embassador[4] as we are informed, from the King of England. Let him, in behalf of the King, and the Americans adjust all their matters according to their agreement at the making of peace—and then you will soon see all things settled among the Indian-Nations, peace will be Spread far and near; Let the president and the Embassador use all their exertions to bring about this settlement (according to their peace) and it will make us all glad & we shall consider both as our real friends

Brother! You continue to hear, be assured we have Spoken from our very hearts and not from our lips only[.] Let us therefore make this observation That when you Americans and the King made peace, he did not mention us and showed us no compassion notwithstanding all he Said to us, and all we had suffered. This has been the occasion of great sorrow and pain, and great

4. William Leete Stone's note: "Mr. Hammond, British envoy to the U.S."

loss to us the five nations. When you asked and he settled the peace between you two great nations, he never asked us for a delegation to attend to our Interests, Had he done this a settlement of peace among all the Western nations might have been effected[.] But the neglecting of this and passing us by unnoticed has brought upon us great pain & trouble

Brother! It is evident that we of the five nations have Suffered much in consequence of the strife between You and the King of England who are one colour and one blood. Our chain of peace has been broken—Peace & friendship have been chased from us. But you Americans were determined not to treat us in the same manner as we had been treated by the King of England[.] You therefore desired us at the reestablishment of peace to Sit down at our ancient fire places, and again enjoy our lands. And had the peace between You and the King of England been completely accomplished,[5] it would long before this time, have extended far beyond the five nations.

Brother Conneh-Sau-ty [Timothy Pickering] you are specially appointed with General Knox to confer with us on our peace and happiness. We have rejoiced in Your appointment and we hope that the great Warrior will remember that though a *Warrior* he is to converse with us about *peace:* letting what concerns *War* Sleep; and the *Counselling* part of his mind, while acting with us, be of *peace*.

Brother! have patience and continue to listen[:] The President has assured us, that *he* is not the cause of the hostilities now existing at the Westward but laments it[.] Brother we wish You to point out to us of the five nations *What You thing [think] is the real cause*

Brother! Agent of the Thirteen United States in the present Council, we now publicly return our thanks to the president & all the Counsellors of the thirteen United States for the words which he has spoken to us. They were good, without any mixture. Shall we observe that he wished that if the errors of the hostile Indians could be discovered he would use his Utmost exertions to remove them? Brother You & the King of England are the two governing powers of this Island. What are we? You both are important and proud: and you cannot adjust your own affairs agreeably to Your declarations of peace[.] Therefore the Western Indians are bewildered[.] one says one thing to them and one says another. Were these things adjusted it would be easy to diffuse peace everywhere.

---

5. William Leete Stone's note: "alluding probably to the British retention of northwestern forts."

In confirmation of our words we give this belt which we wish the president to hold fast in remembrance of what we have now Spoken

(He then delivered to Colonel Pickering the annexed belt)" [Source: "Indian Collection," box 1, folder 1, "Government and Business, 1790–1811," BECHS B-002; Washington 2002, 190–94; also in Stone 1841, 74–80]

On Monday, March 26 (prior to the above speech), the governor of Pennsylvania met the Indians at the State House and delivered a brief welcome, pledging friendship and requesting the Indians to listen carefully to the president.[6] In response to the governor's welcome, Sagoyewatha made following reply on March 28:

Brother Onas*[7] Governor,

OPEN unprejudiced ears to what we have to say. Some days since you addressed us, and what you said gave us great pleasure. This day, the Great Spirit has allowed us to meet you again in this Council-Chamber. We hope that your not receiving an immediate answer to your address, will make no improper impression upon your mind.

We mention this, lest you should suspect, that your kind welcome and friendly address, has not had a proper effect upon our hearts. We assure you it is far otherwise.

Brother, Onas Governor,

In your address to us the other day, in this ancient Council-chamber, where our forefathers have often conversed together, several things struck our attention very forcibly. When you told us this was the place in which our forefathers often met on peaceable terms, it gave us sensible pleasure and more joy than we could express.

Brother, Onas Governor,

Though we have not writings like you; yet we remember often to have heard of the friendship that existed between our forefathers and yours. The picture[8] to which you drew our attention brought fresh to our minds the friendly conferences that used to be held between the former Governors of Pennsylvania and our Tribes, and shewed the love which your forefathers had of peace, and the friendly disposition of our people. It is still our wish, as well as yours, to preserve peace between our Tribes and you, and it would be well if the same spirit existed among the Indians to the Westward, and through every part of the United States.

6. The governor's full speech appears in the *Federal Gazette and Philadelphia Daily Advertiser*, March 27, 1792; and also the *Gazette of the United States*, April 4, 1792.

7. Note in the *Gazette:* " 'Onas,' the name originally given to William Penn."

8. A painting of William Penn's treaty with the Indians.

Brother, Onas Governor,

You particularly expressed, that you were well pleased to find, that we differed in disposition from the Indians Westward. Your disposition is that for which the ancient Onas Governors were remarkable. As you love peace, so do we also; and we wish it could be extended to the most distant parts of this great country.

Brother, Onas Governor,

We agreed in council this morning, that the sentiments I have expressed, should be communicated to you, before the delegates of the Five Nations, and to tell you, that your cordial welcome to this city, and the good sentiments contained in your address, have made a deep impression on our hearts, have given us great joy, and from the heart I tell you so. This is all I have to say. [Source: *Gazette of the United States*, April 11, 1792. Shorter versions in Drake 1841, 105–6; Stone 1841, 70–71]

Sagoyewatha's speech was followed by a short speech by Good Peter, who looked forward to continuing friendship with the United States even though some of the Indians were not all of one mind. The governor responded briefly that he hoped all Indians would do as the Six Nations had done.

Having told the Haudenosaunees about the $1,500 Congressional annuity just passed, Pickering had to work out how the money and instructors of agriculture would be disbursed. On April 10, Sagoyewatha spoke about the Senecas' recommendations for distribution:

Brother Connesauty,

Yesterday when you made your proposals, the Oneidas accepted them and thanked you. They spoke for those Oneidas Onondagas and Tuscaroras who *all lie under one blanket.*[9] We the Senecas have considered them, and are now going to Speak

Yesterday when you proposed *four* establishments and that there should be three men for each, you mentioned the rewards to be given to a certain *number* who should learn quickest—of the *biggest* nations *six*, but those who could not learn fast must be miserable[.] If you do right, you will give to all something to work with as fast as they learn; so that all may be supplied, otherwise a strife will arise. But if all are to be supplied all will be encouraged to learn; Another thing—a great many of our people are poor—women who have no men in their families: now by supplying others, in the manner we

9. Manuscript note: "live in one neighborhood."

have suggested, the fields of the poor may be ploughed. This will rouse the minds of the whole nation to learn what the white people know.

You told us that if we liked what you said, we should say so. If it was deficient we should tell what was wanting; If redundant, we should strike off. You mentioned the places for the establishments. One was at Genneseo, and one at Oneida[.] We have considered that at Oneida there are a great many people, Tuscaroras and Oneidas, who can help one another; and that at Genneseo there are also Oneidas & Tuscaroras who being numerous will want one establishment for themselves. We wish you to use them as you do the Senecas that their minds may be easy—perhaps they will learn quicker, so we desire two establishments at Geneseo.

You must not suppose that we slight any thing that you have offered[.] We accept of all. It is all good. But we hope that you will not think, of making establishments at Buffalo Creek or Obeil's town,[10] *at present.* For there is some shaking (trouble) at the extremity of our house (border of our Country) There may be some danger to the persons who might be employed

There is one thing that might be of great advantage to us which you have not mentioned: That is a saw-mill. This would help us greatly[.] We know the cause of Mr. Allen's leaving our Country.[11] He told us the reason before he went away. And you and we all know that his mill is over the line agreed on last summer before you, and he has gone away, he says, because he owns nothing[.] Allen told us if General Washington would buy the Mill paying him just what it cost, it might be ours, and he allowed it stood on our land[.] And we should rejoice exceedingly if we could become the proprietors of that Mill. If General Washington would buy it and give it to us, the Superintendent might see to the appraisement of it.

You mentioned that this provision was for those of our nations who live on this side of the Lakes. But perhaps our Brothers at Grand River,[12] when they see those things introduced among us, may fall in love with them, and want to come and join us. We therefore wish that the plan may be so formed as

10. Cornplanter's home at Allegany.

11. Ebenezer Allan. See glossary and Turpin (1932). Allan left the Genesee valley for Canada because he could not secure any land for himself.

12. Grand River is a large Six Nations settlement, largely Mohawk and founded by Joseph Brant, sixty miles west of Buffalo in Canada. The Grand River reserve, twelve miles wide as it follows the river, was given to the Mohawks by British general Frederick Haldimand on October 25, 1784, to compensate for the loss of their lands in New York following the Revolution. In order to raise money, Brant attempted to sell off large portions of the Grand River settlement to white investors from 1797 until his death (see Kelsay 1984; and esp. Johnson 1964; map 6).

to comprehend all. For our peace is in a weak languid condition, just expiring, and we would avoid giving offense to any of our Brothers. There are two Roads: perhaps they on the other side of the water (meaning those at the Grand river) may take our road[.] Therefore we wish you to extend your invitation to the whole Six Nations, and press them to join us. when peace shall take place—we shall desire the proposed establishments may be made at Buffalo and Allegany

It was the custom of our fathers, when they had finished any particular business to talk over affairs of general concern—Now we wish Congress to hasten to make peace, with the hostile Indians who are alongside of us. We both have our eyes to the place where the trouble lies

This is all we have to say.

dated Apr 10. 1792

true copy

War department   **X**   J[oh]n Stagg Jr.

Sept 12, 1792   **X**   Ch[ie]f. Cl[er]k.

[Source: "Indian Collection," box 1, folder 1, "Government and Business, 1790–1811," BECHS B-002. Marked "true copy" from War Dept. on September 12, 1792, but probably recopied with several other speeches in folder 1 on "Sep 1822"; also in Stone 1841, 83–86]

A week later, on April 17, 1792, Pickering gave a long address[13] *that expressed optimism for the new path toward civilization that the Six Nations were considering. He also put most of the blame on the western war on the Ohio Indians, who had never put down the hatchet since joining with the British during the Revolution. He delicately asked that if the Six Nations thought they could assure the western Indians of the peaceful intentions of the United States that they might take any steps they felt comfortable taking. The Indians responded to Pickering's request for brokering peace with the Miamis and Wabash Indians on the same day. Farmer's Brother began with a passionate speech*[14] *that lay blame on the brash conduct of the commissioners at the treaties of Fort McIntosh in 1785 and Fort Harmar in 1789, and the massacre of peaceful Indians. Red Jacket continued:*

Brother Connesauty, who have been appointed by the President to represent the United States in the business on which we were invited, now attend—

You spoke to us on our first arrival; and a few days since you opened the

13. The full text of Pickering's speech appears in Stone (1841, 87–92).
14. Farmer's Brother's complete speech appears in Stone (1841, 92–96).

whole business which respects our national happiness—After this you adverted to the troubled state of the nations at the Westward; and mentioned what you supposed were the causes of those troubles among the various nations in that quarter: and you desired us to speak our minds freely on this subject—

Brother,

You have heard the two principal causes of those troubles. Those two causes, as we apprehend were these; The destroying of the Town by the Big Knife, & killing the old man while the nations were met counselling for peace; and the smallness of the number who attended the Treaty at Muskingum & the affair of the lands. For we the five nations had to give up our judgements to what the commissioner dictated; and that was the reason there were so many names to the writing—

Brother,

You have now heard the causes of the uneasiness among the Western Indians you said you wished to know the causes of those hostilities, that you might remove them—Here they are, as we consider them—Now it is our wish that the President & Congress would exert themselves to remove them. You have manifested a desire to put the burthen of bringing you and the Western Indians together, upon our shoulders: but tis too heavy for us to bear without your assistance.

Brother,

You continue to hear. We are not able to go forward with this great business alone. Therefore if you earnestly wish for the restoration of peace as your words have expressed, let us have some assistance—So there be one voice between you and the British who are by our fire side, to effect this object—True you have drawn a line between them & you; and the line comes near to us. But we think you are too proud to act together upon this business. And unless you go to the Western Indians, how will you convince them that you mean to do them justice—

Brother,

We of the five nations have not settled all the affairs pertaining to our peace—and it will give great joy to our minds if you can extend peace to the Western Nations. What we have proposed we think would be a healing medicine. Therefore when we have completed our business with you, we shall be glad to communicate this to the people of our colour at the westward.

Brother,

While you are yet hearing, let us remind you of your own words—"verily you must love those of your own colour; and we believe also that you are friends to us."

Brother, You have spoken truly: we do love both. we also love our common peace. Therefore have we thus advised to this healing medicine, which alone, we think, will complete a cure of all the wounds—

Brother,

This is all we now have to say. You see that it is a pleasant day; an emblem of the pleasure and joy now diffused thro' all here present, for indeed it has been a counselling day—a day of business— [Source:"Indian Collection," box 1, folder 1, "Government and Business, 1790–1811," BECHS B-002. Also in Stone 1841, 96–98]

On April 25, 1792, President Washington spoke a farewell address to the Haudenosaunees, informing them of their $1,500 annuity and offering his condolences about the deaths of the two chiefs during their visit (Washington 2002, 316–17; Stone 1841, 98–99).

Indian Council at the Glaize

SEPTEMBER 30–OCTOBER 9, 1792

FULFILLING THEIR PROMISE in Philadelphia, the Senecas attended the pan-Indian council at the Glaize (Auglaize village, at the forks of the Auglaize and Maumee rivers, see map 1), which got underway during the fall of 1792. At the council, the Six Nations faced the delicate task of trying to convince the western Indians that it was in their best interests to make peace with the United States. They persuaded the western Indians to attend another council with the United States on the lower Sandusky river the following year. However, as the following speeches indicate, the western Indians felt betrayed by the Six Nations, who had done nothing when United States had sent two armies to overrun the Ohio Indians. British lieutenant governor John Simcoe and his Indian agent, Colonel Alexander McKee, both attended the council to offer the western Indians advice and support. Simcoe was interested in building a defensive buffer zone between the United States and Britain, and his agents counseled the western Indians to maintain the Ohio River as the boundary between Indian and U.S. lands (Mohawk 2000, 54; Kelsay 1984, 484).

In the following transcript, Sagoyewatha is called Cowkiller, a name uncharitably conferred upon him during the Revolution by Joseph Brant (see introduction). Because representatives from many different nations were speaking, adequate interpretation was a difficult job, as appears below at the end of a heated exchange on October 5. The manuscript does not specify the interpreters, but among Simcoe's translators were probably Walter Butler Sheehan and William Johnson. Both these interpreters worked for the British Indian department (see glossary), and they attended a follow-up council at Buffalo Creek a month later on Simcoe's behalf.

The following transcript comes from the Simcoe Family Papers, Archives of Ontario, Toronto. The complete text of the other speakers' words can be read in *The Correspondence of Lieutenant Governor John R. Simcoe* (Simcoe 1923, 1:218–29). The editors of Simcoe's correspondence, however, seemed to have worked from a slightly different manuscript, and they are also missing a manuscript page from Messquakenoe's speech on October 7.

The council began on September 30, with Messquakenoe ("Painted Pole"), a Shawnee chief, opening the council with condolence ceremonies and the passing of a pipe. He announced himself as the principal speaker for the western Indians present. Two days later, on October 2, the council resumed. Messquakenoe and Buckange-hallis, a chief of the Delawares, noted that they had not heard from the Six Nations in several years and reminded them that they pledged together four years earlier to be united and defend each other when trouble arose. Red Jacket briefly acknowledged their words and replied that they would be ready to respond the following day. De-layed by bad weather, Red Jacket responded for the Six Nations on October 4:

Cowkiller, a Seneca Chief, with a String of White Wampum

We thank ye all Shawanoes, Delawares &c &c &c (repeating all the different nations) for wiping away our tears and setting our hearts right, for the loss of our friends, our women & children since we last met: And I beg you will now listen to what your Elder Brethren the 6 Nations are now going to say to you.

taking a Black & White String

Brothers We have now come to Council with you, as you sent for us and I beg you will listen attentively, as you desired us to tell you what we had on our minds—We are now following the steps of our forefathers and renewing our ancient friendship, Listen therefore to what we have now to say to you.

Then taking the bundle of Speeches and belts, that were delivered to them the last Council day, thus proceeded.

Brothers We are very glad you have strengthened the Chain of friendship with all the distant Nations from whom you received these Belts and Speeches.—It was always our advice to you to do so, and we are glad you have followed it, and we return you our thanks for the pains and trouble you have taken to accomplish it.

Brothers You told us also of the Creek & Cherokee Nations being now present, we return you thanks for that also, as it will brighten the Chain of friendship with all Nations.

A Pipe[1]

Brothers We thank you for showing us this Pipe of Peace and friendship, which was sent, to be left here for all Nations of our Colour to take hold of—

---

1. This pipe was passed by Blue Jacket.

We now join our hands to it, and leave it to be lodged with you for the purpose you have mentioned.

Black and White Strings.

Brothers I now speak to the Counsellors & Warriors and I desire you will take notice what I say to you—The White People are now looking at us and know what we are about—They were always the instigators of our quarrels; let us now unite and consider what will be the best for us, our women and Children, to lengthen our days and be in Peace.

Several Strings of White Wampum.

Brothers I address myself to all the Nations—You know, that 4 years ago we met in Council at the foot of the Rapids; you well remember all that passed there.—You invited us now to come here, as we had not seen you for 4 years; And you suppose we were doing something all that time for your good: I now tell you we have been endeavouring to do something for your good, the last two years in our Councils.

Brothers When the White People on this Island were as one Man, they asked us at Fort Stanwix for land; we granted it.—A few years afterwards, they fell out among themselves.—

The King our Father told us he was going to chastise his Son and nobody else, and it would be over in a short time.—Soon after we were desired by the people of this Island to sit still and not mind the quarrels of Father and Son. But shortly after that Our Father the King desired us to take part with him, which we complied with. Our Father was defeated by the Americans and then made a Peace and left us alone.

Our Father then desired us to speak to the Americans for as good a peace as we could get for ourselves.—We have been trying to do so in the best manner we could and we now desire you to do the same and to join with us in our best endeavours for that purpose—The Country you live in is a very good one and I like it very much.

Brothers You were fortunate that the Great Spirit above was so kind as to assist you to throw the Americans twice on their back, when they came against your Villages, your women and Children—Now Brothers, We know that the Americans have held out their hands to offer you peace—Don't be too proud spirited and reject it, lest the Great Spirit should be angry with you, but let us go on in the best manner we can to make peace with them.

A Black and White String.

Now Counsellors and Warriors—you have heared what I had to say; I hope you will attend to it:—Your Warriors were lately in the front, but I hope to see the Counsellor's there and they together consulting which is the best means of making peace for the advantage of ourselves, our women, and Children.

A Black & White Belt.

Brothers You have heared what the 6 Nations have said to you. You well remember, the Americans have come when we have been in Council and kicked out our fire—We now kindle it once more that we may settle what is good and proper for peace for our women, our Children and Warriors.

Cochenawaga, a chief of the Seven Nations of Canada, then spoke on behalf of pan-Indian unanimity in relations with the Americans, particularly addressing the Creeks and the Cherokees, and the council broke up for the day. The next day, October 5, Messquakenoe thanked the Seven Nations, and promised the belt signifying their words would be sent west for all to see. Then, taking up the belts of the Six Nations from the previous day, he angrily accused the Six Nations of talking too much to the Americans, and he threw their belts down at their feet. Red Jacket replied:

Brothers We desire you will sit still, we shall move to a little distance, to consult on what answer to give you—You have talked to us a little too roughly—You have thrown us on our backs.

Farmer's Brother picked up the belt and put it across his back. The Senecas retired for an hour to council among themselves. When they returned, Sagoyewatha said:

Brothers, Listen to what the 6 Nations are now going to say to all the Nations of our Colour—You very well know when you returned from Canada last year, you passed by our villages and went by Tiandenaga's[2]

Brothers You tell us that we are always running to the Americans and telling them every thing—We have been talking to them, 'tis true: They sent for us and led us by the hand to Philadelphia where we met the 13 United States and Washington—He told us he has had several meetings with the Indians on this Island at Beaver Creek and several other places—You all know and the Wyandots whom I see there know,—what was said there—it cannot be strange to any of you.

Brothers Washington asked us what was the cause of the uneasiness of the Western Nations—We told him it was in regard to their lands.—He then told us, he would satisfy the owners of the Land, if it had been sold by people who were not the real owners thereof: But he wishes for a Council with all the Nations for that purpose.

2. That is, Thayendanegea's, or Joseph Brant's village on Grand River.

Brothers He did not say he would give up the Lands, but that he would satisfy the Indians for them.

That he wanted nothing so much as the friendship of all his Brothers the Indians throughout this Island—He then desired us to come to you with his Speeches and tell you all he said, and he added that if the forts he had made in the Country gave you uneasiness he would remove them.

Brothers He also told us, that after we had finished our business, it might be dangerous for us to return through the Country; But that you had many Prisoners of his and that you could easily send some of them to tell him what had been determined on.

Brothers These are the Papers and Speeches (taking up a Tin Case) which we received B.[3] and we now give them to you—This is all we have to say, take them to your Father and he will explain them to you.

The council then broke up for the day. As Red Jacket noted in a speech a month later (November 13, 1792), the Six Nations felt that they had unintentionally given offense to their western brethren through bad translation, and the next day they called a private meeting with the western chiefs and another interpreter to clarify the misunderstanding. At that conference, Farmer's Brother said that Washington had not lied to the Senecas over the past two years, and that the president's desire that they take no part in British and American intrigues was something to "consider well." Messquakenoe responded on the following day that over the past two years Washington had sent two armies against them while the Six Nations seemed to be blinded by their "sweet speeches." Messquakenoe concluded by telling the Senecas to take the following message back to the United States: if the Americans wanted peace, they must destroy their forts and withdraw from land north of the Ohio River. Otherwise, the Americans would travel a "bloody road." Red Jacket replied:

Brothers The 6 Nations return you thanks for what you have said to us— You have considered well before you spoke: We now join with you and will put our Heads together, and endeavour to get all our Lands back, where the Americans have encroached upon us, And we will meet you in the Spring at lower Sandusky as you have mentioned [Source: "Official Correspondence," September 1792, F 47-1-2-5, John R. Simcoe Papers, Simcoe Family Papers, Archives of Ontario, Toronto]

---

3. This uppercase "B." signifies "item B" in an attachment not included in the manuscript microfilm.

The council went on for two more days. The Indians notified the Six Nations that they were going to specify that the British agent Alexander McKee, acting as Simcoe's representative, would accompany the Indians to Sandusky to advise them if the United States made an offer. The council ended with the western Indians addressing McKee, expressing their thanks to Governor Simcoe for his assistance and friendship.

Council at Buffalo Creek

NOVEMBER 13–14, 1792

THE FOLLOWING COUNCIL was convened to inform the British and the United States of what transpired at the prior month's council at the Glaize. The Six Nations pointed out to the United States that they had fulfilled their promise and that the success of the council would depend on a strong commitment on behalf of both the British and the United States for peace.

The transcript is taken from the official correspondence of Governor Simcoe, but it is an odd mix of summary and quotation occasionally narrated from the Six Nations's point of view. Jasper Parrish was interpreter for the Six Nations, and Simcoe's interpreters were William Johnson and Walter Butler Sheehan, both very experienced translators (see glossary). According to William Leete Stone, Parrish wrote an account of the council to be forwarded to the president. Stone reprints it in his appendix, but admits that it is a "curious" document. Part of Stone's concern is that Parrish seems to have inserted accounts of the translation disagreement a month earlier at the Glaize (on October 5 and 6) without clearly noting that he is rehearsing debates that occurred a month before. Some of the speeches Parrish summarizes are highly divergent texts from Simcoe's, but they contain largely the same content.

Tuesday Nov 13, 1792

Present:—By Order of His Excellency Lt. Governor Simcoe. Lt. Colonel [John] Butler, Agt, I.[ndian] D.[epartment]; Major of Brigade Littlehales [representing Gov. Simcoe]; Lt. Talbot 24th Regt.; Lt. Grey 7th or R.F.; W.[alter] B.[utler] Sheehan W[illia]m. Johnson Interpreters.—With the Chiefs of the Seneca, Onandago, Cayuga, Tuscarora Indians and their Allies, Delawares &c, &c., &c. On the part of the United States, Mr. [Israel] Chapin [Jr.] (son of the Superintendent General) Mr. Parrish, Interpreter.

Cow Killer—A Seneca Chief Spoke thus.

Brothers, Give attention to what we are going to say. We are happy to see the King's people and those of the United States side by side. We last winter went by Invitation to Philadelphia; upon our return we reported our proceedings to the King's Superintendant, who seemed pleased.

The United States recommended our mediation in making a peace with our Western Brethren; and being also solicited by them to attend; The King's people furnished us with every assistance, and sent a person with us; We accordingly went to Detroit, where we met with every attention, and were amply provided to the place of our destination.

Brothers, While at the Council of the Glaize, our Brethren called us Elder Brothers; said, they had often sent to us for four years past for our Advice and assistance.

White Belt six Rows of Wampum.

Brothers, After the above was delivered we asked why the great Council Fire was kindled and if they had any thing on their minds?—They replied "*that* was not all they wished to mention; that four years ago they sent an express to their Elder Brethren, informing them of their situation.—The answer the Six Nations returned was, they were all of one colour, and ought to be *firm* and *united*; in consequence of which they received a large bunch of Wampum, containing the Sentiments of twenty different Indian Nations.

Brothers, After receiving the message from our Elder Brethren we took their pipe, and our Confederacy smoked it, and returned the same with all our opinions.

Brothers, "We now return the Pipe, and hope you (our Elder Brethren) will smoke it with the same sentiments you offered it to us.

Brothers, "We the Six Nations after having smoked out of the Pipe, said *we* were all of one mind, in ancient times our Forefathers were at war with each other, some nations occasioned Disturbances amongst us, perhaps it was the will of the great Spirit; We the Six Nations then exerted ourselves to procure peace; in process of time the English *Our Fathers,* came to trade with us, they demanded a small piece of ground; this we granted, they still solicited for more Land. They assisted the Indians when they became settlers in making peace, and recommended all we have hitherto done, that we ought to be of one mind. We told the Hurons we conceived them to be the promoters of the existing troubles and thanked our Brethren in general for defending our property.

Brothers, "Tho' we were happy at your success in repelling the late Invasion of your Territories yet we recommend the advice of the King (our Father) to keep possession of your Country by making an Adequate Peace.

Brothers, "When the White People arrived at Albany, the great King and the Americans were one; our Father Sir William Johnson had the care of us, we then agreed to give the white people Lands East of the Ohio the *Boundary*

Line; selling other Lands to the East of that *Boundary Line,* was the cause of breaking the minds of the Indians.

Brothers, "Attention; we hold this Pipe, you call us Brothers, we wish unanimity, that the chain of Friendship may be brightened; we will cordially assist you to hold it and to carry the heavy burthen."

After delivering the above Speech the Shawanese answered.

Brothers, "Tho' we call you Elder Brethren, we look upon it you do not speak from your *Hearts* as you are but just come from counselling with the Americans, we know you have Intercourse with them." When this was said, they told us they would adjourn, and desired us to make our minds easy, as they would speak more freely. We replyed we shall now go back to (the Interpreter) Johnson and relate what has passed.

On reassembling we spoke as follows.[1]

Brothers, "You consider us as people who speak only from our Lips, and that we converse with what you call *Yankies,* it's true we have held Treaties with the United States, the British have advised it when for our Interest, but we never lost sight of the Confederacy; you seem Jealous of our Intercourse with the States, we are independent people and not biased by British or Americans."

Brothers, "All the time the English and French were at war, they were fighting for this Island, the French were conquered, soon after the people now called Americans disagreed with the English; and in the contest the King was thrown down; and gave up this Country to the States.

This is the Language the States hold forth to us; They consider themselves the proprietors of these Lands, in the same manner the King did; when he took them from the French and could shew them upon paper.

Brothers, This being related our Western Brethren did not appear to comprehend it, owing to the Interpreter, but when it was explained by another Interpreter, the Confederacy were satisfied, and promised to abide by our advice, and thanked us for following the wise measures of our Forefathers.

An unnamed speaker for the western nations replied that they had defeated the last army Washington sent, and they were willing to listen to Washington next spring in Sandusky only if he genuinely came in peace. To show their good will, the western Indians ceded any lands they claimed east of the Ohio River.

1. The speaker for the Six Nations is not here specified but identified as Sagoyewatha later in the day. The pronoun "we" suggests that Parrish is the narrator.

The Cow Killer then continued his Speech having finished repeating the transactions at the Miami.

Brothers, We give it in charge to remember us to the great Man at Niagara,[2] who we understand is lately arrived from England, and has the care of the Indians as well as the White People, in this part of the Country, we urge it to you to request his attendance at the proposed Council, at Sandusky next Spring; Colonel Butler has been long acquainted with our affairs, we therefore solicit his attendance, and hope our Father will consider us, and provide some provisions at the place of meeting; We conclude by observing that if the Governor or his representative does not meet us, and those persons deputed by the United States do not also meet us, we shall suppose they do not wish for peace.

Four Strings of Black & White Wampum.

Addressed to Mr. Chapin.

Brothers, You represent the United States, we were sent by you to the Westward, and have related what passed there.

Brothers, Give attention—We address you in the same manner as the President of Congress;—by his desire, we went to the Westward; the road is opened for him to pursue, and accomplish the desired peace; We have repeated your wishes to the Western Nations and explained them; there is a peaceful path and a bloody one; prevent your armies from proceeding in that Country, and enable us to render that service you seem so desirous of. The Six Nations are now returned, and have contributed as much as possible their assistance, with their Western Brethren, to restore peace; We hope the United States will not by any improper means, defeat the intended purpose; for should such be the case, as it is the wish of the Indians to live in peace, they will look upon the President of the United States as the cause of its not taking place.

A Belt eight rows Black & White Wampum.

We expect sensible persons will be appointed to attend the Council, and that all Records of purchases of Lands, Treaties and Documents, Maps, &c. since the first arrival of the white people among us, will be brought and produced by them, as they will then be particularly investigated.

Four Strings of Black and White Wampum.

We request that what we have now said, may be immediately communicated by *Express* to Congress, and an answer sent back to us as soon as possible without any delay that we may make our Western Brethren acquainted with it; as it is a matter requiring our most serious consideration.

Brothers,

2. Lt. Gov. John Simcoe lived in Niagara.

More particularly addressed to Colonel Butler.

We have related all our Business to the Westward and we now repeat that we cannot negotiate any thing at the proposed place of assembling (viz.) Sandusky, without the Governor's and your (Col. Butler's) presence it being a matter of the most essential Importance to us; we therefore hope you will be prepared to clear up all doubts and to be active and alive to our Interests as Reflections have been insinuated that when we formerly consulted the commanding officers they could not give us final answers, we trust that is now obviated, and that the Governor will make a Speedy Reply.

Brothers, We expect the Governor will bring to Sandusky all papers, Maps, Records and treaties relative to us Indians.

A Belt eight Rows of Black & White Wampum.

Brothers, It gives us great pleasure to see you who represent the King Our Father and the United States sitting in Council together, it has been very different for some years past when you were much divided in your Sentiments.

Adjourned.

The following day, November 14, Major Littlehales, who worked as Simcoe's secretary, told the Indians that Governor Simcoe was happy to see the Indians working for peace. He promised to ask Simcoe to come to Sandusky with all the maps and records the Indians requested. He concluded that Simcoe would work in every way to bring about peace in their interests.

On behalf of the United States, Captain Israel Chapin, Jr. gave his regrets that his father could not attend. Chapin promised to send an express dispatch of the council transcripts to the U.S. Department of War, adding that he would probably also go himself and give a "faithful account" of everything. As he was agreeing with the Indians' request that good persons be sent to the council of Sandusky, he was interrupted by Red Jacket:

Chapin: "Brothers, I shall particularly mention what you said about the meeting at Sandusky next spring and your wish that good persons may be sent to the Council.

"Brothers—(Parrish the American Interpreter translated this Speech to the Indians at the conclusion of every sentence, here, the Cow Killer interrupted him, and said not only good persons, but sensible proper people no Land Jobbers but such as Colonel Pickering") Chapin proceeded that he would ask the United States to bring all necessary maps and documents to the treaty. The council then adjourned. [Source: Simcoe 1923, 1:256–60]

Council with Butler at Fort Erie

June 9–10, 1793

THE FIRST DAY of this council was spent condoling over the death of Colonel John Butler's wife, Catherine, who was buried on May 31. The second day concerned discussion about the pan-Indian council scheduled for Sandusky, which had been agreed upon the preceding fall at the Glaize. Discussion at the Erie council, however, was influenced by news of General Anthony Wayne's advancing forces in Ohio. The interpreters were Walter Butler Sheehan and William Johnson.

"Present: Lt. Col. Butler, Deputy Agent for Indian Affairs; Lt. Master Green, 5th Regiment, Ft. Erie; W. B. Sheehan; Wm. Johnson; Johnson Butler. With the Chiefs of the Six Nations and Mississagua Indians

The Cow Killer, a principal Seneca Chief after going through the usual Ceremony of Condolence addressed himself to Lt. Col. Butler as follows—

Brother We sent for you to say a few words and are sorry in [our] hearts for the Occasion, the accident which has happened in your Family has troubled our minds. It is a Custom handed down to us from our wise Forefathers to Condole with our Brethren for any loss the[y] have Sustained—We therefore with these Strings wipe the tears from your eyes, we clear your throat that you may Speak to us and we wipe the Blood from your Sight that the great loss you have met with may not obstruct you from hearing your Brethren and attending to their affairs as usual[.]

3 Strings of Wampum.

Brother As you long have had the care of us and are acquainted with the Ceremonies that took place in the time of the late Sir William Johnson—as he is now no more we look up to you who know his Custom of treating us, We therefore with these Strings hope to ease your Mind of the Weight with which it is oppressed lest excessive Sorrow Should Deprive us of your Fatherly Care and assistance also. We therefore cover the Grave From your sight with these.

4 Strings Blk & White Wampum

Brother It has always been Customary with us to take the earliest opportunity to remove Sorrow from the Minds of our Friends, and as a tear may Still remain on your Cheek with these Strings we wipe it Dry, and remove all remaining impediments that you may See us clearly as heretofore.

3 Strings White Wampum

Brother We have now finished condoling with you in the name of the Sachems, Chiefs, Warriors, and Chief Women of the Six Nations, We wish ease to your mind & invoke the Great Spirit for your Preservation—

At which Lt. Col. Butler Returned the following Answer

Brethren I have attentively heard what you have said & I thank my Brethren of the Six Nations for the affection the[y] express for me and for the part they take in the misfortune that has happened in my Family and as far as in one lies I will follow their kind advice

4 Strings White Wampum

Brethren On your Second Strings you mention the Customs of your Wise forefathers, and of the late Sir William Johnson, with which I am acquainted and as far as my power extends I shall pursue them, as they must always tend to the advantage of my Brethren the Six Nations and the Indians in General, I return you my gratefull thanks for your affectionate concern for me personally. it is true life is uncertain, but whatever portion of it is allotted me in this world shall be devoted to your true interests & Service.

4 Strings Black & White Wampum

Brothers I am perfectly sensible of the kindness you have Shewn me in taking the earliest opportunity of condoling with [me] and request you will inform all the Six Nations of my thanks for their kind attention to me on this occasion 3 Strings White Wampum

Brethren I am sorry that my Health will not permit me to attend the treaty at Sandusky. I recommend to you unanimity without which nothing you do will have effect

The next day, June 10, Sagoyewatha began the council by addressing Colonel Butler:

Brother You informed us yesterday that In consequence of the ill State of your health you could not proceed to Sandusky, but meant to return from hence, We are sorry to think you would not attend to the call of all the Six Nations and the Western Indians communicated to you in our Speech last fall at our Council Fire at Buffaloe Creek.

The King our Father has always taken care of us by appointing persons who were Capable of Conducting our affairs and who have a knowledge of our Customs—

It is well known that the late Sir William Johnson established peace amongst our Tribes, and you who have uniformly trod in his footsteps and in whom we have Great Confidence, Should by all means attend to assist us in bringing about a peace for us Indians. We Shall stand in great need of your Best advice and assistance with us to Secure to our Western Brethren their Just rights which are now invaded

We therefore hope that for the Sake of the Western Indians and Six Nations that you will lay aside all thoughts of Returning, but proceed and with your Council assist the Interest of the Indians and we hope the Great Spirit will preserve your health when traveling as well as if you Remained at Home

4 Strings Wampum

Brother With these Strings we request you will inform Captain Brant and the Chiefs who are gone to Sandusky that our agreement at the last Council at Niagara was for the Indians at Buffaloe Creek to wait the arrival of the 7. Nations from lower Canada, but as there is no appearance of them and the appointed time past we mean to Proceed in canoes round the Lake to Sandusky. we also request you to explain to Captain Brant & the Chiefs at Sandusky that we are united and are Determined to act steadyly & uniformly according to agreements at the last Council at Niagara[.] We hope therefore that they will make their Mind easy as the Six Nations will always act for the Interest of their own Colour

3 Strings Wampum Black & White

Brother, We now inform you that the Senecas and Onandagos will Proceed immediately to Sandusky in Canoes, The Cayugas & Tuscaroras will go with you in the Vessel, We hope you will Consider us and assist us with Provisions Tobacco & Ammunition for our Journey

To which Lt Col Butler Replyed

Brethren, From what you have now said notwithstanding the Bad State of my health I will comply with your Request, and proceed to Sandusky as the Welfare and Interest of the Indians will always be of the first consideration to me and you may rely on every assistance I can give you, I am happy to find you are unanimous and hope you will act in Conjunction with your Western Brethren, a matter I have so frequently recommended to you

a Small Belt Wampum [Source: "Official Correspondence," 1793, F 47-1-2-12, John R. Simcoe Papers, Simcoe Family Papers, Archives of Ontario, Toronto]

Letter to Pickering, Sent by Mr. Parrish

AUGUST 11, 1793

IN MAY 1793, Timothy Pickering, Benjamin Lincoln, and Beverly Randolph set out from Pennsylvania to Detroit to act as U.S. commissioners at the upcoming Indian council that had been agreed upon at the Glaize in the fall of 1792 (for accounts of the trip, see Moore 1835; Lindley 1832). The Detroit council of Indians was so insulted by the U.S. refusal to give up lands north of the Ohio River (Pickering offered payment instead) that they refused to meet with Pickering. Red Jacket's message to Pickering reflects the anxious state of affairs at Buffalo Creek, where war seemed imminent. According to the preface of the letter, Red Jacket met Parrish in the woods between Geneseo and Buffalo Creek to give Pickering notification that he would not be coming to the council. Parrish then carried the letter to Pickering at the mouth of the Detroit River on August 11, 1793.

Sagoyewatha's letter:

One reason why I did not attend the treaty, was, that when the Six Nations had prepared their belt & speech to deliver to the Deputies of the Western Indians, at the Conference lately at Niagara, the speech was struck down, by Brant:—we were not suffered to deliver it.

Another reason was, that I thought there would be no peace; and that the Six Nations would be called on to join the Western Indians in the war, and I did not wish to have any hand in consenting that my nation should join them as it might be the cause of reflections on me hereafter, in case of any misfortunes by means of the war.

Brother, If peace is not made, I advise you, *in private*, to recommend to the principal chiefs of our nations, not to join in the war: So that if we avoid the war, it may appear to the hostile Indians to proceed from ourselves; and not to have been done by your influence. The chiefs to be spoken to in private are, The Farmer's Brother, Young King, Obeil, New-Arrow, (and another Chief from Allegany whose name Parrish has forgotten), Captain Billy, and Great Sky These Chiefs will consult the warriors.

Five Strings of White Wampum [Source: PP, 59:204–204A]

Treaty of Canandaigua

OCTOBER 19–NOVEMBER 12, 1794

AS ANGLO-NATIVE BOUNDARY CONFLICTS threatened a war in Ohio, the Six Nations faced a boundary dispute concerning Presque Isle and the area called the "Erie" or "Pennsylvania Triangle" that connects Pennsylvania to Lake Erie (map 3). The Americans argued that Pennsylvania twice purchased the area at two earlier councils (Emlen 1965, 313; Prucha 1994, 43–48, 54–58; Manley 1932, 95). The Americans were building a military garrison and settlement in the spring of 1794 at Presque Isle, and the ensuing conflict between Indians and settlers had resulted in several Indian deaths. Afraid of further alienating the Six Nations at a time of instability in Ohio, Secretary Knox asked Chapin to organize a council to settle the question of the Erie Triangle and any other complaints of the Six Nations (Campisi and Starna 1995, 477–78; see also Campisi 1988, 62). The council was large, with 1,600 members of the Six Nations attending. The Treaty of Canandaigua is important because it established federal responsibility for all later treaties and land sales the Haudenosaunee made after 1794 (see Jemison and Schein 2000; Campisi 1988).

Although some fragments from Sagoyewatha's speeches at the treaty appear in Timothy Pickering's Papers, the most complete account of his speeches appears in the *Journal of William Savery*. Savery was one of several Quakers (including David Bacon, James Emlen, and John Parrish) who attended the treaty negotiations. Pickering's interpreter was Jasper Parrish, and it is likely that he also provided translations for Savery. Taken as a group, the Quaker journals provide a rich account of the council, which is only briefly sketched here.

After preliminary introductions, the council proper began on October 22 when Cornplanter and Red Jacket gave speeches that explained the history of the problems with the whites from their arrival on the Island to the treaties of Fort McIntosh (1785) and Fort Harmar/Muskingum (1789). Cornplanter proposed peace by setting a new boundary line that gave the lands of the Erie Triangle to the Six Nations

(Emlen 1965, 307–8). Neither of these speeches were saved by Pickering, and exist only in the summaries written by the Quakers who listened to Pickering's response the next day.

The following day, October 23, the Clan Mothers expressed their desire to speak. Three elderly women said that because a white woman had been permitted to speak in council (alluding to a prayer spoken by Jemima Wilkinson on October 21) they might also be allowed the same liberty. Their spokesman was Red Jacket, who said that:

they felt a deep interest in the affairs of their nation, and having heard the opinions of their sachems, they fully concurred in them, that the white people had been the cause of all the Indians' distresses; that they had pressed and squeezed them together, until it gave them great pain at their hearts, and that the whites ought to give them back the lands they had taken from them. That one of the white women had yesterday told the Indians to repent; and they now called on the white people to repent, for they had as much need as the Indians, and that they should wrong the Indians no more. [Source: Savery 1837, 112]

According to James Emlen's account of the same event, the women, speaking through Red Jacket, "expiated on the importance of their Sex saying that it was they who made the Men, that altho' they did not sit in council, yet that they were acquainted from time to time with the transactions at the Treaties, they had understood that the White Woman had told the Indians to repent & turn from their evil Deeds & they now had to say the same to the White people to repent & turn from our [their] evil Deeds, but that their principal desire was that the U.S. would grant the request made yesterday by the Men,[1] that they had found themselves much distressed by being hemmed in, but if the request was granted they should feel themselves much relieved & more at liberty: after expressing their desire that the Great Spirit might influence & direct us in effecting the good work of peace, they retired" (Emlen 1965, 306).

The death of an Oneida chief and heavy snow put off discussion for several days. On October 28, Pickering told the Indians that the Erie Triangle had been twice paid for by Pennsylvania and they were not going to give it up, but the Six Nations could be given back all their lands between Buffalo Creek and the Triangle. He said he was empowered to add another $3,000 to the annuity promised them at Philadelphia in 1792, and that he had $10,000 in gifts to distribute. In exchange, he asked for a quitclaim on the Triangle and the four-mile-wide swath between Lake

1. Cornplanter's proposal to get back the Erie triangle.

Erie and Ontario (but allowing the Indians hunting and fishing rights). The Indians
counseled among themselves for several days on Pickering's offer.

The following excerpts are from the 1837 edition of Savery's journal:

"October 31st, 1794: "Red Jacket, Clear Sky, Sagareesa,[2] and a chief of the
Cayugas, waited on us at our lodgings, being a deputation from the Indian
council that has been deliberating several days upon the proposals of the commissioner, bringing with them the interpreter. Several Indians and some white
people being in the room with us, they were desired to depart, as the business
they came about would not admit of their presence. Apprehending that we
should be interrupted in the house, we retired to a distance, and sat down
upon some logs, when Red Jacket spoke nearly as follows:

"Brothers,—You see here four of us of the Six Nations, who are assembled
at this place, in the will of the Great Spirit, to transact the business of the
treaty. You have been waiting here a long time, and often visited by our chiefs,
and as yet no marks of respect have been shown you.

"Brothers,—We are deputed by the council of chiefs assembled, to come
and see you. We understand that you told Sagareesa, that you should not have
come, but at our request, and that you stood ready to afford us any assistance in
your power.

"Brothers,—We hope you will make your minds easy. We who are now
here are but children; the ancients being deceased. We know that your fathers
and ours transacted business together, and that you look up to the Great spirit
for his direction and assistance, and take no part in war. We expect you were
all born on this island, and consider you as brethren. Your ancestors came over
the great water, and ours were born here; this ought to be no impediment to
our considering each other as brethren.

"Brothers,—You all know the proposals that have been made by Cunnit-
sutty (Colonel Pickering, the commissioner), as well as the offers made by us
to him. We are all now in the presence of the Great Spirit, and we place more
confidence in you, than in any other people. As you expressed your desire for
peace, we now desire your help and assistance—we hope you will not deceive
us; for if you should do so, we shall no more place any confidence in mankind.

"Brothers,—We wish, if you know the will of Congress, or the extent of
the commissioner's powers, that you would candidly inform us.

"Brothers,—We desire that what we are now about communicating, may
be kept secret. We are willing to give up the four-mile path, from Johnson's
landing-place to Cayuga-creek, agreeably to our compact with Sir William

2. Sagareesa was a principal Tuscarora chief.

Johnson, long ago. The other part proposed by Colonel Pickering to be relinquished by us; that is, from Cayuga to Buffalo-creek, we wish to reserve on account of the fisheries; that our women and children may have the use of it for
that purpose. We desire to know if you can inform us, why the triangle on Lake
Erie cannot be given up.

"Brothers,—Cornplanter and Captain Brandt, who were only war chiefs,
were the persons who attended the treaty at Fort Stanwix, and they were to
have sent forward the proposals for our more general consideration. At that
time Old Smoke[3] was alive, who was a man of great understanding; but they
were threatened into a compliance, in consequence of which Captain Brandt
went off to Canada, desiring Cornplanter to do the best he could."

"They delivered us seven strings of wampum" [Source: Savery 1837, 127–29]

*The following day, November 1, Savery responded to Red Jacket's speech, returning
the seven strings, and making three points in return, but Savery did not specify the
details. On November 2, the main council resumed and Savery continued:*

"The business was introduced by Clear Sky, an Onondaga chief, in the following manner: He expressed a hope that there would be no hard thoughts entertained, on account of their having been several days deliberating on an
answer; the subject was of importance, and he wished his brethren to be preserved in unanimity. Then Red Jacket being principle speaker, said,

"Brothers,—We request that all the nations present will attend to what
we are about to deliver. We are now convened on one of the days of the Great
Spirit; Then addressing Colonel Pickering:—

"Brother,—You now represent the President of the United States, and
when you spoke to us, we considered it as the voice of the fifteen fires. You desired that we would take the matter under our deliberate consideration and
consult each other well, that where the chain was rusty, it might be brightened. We took General Washington by the hand, and desired this council-fire,
that all the lines in dispute might be settled.

"Brothers,—We told you before of the two rusty places on the chain,
which were also pointed out by the sachems. Instead of complying with our request, respecting the places where we told you the chain was rusty, you offered
to relinquish the land on Lake Erie, eastward of the triangular piece sold by
Congress to Pennsylvania, and to retain the four-mile path between Cayuga
and Buffalo-creek, by which you expect to brighten the chain.

---

3. Old Smoke was reputed to be one of the founders of the Seneca settlement at Buffalo
Creek.

"Brothers,—We thought you had a sharp file to take off the rust, but we believe it must have been dull, or else you let it slip out of your hands. With respect to the four-mile path, we are in want of it on account of the fisheries; although we are but children, we are sharp-sighted, and we see that you want that strip of land for a road, that when you have vessels on the lakes, you may have harbors, &c. But we wish, that in respect to that land, the treaty at Fort Stanwix may be broken. You white people have increased very fast on this island, which was given to us Indians by the Great Spirit; we are now become a small people, and you are cutting off our lands, piece after piece—you are a very hard-hearted people, seeking your own advantages.

"Brothers,—We are tender-hearted, and desirous of peace—you told us what you would give us for our land, to brighten your end of the chain. If you will relinquish the piece of land we have mentioned, our friendship will be strong. You say you are not proud; neither are we. Congress expects we are now settling the business with regularity; we wish that both parties may have something to say in settling a peace. At the time we requested a conference, we also requested that our friends, the Quakers, should come forward, as they are promoters of peace, and we wanted them to be witnesses to what took place; we wish to do nothing in private. We have told you of the rusty part, which the file passed over without brightening it, and we wish you to take up the file again, and rub it very hard; you told us, if it would not do without, you would apply oil.

"Brothers,—We the sachems, warriors and others, all depend upon you; whatever is done, we regard as final and permanent; we wish you to take it into consideration, and give us an answer.

"Colonel Pickering replied, If I understand you right, your minds are easy excepting with respect to the strip of land between the two lakes. He then recapitulated what Red Jacket had expressed, which is the usual custom of the Indians in their answers; reminding them why they decreased, and the white people increased, and gave them advice in what manner they might increase also; observing that he did it as their friend, for he wished to see them rise and become a great people. Here Red Jacket called out earnestly, in his language, 'keep straight.' The commissioner proceeded." [Source: Savery 1837, 131–34]

In his response, Pickering acknowledged their concern that a road might get wider and wider in the future but he felt that it was only a small concern. On November 4, the treaty was about to conclude. Pickering asked the Quakers to sign, but they refused. Savery writes, "We told him [Pickering], on hearing what was proposed, that we apprehended for reasons given, we could not be free to sign the treaty; which did not appear to be agreeable to him; but we have not now to begin to learn to suffer at Indian treaties. At two o'clock, an Indian messenger from the council, came to inform us that they were assembled and waiting for us, the Indians not being disposed to proceed in our absence: a great number were assembled, and Red Jacket addressed the commissioner:

"Brothers,—We, the sachems of the Six Nations, will now tell you our minds. The business of the treaty is, to brighten the chain of friendship between us and the fifteen fires. We told you the other day, it was but a very small piece which was the occasion of the remaining rust in the chain of friendship.

"Brothers,—Now we are conversing together, in order to make the chain bright. When we told you what would give us satisfaction, you proposed reserving the piece of land, between Cayuga and Buffalo-creek, for building houses, &c., but we apprehend, you would not only build houses, but towns. You told us, these houses would be for the accommodation of travellers in winter, as they cannot go by water in that season, and that travellers would want a staff to help them along the road. We have taken these matters into serious consideration.

"Brothers,—We conclude that we do not understand this as the white people do; if we consent to your proposals, we know it will injure us. If these houses should be built, they will tend to scatter us and make us fall in the streets, meaning, by drinking to excess, instead of benefiting us: you want land to raise provisions, hay, &c.; but as soon as the white people settle there, they would think the land theirs, for this is the way of the white people. You mentioned, that when you got possession of the garrisons,[4] you would want landing-places, stores, fields to plant on, &c.; but we wish to be the sole owners of this land ourselves; and when you settle with the British, the Great Spirit has made a road for you, you can pass and repass by water; what you want to reserve is entirely in your own favor.

"Brothers,—You told us, when you left Philadelphia, it was not expected by the President you would release a foot of land. We thank him for having left you at liberty to give up what you please.—You have waited with patience at this council fire, kindled by General Washington; it is but a very small thing that keeps the chain from being brightened; if you will consent to give up this small piece and have no houses on it, the chain will be made bright. As to harbors, the waters are between you and the British; you must talk to them, you are of the same color. I see there are many of your people now here, watching

---

4. In violation of the peace of 1783, the British continued to hold the forts of Oswego, Niagara, and Detroit until after Jay's Treaty, concluded in late November 1794.

with their mouth open to take up this land: if you are a friend to us, then disappoint them, our patience is spent; comply with our request; dismiss us, and we will go home." [Source: Savery 1837, 137–39]

In response, Pickering withdrew his original request for a road westward from Buffalo Creek to Canandaigua, asking instead for permission to clear stumps out of the existing road from Fort Schlosser in Niagara to Buffalo Creek. He added that the road would be opened under the supervision of the superintendent agent of the Six Nations. He sat down to wait for the Indians' answer. The sachems consulted for half an hour and Savery's journal records Red Jacket's response as follows:

"General Washington, now listen; we are going to brighten the chain of friendship between the Six Nations and the Americans. We thank you for complying with our request, in giving up the particular spot in dispute. You mentioned that you wanted a road through our country; remember your old agreement, that you were to pass along the lake by water; we have made up our minds respecting your request to open a road. Colonel Pickering writing what was said, Red Jacket would not proceed till he looked him in the face.

"Brothers,—It costs the white people a great deal to make roads, we wish not to put you to that great expense; we don't want you to spend your money for that purpose. We have a right understanding of your request, and have agreed to grant you a road from Fort Schlosser to Buffalo-creek, but not from Buffalo-creek down this way at all. We have given you an answer; if, on considering it, you have any reply to make, we will hear you.

"Commissioner. I confess, brothers, I expected you would have agreed to my proposal; but as this is not the case, I will give it up, only reserving the road from Fort Schlosser to Buffalo. There has been mutual condescension, which is the best way of settling business." [Source: Savery 1837, 140]

The principal terms of the treaty being agreed upon, a disagreement broke out over the means of payment. While Pickering attempted to work out how the goods and annuities should be distributed, on November 6 a major dispute arose concerning the Six Nations' relinquishment of Presque Isle. Several of the chiefs had found out that Cornplanter and Little Billy had been given $2,000 in goods at Muskingum and another $2,000 in goods at Philadelphia as payment for Presque Isle before the treaty. On November 9, Cornplanter asked his warriors not to sign the treaty. Pickering responded by saying that if they would not sign it, he would not have anything to do with it either. After a moving speech on Indian unanimity by Eel, an Onondaga chief, the warrior chiefs signed on November 11, 1794 (Savery 1837, 140–52).

On the Death of General Israel Chapin Sr., and Request for a Blacksmith

APRIL 28–29, 1795

GENERAL ISRAEL CHAPIN, who had served as U.S. superintendent of Indian affairs to the Six Nations for several years, died in February 1795. A condolence council addressed to his son, also named Israel, was held in Canandaigua on April 28, attended by Farmer's Brother, Red Jacket, Clear Sky, other chiefs from Buffalo Creek, as well as Onondagas, Cayugas, and Oneidas from Canawagaras. The following day, Chapin met the Six Nations to inform them that he had been appointed superintendent of Indian affairs to the Six Nations. The Six Nations responded by asking him for a second blacksmith at Canandaigua, the existing one—"Jones"—having poor skills with gun repair. Chapin denied their request for a second blacksmith because he thought they could draw on two local blacksmiths instead (ORWM, vol. 11, item 16).

Jasper Parrish, who lived in Canandaigua at this time, interpreted, and these texts seem to be his speaking notes taken at the council. The torn and water-damaged manuscripts contain many abbreviations and illegible sections. Stone's clean version of the April 28 speech must have used a recension related to this manuscript because he simply eliminated the most difficult passages.

April 28, Sagoyewatha to Captain Chapin:

Brother—I wish you to pay atten^tn [attention] to what I have to say. You will Recollect you forward[e]^d a mess[age] to us informing us of the loss of our g.[ood] fr.[ien]^d and that the loss is great for us as well as you[.] Yet you would hear what we should have to say & I wish you to pay att[entio]^n to what we shall say

We und.[erstan]^d we have met with a g[rea]^t loss we the 6 N^ts [Six Nations] as well as the US—a person who we look[e]^d to as a f[a]^thr and a person ap[poin]t^d to st[an]^d. between the Six N^ts. & the US—it gives our minds a

68

great deal of uneasyness to think we have lost so valuable a f[rien]ᵈ· who has taken so much pains to B[righ]ᵗⁿ the Ch[ai]ⁿ· of frendship between the Six N ᵗˢ· & the US[.] it app[ear]ˢ· to us that agreeableness friendsh[ip] which has been held up bet.ᵂᵉᵉⁿ us has gone and let us prevent it failing if we can.

Br[other]. As it has been custom[a]ʳʸ am[on]ᵍ the 6 Na[tion]ˢ in case of loosing a f[rien]ᵈ I[srael] C[hapin] they have all waies taken p[ain]ˢ too keep the ant R se [ancient Rules] then is to [throw?] a belt in the place aft[er] he is dead and gone

As we have lost so many of late we are destitute of a belt & in the place we present you these strings

s.[trings] of B[lack] & W[hite] wampᵘᵐ

Brs—As it was custom[a]ʳʸ being hand[e]ᵈ down to us from our Fore Fath ᵉʳˢ to keep up these your old ant[cient] Rules now we level the grave of our f[rien]ᵈ—we geather Leaves & we[e]ᵈˢ & strew them over the greave [grave] & end[eavo]ʳ· to banish grief from our minds as much as we can

14 s[trings] of B[lack] & W[hite] wampum

Brs. You the 15 Fʳˢ [Fires] listen ag[ai]ⁿ· to the voice of the 6 N.ᵗˢ The person who you app.[oin]ᵗᵈ for us to communicate our minds to is now left us and gone to anoth[e]ʳ world we are now at a loss who [to] open our minds to[.] if there was any thing to be communicated from one to the other we used to reveal it to him

B.ʳˢ You of the 15 fʳˢ we think you feel this great loss as well as we the 6 N ᵗˢ that agree alike comm ᵗᵉˢ [communications] being cut of[f] between the 6 N ᵗˢ & ye [the] US[.] A person who spar[e]ᵈ no pains to keep ye [the] Ch[ai]ⁿ of F[riendship]ᵈ B[right]—and while he had the conducting of Bus[ines]ˢ wh[ile] app.[ointe]ᵈ the US sat close by our sides if we had any thing to commᵗʰ [communicate] it [was] conducted with the greatest care to the g[rea]ᵗ Council fire[.] Now as we have lost our [guide?] it troubles our minds to find out in what manner we shall proceed to keep up that friendship that we have heretofore—

B.ʳˢ of the US it is a [illegible word] waity matter [which?] we ar[e] now about to relate[.] you will p.[oin]ᵗ out some way more agreeable to keep up this friendship better than we [could?]

Bʳˢ· You will allow us to make use of our sentiments to mention in what manner this busⁿˢ [business] should take place[.] when you app[oin]ᵗᵈ· a person to come forward to att[en]ᵈ· to the Six N ᵗˢ you app[oin]ᵗᵈ· the person that gave satisfaction to us & we believe he did to you—it was frequently thronged with busⁿˢ· [business] men then he would att[en]ᵈ· to himself[.] some times [he] could not att[en]ᵈ· on acc[oun]ᵗ· of sick[nes]ˢ· at these times sent forward his son C— [Chapin] to act on his behalf[.] we consider ourselves being well acqua[in]ᵗᵈ·

with the [disposition?] of this y.[oung] man as we have frequently transacted bus[ns] [business] with him we found his mind to be good

B[rs.] he being very well acqu[ain][td.] in the manner the bus[ns] [business] was formerly conducted and all the papers Belts wampum &c left in his hands we cannot conceive any other person any more suitable to fill his f[athe][rs] seat than [two illegible words] the former app[ointmen][t.] was done by the US[.] now grant us priveleg [privilege] to mention one we think will give satisfaction to us, perhaps you think it a favor further than we can ask [still?] grant us the privilig[e] this our request I[srael] C[hapin] & w[ish] of the 6 Na[ts] that his son may fill [his] seat.

B[rs.] You of the 15 F[rs] [Fires], this is the 2[nd.] pettition of this kind we have laid befor[e] you requesting a person to who should be app[oin][td.] to conduct the aff[ai][rs] of the Six N[ts.] Last our pettition before was not taken into consid[era][tn.] whether you would grant our request or not[.] this being the 2[nd.] time we have in our pett[itio][n.] pointed out a person to the office[.] we hope you will notice it—we should not attempt any thing of the kind, were we not acqua[i]nted with the person we mention[.] we have reason to think he will walk in ye [the] steps of his f[athe][r.] if this should be the case we think it would satisfy you and the 6 Na[ts.]

B[rs.] I expect you have listened with atten.[tn] to the voice of the Six Nat. now it is our earnest request you should forward this to the g[rea][t.] C[ouncil] fire of the US as soon as posiable [possible] and that we might receive an answer as soon [as] it can be sent back[.] it is customary among the W[hite] People to set a particular time when a p[ape][r] [illegible word] of Bus[ines][s] shall be completed and you will now [illegible word] give us a time to receive an answer[.] We have laid before you all the Bisn[e][ss] we can & we shall soon return home to our seats & upon our return our faces will be this way to receive an answer[.] we shall still look till we receive an answer etc.

13 Long S.[trings] of B[lack & White wampum] [Source: ORWM, vol. 11, item 14. Also in Stone 1841, 146–47. Stone thanks John Gregg, Esq. for the text (usually spelled "Greig"). Greig married Israel Chapin Jr.'s daughter and became a prominent attorney and landowner. Greig gave Stone copies of several manuscripts for Stone's Red Jacket biography]

April 29, Sagoyewatha to Chapin:

Br[other] with a g[reat] deal [of] att[entio][n.] we have listened to what you have s[ai][d.] to us informing us of y[ou][r.] app[ointmen][t.] & to our satisfaction

B[r.] we come into Coun.[ci][l] prep[are][d] to make a small speech to you as we know the mind of the US being good & wishing to serve us in any thing to our advantage[.] there is one thing we stand in need of that is a Bs [blacksmith] at this place being ye [the] prin[cipa]ˡ place where the W[arrio]ʳˢ come that the W[arrio]ʳˢ would be helped to things they want for hunting as yo[u]ʳ f[athe]ʳ had none here[.] we hope you get one for us—

Bʳ The reason we make this Request we have it granted by the US G[eorge] W[ashington] &c—we were to have them as we should want now we would wish a man who should understand the business we want[.] done—because they do not [k]no[w] in general one person can do the bus[i]ⁿˢ of both trades

Bʳ In reply to this y[ou] al[ready] say we have one[.] true we have but to no service[.] we take our things to him and there they lye till they are lost[.] we have tried him some time but are discouraged as we receive no service from him

Bʳ we were told by G[eorge] W[ashington] & C[olone]l P[ickering] that so much mo[ney] was given for the 6 Nᵗˢ that sh[oul]ᵈ be paid into the hands of the I[ndian] P[erso]ⁿ & should make use of it for the best use of the Six Nᵗˢ. we heartily thank them for the same—and we consider the mo[ney] lost that [was] given to Jones because we can't get any thing done by him—

Br—We remember what C[olonel] P[ickering] told us at the late Treaty[1] at this place[.] the sum was ment[ione]ᵈ that sh[oul]ᵈ be grant[e]ᵈ yearly but the busin[ess]ˢ was not finished on our par[t] to tell him what we would wish is in to our best advantage—we consider the US being liberal with their mo[ney][.] in Regard to the goods Last fall &c They de[livere]ᵈ a q[uanti]ᵗʸ of thread awlls wire & needls knives these things did not do us much good—we would not wish to have these articles procured for us as we can get them ourselves, but the mo[ney] grant[e]ᵈ we would wish to have it in blankets [shrouding?] shirting legging and these not to be rotten—As Co[lone]ˡ P[ickering] has the conducting of bus[i]ⁿˢ I hope he will get that which is good and pains taken that it shall not be damaged and when you receive it should be good—another article we would wish ie[:] kittles [kettles] we would wish small kittls, as they are best &c—The kittles we wish we would wish brass[.] Also good powder for the War[rior]ˢ Lead Shot guns if they can be had—by our powder we get our living & we want good

Bʳ When these goods come to y[ou]r hand we wish to have them dealt out in a different manner than what they have been—we wish to receive them all at once divided out equal to the several Nat[ion]ˢ. We want a [return?] made out to Cl. P[ickering] and for him to give an answer—One thing we have not ment[ione]ᵈ· We do not pett[itio]ⁿ for Liquor we can get it in the Country. [Source: ORWM, vol. 11, item 15]

1. Treaty of Canandaigua, 1794.

In Hartford, Connecticut

CA. 1795

IN STONE's *Life and Times of Red-Jacket,* he prints a speech that occurred when a deputation of Seneca chiefs traveled to address the Connecticut General Assembly in Hartford some time after it put up the lands of the Western Reserve for sale in May 1795 (Rose 1950, 22). Stone's source was a manuscript, now lost, held by Joseph Moulton (Stone 1841, 164). Stone writes that the text was drawn from the recollection of Gideon Granger, a partner of Oliver Phelps in the Connecticut Company, and later a resident of Canandaigua. Granger said he was present when Red Jacket gave this speech. In 1805, Joseph Brant also claimed that Red Jacket had addressed the Connecticut Assembly and had even kissed a portrait of George Washington to prove his fidelity to the United States (Stone 1845, 2:417). Newspaper accounts of Sagoyewatha's visit are not extant. Given the speech's biblical allusions and similarities to Jefferson's "who mourns Logan?" speech, it is likely that this is not an accurate text.

We stand a small island in the bosom of the great waters. We are encircled,— we are encompassed. The evil spirit rides upon the blast, and the waters are disturbed. They rise, they press upon us, and the waves once settled over us, we disappear forever. Who then lives to mourn us? None. What marks our extermination? Nothing. We are mingled with the common elements. [Source: Stone 1841, 164]

To Moses Cleaveland at Buffalo Creek

June 6–23, 1796

SEVENTEENTH-CENTURY ROYAL CHARTERS gave several of the New England states land claims that extended to the Pacific Ocean. In September 1786, Connecticut gave up most of its westerns claims to the federal government. The area of northern Ohio it withheld—henceforth called the "Western Reserve"—was a three and a half million acre area south of Lake Erie whose western boundary ended 120 miles from the Pennsylvania border (and was limited on the south by the forty-first parallel, see map 4). In 1792, Connecticut set aside the western 500,000 acres for citizens who lost property during the war by fire or other means, the "Fire Lands." The three million acre remainder they sold in May 1795 to a group of investors called the Connecticut Land Company (Rose 1950, 22). Moses Cleaveland, one of the company's directors, led the company's forty-man surveying party in May 1796.

Although the Senecas had explicitly given up any claims to Ohio lands at the Treaty of Canandaigua in 1794, the Connecticut Company believed that they might make trouble if they were not consulted about the transfer. Oliver Phelps, the company's primary stockholder, explicitly told Cleaveland to avoid the language of "sale" and to offer money only as a respectful gratuity. Cleaveland arrived at Buffalo Creek on June 21, and gave a speech announcing his intentions to survey the Ohio lands (this speech is extant at the Western Reserve Historical Society, WRHS, in Cleveland, Ohio). Brant responded the following day, and that night the Indians held a dance. On June 23, there were several speeches exchanged between Brant, Red Jacket, Chapin, and Cleaveland, and the business was settled. The lands covered by the Buffalo Creek agreement were only those between the Cuyahoga River and the Pennsylvania line. The exact amount of the settlement is unclear, but it was in the area of $2,000. According to Seth Pease's journal, the "western Indians" (that is, those from Grand River) accepted goods worth 500 pounds in New York currency (about $1,000), and the "eastern Indians" (mostly New

York Senecas) accepted two beef cattle and 100 gallons of whisky for their consent to let Cleaveland's party go on to Ohio.[1]

Cleaveland kept good records of the speeches and correspondence with the Indians, but these papers, along with his journal, were lost in the mid-1800s, sometime after Orrin Harmon copied extracts from Cleaveland's journal in his "Historical Notebook" (Harmon Family Papers, WRHS). Cleaveland's journal for June 1796 no longer exists, but the journals of his surveyors, John Milton Holley and Seth Pease, do. In 1971, a few of the speeches from Cleaveland's Buffalo mission were donated to the Western Reserve Historical Society. They do not include the speeches of the primary council day, June 23. The three extant documents (no. 7, from June 6; no. 11, an undated invitation to council; and no. 13, June 21) were presumably part of a complete series Cleaveland kept for the company.

On June 6, the Senecas sent the following letter to Cleaveland at Canandaigua:

The Red Jacket a principal Sachem of the Seneca Nation Speaker—

Brother we have this day received your Speech forwarded by our Interpreter M,ʳ Parrish by which we find that you are desirous of having a Conference with the Chiefs of the Six Nations as soon as may be Convenient to us here at our Council Fire.

Brother Having considered this matter we have Concluded to meet you hear in eleven days from to day[.] we will therefore immediately dispatch runners to the Cornplanter and the Grand River that the meeting may be General when you may explain what right you have to the lands you wish to settle.

Brother In your Speech you have not mentioned any Provision for those who attend the Council[.] Some of the Chiefs have to come from a great

1. Holley's journal notes that in addition to the payment for the Ohio land during the council, Brant requested that Cleaveland try to get a $500 annuity from the federal government, and if that failed, the Connecticut Company should give another $1,000 to the Grand River Indians for the land, $100 of which would go to the Senecas. A year later, Superintendent Chapin wrote to Cleaveland on behalf of the Grand River Indians about the annuity. On the same day he wrote to Cleaveland, Chapin also wrote to the secretary of war that Brant was on his way to Philadelphia to obtain a $1,200 cash payment or a $500 annuity for the lands (Chapin to Cleaveland, February 6, 1797, Cleaveland Papers, WRHS; Chapin to Secretary of War Henry, February 6, 1797; ORWM, vol. 15, item 8). The federal annuity was never paid, but neither, apparently, was the $1,200.

distance and as we are Scant ourselve[s] we request you will consider this matter.

Brother It is our desire that when you come on to meet us in General Council that those people who are wishing to Settle the land in question may remain where they are untill this business is finally Settled

Brother It is also the desire of the Chiefs assembled in Council that you will take our Brother Capᵗ, Chapin by the hand and lead him to our fire place as he is the Person appointed by the Great Chief General Washington to take Care of us,

Brother from what we Can larn provision may be procured Cheaper near this than where you are[.] we also wish you to understand that the provision required is only for the Support of those who come from a distance on this Public business

Brother. We return you thanks for uncovering the Council fire at this place[.] this this [*sic*] is perfectly agreeable to our Customs and is the place where we wish all business of importance to be transacted as all our People can then have an opportunity of hearing what passes.

Brother It gives us pleasure to find by your Speech that you mean to meat us as a friend and Brother and to deal honorably[.] we therefore take this opportunity of assuring you that you will find your Brother of the Six Nations in the same disposition.

    Farmer Brother   **X**
    Red Jacket   **X**
    Young King   **X**

[Source: "I" vertical file, Iroquois Indians, Red Jacket, "Reply of the Chiefs . . . ," WRHS. Speech is identified on back of page as "No. 7"]

The evening of the sale, June 23, there was a general dinner attended by the Connecticut Company men and Red Jacket, Farmer's Brother, and Little Billy. John Milton Holley, one of the surveyors for the company, left the following account in his journal:

In the course of conversation, Red Jacket gave his sentiments upon Religion, which were to this purpose—You white people make a great parade about Religion—you say you have a Book of Laws & rules which was given you by the great Spirit—but is this true, was it written by his own hand & gave to you—No, says he—'twas written by your own people.—they do it to deceive you—Their whole wishes center here—(pointing to his pocket) all they want is the money (it happened there was a priest in the room at the same time who hear[d him]) he says white people tell them they wish to come & live among them as brothers, & learn them agriculture &c. they bring on Implements of husbandry, & presents, tell them good stories, and all appears honest but when they are gone all appears as a dream—our land is taken from us & still we don't know how to farm it &c &c &c &c &c. [Source: Holley 1796; reprinted in Blanchard 1880, 226]

Council at Fort Niagara

September 21–23, 1796

WHEN THE POSSESSION of Fort Niagara was finally ceded by the British to the United States after Jay's Treaty, the Senecas were invited to a council by the new U.S. commander of the fort, Captain James Bruff. On September 21, 1796, Bruff gave a speech welcoming them to Niagara. He presented them with a U.S. flag declaring that "the light of its stars" might "illuminate the western world." He added his hope that the "the increase of its *stripes* give to our friends a confidence of our ability to protect them" and "may they also admonish such as would disturb our peace, of our power to chastize them." He also gave them a keg of rum so that they may "drink to the prosperity of the United States and Washington." He requested two things of the Indians: first, that the Indians would not allow themselves to get involved in British-U.S. affairs, nor would they let themselves be hired by the British to hunt for their deserters in New York; and second, that they allow a road to be widened and straightened from Niagara to Canawaugus (an Indian village near Avon on the Genesee River).

When Red Jacket's forceful reply to Bruff was sent to President Washington, it convinced him that the Senecas did not want to sell their lands. Washington refused Morris's requests that he appoint a commissioner to oversee a land sale. The two interpreters were Horatio Jones and William Johnson, assisted also by Mr. Ransom, who, like Johnson, lived in Buffalo. The only surviving copy of the text is at the New York Historical Society.

On September 23, the Senecas made their answer to Bruff:

The Farmers Brother, began by calling the attention of all present, to what was to be considered the answer & voice of the Nation, and hoped that the Warriors would make their minds easy, altho' the answer of the Chiefs (their uncles) should be a great way from their Expectations.—

. . .

Red Jacket, then rose and spake literally or in substance what follows

Brother—We have heard remember and have well considered your talk.—I therefore beg your attention, and the attention of the Warriors and chief Women while I speak for the Nation.—

Brother—you have spoke against our pursuing Deserters and the consequence of our interfering with disputes between white People—We are well pleased with what you have said on that subject, agree with you in Opinion that Indians have nothing to do with your affairs, we therefore grant your Request about Deserters.—

Brother—You have presented us a Flag of your Nation and hope that the American Stars may enlighten the Six Nations and their western Brethren— We accept the Flag, but must remark, that our Chiefs have never been much enlightened by them, except when you have burnt our Towns where they have been flying; for such a Flag was once presented to the Onondaga Nation with a pipe and Protection, yet your People came and burnt their Town without regard to either Protection or the Flag that was flying in it.—

Brother—You hope we all will bury the remembrance of last war, we have done that long ago, but are apprehensive you have not—Your mind we suspect is a good deal on War, Ours on saving our Land—You are a cunning People without sincerity, and not to be trusted, for after making Professions of your Regard, and saying every thing favorable to us, you then talk about a Road and tell us that our Country is within the lines of the [United] States—This surprises us, for we had thought our Lands were our own, not within your Boundaries, but joining the British, and between you and them, But now you have got round us and next [to] the British, you tell us we are inside your Lines—

Brother—You spoke yesterday more at large about the Road and said, the priviledge now asked was not the same, nor as extensive as that asked by Col. Pickering—You only wanted permission to widen mend and straighten our Path from this to Cannowagaras [Canawaugus] which would be a benefit not only to you, to your Settlements and your British neighbors but to us also, that the Lands and the Road would remain as much ours as before, we therefore could not be injured by the Grant.—

Brother—We hope you will consider the present situation of the Six Nations, that it is critical, that we are poor, helpless distressed and perplexed. The great Spirit looks down, sees this and how hard we are used by the white People, who after getting between us and the British tell us we are within the territories of the United States—We had always thought that we joined the British and were outside your lines—We are perplexed & beg you will not ask too much of us.—

Brother—Our nation grants you the privilege of widening mending and straightening our path from Niagara to Canowagaras as you request, for one waggon to pass at a time, or not more than three fathoms wide—We hope this will satisfy you, and that you will ask no more.—for we know you white people are witches, too cunning and hard for us.—

Brother;—And now we have granted you all you ask.—We have something to ask in turn, the granting of which will be a better proof of our Brotherhood and your Regard for us than sending us a flag—We are much disturbed in our Dreams about *the great Eater with a big Belly* (Mr. [Robert] Morris) endeavoring to devour our Lands—We are afraid of him, believe him to be a Conjurer, and that he will be too cunning and hard for us, therefore request Congress will not licence nor suffer him to purchase our Lands.—

Brother—We hope you do not consider yourself as only spoken to, but that we speak to Congress also who has assured us of their Protection and that they would always inform us before they gave any the Permission to buy our Lands.—Now as we have accepted your Flag and granted you every thing you have asked, we expect that Congress will grant our Request, and assure us of it as soon as possible in an answer to this.—

Red Jacket sat down, and Farmers Brother concluded by saying:

Brother—You have the answer of the men by Red Jacket. The women wish to be heard a few words by me.—As they sat in Council, and the Land and the warriors belong to them, they hope the Requests of the warriors about the Road may be attended to, and that it may only be straightened and widened for one Carriage to pass at a time—They are surprised to find themselves within the Boundaries of the United States, they also dream much & think a great deal of Drums, are much disturbed in them about the Great Eater devouring their Lands, and join in the Request that he may not be permitted to purchase them.— [Source: ORWM, vol. 15, items 39–41]

Captain Bruff replied that the United States claimed the same jurisdiction that Britain had over the Indians, and that the United States claimed up to the Great Lakes as well as lands around their forts.

Letter from Thomas Morris

May 29, 1797

IN PREPARATION for the land purchase known as the Treaty of Big Tree (1797), Robert Morris sent his son Thomas on a preliminary expedition into Seneca country to lobby support for the sale. Robert Morris had owned the preemptive rights to the four million acres of Indian country since 1791, and he was anxious to extinguish the Indian claims to validate land sales he had already made to English investors and the Holland Land Company (see maps 2 and 3; Chernow 1977). In a letter to his father, young Morris wrote that he went to a Buffalo Creek tavern three miles from the Indian village and sent out word that he wanted the chiefs to assemble. The next day, about sixty showed up, suspicious of his motives. Dissembling, Thomas told them he was merely on a pleasure jaunt bound for Detroit but he became tired. Thomas mentioned that he was in Philadelphia when the president was read Sagoyewatha's September 23, 1796, reply to Captain Bruff about their fear that Robert Morris would attempt to devour their lands. Young Morris told Red Jacket that he had no reason to fear and that if they wanted to hold a land sale council, everyone would be invited, including Superintendent Chapin and Captain Bruff, and they would see that all was done fairly.

Thomas Morris narrates:

Red Jacket thanked me for the speech which I had made, he said they were all very glad to see me at the place of their abode and particularly so at the present time. that the Interpreters who had interpreted his speech to Capt. Bruff were both present[1] and would know that he was either misrepresented or misunderstood, that whatever was said with regard to you was said in jest and that it was never intended by him that a Syllable of it should go to the Presidents Ears. he said that he had never expressed an aversion to your holding a Conference with them, but as Genl. Cleveland (the Agent of the Con-

1. Horatio Jones and William Johnson.

necticut Company) had sometime before their meeting told them on his way
to New Connecticut (to a part of which the Six Nations made some Claim)
that he had made a purchase from one of the States and had none to make of
them, that they were afraid that the United States might without consulting
them sell to you a permission to take possession of a part of their Lands. he appeared to be very much mortified at having called you the *big Eater*. he said
that there were so many large Men in the United States that if he had called
you the big Man that the Indians would have been at a loss to know whom he
meant, but having dined with you at the Green House out of Town they observed you eat very heartily and he knew that they would know whom he
meant when he called you the big eater. he concluded by saying that the Cornplanter and his party had stirred up some Confusion in their Counsels and that
they had determined upon creating some new Chiefs to assist them in the
business of the Nation, that that business must be ended before any other
could be done, that a few days would complete it, and that then they would let
me know whether they wished you to come on this Summer or not & if they
did whether they would ask you to come on full or empty handed or leave it to
yourself to come as you pleased. [Source: ORWM, vol. 15, items 46–46A]

*Thomas's letter to his father then states that the following events had since occurred:
When Thomas returned to Buffalo a few days later, the Indians still were not ready
to give him an answer about the council, and took another four days to make their decision. Finally Red Jacket and Farmer's Brother agreed to go to Canandaigua with an
answer. At the same time, however, Horatio Jones privately told Thomas that the
Senecas had already decided to accept Morris's offer of a land sale council. Thomas
also learned from Cornplanter's son that Cornplanter was calling a private meeting
of warriors where he would argue that the Nation should divide its property and let
the Warriors sell land separately from the sachems. Thomas wrote that Cornplanter
had already promised both Red Jacket and Farmer's Brother that they would get $60
a year for life if they supported the land sale. Thomas claimed that Red Jacket asked
him for a bond, but Thomas said he would give him the bond after the purchase.
Thomas stated that he had hired Horatio Jones, Jasper Parrish, and William Johnson
as interpreters. Thomas concluded the letter by writing that he thought the Senecas
would only sell part of their lands.*

To Peter Russell, President of Upper Canada, on New Province

July 27, 1797

THE FOLLOWING SPEECH, made on the last day of a three-day council at Fort George or Newark, reflects anxiety over the creation of the new province called Upper Canada (Upper Canada refers to the Ontario area "up" the rivers, or westward from the Atlantic). The Indians were concerned that the division of the province would undermine the power of their superintendent, Sir John Johnson. Earlier in the day, President Russell reassured them that the reorganization actually gave Johnson direct power to help them engage in land leases without consulting the king's advisors in England, but Russell cautioned them about selling land. Later that day Red Jacket responded.

Previous days of the council had focused on the desire of Joseph Brant to sell several hundred square miles of the Grand River Reserve to investors on five tracts (see map 5). The British did not favor the sale. As Russell reminded Brant earlier in the council, Lord Dorchester and General Frederick Haldimand had given the Indians the Grand River land in October 1784 to help them protect their national integrity following the loss of Mohawk lands in the United States after the Revolution. Nonetheless, Brant had been attempting to sell portions of the reserve for several years, and by 1797, the British reluctantly began to comply. For more on Grand River land sales, see Kelsay (1984), Charles Johnson (1964), and also the council of July 27, 1801.

David Price, who translated often for British-Indian councils, interpreted. The transcriptions are microfilm copies of the papers of Deputy Indian Superintendent William Claus, who was also present at the council.

Red Jacket:

Brother—We have listened to what you said to us yesterday and considered it seriously.

Brother—You was pleased to give us a full explanation concerning the new arrangements of the Indian Department in answer to our speech delivered by the Farmer's Brother last month that might remove our doubts & uneasiness on that subject.—

Brother You said that when the two Canadas formed but one Province, the Indian concerns in this part were managed by the officer Commanding this majesty's warriors in it, and the Superintendants.—

Brother You also stated the tedious delays business met with in this arrangement on account of the great distance from Head Quarters where all matters of importance was obliged to be carried, and which might cause disappointments; And that our Father the King having taken into consideration this inconveniency, which it had been long wished to remedy, has now made the new arrangement, and that you are Commanded to take charge of the whole Indian concerns in this quarter; And you also said that the King our Great Father, by so doing, as it were brought us nigher to his person as we were now in a manner face to face, And that we could have an answer to any thing without sending to so great a distance as formerly, as in your person we saw the Representative of the King.

Brother—For this cause and that we might remove all uneasiness and not listen to bad birds—you said the King is too well satisfied with the conduct of our friend Sir John Johnson for to have him removed and the Superintendants under him, And you said that the Council fire is still to be kept up in the old place and also the presents.

Brother—You assure us that the Kings regard and friendship for us will never cease—that his friendship will be always clear and his covenant chain kept bright and that the only difference we will experience in this change will be in the attention and pleasure you will have in listening to whatever we might propose.

Brother We give you thanks for the candid information you have given us.

(A large bunch of wampum consisting of Eleven strings, black & white, marked C. in Captain Claus's possession)

Brother—We are happy to find by the whole tenor of your speech that the covenant Chain will be brighter than ever as we now are as it were Face to face with the King our Father—Any business we may have to do or any thing we may have to say will now be decided and settled in a moment.

Brother—As we have ever been well satisfied in every respect whatsoever with our friend Sir John Johnson as well as with his Father Sir William Johnson and the more particularly as his Father and himself ever fought the same Battles with us and always shared the same fate as ourselves, We could not help but feel ourselves much hurt when we heared of a change; and we supposed if this should be true there would be an end to the pursuing of our old Customs as well as to our friendship and regard.

Brother We hope however that matters are now so settled that there will in future be no occasion to say we must wait to send or hear across the Great Waters; And as we have good reason from your explanation to think that we will be happier as business will now be carried on immediately at our own fires, which must be more to our satisfaction as the delays will be removed and as we are now as it were in the presence of the King our Great Father; We therefore cannot but expect that every thing to be done for us now must exceed what has been done heretofore when he was at so great a distance as across the Great Water; otherwise the change will not be considered by us in so favourable a light.

Brother We hope you would not suppose that we would interfere in the movements or arrangements of the King our Great Father but as they immediately relate to ourselves.

Brother The Dividing the Indian Department is a matter opposite to our customs, and by that means our chain of correspondence may in the end be broken, 'tis therefore against our Interest as we are in a manner separated from our Brethren in Lower Canada.

Brother You have expressed to us in the clearest manner that our Brother Sir John Johnson is not removed from us, nor are the Deputy Superintendants, in which case we shall pursue our former customs and transactions and therefore we will now send Deputies down to Sir John Johnson concerning the business of this new arrangement, and our wishes to have a conference with the Lower Canada Indians

Brother—We hope that you would not listen to the many wicked Birds that may fly round your Ears; and we would have you to believe that our forefathers ever were, and that we ourselves are capable of acting for ourselves; And that we are ever true to our engagements.—

We therefore hope you will put confidence in our Speeches, And we will always be as candid to you, that when we have any thing to say we ourselves will make it known to you.

A bunch of wampum

(Fourteen Strings of Black & White Wampum marked D. in Capt Claus's possession) [Source: "Records of the Councils and Speeches to and by Indian Nations in Upper Canada, 1796–1803," BV Indians, Misc. Microfilm, reel 24, pp. 36–41, NYHS]

The Treaty of Big Tree

THE TREATY OF BIG TREE was one of the most important Indian land sales in New York State history. It had a complex background, hinging on the transference of *preemptive* or *presumptive right* to buy Indian lands (see Chernow 1977; Evans 1924; Osgood 1892; Turner 1850, 1851; Wilkinson 1979). Because Oliver Phelps and Nathaniel Gorham defaulted on two-thirds of their payments to Massachusetts, in 1791 Robert Morris bought the preemptive rights to what Phelps and Gorham were unable to pay for—four million acres of lands, virtually all of present-day New York State west of Geneseo (or, as the town was called then, Big Tree. See maps 2 and 3). In 1792, Morris sold the western majority of those lands (reserving some sections for himself), to the Holland Land Company, a collection of Dutch investors. Because Morris did not actually own the lands he sold, he had to convince the Indians to sell their lands to him so he could fulfill his promise to the Holland Company. At Big Tree, the Senecas sold most of their lands for $100,000, reserving only ten reservations totaling about 300 square miles. Many of the participating sachems and warriors were paid bribes in advance and given personal annuities afterward (Wilkinson 1979, 275).

Although Sagoyewatha opposed the sale, a large group of the Seneca warriors successfully worked to advance it. In the end, Red Jacket signed the treaty and received $600 cash and a $100 annuity for life. Readers should be advised that most historians criticize Red Jacket for duplicitous conduct at Big Tree (Morris 1844; Stone 1841, 237–49; Wilkinson 1979). For alternative views, see Densmore (1999) and Ganter (2000).

Thomas Morris was assisted by Charles Williamson, an agent of British investors to whom Robert Morris had already sold extensive Genesee lands. Jeremiah Wadsworth, a successful Connecticut investor, served as U.S. commissioner. General William Shepherd, Revolutionary War veteran and congressman, represented Massachusetts. William Bayard represented the New York bank handing the Dutch interests. He was accompanied by Jan (John) Lincklaen, Garret Boon, and two members of the Dutch Van Staphorst banking family. Joseph Ellicott was a Holland Company surveyor who later became an agent for the company (Wilkinson 1979, 266). James Rees acted as treaty secretary (Morris 1844, 31). Council interpreters were Jasper Parrish, Horatio Jones, and William Johnson.

The following transcripts are taken from Thomas Morris's revised daily account of the negotiations, as submitted to his father's business associates ("Diary of Big Tree," Holland Land Company Papers, reel 28 of 202, SUNY Fredonia). This manuscript gives a fairly reliable account of the negotiations, although it offers condensed versions of several events and speeches. James Rees's original notes for this diary, which contain numerous revisions and lengthier speeches, are in the Henry O'Reilly Collection of Western Mementos at the New York Historical Society. I have included short extracts where they diverge significantly from the Holland Land Company papers.

After a week of condolence ceremonies and gift disbursements, the council business began on August 28. Wadsworth and Shepherd gave their assurances to the Indians that Morris was the only man allowed to treat with the Indians according to the U.S. Intercourse laws, and that Thomas Morris and Charles Williamson were his agents. Thomas Morris read a letter from his father, apologizing that he was too "corpulent" to attend himself but that he looked forward to the outcome of the negotiation. The next day, August 29, Red Jacket spoke for the Indians. Morris narrates, usually referring to himself in the third person:

This day the Indians were counciling among themselves on the speeches delivered to them untill late in the afternoon, when the commissioners, Mr. Morris, &c were sent for, and soon after they were seated, Red Jaquet rose and noticed the Speeches delivered yesterday—thanked the Great Spirit for his care of the Commissioners and confessed they were satisfied with the appointments made by the President, Governor of Massachusetts, and their friend who called for this council fire, but turning to Mr. Th.[oma]ˢ Morris, observed that from the Speeches delivered to them, by him, it appeared something was kept back and, from the candor and Sincerity promised by him, they hoped all would be laid before them fairly. On which he [Morris] rose and informed them, that it was his intention to act with sincerity and fairness towards them, and was then ready to lay before them, more particularly, the business for which they were assembled, if they were then disposed to hear him. Red Jacket replied, that the sun was nearly down, it would perhaps be well to leave it untill tomorrow, to which he [Morris] consented and the council fire was covered over.

The next day, August 30, Morris gave a long speech explaining why it was in the Indians' interest to sell. He noted that their game was decreasing each year, and an annuity from a land sale would remain constant. He emphasized that Robert Morris was the only person allowed to make them this financial offer. The Indians counseled among themselves for two days, apparently distracted by liquor sales at their camps. On the afternoon of September 2, the Senecas were ready to reply:

Farmers Brother addressed the nation, requesting attention, as it was then intended to make an answer to Mr Morris's speech.

Red Jacquet then rose and after recapitulating Mr Morris's speech observed in answer, that many disadvantages would attend the sale of their lands, that experience had proved, that whenever they parted with their Territory, they also parted with their consequence; and in order to elucidate this, he instanced the situation of the Oneidas, formerly, he said they were a great people and formed a powerfull part of the Six Nations, that they had been usefull to them in their councils untill the State of New York purchased their lands, that since that period their importance had diminished, and that altho' they were more wealthy than before, yet their national weight was lessened, as it caused a separation from the Six Nations.—that the Senecas had not more land than they wanted—a great deal of what they formerly owned, was sold, and the Money spent, they of course were now no richer than if none had been sold. That they had been told a great deal of money would be offered for their lands, they did not know how much as Mr. Morris had not yet told them, but they supposed he would now come forward with a great deal of money to shew them, but requested he would hold his fists close, as they would rather have their lands than money.

Mr. Morris in reply pointed out the benefit which would accrue to them from a sale with the manner he proposed. He adverted to the arguments used in his speech of the 30th and impressed upon them the advantages of an annuity, and told them that if their forefathers had disposed of the purchase money which they received for their lands, in the way he proposed, complaints of fraud and their being now no richer for those sales, would not be heard. He then expressed his astonishment at hearing them impute the separation of the Oneidas to the purchase of their lands by the State of New York, and asked them wether the impression made by the last war was so slight, as to be suddenly forgotten. It was that event which disunited your councils. Many years before the purchase by New-York you had taken up the tomahock against each other and never met but in the field of battle. But as the Oneidas had been mentioned he would contend that they were happier since than before the sale; their reservations were more than sufficient for them, and their annuity made them easy and wealthy. As to other Indians surrounded by white people he admitted that many of them were poor and unhappy; but it was not to be ascribed to their selling their lands, but to their improvidence in spending the money received; this was a stronger reason why the Senecas should avail themselves of the plan proposed for securing the happiness of themselves and future generations.

After a short address from Red Jacket to the Indians the council fire was covered over by Mr. Morris at their request.

In the evening a private conference was held with the principal chiefs, at which Mr. Morris offered 100,000 dollars for the whole of their lands, which might be invested in Bank stock of the United States and would bring them at least 6000 d.[ollar]s annually forever; this offer they requested he would State in public council on which the conference concluded.

September 3d

This day Red Jacket sent a private message to Mr. Morris stating that his speech of yesterday was not his own sentiments, but made to please some of their people—The next speech would not be quite so harsh, and that he [Morris] would finally answer his purpose if he persevered in the business. In the afternoon a public council was called at which

Red Jacket rose and said, Brothers, we yesterday made you a speech and you immediately answered it. We told you then and we tell you now that our seat is not too large for us to sit down upon comfortably. Once the Six Nations were a great people and had a large council fire which was held at Onondaga, but now at Buffaloe, and soon may be removed from there. Now the Onondagas are nobody, have no lands of their own, but we ever hospitable to our bretheren, let them sit down on our lands. We are still a great people and much respected by all the Western Indians, which is allowing to our having land of our own. You wish to buy all our lands, except such reservations as you might make for us to raise corn on. It will make us nobody to accept such reservations, and where you may think proper—if this should be the case we could not say we were a free people. Brothers, we mentioned before that our fore fathers had sold their lands and had eat up all the money they got for them. Brothers, we wish to reason on this business coolly and calmly,—it is of great magnitude and we thank you for putting us in mind of this and hope you will stick to the same advice you give us. Brothers, we wish you to put your speeches in writing so that we can read them when we are old; there are great many of our people that cannot remember long; but if they are wrote down they can be read to them when they are old, and we shall know what has been said to us.[1]

Morris responded by saying that he did not think the Senecas were held in very high repute by the western Indians, alluding their reception at the Glaize in 1792. He also emphasized that if the Indians did not want to sell now, Robert Morris would never make a second offer to them. A significantly longer version of Morris's reply appears in Morris's "Rough Memoranda." Because Sagoyewatha later responds to ideas only mentioned in this version, the alternative text is worth reproducing in full. Most of the strikeouts are inconsequential except for Morris's consistent substitution of the plural "we" for the "I" that initially appears throughout the text. Morris speaks:

Brothers of the Seneca Nation

We have listened attentively to your Speech and we request the same attention from you while I am delivering our answer to it.

You say Brothers that when you became surrounded by the White people that altho' your Wealth will increase your importance will diminish, and to prove this assertion you desire me to look at the situation of those Indians who have sold their Lands and who live on Reservations surrounded by the White People—You also say that you are now respected by the Western Indians that they look up to you as their elder Brothers and that you have obtained this Consequence by the Land which you own. you further mention that you have not only your importance as a people to preserve, but that other Nations seated on your Lands look up to you as their elder Brothers for protection, that these are dependent on you and that it would be unjust in you to disturb them.—You desire us to look back, and discover if we can [see] near the old Onondaga any vestige of the place where your great Council fire was formerly held. You say that you are afraid that that Council fire will be also extinguished at Buffaloe Creek if you sell your Lands. You also say that altho' by the Sale of your Lands you will become possessed of a great deal of Money, yet that you understand but little about the Value of Money and your speaker [Red

1. Stone gives a different version of the above speech. He reports that while Red Jacket was explaining the peace of mind that the possession of their lands gave them, he said, "That knowledge is every thing to us. It raises us in our own estimation. It creates in our bosoms a proud feeling which elevates us as a nation. Observe the difference between the estimation in which a Seneca and an Oneida are held. We are courted, while the Oneidas are considered a degraded people, fit only to make brooms and baskets. Why this difference? It is because the Senecas are known as the proprietors of a broad domain, while the Oneidas are cooped up in a narrow space" (Stone 1841, 151). Although colorful, and indicative of the literary energy for which Sagoyewatha was acclaimed, Thomas Morris (Stone's source) was probably just pulling it from memory.

Jacket] declares that if he had His home full of it that his arm would never be tired in handing to storekeepers for the fine things which they expose for sale in their stores.

You also remind us that we have called upon you to deliberate coolly and dispassionately upon the proposals which we have made to you

Brothers We are happy to find out that you have attended to our advice and that you are convinced of the propriety of our doing our business in a calm and temperate manner. We recommended it to you because we thought it would be of service, and we sincerely rejoice that you agree with us in Sentiment in this particular.

Brothers We were astonished to hear you speak of your apprehensions of being surrounded by the White People, and of the disadvantages what you would experience when so situated. you are already surrounded by the White People, there is not a single direction by which you can leave your Country with out coming to our settlements and if you have been until now without experiencing inconveniences from being so situated, you will have none to expect hereafter. As to the Indians who have sold their Lands and now reside among the White people some of them to be sure are poor and miserable others are better off than they would be if they still retained their Lands. but what has occasioned the poverty and misery of those whose situations you lament[?] it has not been occasioned by their selling their lands but by their spending all the money which they got for them[.] If when they sold they had done what we now wish you to do, if they had reserved to themselves an annual payment forever, they would have still maintained their Consequence and their Wealth.

Brothers We were also surprised at your mentioning the importance which your lands give you among your younger brothers the Western Indians. let us look back together and recollect what happened only a few years ago. Motives of friendship both for the United States and for them induced you to accompany our Commissioners into the Country of your Western brethren. did they then listen to the wholesome advice which you gave them, no they shut their Ears against your Admonitions, and your situation among them became dangerous. I mention this to show to you that your Lands do not give you that Consequence among your Western brethren that you imagine

Brothers the protection which you have given to other Nations by seating them upon your Lands will not be withdrawn if you sell. We agree with you that it would be improper to remove them and we shall be ready to confirm to them the privilege which they heretofore have had of living on and cultivating the Ground which they occupy. You certainly have no reason to fear that your Council fire at Buffaloe Creek will be extinguished by a Sale of your Lands. Your principal reservation will undoubtedly be at Buffaloe Creek and your Council fire will burn there as well after the Sale of Lands adjoining that place as before. Union and harmony will be promoted by your drawing near to each other and your business will be better conducted and your Councils attended by all of you with more ease than when you were scattered all over your Country. your former Council fire was not destroyed by the Sale of your Lands, but by that unfortunate misunderstanding between us which gives us all pain to think of and which you properly observed the other day ought always to be kept out of sight. Neither Brothers can the Situation of our friend Capt. Chapin be affected by your determination at present, if you are assembled in a few places he will meet with you with less trouble than he heretofore has had in counselling with you, and his advice will be as important to you as ever it has been. besides Brothers he is so disinterested a friend of yours that even if his office was affected by it, which it will not be I am persuaded that he would wish you to attend to the good of your Nation

Brothers—You suppose that money is not as valuable to you as to the White people because you do not use it with the same Economy[.] why do you not, because you never yet have recieved annually a Sum adequate to your Wants. When heretofore you have sold Land your necessities have been so many that your money has been instantly swallowed up by them. you have recieved so little of it at a time that after spending it all you were yet unfurnished with many things useful to yourselves and families. but if you were enabled every Year by the reciept of a Sum of money to provide yourselves with Cloathing and other necessaries you would soon become as well acquainted with the Use and Value of Money as the White People are. you would find so many advantages arising from a proper Economy that you would soon become more anxious to save your Money and my friend [Red Jacket] himself would after a little while be quite as unwilling to throw it away upon the fine things of a store as at present he would be to dispose of his Land for the same purpose.

Brothers I think it necessary to repeat to you again the proposals which I have made to you. I have offered you one hundred thousand dollars for all your Lands excepting such Reservations as it may be necessary for you to make. if these reservations are small, I shall make no deduction from the Sum just mentioned[.] if on the contrary you make them large the quantity of money which you receive will lessen in proportion to the Land reserved. the Sum of money which I have offered to you is very considerable, so considerable Brothers that you ought to have the best Security that our Country can afford. I therefore proposed that it should be vested in the stock of the Bank of the

United States in the name of the President your father. being thus invested it will not only always be safe but it will annually furnish you and your Children after you with Money enough to make you rich & happy as a Nation.

Brothers. the diminution of your game annually decreasing the wants of your old and poor people the ease and happiness of your Women and Children and the many Comforts with which the Money will furnish your Nation forever are strong reasons why you should accept of my offer

Brothers you will never again have as good an Opportunity of doing complete Justice to your Nation. my father alone can buy your Lands and if after making you the greatest offer that ever yet has been made to Indians for Lands you reject it he will never again treat with you on the same favorable terms. If he should ever be induced to meet you after this for a similar purpose he will not be able to come forward as full handed as he at present is. he cannot keep so much money long together, he will apply it to other Uses and you must expect if you sell in future to get no more than you have got for the Land upon which we now are

Brothers I have now opened my mind to you fully, I have nothing more to say, I have made you all the offers that I can make and I expect that your next answer will explicitly mention whether you will sell or not and if you do sell what reservations you will make. [Source: ORWM, vol. 15, item 69]

Over the next two days, September 4 and 5, it became clear that the Senecas disagreed among themselves over whether to sell. Cornplanter gave a speech expressing his disappointment that the sachems had "shut the warriors out." On September 6, Little Beard, a warrior, gave a speech saying that the warriors had agreed to abide by the decision of the sachems, and then Red Jacket spoke:

Red Jacket then rose, and particularly addressing himself to the commissioners, Mr. Morris, and Cap[t.] Williamson, observed that with respect to our Nation not being of consequence among the Western Indians, as had been stated at a former council from the lands they held, the true reason if they were not respected, was that they were too much in company with United States commissioners; but as this subject had nothing to do with their present business, it should be buried, that business might go on.

Brothers

I wish your attention to what I shall now say. We have made up our minds to try the Value of our lands. We will let you have a Tract of six miles square, beginning at the corner of Gorham & Phelps purchase and the Pennsy[lvani]ª line at one dollar p.[er] acre; this is our price, therefore you need not offer us half that price, nor expect more land, our friend Col. Wadsworth will see that this bargain is just, and will confirm it, that the writings may be drawn. Brother Mr. Morris you know the value of land round a town you settle, and therefore, we hope you will deal honorably with us. You get six dollars p.[er] acres, and we offer to sell at one, therefore you ought to make your mind easy. Tomorrow will be time enough to give us an answer to this offer, or it may be given now, as your friend Capt. Williamson is present, after consulting him, perhaps an answer may be given immediately. That he had spoken his mind in a few words, very short.

Mr. Morris then rose and promised to be as short in speaking his mind. At different councils he had stated this business truly and believed it was understood by them. The offer now made did not require a moment's consideration, it could not be accepted, and if as had been said, it was their fixed determination and that nothing farther was to be expected, they might as well cover the council fire—but if they were desirous again to consider the proposals he had made, he would wait their answer.

The moment he had sat down, Red Jacquet again rose and in great passion said: Agreed, let us cover the council fire over and furiously stretching his hand across the table—let us shake hands upon it and part friends; and thus the business was considered as unfortunately closed; but soon after the council was broke up, Farmers Brother came to Mr. Morris and enquired wether he was going home early in the morning, to which he answered, he would perhaps take two days having so many things to pack up and on that account he would be detained; that notwithstanding the business was ended in the manner it was, yet he did not want to leave his brothers out of temper, that it was he who had kindled the council fire, and of course, it was his and not Red Jacket's place to put it out, that as things were situated they might again meet for the purpose of being reconciled to each other and parting friends.

On the morning September 7, Morris visited the chief women and emphasized how much money he was going to give them. In the afternoon, Cornplanter expressed his dissatisfaction that the sachems had covered up the council fire too soon, and Farmer's Brother then spoke to officially turn the decision over to the warriors and chief women. On September 10, Cornplanter announced that the Senecas were ready to sell. Little Billy announced that each village would appoint representatives to negotiate the size of their reservations. In his accounts of the wrangling over reservation size, Morris writes that over September 14 and 15, Red Jacket was very difficult:

Of all the tribes the Buffaloes were the most difficult to bring over. Red Jacket insisted on a reservation that would have taken 980,000 acres for the

Buffaloes only. he contended with extreme violence that their national char-acter and pride would be lost, unless they claimed this much, and pressed with great animation a settlement on these terms; but Mr. Morris on the other hand insisted on the unreasonableness of their demand that he had offered them what the whole of their country was worth, and generously gave them what land they might, in reason, wish to retain; but they in abuse of his goodness wished, under the name of reservation to take half the land back. Red Jacket still persisted and M. Morris told him he would not acquiesce, that his father would suppose him unfaithfull in his duty, and upbraid him with folly. After several conferences on this subject, M. Morris told them he would make them the generous offer of 100 miles square for them and the Tonawantas—this they rejected, and told him they would have the reservation first mentioned— the loquacious Red Jacket insisted, that they were the sellers, they were not to be told what they should part with—they would sell only what they pleased. M. Morris in answer told them, that as he was payer he would only pay for what he pleased, on this he was asked, if they made this reservation what sum he would deduct from the 100,000 dollars offered, to which he replied 25,000 d^{ls} [dollars]. to this they consented and requested the writings might be drawn, on which he left them; but it seems many of the chiefs who were restrained from speaking by the forwardness of Red Jacket in Morris's presence, spoke their mind freely after he had withdrawn, and insisted on the reservation being reduced, so that no reduction should be made from the money. The Young King and Farmers Brother came out to talk the matter over with M. Morris & Cap$^{n.}$ Williamson. They mentioned many inconveniences which would attend a deduction from the 100,000 dollars and finally asked whether they would allow them to make for themselves and the Tanawanta Tribe, 200 *square miles* instead of what had been asked. on this they at length yielded, as a denial in all probability, would throw all up in the wind again. [Source: Holland Land Company Papers, reel 28 of 202]

The deed was finally signed by candlelight the night of September 16.

To Joseph Ellicott and Capt. Chapin on Dissatisfaction with the Treaty of Big Tree and Requests for Boundary Adjustments to the Reservations

June 21, 1798

AT A COUNCIL held at Buffalo Creek a year after the Treaty of Big Tree, the Senecas met to voice their complaints about their treatment following the sale of their lands to Robert Morris and the Holland Land Company. Joseph Ellicott, the brusque surveyor and agent of Holland Land Company, came to the council bearing papers describing the Seneca deposits in the Bank of the United States and a commission to survey Seneca lands. Although the transcripts are not clear about the Senecas' largest request, they seem to be asking that the United States amend the Big Tree purchase. They also asked Ellicott to make smaller adjustments to their reservations, particularly to the Cattaraugus reserve, which had a thin strip they wanted to exchange for a larger centralized block. Chapin and Ellicott responded that the terms of Big Tree could not be altered. On behalf of the Indians, however, Chapin successfully requested to Secretary of War Henry that the boundaries of the Cattaraugus reserve be amended (Chapin to Henry, June 28, 1798; ORWM, vol. 13, item 17). The Holland Land Company also cooperated in revising the Cattaraugus boundaries, and they also agreed to give the Tuscaroras a one-mile-square reservation (provisions for their reservation had been forgotten at the 1797 Treaty of Big Tree; see Ellicott 1937).

The following are two speech transcripts from the council. Sagoyewatha speaks for the clan mothers at the end. The manuscripts contain no introductory material and do not state who interpreted the speeches, but the shorthand resembles Jasper Parrish's. The speech texts sometimes shift from speech to narrative summary without explicit signal:

"Red Jackit spoke as follows: "First cal[le][d.] on his people to att[en][d.] s[ai][d.] something of the treaty with Mr Morris that the Chiefs at that treaty attended to the bus[ines]ˢ˒ but now the matter of bu[sines]ˢ˒ at this C[ounci]ˡ˒ would be referred to the Warriors to act in place of the sachems.

Abeil [Cornplanter:] B[rothe]ʳˢ We met you here yesterday as the man who has the charge of our business to converse respecting our lands and you told us that the money for the sail of our Country to Mr. M[orri]ˢ was duly deposited in the B[an]k of the US by reading certain papers to us which were sent by the Secʸ˒ at War & we were also told that we might receive the mo[ney] half yearly, or yearly as we pleased.

B[rothe]ʳ˒ We give the P[resident] great thanks for his care of our business in attending to our aff[ai]ʳˢ.

We also understand that Geo[rge] W[ashington] has witnessed to our money being placed in the B[an]k of the US, for which we return him our thanks

Bʳ—We have thought for the last winter that the Rich Man Mr. Mʳˢ [Thomas Morris] must be well pleased with the bargain he has made with the Ind.[ian]ˢ and suppose he would be disposed to do every thing in his power to fulfill agreements. And that his Father [Robert Morris] must be well pleased and would see that every thing that was promised should be strictly complied with.

Bʳ˒ Ellicot, I wish to ask you one question, whether you can comply with every article of the treaty made with Mr R Mori [Robert Morris] and grant us answers to such questions and grant other things that we may ask of you relating to the bargain. Br. this young Rich Man conducted irregular & we would wish to let his Father know of it and at the same time handed certain papers to Mr. Ellicot & requested him to tell them whether he could ensure to them the sums of mo[ney] ment[ione]ᵈ in them as long as the sun [rises?] & water runs.

And there are some other matters T. Morris [often referred?] to his Father which we wish to know whether they will be confirmed as we have not as yet learnt [respecting?] them. (being a letter to M[r.] R[obert] Morris from his son TM [Thomas Morris])

Capt. Abeel[:] Peo[ple] of the US we have heard what you have s[ai]ᵈ˒ to the papers I hold in my hand being Mr. M[orris's] notes—I formerly thought I should not have the diff[icult]ˡʸ I now finde as I have [been?] [willing?] the wh[ite] Peo[ple] sh[oul]ᵈ have privileges as well as our selves but I am not diss[appointe]ᵗ but am anx[ious] that my peo[ple] shall have some advantage from the country once ours. The Landˢ now in question fell in to Mr. M[orris's] hand & has not seen us at the tim[e] of doing business (meaning R[obert]

Mo[rris]) and wishes all w[oul]^d consider and have Mr M[orri]s come forward tho we do not wish to have any compulsion for his immediate presence as he may come more conveniently next winter & at the place where it wou[l]^d be proper to meet w[oul]^d be at the place where we held our treaty last —Big Tree—

Red Jacket[:] Peo[ple] of the US I wish you to listen[.] you just heard what our war[io]rs just s[ai]$^{d.}$ we finde we are of late less taken notice of[.] we frequently r[eceive]^d me[ssages?] of the US & their request[.] we always complied with it[.] it came to us by Col[onel] P[ickering.] his voice was good & smooth[.] we told him we were afraid he d[e]l[iver]d his w[or]^{ds} from his lips[.] he told us it was from the heart—the US made a request of us resp[ectin]^g diff[icultie]^s towards the setting of the sun & did all in our power & now these diff^{ts} [difficulties] are settled we finde ourselves neglected. at the time of delivering this [message?] the US made proposals to be of use to us in send[in]^g men to teach us husb[an]^{dy} &c but now all is peace & you set your eye on our land—the rich M[orris] bought [presumptive right] of Ph[elp]^s & after holding it a short time he came for[war]^d with his eyes wide open for our lands and at the treaty last Fall we attended with our [two illegible words] they place & there the wish of the rich M[orris] was made known to us & after holding a long talk we made a proposal to let him have a tract of our land [two illegible words] Bay—but they w[oul]^d not comply with our request but at last we sold [illegible word] C[oun]^{ty} as we did. We when thinking the winter past concerning the situation of our [reserves?] being such as to give us trouble & to ease the mind of our Br[other] we would wish the first proposed line to take place, & want the P[resident] of the US to use his influence to bring the matter about. Mr. E[llicott] you ever Jaunt forw[ar]^d to survey our land & we wish you to rest & the money placed in the B[an]k to remain in the situation it is and also the land. altho we do not expect the bargain to be broke but to have the business remain as it is.

Possibly the next day, June 22:

Far[mer's] B[rother] call[e]d their attention &c—

Red Jacket[:] B[rothe]^r, Capt. Chapin, & Mr. Elicot attend[.] Yesterday y[ou] made several replies to the speech you made before & it seems by what you say you think we cast some [aspersions?] on Gov[ernmen]^t you told us Congress were not cons[ulted?]^q in any of our land & that you judged by what we s[ai]d Gov^t had forgot us but you told us it was not the case[.] you told us Govt still continued their charity [still?] to us—then you ask[e]^d us where

Congress had rec[ceive]ᵈ any benefit from you[.] we wish to inquire what has become of our lands—

This Isl[an]ᵈ was given us by the G[rea]t Spirit on which you live and receive every advantage from. You are a great people now on this isl[an]d and have become rich & numerous—

Bʳ When we sent for you we looked to you for advice & expected we should have your assistance but you overset all our request. You told us the barg[ai]ⁿ respecting our land was made strong by Govt, & that we understood the whole bargain of our lands & what was confirmed would not be altered & you refused to assist to alter the agreement. Br. I allways conceiv[e]ᵈ you were to listen to our request[.] the other day we told you our wishes & we have found since we made our bargain we missed it, as we have made our seats so small we have ruined them. being many peo[ple] shall soon overrun it & be obliged to move on ac[coun]t of having so many diferent nations among us to occupy the ground. Since we return[e]d from the treaty we have found we have missed it very much & we now acknowledge we have injured our women & children in the sail of our country.

Bʳ—We have determined M[r.] Morris shall hear our distressed situation as we can not be reconciled without—Bʳ—It is necessary we sh[oul]ᵈ have room to walk about & not be crowded by wh[ite] Peo[ple] as the peace of both parties will be disturbed and we want a large seat here that all may have a privilig[e] to set down on this ground. [Source: ORWM, vol. 12, item 66]

The manuscripts continue with other fragments of speeches from this council:

Capt Abeel [Cornplanter], speech

Br.[other] It is the wish of the Catargara [Cattaraugus] Ind[ian]ˢ as they have made a great mistake in laying off their reservations being not compact enough, which is a reason we forbid the present survey being made and we want to know whether the Se[cretar]ʸ at War or the President will confirm the reservation if it shall be altered more to their mind. & we wish the Sec[retar]ʸ at War to hear us and grant our request and the sooner it can be done the better we shall be pleased.—

Red Jacket's speech

B[rothe]ʳ The Weorer [warrior's] request made by Abeel is the wish of all the Council present to have the Cat P [Cattaraugus Preserve] reservation laid off in a compact piece as we consider it more to their advantage.

. . .

Speech—[1]

B[rothe][rs]—Listen in regard to the treaty at Geneseo last fall between the R[obert] M[orris] & the Ind[ian][s.] we were surprised when we found what had taken place, at the treaty we had reason to think too much use of Liquor was made, & turned their minds.

I am surprised the treaty took place as it did, we women, are the true own-ers[.] we work on it & it is ours & if it is the will of the g[rea]t S[pirit] [we very uneasy?] & now we are sorry our seats are so small. as We women since the bar-gain it has given our minds much uneasyness to think our seats are so small[.] you will remove these feelings from our breasts if these comp[lain][ts] can be re-moved & also if all these that are possessed of thought—Now you have heard the request of the women & by your white Peo[ple] complying with our re-quest will ease our minds & when we finde we have not got enough for a thing we go back with it & get [alteration?] which satisfies our minds. Now we have made our request to you[.] the line has been pointed out by our sachems to which we agree & if the Sec[retar][y] of War will agree to the same we will then think he has regard for us—Our request is now free from liquor which ought not to be used to take advantage of Ind[ian][s.] we now speak soberly—Now you have heard the voice of the women & when you return the answer from the Sec[y] of War return these strings.

6 strings of wampum [Source: ORWM, vol. 12, item 69]

Ellicott replied that the Holland Company was expending huge sums of money—upward of $100 a day—and they would lose all this money if they complied with the Indians' request. In a long speech following, Cornplanter asked for Allegany annu-ities to be paid at Fort Pitt, and that he wanted to swap some of his New York land for land in Pennsylvania. He also repeated his request that Ellicott stop his surveying until the Indians were satisfied. Ellicott did not stop surveying but he did get the Cat-taraugus and Tuscarora reservations quickly adjusted (Ellicott 1937, 42–52; ORWM, vol. 12, item 70).

1. Sagoyewatha speaks here for the clan mothers.

To William Claus on the Ferry at Black Rock

OCTOBER 30, 1799

THREE MILES above the village of Buffalo, the area known as Black Rock was the customary departure point for Senecas to cross the Niagara River to Canada (see map 5). The Indians requested that Claus intervene in the business of two rival ferrymen. Claus's response is not recorded in the papers. Others present were Senecas from Buffalo Creek; Robert Kerr, Indian Department surgeon; Lt. R. McDonell, R.C.V.; Lt. Bromhead, 24th Regt.; Mr. Chew,[1] Indian Department; David Price, interpreter. The council took place at Fort Erie, Canada. The speech is a copy from the William Claus Papers.

The usual ceremonies of condolence being gone through, Red Jacket, a principal Seneca Chief spoke as follows:

Brother Our minds for some time have been a good deal uneasy and we now wish to acquaint you of the Cause.

We have always found great difficulty in crossing from the opposite Shore[2] and we at last found a man who engaged to take us over for nothing on consideration of giving him the Ferry on our side, allowing him to build a House and inclose some ground to plant which we complied with but we are sorry to tell you that there is a man on this side[3] of the water that keeps a Boat and as soon as he sees a Waggon or Horsemen at the point above the Black Rock he goes over and brings them to this side of the water for less than our man can afford, We have deferr'd hurting his Boat until we mentioned this business to you and hope that you will get the matter settled so that it may pre-

---

1. Joseph Chew was Guy Johnson's secretary; he was briefly Indian superintendent after William Johnson died in 1774; "Mr. Chew" may have also been one of Joseph's sons, William Johnson Chew or Benjamin Chew (Kelsay 1984, 140, 564)

2. The U.S. side.

3. The Canadian, or British side.

vent any harm from happening to the man that makes the Whiskey, his continuing to come over for people that are on our side of the Water may bring us all into trouble. We have now opened our minds to you and shall wait to see what you will do for us. [Source: "Records of the Councils and Speeches . . . ," BV Indians, Misc. reel 24, p. 80, NYHS]

To Rev. Elkanah Holmes at Seneca Castle

October 20, 1800

FOLLOWING THE REQUEST of the United States that the Six Nations develop agriculture and education, the Senecas initially let Christian missionaries come onto their reservations who claimed to be teachers. Elkanah Holmes was among the first. He was given $190 by the New York Missionary Society for a school at Buffalo Creek, but he ended up living with the Tuscaroras, who were more responsive to his efforts (Howland 1903, 126; Houghton 1920, 141. See also missionary accounts of Red Jacket at Buffalo Creek: Holmes 1801; Hyde 1903; Alden 1827; Bacon 1903; Covell 1804; Cumming 1979; and esp. Harris 1903b). In early October 1800, Holmes arrived at Seneca Castle at Buffalo Creek, and arranged a meeting attended by more than one hundred Senecas. Holmes told the Senecas that he would like to preach to them and wanted to know what their answer was. Some young Seneca listeners laughed in response, and one of them probably broke wind, a typical gesture of disrespect (the phrase Holmes uses is "one made a very indecent report" [1801, 65]). After the chiefs consulted for half an hour, Sagoyewatha welcomed him "in a very decent manner and in flattering language," saying that they feared no deceit and agreed to let him preach the following morning. Holmes preached several times over the next week.

The following is an account of Red Jacket's speech to Holmes on October 20, 1800. The interpreters were William Johnson and Nicholas Cusick (Holmes spells his name "Cusock"). Holmes hired Cusick for $15 a month to serve as his interpreter and guide. The following text appears as it was first published in the *New York Missionary Magazine* in 1801.

Red Jacket introduced Holmes:

"FATHER,

WE are extremely happy that the Great Good Spirit has permitted us to meet together this day. We have paid attention to all that you spoke to our ears at our last meeting. We thank the Great Spirit, who has put it into the minds of the great society of friendship at New-York, to send you to visit us. We also hope that the Great Spirit will always have his eyes over that good society, to strengthen their minds to have friendship toward the poor natives of this Island.—We thank the Great Spirit, that he has smoothed your way, and has protected you through the rugged paths, and prevented any briars or thorns from pricking your feet.—As you came on your way to visit us, you called on our brothers (the Oneidas, Muhheconnuks,[1] and Tuscaroras) who were well acquainted with you. We thank them for the pains they have taken in sending this good talk with wampum. (*At the same time holding the talk and wampum in his hand.*) We are convinced that what they say of you is true, that you come purely out of love to do us good, and for nothing else; and that there is no deceit in your business, or in the good people that sent you.

"Father, we now request you to speak something to us about Jesus Christ, and we will give attention."

He [Red Jacket] then addressed his people, and requested them to give good attention to what I was about to say, and make no noise, but behave in a becoming manner.

I then proceeded, and endeavoured to preach Christ to them.—When I had concluded, Red Jacket rose and made the following speech to me, after consulting the chiefs:

"Father; we thank the Great Good Spirit above, for what you have spoken to us at this time, and hope he will always incline your heart, and strengthen you to this good work. We have clearly understood you, and this is all truth that you have said to us.

"Father, we believe that there is a Great Being above, who has made Heaven and earth, and all things that are therein, and has the charge over all things—who has made you whites as well as us Indians; and we believe there is something great after death.

"Father, what you say about our loving the Great Spirit, we know to be truth, as he has eyes over all things, and watches all our movements and ways, and hears all we say, and knows all we do.

"Father, we Indians are astonished at you whites, that when Jesus Christ was among you, and went about doing good, speaking the good word, healing the sick, and casting out evil spirits, that you white people did not pay attention to him, and believe him, and that you put him to death when you had the good book in your possession.

1. Mahicans, or Stockbridge.

"Father, that we Indians were not near to this transaction, or could we be guilty of it.

"Father, probably the Great Spirit has given to you white people the ways that you follow to serve him, and to get your living: and probably he has given to us Indians the customs that we follow to serve him (handed down to us by our forefathers) and our ways to get our living by hunting, and the Great Spirit is still good to us, to preserve game for us. And father you well know, you white people are very fond of our skins.

"Father, you and your good people know that ever since the white people came on this island, they have been always getting our lands from us for little or nothing.

"Father, perhaps if we had had such good people as you and your Society to have stepped in and advised us Indians, we and our forefathers would not have been so deceived by the white people, for you have the great and good God always in your sight.

"Father, we repeat it again—We wish you and the good people of your Society, to make your minds perfectly easy, for we like what you say, and we thank the good Society for their good intentions, and that they have sent you to visit us.

"Father, you do not come like those that have come with a bundle under their arms, or something in their hands, but we have always found something of deceit under it, for they are always aiming at our lands; but you have not come like one of those; you have come like a father, and a true friend, to advise us for our good; we are convinced that there is no snare in your business; we hope that our talk to you at this time, will be communicated to your good Society at New-York, and that the Good Spirit will protect you and them in this good work that you and they have undertaken; and we expect that the bright chain of friendship shall always exist between us; and we will do every thing in our power to keep that chain bright, from time to time."

He then took up the strings of wampum that accompany this talk, and continued his speech to me as follows:

"Father, you and your good Society well know, that when learning was first introduced among Indians, they became small, and two or three nations have become extinct, and we know not what is become of them: and it was also introduced to our eldest brothers the Mohawks; we immediately observed, that their seats began to be small; which was likewise the case with our brothers the Oneidas. Let us look back to the situation of our nephews, the Muhheconnuks; they were totally routed away from their seats. This is the reason why we think learning would be of no service to us.

"Father, we are astonished that the white people, who have the good book called the Bible among them, that tells them the mind and will of the Great Spirit, and they can read it and understand it, that they are so bad, and do so many wicked things, and that they are no better.

"Father, we know that what you have said to us, is perfectly good and true—We here (pointing to himself and the Farmer's Brother) cannot see that learning would be of any service to us; but we will leave it to others who come after us, to judge for themselves.

"Father, if it should be introduced among us at present, there might be more intrigue or craft creep in among us; it might be the means of our fairing the same misfortunes of our brothers; our seat is but small now; and if we were to leave this place, we would not know where to find another; we do not think we should be able to find a seat among our western brothers.

"Father, we repeat it again—We hope that you and your good Society will make your minds perfectly easy, for we are convinced that your intentions are good."

He then presented me seven strings of wampum, saying, "We wish that this may be delivered with our speech, to your good Society that sent you to visit us."

WE the subscribers, assisted as interpreters when the foregoing Address was delivered, and assisted the Rev. Elkanah Holmes to commit it to writing—And do hereby certify, That the above is as near to the phraseology and ideas of the speaker, as we are able to recollect.

WILLIAM JOHNSTON
NICHOLAS CUSOCK

[Source: *New York Missionary Magazine* (1801): 68–75; reprinted in "Letters of the Rev. Elkanah Holmes from Fort Niagara," *Publications of the Buffalo Historical Society*, vol. 6, ed. Frank Severance (Buffalo, 1903), 187–206]

The next day, October 21, Farmer's Brother gave a speech to Holmes at John Palmer's house in Buffalo village and discussed the fate of his first grandson, who went to Philadelphia to be educated. When Farmer's Brother visited him, he found him in a tavern drinking, gaming, and whoring. Farmer's Brother offered to Holmes, however, a second grandson whom he wanted to be educated by the society in "good" education, not bad habits. In his reply to Farmer's Brother, Holmes confessed that he was unprepared to accept the boy, but he promised if he were sent later by the Senecas with supplies and money, the boy would be educated by the Missionary Society.

In Washington on the Murder of Two Haudenosaunees

FEBRUARY 11, 1801

THE MURDER OF TWO MEMBERS of the Six Nations while hunting at Big Beaver, west of Fort Pitt, caused a deputation of Tuscaroras and Senecas to go to Washington to protest. This was Red Jacket's first trip to Washington, D.C. President Adams was just finishing up his term. The Indian deputation, headed by Sagoyewatha, was addressed by the acting secretary of war, Samuel Dexter, on February 10. Sagoyewatha's response came the next day, February 11. He complained of numerous offenses against the Indians, particularly on the Pennsylvania frontier. At the end of the speech, he refers to Major John Jacob Ulrich Rivardi, former U.S. commander of Fort Niagara. The only record of this speech is from Stone's biography in 1841. The interpreter was probably Jasper Parrish.

"BROTHER:—We yesterday received your speech, which removed all uneasiness from our minds. We then told you that should it please the Great Spirit to permit us to rise in health this day, you should hear what we have come to say.

"BROTHER:—The business on which we are now come, is to restore the friendship that has existed between the United States and the Six Nations, agreeably to the direction of the commissioner from the fifteen fires of the United States. He assured us that whensoever, by any grievances, the chain of friendship should become rusty, we might have it brightened by calling on you. We dispense with the usual formality of having your speech again read, as we fully comprehended it yesterday, and it would therefore be useless to waste time in a repetition of it.

"BROTHER:—Yesterday you wiped the tears from our eyes, that we might see clearly; you unstopped our ears that we might hear; and removed the obstructions from our throats that we might speak distinctly. You offered to join with us in tearing up the largest pine tree in our forests, and under it to bury the tomahawk. We gladly join with you, brother, in this work, and let us heap rocks and stones on the root of this tree, that the tomahawk may never again be found.

"BROTHER:—Your apology for not having wampum is sufficient, and we agree to accept of your speeches on paper, to evince our sincerity in wishing the tomahawk forever buried. We accompany a repetition of our assurances with these strings. (*Strings of wampum.*)

"BROTHER:—We always desire, on similar melancholy occasions, to go through our customary forms of condolence, and have been happy to find the officers of the government of the United States willing in this manner to make our minds easy.

"BROTHER:—We observe that the men now in office are new men, and, we fear, not fully informed of all that has befallen us. In 1791 a treaty was held by the commissioners of Congress with us at Tioga Point, on a similar occasion. We have lost seven of our warriors, murdered in cold blood by white men, since the conclusion of the war. We are tired of this mighty grievance, and wish some general arrangement to prevent it in the future. The first of these was murdered on the banks of the Ohio, near Fort Pitt. Shortly after, two men, belonging to our first families, were murdered at Pine Creek; then one at Fort Franklin; another at Tioga Point; and now the two that occasion this visit, on the Big Beaver. These last two had families. The one was a Seneca; the other a Tuscarora. Their families are now destitute of support; and we think that the United States should do something toward their support, as it is to the United States they owe the loss of their heads.

"BROTHER:—These offenses are always committed in one place on the frontier of Pennsylvania. In the Genesee country we live happy, and no one molests us. I must therefore beg that the President will exert all his influence with all officers, civil and military, in that quarter, to remedy this grievance, and trust that he will thus prevent a repetition of it, and save our blood from being spilled in [the] future. (*A Belt.*)

"BROTHER:—Let me call to mind the treaty between the United States and the Six Nations, concluded at Canandaigua.[1] At that treaty Col. Pickering, who was commissioner on behalf of the United States, agreed that the United States should pay to the Six Nations four thousand five hundred dollars *per annum*, and that this should pass through the hands of the superintendent of the United States, to be appointed for that purpose. This treaty was

---

1. In 1794.

made in the name of the President of the United States, who was then General Washington; and as he is now no more, perhaps the present President would wish to renew the treaty. But if he should think the old one valid, and is willing to let it remain in force, we are also willing. The sum above mentioned we wish to have part of in money, to expend in more agricultural tools, and in purchasing a team, as we have some horses that will do for the purpose. We also wish to build a saw mill on the Buffalo Creek. If the President, however, thinks proper to have it continue as heretofore, we shall not be very uneasy. Whatever he may do we agree to; we only suggest this for his consideration. (*A Belt.*)

"BROTHER:—I hand you the above mentioned treaty, made by Col. Pickering in the name of Gen. Washington, and the belt that accompanied it; as he is now dead, we know not if it is still valid. If not, we wish it renewed—if it is, we wish it copied on clean parchment. Our money got loose in our trunk and tore it. We also show you the belt which is the path of peace between our Six Nations and the United States. (*Treaty and two Belts.*)

"BROTHER:—A request was forwarded by us from the Onondaga nation to the governor of New-York, that he should appoint a commissioner to hold a treaty with them. They have a reservation surrounded by white men which they wish to sell. The Cayugas, also, have a reservation so surrounded that they have been forced to leave it, and they hope that the President's commissioner, whom they expect he will not hesitate to appoint, will be instructed to attend to this business. We also have some business with New-York, which we would wish him to attend to.

"BROTHER:—The business that has caused this our long journey was occasioned by some of your bad men: the expense of it has been heavy on us. We beg that as so great a breach has been made on your part, the President will judge it proper that the United States should bear our expenses to and from home, and whilst here.

"BROTHER:—Three horses belonging to the Tuscarora nation were killed by some men under the command of Major Rivardi, on the plains of Niagara. They have made application to the superintendent and to Major R.[ivardi], but get no redress. You make us pay for our breaches of the peace, why should you not pay also? A white man has told us the horses were killed by Major R.[ivardi]'s orders, who said they should not be permitted to come there, although it was an open common on which they were killed. Mr. [Israel] Chapin [Jr.] has the papers respecting these horses, which we request you to take into consideration. [Source: Stone 1841, 169–72]

According to Stone, Dexter responded five days later on February 16. He promised to pay for their expenses and thoroughly investigate the circumstances of the murders, land-sale issues, and recompense for horses. During Red Jacket's defense of Stiff-Armed George the following year, it seems that Dexter settled the government's debts amicably because the Senecas later claimed satisfaction with his conduct.

The Trial of Red Jacket

JUNE 1801?

DE WITT CLINTON'S ACCOUNT of Red Jacket's trial for witchcraft appears in his address on the Iroquois, given to the New York Historical Society on December 6, 1811. Because it is the literary source of John Mix Stanley's celebrated 1868 portrait of Red Jacket defending himself at a council, it is worth reprinting despite its hazy veracity. According to Anthony Wallace, there was a Seneca council held at Buffalo Creek in June 1801 where Red Jacket, among others, was accused of witchcraft by Handsome Lake, following the illness of one of Cornplanter's daughters (see Wallace 1972, 239–59; Parker 1968, 68; *National Intelligencer*, March 4, 1801; Blacksnake n.d., 20, 31, 36; see also introduction). Wallace asserts that Red Jacket and Handsome Lake's disagreement over the upcoming sale of the Mile-Wide Strip was an unspoken element of his indictment (1972, 259; see also the speech of November 12, 1801).

According to an account written by De Witt Clinton ten years later, Sagoyewatha successfully defended himself in council for three hours, pointing out that Handsome Lake's attacks were merely trying to rehabilitate the influence of Cornplanter's family. Other than Clinton's story, however, there are no records of what Red Jacket said. There are later accounts, published long after the summer of 1801, of tension between Red Jacket and Handsome Lake, but the nearest validating source of this event is a report in the June 1803 *New York Missionary Magazine* that Sagoyewatha had recently endured a "storm" of conflict with the Prophet (203). See also the *Evangelical Intelligencer* 1 (1807): 92–93; *The Panoplist* (January 1807): 386–87.

Clinton writes:

Within a few years, an extraordinary orator has risen among the Senecas, his real name is Saguoaha, but he is commonly called Red Jacket. Without the advantages of illustrious descent, and with no extraordinary talents for war, he has attained the first distinctions in the nation, by the force of his eloquence.

His predecessor in the honors of the nation, was a celebrated chief, denominated The Cornplanter. Having lost the confidence of his countrymen, in order to retrieve his former standing, as it is supposed, he persuaded his brother to announce himself as a prophet, or a messenger from Heaven, sent to redeem the fallen fortunes of the Indian race. The superstition of the savages cherished the impostor, and he has acquired such an ascendancy, as to prevail upon the Onondagas, formerly the most drunken and profligate of the Six Nations, to abstain entirely from spirituous liquors, and to observe the laws of morality in other respects. He has obtained the same ascendancy among the Confederates, as another impostor[1] had acquired among the Shawanese, and other western Indians; and like him, he has also employed his influence for evil, as well as for good purposes. The Indians universally believe in witchcraft; the prophet inculcated this superstition, and proceeded, through the instrumentality of conjurers selected by himself, to designate the offenders, who were accordingly sentenced to death; and the unhappy objects would have been actually executed, if the magistrates at Oneida and the officers of the garrison at Niagara had not interfered. This was considered an artful expedient to render his enemies the objects of general abhorrence, if not the victims of an ignominious death. Emboldened by success, he proceeded, finally, to execute the views of his brother, and Red Jacket was publically denounced at a great council of Indians, held at Buffalo Creek, and he was put upon his trial. At this crisis he well knew that the future color of his life depended upon the powers of his mind. He spoke in his defense for near three hours. The iron brow of superstition relented under the magic of his eloquence; he declared the prophet an impostor and a cheat. He prevailed: the Indians divided, and a small majority appeared in his favor. Perhaps the annals of history cannot furnish a more conspicuous instance of the triumph and power of oratory, in a barbarous nation, devoted to superstition, and looking up to the accuser as a delegated minister of the Almighty. [Source: Clinton 1849, 241–42]

---

1. Tecumseh's brother, also known as the Prophet, Tenskwatawa, or Elkswatawa.

Pan-Indian Congress at Fort George, Canada

July 27–29, 1801

THE POLITICAL BACKGROUND of this council was a growing distrust between William Claus and Joseph Brant over the sale of Grand River lands. Although the British Executive Council had voted to approve Brant's land sales in 1798, they also appointed several trustees to oversee the sales, one of whom was Deputy Indian Superintendent William Claus, who had the king's interests to protect. Because Brant's purchasers were largely unable to make payment, Brant was always trying to advance another sale, and this put him at cross purposes with Claus. Tired of Claus's obstructions, Brant asked the western Indians to rally behind him and the Six Nations. Brant argued that the British were ungrateful to their Indian allies. At a council at Detroit, he asked a group of Chippewas, Ottowas, and Potawatamies to go to Buffalo Creek and agree to what was said there about unity (see Kelsay 1984, 528–626; Johnson 1964). Two months after this council, Claus and Brant would begin to fight openly, with Claus leaving council when Brant spoke.

Present were chiefs and warriors of all the Six Nations as well as representatives from the Munsees on the Thames River. The British present were William Claus, deputy superintendent general; Major Spencer, R.C.V.; Lt. Johnson, R.C.V.; Lt. Malhiot, R.C.V.; Capt. McDonell, R.C.V.; Honble. James Baby; Doctor Kerr; Prideaux Selby, secretary to the superintendent of Indian Affairs; David Price, interpreter. These manuscripts are validated as "true copies" by Secretary Selby.

Red Jacket spoke thus

Brothers Hear patiently what we have to say: All the Nations here jointly salute you and we hope the goodness of the Great Spirit will guard and protect you; We have been engaged in a business, long under our consideration, and have come to let you know the purport of what we have been doing at Buffaloe. We hope you will not think hard Brother that so many of us have come to this place when we inform you that Provision is very scarce with us; but this was not our only motive; We heared that Sir John Johnson who has been so long at the head of our affairs was expected here and our women and Children came to see the person who is at the Head of us

Brother We all Salute you and hope the Great Spirit will protect you

Delivered three Strings White Wampum.

The Deputy Superintend[en]ᵗ General

Returned their Compliment and expressed his concern at the scarcity of Provisions with them. He then went thro the ceremony of opening their Eyes &c &c and added, that he would order them some provisions

Delivered five Strings Black & White Wampum

Over the remainder of the council that day, Captain Brant voiced the concern of the Six Nations that several of the Seven Nations of Canada and some representatives from the western nations had been discouraged from attending the council. Brant also delivered strings to mark the promotion of four young men to chief, as well as condolences on the deaths of members of the western nations. Claus received the strings, spoke of his satisfaction about the new chiefs, and assured them that the king harbored only good intentions toward them. Two days later, on July 29, another council was held with slightly different British attendees: "Captain Claus; Capt. McDonell RCV; Lt. Fraser RCV; Lt. Malhiot RCV; Ens. Boucherville RCV; Adjt Crampton RCV; William Johnson Chew;[1] Prideaux Selby, Asst. Secretary General Indian Affairs; David Price, Interpreter."

Red Jacket spoke as follows

Brothers We had a consultation yesterday with the Mohawks on some particular business, and if you are ready to hear us, I will now mention it,

Brother You know when we *last* spoke to you, we had some wampum remaining, and we have requested this meeting to finish what we had to say. We wish to send a message to the Westward, and also six of our people to Lower Canada, to know the reason why they were so heavy and inattentive to our invitation to come up.

Brother A Belt will remain at Buffaloe until the Cherokee's meet the western Indians at the Council to be held at the Wyandot Village And we must request your assistance Brother to forward the message we mean to send to them, to the Superintendant above, that he may communicate it to the Shawenoes, Ottowa's and Chippawa's with our wampum—.

Brother We asked you why the seven Nations of Canada and the Western Indians did not come to our Council at Buffaloe and you said you did not know

---

1. His rank is indecipherable, but he was the son of Joseph Chew of the Indian Department.

the reason, but we still think they have been stopp'd by the Indian Department, and we wish to know also why the Messassagues [Mississaugas] have not
come for we see no reason why they should not as formerly unite in our Councils: It is hard the Messassagues should drop off, we should have been glad they
had come: it is a material hurt to us that they have not come and we wish to
know if there be any reason to prevent our Counselling together as formerly

Delivered four Strings White Wampum. [Source: "Records of the Council
Speeches . . . ," BV Indians, Misc. reel 24, pp. 166–72, NYHS]

*Claus, referring to the proceedings of a council held on October 13, 1801, answered
that he was presently no longer the superintendent of the Mississaugas and Munsees
(James Givens was), and that he refused sitting with them in council at the beach
only because of the smallpox epidemic that was then raging. In the remainder of the
council, Claus agreed to help the Six Nations carry their messages to the western
Indians.*

To Chapin on Annuities, Husbandry, and Proposal to Sell the Mile-Wide Strip

November 12, 1801

THE COUNCIL WAS HELD with Captain Chapin at Geneseo to distribute the annuities. This address underscores the motives that drove the Six Nations to sell much of their land during the period. Discussion of this particular sale, however, goes back to Timothy Pickering's request at Canandaigua in 1794 for a four-mile-long swath running along the Niagara River, stretching from Lake Erie north (maps 3 and 5). As the Senecas found their finances insufficient to their needs, they began to warm to the idea of selling their Niagara riverfront access north of Buffalo Creek, provided they could retain fishing rights. As Anthony Wallace notes, the Six Nations' proposal to sell was complicated by Handsome Lake's initial opposition (1972, 259; Densmore 1999, 54–57; Hauptman 1999, 133). Their decision had been long coming, however. On their return from Washington at the end of February 1801, the Senecas stopped in Albany to inform Governor John Jay that they were ready to begin negotiations to sell the strip (*Western Constellation*, March 16, 1801).

Present: "Principal chiefs of the Senecas, Onondagas, Cayugas, and Delawares. Jasper Parrish interpreter."

Red Jacket Chief speaker of the Seneka nation spake as follows

Brother Capt. Chapin & Parish Interpreter Listen. We have assembled at this time for the purpose of receiving our annuity of goods from the US & have, as relates to that part of business accomplished it. We have a word however to say on that subject. We wish for the next year our goods may come different, we wish fine broadcloths to be ommitted & coarser wollen cloths sent in their place, as they only serve to mock our wishes rather than to warm our limbs. Our old men & women & children are looking to you for something to screen them from the cold winter blasts & snow, and if we have a greater proportion of coarse cloth flannels &c we may expect a small portion divided to all. Brother Our warriors want powder & lead, at this season of the year our young men betake themselves to the forrest to pursue game, and as they are willing the old men & women should have a greater share of clothing they feel disirous of having some ammunition to help themselves with—and as many have not the means to purchase are obliged to starve for the want thereof.

Brother One thing more we wish you to make known to the President of the United States.

We have now concluded to receive the proposals of the President made to us some years ago.[1] He told us it would be necessary for us to quit the mode of Indian living and learn the manner of White people[.] And that the US would provide us oxen to plow the ground which would relieve our women from digging—that we should be provided with cows & we must learn our girls to milk & make butter & chees. That we should be furnished with farming utensils for cultivating the ground & raise wheat & other grain—that we must have spinning wheals & learn our children to spin & knitt—We were told we must make use of Cattle instead of Moose Elk etc & Swine in stead of beans, sheep in place of dear etc etc.

Brother We desire you to make known to the President who is in place of Gen. Washington that we agree to accept of his offer. We finde ourselves in a situation which we believe our fore Fathers never thought of—instead of finding our game at our doors we are obliged to go to a great distance for it, & then finde it but scarce compared to what it us'd to be. The White people are seated so thick over the Country that the dear have almost fled from us, and we finde ourselves obliged to pursue some other mode of geting our living, and are determined in all our Villages to take to husbandry, and for this purpose we want to be helped to a number of pair of cattle viz four for Buffaloe Creek two for Tonawanda & some for Alleghana and Cataragaras. Brother You may perhaps say that we shall make but bad use of such property on account of some of our people who drink to excess—but you may be assured it will not be the case, as we have all agreed to quit the use of liquor which you must be in some measure convinced of from what you see at the present meeting. Brother You will not hesitate to make known to the President the whole of our speech & to urge his compliance, and bring us his answer on your return.

Brother We wish you to bring forward the use or interest of our money under the direction of the President of the US and also the money due from the Land Company & interest due on the same. Br.[other] We wish Mr. Phelps's payment of $500 dollars p^r annum[2] to be deposited in the Bank of the

1. Philadelphia 1792.
2. Under the terms of the Phelps and Gorham Purchase of July 4–8, 1788.

US under the direction of the President, and all our payments to come forward at one time.

Br.[other] We wish you to call on Mr. Busti[3] and bring an answer from him respecting exchange of land as we are desirous to have our reservation at Buffaloe Creek inlarged.

Br.[other] You will call on the Governor of New York & renew our petition of last year and urge him to appoint Commissioners to come forward to B[uffalo] Creek about the middle of May as it is a time that fish may be taken in abundance & we will have no [reason?] to put them to exp[ense][u] for provisions as we conceive the price of our land is lessened on acc[oun][t.] of being furnished supplies. We wish to sell the strip of land along the Niagara River as it is a narrow strip and we fear incroachments, a party of men having made a beginning there last summer.

Br.[rother] We speak also for the Onondagas & Cayugas our voices are one, They with us wish to sell—they have but some small pieces that remain which are surrounded by W[hite] People and are desirous to put them off. We therefore are desirous that Comm[issione][rs], from the US & the State of NY may come forward that the sails may be duly made. [Source: ORWM, vol. 14, item 12]

3. Paul Busti, agent general of the Holland Land Company.

Defense of Stiff-Armed George

AUGUST 3, 1802

ON JULY 25, 1802, a white man named John Hewitt was stabbed and killed in an altercation near Buffalo Creek by Stiff-Armed George, a Seneca. There were no Indian witnesses present to contravene the account that George started trouble without provocation (Chapin to Dearborn, August 1, 1802, ORWM, folder 14, item 25). At the trial six months later, however, it was revealed that the whites apparently recognized that George was drunk, and they chased him when they saw he had a knife. They hit him with a brick and knocked him with a club. In response, George cut one of them in the face and fatally stabbed Hewitt (*Albany Centinel*, March 15, 1803). The Indians did not want George to be surrendered to white authorities. Because of the 1794 Treaty of Canandaigua, they believed that George should be tried by Haudenosaunee laws. They initially hid him from the sheriff, pointing out that they did not forfeit their national sovereignty at Canandaigua. But after the intervention of some neighborhood whites, they reluctantly allowed him to be taken into custody. Although George was condemned to death on February 23, 1803, Judge Brockholst Livingston wrote a letter persuading Governor Clinton to pardon him, citing in particular Red Jacket's speeches during the trial (*Albany Centinel*, March 15, 1803; for more on the pardon, see also *ASPIA*, 1:667).

The following speech occurred just after George was taken into custody at a public meeting held by the Seneca chiefs at the Canandaigua courthouse on August 3, 1802. Speaking on George's behalf, Sagoyewatha complained that part of the problem was that the Six Nations no longer had an agent to buffer disputes with the whites. Superintendent Chapin had just lost his post in July at the hands of the incoming Jefferson administration. He later was replaced by Captain Callender Irvine, which made the Senecas furious because they liked Chapin (Fairbank n.d., 88; *Albany Centinel*, August 20, 1802). Because of the speech's frank criticisms of the Jefferson administration, Secretary of War Henry Dearborn complained to Chapin that he thought Chapin had written it or had otherwise "artfully managed" the Senecas to take up his cause

(ORWM, vol. 11, item 35). To placate the Indians, Jasper Parrish was appointed Irvine's subagent in February of 1803, a position he held until 1829.

The speech was initially published in the August 12, 1802, *Ontario Gazette* (no longer extant) and subsequently circulated in other newspapers over the following two months, where it set off a minor debate about whether the speech was actually anti-Jefferson propaganda published under Red Jacket's name (see *National Intelligencer*, September 15, 1802). The earliest extant copy appears to be in the September 3, 1802, *Albany Centinel*. James D. Bemis, the Canandaigua printer who worked for the *Ontario Gazette*, republished the speech in an 1811 pamphlet called *Native Eloquence*. The two versions are very similar, and although Bemis would have had access to the *Ontario Gazette* copy, I have chosen the earliest extant text from the *Centinel*. The translator was Horatio Jones (G. Harris 1903).

At a Council, held at the Court House, in Canandaigua, the 3d day of August, 1802.

PRESENT—The Principal CHIEFS and SACHEMS of the *Seneca, Onondaga and Cayuga* Indians; and a number of the principal inhabitants of the town of Canandaigua.

RED JACKET, the principal speaker of the Seneca Nation, spoke as follows:
Brothers,

OPEN your ears and give your attention. This day is appointed by the Great Spirit to meet our friends at this place. During the many years we have lived together in this country, good will and harmony have subsisted among us.

Brothers—We have now come forward upon an unhappy occasion;—We cannot find words to express our feelings upon it. One of our people has murdered one of your people: So it has been ordered by the Great Spirit, who controuls all events. This has been done; we cannot now help it. At first view, it would seem to have the effect of putting an end to our friendship; but let us reflect, and put our minds together. Can't we point out measures whereby our peace and harmony may still be preserved? We have come forward to this place, where we have always had a Superintendant and Friend to receive us, and to make known to him such grievances as lay in our minds; but now we have none; and we have no Guardian—no Protector—no one is now authorized to receive us.

Brothers—We therefore now call upon you to take our Speech in writing, and forward our ideas to the President of the United States.

Brothers—Let us look back to our former situation. While you were under the government of Great-Britain, Sir William Johnston was our Superintendant, appointed by the King. He had power to settle offenses of this kind among all the Indian Nations, without adverting to the laws. But under the British government you were uneasy—you wanted to change it for a better. General WASHINGTON went forward as your leader. From his exertions you gained your independence. Immediately afterwards, a Treaty was made between the United States & the Six Nations, whereby a method was pointed out of redressing such an accident as the present. Several such accidents did happen wherein we were the sufferers. We now crave the same privilege in making restitution to you, that you adopted towards us in a similar situation.[1]

Brothers—At the close of our Treaty at Philadelphia,[2] General WASHINGTON told us that we had formed a chain of friendship which was bright: He hoped it would continue so on our part: That the United States would be equally willing to brighten it, if rusted by any means. A number of murders have been committed on our people—We shall only mention the last of them. About two years ago, a few of our Warriors were amusing themselves in the woods, to the westward of Fort Pitt. Two white men, cooly and deliberately, took their rifles, travelled nearly three miles, to our encampment, fired upon the Indians, killed two men and wounded two children. We then were the party injured. What did we do? We flew to the Treaty, and thereby obtained redress, perfectly satisfactory to us, and we hope agreeable to you.[3] This was done a short time before President ADAMS went out of office: complete peace and harmony was restored. We now want the same method of redress to be pursued.

Brothers—How did the present accident take place? Did our Warriors go from home cool and sober, and commit murder on you? No. Our brother was in liquor, and a quarrel ensued, in which the unhappy incident happened. We would not excuse him on account of his being in liquor; but such a thing was far from his intention in his sober moments. We are all extremely grieved at it, and are willing to come forward and have it settled, as crimes of the same nature have been hitherto done.

Brothers—Since this accident has taken place we have been informed, that by the laws of this state, if a murder is committed within it, the murderer must be tried by the laws of the state, and punished with death.

1. That is, financial restitution to victims' families.
2. March 1792.
3. Viz. speech on February 13, 1801.

Brothers—When were such laws explained to us? Did we ever make a treaty with the state of New-York, and agree to conform to its laws? No. We are independent of the State of New-York—It was the will of the Great Spirit to create us different in colour: We have different laws, habits and customs, from the white people. We will never consent that the government of this state shall try our brother. We appeal to the government of the United States.

Brothers—Under the customs and habits of our forefathers, we were a happy people; we had laws of our own, they were dear to us. The whites came among us and introduced their customs; they introduced liquor among us, which our forefathers always told us would prove our ruin.

Brothers—In consequence of the introduction of liquor among us, numbers of our people were killed. A Council was held to consider of a remedy, at which it was agreed by us, that no private revenge should take place for any such murder—that it was decreed by the Great Spirit, and that a Council should be called, to consider of redress to the friends of the deceased.

Brothers—The President of the United States is called a Great Man, possessing great power—he may do what he pleases—he may turn men out of office; men who held their offices long before he held his. If he can do these things, can he not even control the laws of this state? Can he not appoint a Commissioner to come forward to our country and settle the present difference, as we, on our part, have heretofore often done to him, upon a similar occasion?

We now call upon you, *Brothers*, to represent these things to the President, and we trust that he will not refuse our request, of sending a Commissioner to us, with powers to settle the present difference. The consequences of a refusal may be serious. We are determined that our brother shall not be tried by the laws of the state of New-York. Their laws make no difference between a crime committed in liquor, and one committed coolly and deliberately. Our laws are different, as we have before stated. If tried here, our brother must be hanged. We cannot submit to that—Has a murder been committed upon our people, when was it punished with death?

Brothers—We have now finished what we had to say upon the subject of the murder. We wish to address you upon another, and to have our ideas communicated to the President upon it also.

Brothers—It was understood, at the treaty concluded by Col. Pickering,[4] that our superintendant should reside in the town of Canandaigua, and for very good reasons: That situation is the most central to the Six Nations; and

4. Canandaigua, 1794.

by subsequent treaties between the state of New-York and the Indians, there are still stronger reasons why he should reside here; principally on account of the annuities being stipulated to be paid to our superintendant at this place. These treaties are sacred. If their superintendant resides elsewhere, the state may object to sending their money to him at a greater distance. We would therefore wish our superintendant to reside here at all events.

Brothers—With regard to the appointment of our present superintendant, we look upon ourselves as much neglected and injured. When general Chapin and captain Chapin[5] were appointed, our wishes were consulted upon the occasion, and we most cordially agreed to the appointments. Captain Chapin has been turned out, however, within these few days.—We do not understand that any neglect of duty has been alleged against him.—We are told it is because he differs from the President[6] in his sentiments on government matters. He has always been perfectly satisfactory to us; and had we known of the intention, we should most cordially have united in a petition to the President to continue him in office. We feel ourselves injured—we have nobody to look to—nobody to listen to our complaints—none to reconcile any difference among us. We are like a young family without a Father.

Brothers—We understand that the President has appointed a superintendant who is altogether unknown to us, and who is unacquainted with Indian affairs, we know him not in our country. Had we been consulted upon the subject, we might have named some one residing in this country who was well known to us. Perhaps we might have agreed upon Mr. Oliver Phelps, whose politics, coinciding with those of the President, might have recommended him to the office.

Brothers—We cannot conclude without again urging you to make known all these our sentiments to the President. [Source: *Albany Centinel*, September 3, 1802; *Native Eloquence* 1811, 18–24; *Ontario Gazette*, August 12, 1802 (no longer extant); Stone 1841, 173–78]

---

5. General Israel Chapin and Captain Israel Chapin.
6. Jefferson.

To Gov. Clinton on Sale of the Mile-Wide Strip

AUGUST 18–20, 1802

IN 1802, New York State wanted to sell the port of Black Rock to the United States for use as a military base, but the Senecas held title to the Mile-Wide strip that ran along the Niagara River from Buffalo Creek to Stedman's farm (near Niagara Falls, see maps 3 and 5). The Six Nations had clearly announced a desire to sell the strip in Sagoyewatha's speech of November 12, 1801, but Handsome Lake counseled against the sale. During the last two weeks of June 1802, the first attempt of the U.S. commissioners ended in failure. (For their detailed July 12 report to Governor Clinton, largely blaming Handsome Lake's interference, see Paul Reilly Papers, box 41, item 8.)

Despite the opposition of Handsome Lake, a deputation of Seneca chiefs arrived in Albany in mid-August with several items of business to discuss with the governor, the most pressing of which was their attempt to get Stiff-Armed George bailed (see speech of August 3, 1802). Although they were unable to get George out of prison, the Senecas sold their rights to the strip for $5,000 (*ASPIA*, 1:668; Prucha 1994, 113–15). In the same treaty, Horatio Jones and Jasper Parrish each received gifts of one-mile-square pieces of land near Niagara (see map 5). Since November 21, 1798, the Senecas had requested that New York State ratify their gifts to Parrish and Jones, but apparently the state still had not taken action (ORWM, vol. 13, item 34). Although not specified in the federal act of the sale, the Indians also received hunting and fishing rights, and use of the Black Rock ferry without toll (Hauptman 1999, 133). In the following addresses, Sagoyewatha is speaking to John Tayler, U.S. commissioner, and Governor George Clinton. The interpreter is unknown but likely was Jasper Parrish. The text is as it appears in manuscript in the Paul Reilly Papers held at Buffalo State College.

Albany 18th August, 1802

Red Jacket, the principal Orator of the Nation, addressing himself to his Excellency the Governor spoke, in substance, as follows

· · ·

(1ˢᵗ Speech)

Brother

Altho' the matter we have to communicate to you on this occasion is of a disagreeable and melancholy nature, yet we hope you will open your Ears to what we shall say, and reflect seriously on the subject

You have doubtless already heard of the murder which has been committed by one of our men, on one of your children; We consider you as the Father of a great people, commanding extensive territories; and you must necessarily feel interested when any thing happens to any of your people

Before we were told by your officers that our friend was to be taken, and punished by the laws of your state, we always thought that we were answerable to the United States only under our existing treaties with them. We were always told so by the Commissioners of the President.—Five instances have heretofore happened where the White people have committed murders on our people, and in every instance we have applied to the United States; and not to the states in which the acts were committed, for redress; and we have always recieved satisfaction, by presents sent to us and particularly to the injured family, but in no instance have they been punished with death. Now therefore, altho it is true that this crime was committed within the Limits of your State, we know of no Treaty with the State by which we are bound to give satisfaction; but we are perfectly willing to treat with the United States, and to give them satisfaction in the same manner we have heretofore recieved when we were the injured party—

Brother—We have sent on our speech to the President of the United States about this business, and now present you with a copy thereof, and also of our Treaty with them: being informed however that our friend is to be tried for this crime by this State we have thought proper to speak to you on the subject and we hope you will take it into serious consideration

Brother—We should be very sorry, if our friend was to suffer death for this crime. In the instances which we have mentioned, by which we were the sufferers, the murders were committed in cool blood; but in this instance it was done under intoxication and passion, which differs very much from those committed with deliberation and premeditated design—We hope therefore you will use your influence to settle this business in a peacable way, and keep the chain of friendship between us bright.

(2ⁿᵈ speech)

Brother

"You have given us a full explanation of the origin of our connection with the white people and of the nature of your Laws—&c &c (*here the orator reca-pitulated what his Excellency the governor had said to them in reply to the preceeding speech*)

—"But we notwithstanding think it a little strange that our friend should suffer imprisonment under your Laws for a long time before trial when none of the white people have ever been punished for killing our people—Impris-onment to an Indian is worse than death, being accustomed to roam the wilderness at liberty, it is hard for him to be confined in a *large house*; and and [*sic*] as in this instance the crime was attended with extenuating circum-stances, we are willing to enter into bonds for any reasonable sum to deliver up the prisoner at the time of trial. We think this a reasonable and just request and hope it may be granted.—we would further mention that the prisoner was always a good civil man when sober, and a near relation to the first chief of our Nation, as were also some of those Indians formerly killed by the White people.—

August 19th 1802

Red jacket, addressing himself to the Commissioner on the part of the United States, and to his Excellency the Governor, began as follows

(3rd speech)

Brothers

We are now come to renew the business on which your commissioners were some time ago sent to us. It will be unnecessary for us to repeat what we told them in our speeches, as you are doubtless informed of it—We will men-tion however that one reason why we wished to reserve the spot at Black Rock was because it is the best fishing place on the River—Since that time however shortly after your commissioners went away we held several councils among ourselves and as you wished very much to purchase this land we agreed at last, notwithstanding all our difficulties to let you have it.—

We propose to sell you the whole tract, with the reservation however of all the Islands; the line to run at the edge of the Water, but the use of the river to be free to you—We wish to reserve also the privileges of using the beach to encamp on, and wood to make fires, together with the uninterrupted use of the river for the purpose of fishing; And likewise the privileges of passing the bridge and turnpike, when made, free from Toll, and of keeping a ferry across the River—For the whole tract we ask, $7500. We think this reasonable, and that in a few years it will refund you much more than this sum:—

Brothers—with respect to this price, you may perhaps think it high, and much more than you have heretofore given for any lands, but you must also acknowledge that this land, from its situation and other circumstances is more valuable than any other land you have purchased—

Brothers—Let us reflect a few years back.

When the white people first came to our country we considered them poor and sold them large tracts of land, by which they became rich; and our land being diminished, it is reasonable that we should now value it higher than formerly—This sum will be but a small thing to you, but we acknowledge it will be considerable to us. Our hunting ground being occupied by the white people, it becomes necessary that we should resort to some other means of living.—

Brothers—We desire that, to the two Families which reside on the land, to assist them in moving off, the presents may be given which were promised by your commissioners—They also proposed to make us presents of $500 Dollars worth of calico for our Women, which we expect will be complied with—

Brothers—This being the first Treaty held with you since the close of the War, we hope it may brighten the chain of friendship between us, & last as long as the water runs, and the grass grows.—

Brothers—We have now opened our minds to you and we are happy of this opportunity, to speak to you on this subject personally—We hope the great Spirit will preserve us all in health 'till we have closed the business.—

August 20th 1802

The orator addressing himself to his Excellency the Governor, proceeded (4th Speech)

"Brother"

"The other day we came forward and made known our minds to you about the melancholy affair which has happened amongst us. You told us you would refer the matter to the judges we were then in hopes that our request would have been granted, to have our friend bailed and set at Liberty 'till he could be tried, but we are now told that it cannot be done consistent with your Laws, and our request which we considered as a reasonable one, is altogether refused. You may doubtless think your Laws are right, but to us in this case they appear peculiarly hard; we would not however wish you to think that we desire to encourage acts of this kind: far from it, we have uniformly done whatever we could to preserve peace and good order—

Brother—You also told us the other day that we would retain our antient Laws and Customs unimpaired, but we can see no reason, in this instance why we should not be permitted to give satisfaction for this offense in the manner we have heretofore recieved in the five cases we have mentioned, and as we have no representation in your government, and we know of no treaty by which we are amenable to the State, we consider it extraordinary, that our men should be punished by your Laws

Brother—You have given us an ample explanation of your Laws, but we think it unnecessary to give you an account of our Laws & customs as it would be useless—

Brother—We find that your Judges here are not so humane as your officers among us, there they permitted us to keep our friend for some time, 'till the wounds & bruses, he had recieved in the affray, were healed—

Brother—We mention these things only because we are sorry that our request is refused."

(after a short pause the orator proceeded)

Brother—We came forward with a great deal of confidence, to have our friend bailed; for the reasons before mentioned, but another reason is because we voluntarily delivered him up, when we might easily have helped him to escape; but we despised doing this because it would not have been perfect Justice—We had also hopes that coming down to the great Chief of the nation, we would have succeeded in our request, especially as we were informed by some of your lawyers that in this case the prisoner might be bailed consistent with your Laws

Brother—It is needless to say any thing more on this subject—we will therefore drop it, as we suppose you have said all you can—We now proceed to the other business: and although you cannot grant our request, we will not however for that reason refuse to comply with your wishes—and on this subject we desire the commissioner of the United States also, to listen to what we shall say

Brothers—We have agreed to consent to the proposals you have made to us, on condition however that some additional presents be given to some Chiefs which we have lately made—and it is understood that you will grant to our adopted children Jasper Parrish & Horatio Jones each one mile square—

Brothers—Our business being now concluded and we having come to an understanding on this subject after some considerable time spent therein, we hope you will use your influence and write to the magistrates to prevent the White people from abusing and hurting the Indians, as they frequently do without any provocation

Brother—We request one thing more—we wish you to prevent the sale of spirituous Liquors on our own ground as well as on your's—We see the evil consequences of this now before our eyes in the late unhappy affair, and hope it may be prevented. [Source: Paul Reilly Papers, box 41, item 12, Buffalo State College. Also in the Records of the New York State Legislature, Legislative Assembly Papers, vol. 40: 393–404, NYSA]

To Rev. Elkanah Holmes at Buffalo Creek

September 28, 1803

THE FOLLOWING EXCHANGE between Red Jacket and Elkanah Holmes appears in the appendix of the journal of Rev. Lemuel Covell, a Baptist minister who visited Rev. Holmes at the Buffalo Creek reservation in 1803. Covell and his associate, Obed Warren, stayed with Holmes for several days at Buffalo in late September to witness the outcome of a proposition Holmes had made to them to build a church-school. As appears in the following speech, the Senecas eventually agreed to his proposal, but it caused a great rift between the followers of Handsome Lake and the Buffalo Creek chiefs. The building was never completed (Houghton 1920, 141). As Covell notes, Holmes believed that the primary resistance of the Senecas was due to Handsome Lake.

The affidavit attached to the speeches lists "Messrs. Johnson and Smith" as the interpreters—probably William Johnson and Joseph Smith. The following comes from Covell's journal, with a preface to the speech by him.

"The reader will recollect, that mention has been made of a council, held at the Seneca village, on the subject of building a house at said village, for public worship, and for educating their children; that Elder Holmes was waiting for their answer, when we arrived at Buffaloe. This council was occasioned by the opposition of a part of the nation, headed by a certain influential *Chief*, by the name of OBAIL,[1] and a brother of his, who pretends to be a prophet,[2] against the building of the house, receiving any books from the white people for the instruction of their children, or harkening to the gospel and the maxims of civilization. At this council, the principal chiefs Onandaga and Cayuga nations were present. The object was to effect a reconciliation between the two contending parties, so that the house might be built, the missionary received, and the nation instructed in the principles of the gospel and civiliza-

1. Cornplanter.
2. Handsome Lake.

tion, by general and amicable agreement.—Much depended on the result of this council. The famous orator, RED JACKET, was a strenuous advocate for receiving the gospel and building the house; and a majority of the nation were on his side. After counselling together on the subject upwards of ten days, they came to a conclusion to have the house built; and invited Mr. HOLMES to meet them at their council house, where RED JACKET delivered him the following speech, in the presence of the nation, and of the gentleman hereafter named, who committed the same to writing, as appears by the annexed certificate, bearing their signatures.

Delivered by RED JACKET, a Sachem of the Seneca Nation of Indians, in Council with the principal Sachems of the Seneca, Onondaga and Cayuga Nations, to the Rev. ELKANAH HOLMES, missionary to the North-western Indians.

FATHER—

WE thank the Great Spirit above, for the opportunity of meeting together this day. We are sorry that we have made so many delays on our part, and for not letting the Missionary Society know our minds before.

Father—We are sorry that you have been detained so long on our account. We have now made up our minds, and concluded, in a general council, that hereafter there shall be no difficulty arising on our part.

Father—We have heard the advice which you have repeatedly given us, and have taken it coolly into consideration, so that all our people may understand it. Your customs are different from ours: We agree to yours; but are not content to forget some of our own customs, which have been handed down to us by our forefathers.

Father—Some years ago, the reason which we assign for our forefathers not laying hold of the gospel, and the customs of white people, is, that they supposed that they inhabited a tract of country sufficiently extensive to render them independent of the white people; but you passed by and looked over us, and went to visit more western nations.

Father—Our friends, the Indians, have found the evil of not attending to good advice. For instance, here are a number of different nations—Delawares, Tuscaroras, and others—who, from a want of education and a knowledge of your customs, have been deceived by the white people, and become their slaves, and have been seen at their doors, cutting wood and making brooms, to earn their bread; when, if they had followed the customs of their forefathers, they would have known better, and would not have been there.

Father—This is the reason why we *gradually* comply with what the Missionary Society has recommended to us, that we may not be deceived and taken advantage of, like those we mentioned before. We have great hopes from the information we have received from the young Chief, whom the Missionary Society have now under their care, that he will be of great service to us, and be able to read our papers, and explain all writings which we may receive from the Missionary Society, or on any other business.

Father—It has been recommended to us by your great Chief, General WASHINGTON, that we should be united as friends and brothers, and learn to cultivate the soil, and attend to every thing that would be for our comfort and happiness.

Father—You have been sent here by a number of those who wear the same cloth with yourself: Their good intention in sending you among us was to open eyes, and to instruct us in those things which will be for our own good.

Father—We are convinced that the Missionary Society are friends to the Indians.

Father—You have taken a great deal of pains and trouble, in coming among us to instruct us for our good. But we make not the smallest doubt that there are a number of white people who have doubted whether we shall ever lay hold of the gospel, and of the good instructions which you have come so far to give us: But we hope to convince those of that opinion, that our children will lay hold of all the good advice which you have, from time to time, given us.

We, the chiefs of the Seneca, Onondaga, and Cayuga nations, have agreed to listen to what has been recommended to us.—Not that we say that *all* will listen; but that the *greater part* have agreed to hearken to what our fathers, the Missionaries, have said to us.

Father—We have been a long time counselling among ourselves about building the house for worship, and for educating our children, which you have recommended to us; and are now all agreed that it shall be built, at the place where you have stuck the stake; and hope that it may become useful to our children, and make them wise.

Father—We thank the Great Spirit above, and the Missionary Society, for sending you among us. We have heard the good effect it has had, by the care they have taken of the young chief. We return our fathers, the Missionary Society, thanks for their attention and care of him, and for the benefit we hope to receive from him hereafter.

Father—We have given up this young chief to your charge: but we cannot say how far you are going to carry him in learning; but will leave it to our fathers, the Missionary Society, to say how far they think proper to carry him; so that, when he returns to us, he may be capable of transacting our public business equal to the white people.

Father—Upon this subject we will stop; but probably say something further on another subject.

Father—Look around the room, and you will see a number of us with the appearance of *old age* upon our countenances, who have no idea of leaving off *some* of our ancient customs; but we will leave our children to judge for themselves.

Father—You have visited us at our villages when we were attending to our customary worship, about the middle of cold weather. We make it a custom to meet together at that time, at our several villages, (which is a custom handed down to us by our forefathers) to return thanks to the Great Spirit above, for the success we have had in hunting our game for the support of our families.

Father—There is another time when we return thanks to the Great Spirit: It is when our crops become fit for use—it being from Him that we receive all those good things.

These customs now mentioned we intend to continue in; and we hope you will have no objection to our following them.

Father—You would not like to have us deprive you of any of your customs! How would you feel if we were to insist on your leaving off your customs, and adopting ours?—For this reason, *Father*, we will retain the customs before mentioned, and attend to yours; and pray to the Great Spirit, that *both* may lead us to happiness.

Father—This is all we have to say at this time—only that we wish that a copy of the Talk delivered this day may be sent to our fathers, the Missionary Society, and that one may be left with us; so that if it should be forgotten by our old men, it may be seen and understood by our children hereafter.

An extemporaneous Reply to the foregoing Talk, by the Reverend ELKANAH HOLMES, Missionary

MY CHILDREN—

I THANK the Great Spirit above, that I am allowed to meet with the chiefs of the Senecas, Onondagas and Cayugas on this day. I thank you all, my children, that you have been so kind as to meet me here at this time. I have had a great desire, ever since I met you, at your fire-place, last fall, to meet to you again in council.

I observe that you have said to me, that you are sorry that you have occasioned any delay: But I remember, that when I first came to visit you, I requested you to be deliberate, and cool; and do nothing in a hurry. You doubtless, remember, that I have often told you that it was a great thing to receive and obey the gospel of JESUS CHRIST. I have also often told you, that if you were hasty in making up your minds, you would be hasty in forgetting: that, therefore, there was a necessity of calm deliberation upon matters of such importance.

I have been well acquainted, ever since last fall, that you have had a great deal of trouble and difficulty in your nations; and I have been much concerned about it. Since that time, I have often prayed to the Great Spirit above, that he would help you to settle your difficulties, in a way that would make for peace. Now I thank the Great Spirit that he has heard my prayers so far, that you have peace and good-will among you.

Now, Children, if I had time, I would be glad to remark upon every thing that you have spoken to me this day; but I have not time at present: But I will tell you this, I am well pleased with the most of what you have said,

Now, one more thing, Children, I will say to you. I hope, by the leave of the Great Spirit, to return home, and to consider of the Talk that you have delivered to me at this time; and to return with my interpreter, and give you an answer in writing; that you, and your children after you, may always have it in your power to know what I say, in reply to what you have spoken this day: and also to send a copy of it to the Missionary Society, that they may know what I have said to you. I will, according to your request, send them a copy of your Talk to me at this time, and also leave one with you.

All that I have further to say, is, that I pray that the Great Spirit may bless you with peace and good-will among yourselves, and make you happy in this world, and prepare you for happiness after death.

Buffalo Creek, 28th Sept. 1803.

"*We, the subscribers, do hereby certify, that we were present when the speech of RED JACKET, a Sachem of the Seneca nation of Indians, was delivered to the Rev. ELKANAH HOLMES, Missionary to the North-western Indians; and that the above is a correct translation of it, as interpreted to us by Messrs. Johnson and Smith, Indian interpreters.—And likewise, that the extemporaneous reply of the Rev. ELKANAH HOLMES to the Sachems of the Seneca, Onondaga and Cayuga nations, assembled in council at the time of the delivery of the aforesaid speech, is also correctly stated.*

"David Thompson

"Justice of the Peace, County of Genesee

"John W. Brownson

Lieut. of 11th Reg. U. States Infantry

[Source: Covell 1804, 28–34]

To Quakers at Buffalo Creek on Alcohol

OCTOBER 2, 1803

IN 1803 a group of Quakers, including Isaac Bonsall, Isaac Coates, Thomas Stewardson, and John Shoemaker, set out to obtain a small portion of land near the Allegany Senecas to help them assist the Senecas with agriculture (see Barton 1990; Jackson 1830; 1952). On their way to speak with the Holland Land Company's agent, Joseph Ellicott, in Batavia, New York, they stopped at Buffalo Creek. In a December 14, 1803, account of their journey to the Philadelphia Yearly Meeting's Indian Committee, they reported that Sagoyewatha said the following. The text is from the papers of Joseph S. Elkinton (1830–1905), who copied the Bonsall letter, among many other documents, into book-sized collections presently held at Haverford College.

Red Jacket replied on behalf of the nation that about two years since some of their people began to help their women and to leave off drinking whiskey, that such as had done so lived more comfortably than they used to do.—the women and children of such were now comfortably fed and clad,—formerly they were almost naked and hungry;—That they were all come to the resolution of leaving off drinking and hoped they would quit it before long,—they knew it was bad for them,—if we or any of our friends would come and see them in two years they would be glad to meet us, and then we should find them better farmers and not in the practice of using very strong drink &c [Source: "Indian Records, 1801–1820," AB 25, p. 47, PYMIC, Haverford College]

Removal of Chief Joseph Brant

MARCH 30–APRIL 8, 1805

ALTHOUGH JOSEPH BRANT'S 1797–98 sale of the Five Townships at Grand River was a diplomatic triumph, it was short-lived. As Isabel Kelsay notes, the financial default of Brant's investors made both his Indian peers and the British uneasy (1984, 628–29). In November 1802, Lt. Governor Peter Hunter (who replaced Simcoe in 1799) forbid the further lease of Indian lands and ordered an investigation of Brant's land sales. Sensing that the British authorities in Canada would continue to interfere in Indian business, in 1804 Brant secretly sent his friend John Norton (whose Indian name meant "snipe" or "plover") to England with letters of recommendation to try to confirm Indian rights to sell Grand River lands without British supervision. Norton, a Scotsman who had been adopted by the Mohawks, wore Indian-style decorations and piercings, and he would often claim in Euro-American company that he was a Mohawk chief (he was, however, only an adopted chief). When other Haudenosaunee leaders heard that Norton was advertising himself as a chief in England, and carrying papers they knew nothing about, they met to disavow Norton's claims and censure Brant's conduct (J. Norton 1970, 629–38).

The following speeches are the result of their decision to "put down" Brant as chief. Brant did not take the resolution very seriously. He argued that it was simply the result of political friction between him and the Buffalo chiefs. However, in the meantime, Claus forwarded the text of the deposition councils to England, where they effectively destroyed Brant's chance to get the Haldimand grant confirmed.

On April 8, 1805, a large council met with Superintendent Claus at Fort George, Canada, to report their decision to put down Brant. David Price and Benjamin Fairchild interpreted, and the transcripts are copies of Claus's official report, authorized by his secretary, Prideaux Selby.

Red Jacket speaker for the 6 Nations said

Brother I speak in the name of the Six Nations when I salute you & say that we are glad to see you well & thank the Great Spirit that he has permitted us to see each other this day

Brother We are met here to communicate to you the result of our deliberations at our General Council fire at Buffaloe Creek which closed Ten days ago, where the Six Nations were called from all around to consult on different matters that lay heavy on their minds. We therefore Brother open your Ears that you may hear plainly and distinctly the resolution we have come to.

When our Father the King gave us the Lands on the Grand River, he did not intend it should be settled by white people, but through his regard for us, allowed a part to be disposed of for the benefit of those living there

But Brother, there are many more white people settled there, than ought to be, particularly on the road going to Long point,[1] and should we move over there we would find it difficult to get a spot that is good as these white people have taken care to pick out the best ground: We understand that Capt Brant and some of the Chiefs gave or sold those Lands without the knowledge of those who should be consulted and we the six Nations can not consent to have what the King gave to us in common disposed of in the way it is, we have too much regard for our posterity for whom we wish it to be preserved.

Brother We have consulted & taken time to examine all the complaints between the Chiefs & Warriors which have for these several years existed, and find that some of the Chiefs have been in the wrong & much to blame.

We have therefore now come to a resolution to put Capt Brant down & to this resolution one hundred and one Chiefs have put their marks & hereafter no body must hear what he says. There is one thing more Brother that has caused us to be uneasy. the little News Bird that flies about has informed some of our people that the Plover (Norton) went across the great Water to England with a paper or complaint from the Six Nations to the King. You know that no business of any consequence can be done but at Buffaloe Creek the general Council fire for the six Nations. If it is true that the Plover went across the Water with a paper or message from the six Nations, it was done underground and we know nothing about it. We have had a Council at Buffaloe Creek at which were collected the six Nations, there were those that lived, far as Ohio, Allegany mountains, & Oneyda, and not one of the[m] know any thing about it.—

That our Great Father the King may not think us such a poor race as to do a thing in so underhanded a manner, we desire that you will send him the proceedings of this day held at this Council fire

Brother The promise between you and us was that when any thing of moment happened we were to acquaint each other of the same, & as we always

1. West of Grand River.

wish to keep our word, we have come down to inform you in a few words what we have been doing at our last Council. It was a custom that we always followed with your Grandfather: we have now done. It was us that lighted your fire, we now cover the same.

Selby here inserts his copy of the council held ten days earlier at Buffalo Creek, with a list of 101 chiefs who agreed with the council's decision. The list of chiefs includes some not present at the March 30 council, but they did come to Fort George on April 8 to deliver the document, and they wished Selby to add their names. Among those who signed were Handsome Lake and Red Jacket (whose name is translated "Disturber of Sleep"). Red Jacket speaks:

Buffalo Creek 30th March 1805.

Brother The Kings officer hear a few words strait forward from us, what we the six Nations have concluded upon at our Council fire at Buffaloe Creek

Brother The old Chiefs have desired us to inform them wherein they have done wrong & we have laid every thing open at the Council fire that we know & have seen

Brother We have seen the conduct of those Old Chiefs & find that they have cheated us a great deal

Brother We have taken a great deal of time & consulted each other, that we the Six Nations have come to a determination that we break Captain Brant and that no body hereafter shall hear what he says. [Source: "Records of the Councils . . . ," BV Indians, Misc. reel 24, pp. 178–84, NYHS]

A list of 101 chiefs follows. After Red Jacket's speech of April 8, Claus acknowledged receipt of the deposition and promised it would be forwarded to the king. He concluded, however, by saying, "I can only say to you what I have before, respecting your lands, that you are at liberty to remove any settlers from your ground that have taken upon themselves to settle there, except those who will be put in possession of the Townships which were sold at your particular request & care will be taken that those places shall not be occupied until you are perfectly secured in the payment for the same."

Reply to Rev. Jacob Cram

November 1805

THE MOST FAMOUS SPEECH of Sagoyewatha's is his reply to the missionary Rev. Jacob Cram. Cram was an experienced missionary and had been sent into Six Nations territory by the Massachusetts Missionary Society to plant a missionary station among the Senecas (see Stone 1841, 272; and especially Densmore 1987, 1999). Although the speech has been reprinted for nearly two hundred years, its authenticity has recently been scrutinized by Harry Robie and Christopher Densmore. Densmore points out that the speech's preface states that it was given in the summer of 1805, but because Cram did not arrive at Buffalo Creek until November, the summer date seems to be incorrect (1999, 67). Densmore also notes that in Cram's journal entries during this period, he did not acknowledge that any important Indian speeches were made to him at Buffalo, noting only that "instead of complying with my request, they [the Indians] embraced the opportunity of stating their usual objections, and seemed not disposed to go into any inquiry" (*Massachusetts Missionary Magazine* [April 1806]: 436). Further, the first publication of the speech text itself came nearly three years after the event, in April 1809. It was sent by an anonymous source from Canandaigua, who wrote that "the speech of Red Jacket, I think, discovers the same beauties of imagery, united with a shrewdness of remark, and an extent of information, far beyond what we should have expected to find in the wandering tribes of Indians" (*Monthly Anthology* [March 1809]: 156; Densmore 1999, 65–66). With no other records of origin, collaborating accounts, or translators mentioned, there is less known about this speech than many others of the period. However, it is unlikely that this is simply a document of "fakelore" because the Senecas were very conscious of what was circulated about them. Furthermore, mention of the attendance of the U.S. Indian agent Erastus Granger would have made misrepresentation of federal consequence. The interpreter was probably Jasper Parrish.

This text is the first publication in the *Monthly Anthology and Boston Review* (April 1809): 221–24. It was republished widely for several years in other newspapers, in broadsides, and as a pamphlet (*Ontario Repository*, November

7, 1809; *Indian Speeches* 1809, 4–8; *American Watchman*, March 14, 1810; *Poulson's Daily Advertiser*, April 27, 1810; see also Densmore 1987; Robie 1986, 1987). In 1841, Samuel Drake published a version of the speech that added a new paragraph. There is no precedent for it. It appears below as a footnote where Drake inserted it, but it is of suspicious origin. It is likely an artifact of the 1820s when Sagoyewatha frequently complained of missionaries on the reservations who expected financial support from the Indians.

(In the summer of 1805, a number of the principal Chiefs and Warriours of the Six Nations of Indians, principally Senecas, assembled at Buffalo Creek, in the State of New York, at the particular request of a gentleman Missionary from the State of Massachusetts.[1] The Missionary being furnished with an Interpreter, and accompanied by the Agent of the United States for Indian affairs, met the Indians in Council, when the following talk took place.)

FIRST, BY THE AGENT.

"*Brothers of the Six Nations;* I rejoice to meet you at this time, and thank the Great Spirit, that he has preserved you in health, and given me another opportunity of taking you by the hand.

"*Brothers;* The person who sits by me, is a friend who has come a great distance to hold a talk with you. He will inform you what his business is, and it is my request that you would listen with attention to his words."

MISSIONARY. "My *Friends;* I am thankful for the opportunity afforded us of uniting together at this time. I had a great desire to see you, and inquire into your state and welfare; for this purpose I have travelled a great distance, being sent by your old friends, the Boston Missionary Society. You will recollect they formerly sent missionaries among you, to instruct you in religion, and labour for your good. Although they have not heard from you for a long time, yet they have not forgotten their brothers the Six Nations, and are still anxious to do you good.

"*Brothers;* I have not come to get your lands or your money, but to enlighten your minds, and to instruct you how to worship the Great Spirit agreeably to his mind and will, and to preach to you the gospel of his son Jesus Christ. There is but one religion, and but one way to serve God, and if you do not embrace the right way, you cannot be happy hereafter. You have never worshipped the Great Spirit in a manner acceptable to him; but have, all your

---

1. A note at the bottom of page in the original: "Rev. Mr. Cram."

lives, been in great errours and darkness. To endeavour to remove these errours, and open your eyes, so that you might see clearly, is my business with you.

"*Brothers;* I wish to talk with you as one friend talks with another; and, if you have any objections to receive the religion which I preach, I wish you to state them; and I will endeavour to satisfy your minds, and remove the objections.

"*Brothers;* I want you to speak your minds freely; for I wish to reason with you on the subject, and, if possible, remove all doubts, if there be any on your minds. The subject is an important one, and it is of consequence that you give it an early attention while the offer is made you. Your friends, the Boston Missionary Society, will continue to send you good and faithful ministers, to instruct and strengthen you in religion, if, on your part, you are willing to receive them.

"*Brothers;* Since I have been in this part of the country, I have visited some of your small villages, and talked with your people. They appear willing to receive instruction, but, as they look up to you as their older brothers in council, they want first to know your opinion on the subject.

"You have now heard what I have to propose at present. I hope you will take it into consideration, and give me an answer before we part."

(After about two hours consultation amongst themselves, the Chief commonly called, by the white people, Red Jacket,[2] rose and spoke as follows:)

"*Friend and Brother;* It was the will of the Great Spirit that we should meet together this day. HE orders all things, and has given us a fine day for our Council. HE has taken his garment from before the sun, and caused it to shine with brightness upon us. Our eyes are opened, that we may see clearly; our ears are unstopped, that we have been able to hear distinctly the words you have spoken. For all these favours we thank the Great Spirit; and HIM *only*.

"*Brother;* This council fire was kindled by you. It was at your request that we came together at this time. We have listened with attention to what you have said. You requested us to speak our minds freely. This gives us great joy; for we now consider that we stand upright before you, and can speak what we think. All have heard your voice, and all speak to you now as one man. Our minds are agreed.

"*Brother;* You say you want an answer to your talk before you leave this

2. A note at the bottom of page in the original: "His Indian name is, Sagu-yu-what-ha; which interpreted is, *Keeper awake*."

place. It is right you should have one, as you are a great distance from home, and we do not wish to detain you. But we will first look back a little, and tell you what our fathers have told us, and what we have heard from the white people.

"*Brother*; Listen to what we say.

"There was a time when our forefathers owned this great island. Their seats extended from the rising to the setting sun. The Great Spirit had made it for the use of Indians. HE had created the buffalo, the deer, and other animals for food. HE had made the bear and the beaver. Their skins served us for clothing. HE had scattered them over the country, and taught us how to take them. HE had caused the earth to produce corn for bread. All this HE had done for his red children, because HE loved them. If we had some disputes about our hunting ground, they were generally settled without the shedding of much blood. But an evil day came upon us. Your forefathers crossed the great water, and landed on this island. Their numbers were small. They found friends and not enemies. They told us they had fled from their own country for fear of wicked men, and had come here to enjoy their religion. They asked for a small seat. We took pity on them, granted their request; and they sat down amongst us. We gave them corn and meat, they gave us poison (alluding, it is supposed, to ardent spirits) in return.

"The white people had now found our country. Tidings were carried back, and more came amongst us. Yet we did not fear them. We took them to be friends. They called us brothers. We believed them, and gave them a larger seat. At length their numbers had greatly increased. They wanted more land; they wanted our country. Our eyes were opened, and our minds became uneasy. Wars took place. Indians were hired to fight against Indians, and many of our people were destroyed. They also brought strong liquor amongst us. It was strong and powerful, and has slain thousands.

"*Brother*; Our seats were once large and yours were small. You have now become a great people, and we have scarcely a place left to spread our blankets. You have got our country, but are not satisfied; you want to force your religion upon us.

"*Brother*; Continue to listen.

"You say that you are sent to instruct us how to worship the Great Spirit agreeably to his mind, and, if we do not take hold of the religion which you white people teach, we shall be unhappy hereafter. You say that you are right and we are lost. How do we know this to be true? We understand that your religion is written in a book. If it was intended for us as well as you, why has not the Great Spirit given to us, and not only to us, but why did he not give to our forefathers the knowledge of that book, with the means of understanding it rightly? We only know what you tell us about it. How shall we know when to believe, being so often deceived by the white people?

"*Brother;* You say there is but one way to worship and serve the Great Spirit. If there is but one religion; why do you white people differ so much about it? Why not all agreed, as you can all read the book?

"*Brother;* We do not understand these things.

"We are told that your religion was given to your forefathers, and has been handed down from father to son. We also have a religion, which was given to our forefathers, and has been handed down to us their children. We worship in that way. It teaches us to be thankful for all the favours we receive; to love each other, and to be united. We never quarrel about religion.

"*Brother;* The Great Spirit has made us all, but he has made a great difference between his white and red children. HE has given us different complexions and different customs. To you HE has given the arts. To these HE has not opened our eyes. We know these things to be true. Since HE has made so great a difference between us in other things; why may we not conclude that HE has given us a different religion according to our understanding? The Great Spirit does right. HE knows what is best for his children; we are satisfied.

"*Brother;* We do not wish to destroy your religion, or take it from you. We only want to enjoy our own.[3]

"*Brother;* We are told that you have been preaching to white people in this place. These people are our neighbours. We are acquainted with them. We will wait a little while, and see what effect your preaching has upon them. If we find is does them good, makes them honest and less disposed to cheat Indians; we will then consider again of what you have said.

"*Brother;* You have now heard our answer to your talk, and this is all we have to say at present.

"As we are going to part, we will come and take you by the hand, and hope the Great Spirit will protect you on your journey, and return you safe to your friends."

As the Indians began to approach the missionary, he rose hastily from his seat and replied, that he could not take them by the hand; that there was no fellowship between the religion of God and the works of the devil.

3. Drake here inserts a paragraph from an unknown source: "*Brother;* you say you have not come to get our land or our money, but to enlighten our minds. I will now tell you that I have been at your meetings, and saw you collecting money from the meeting. I cannot tell what this money was intended for, but suppose it was for your minister, and if we should conform to your way of thinking, perhaps you may want some from us" (1841, 99).

This being interpreted to the Indians, they smiled, and retired in a peaceable manner.

It being afterwards suggested to the missionary that his reply to the Indians was rather indiscreet; he observed, that he supposed the ceremony of shaking hands would be received by them as a token that he assented to what they had said. Being otherwise informed, he said he was sorry for the expressions. [Source: *Monthly Anthology and Boston Review* (April 1809): 221–24. See also Stone 1841, 188–93; Drake 1841, 99; Densmore 1999, 135–40]

A Variant Text of the Reply to Cram

AS CHRISTOPHER DENSMORE NOTES, there is a curious manuscript in the Buffalo and Erie County Historical Society whose introductory material also claims to be a transcript of Sagoyewatha's reply to Cram (1999, 67–68). Although it contains largely the same content as the *Monthly Anthology* version, it is significantly different because Sagoyewatha asks the whites to convert to Indian religion. The manuscript is not dated. The first lines are "Doctr Chapin who was present gives the following speech Red Jacket to Cram a missionary 1805–in reply to a speech delivered by Mr. C. that he was sent by their ancient friends to preach the Gospel among them."

The same variant, without the preface, was also published by William Leete Stone. For some reason, Stone felt the text was not a variant, but an entirely different speech from the same period. He dates it from between 1805–1811 but states nothing of its context. Stone's footnote declares that he received the speech from Joseph W. Moulton (the New York historian), from Cyrenus Chapin, in turn from Jasper Parrish.

Cyrenus Chapin was very well known in Buffalo, but his frontier personality does not inspire confidence in his academic judgement. Settling his medical practice in Buffalo in the early 1800s, he became close to the Senecas as their visiting doctor. He developed a reputation for being a heavy drinker as an officer during and after the War of 1812 (Ketchum 1864–65, 1:156–64). To the dismay of the American military, Chapin was known to enjoy plundering more than fighting. Later, he was frequently involved in financial lawsuits, both as plaintiff and defendant (Chazanof 1970, 198; Chapin folder, BECHS). He made sure newspapers printed stories about difficult medical operations he performed, such as trephinating the depressed skull fracture of a Seneca chief in the early 1820s.

This speech employs a more sophisticated vocabulary than most Red Jacket manuscripts.[1] Given Dr. Chapin's role in the transmission history of

1. The purple prose resembles the language of Chapin's agricultural address published in the February 20, 1821, edition of the *Niagara Patriot*. Chapin's literary style is evident also when

the following text, it is likely that he is responsible for the references to Ajax and Achilles, and the summary paraphrase appearing in the middle of the speech, if not for the ornamentation throughout. If Christopher Densmore is right to suggest that the circulation of the original Cram speech may have been prompted by sectarian disputes among Protestants, perhaps the hard-drinking Chapin simply enjoyed popularizing material that would make missionaries wince. This playful aspect of his personality is suggested by Chapin's business partner, John W. Clark, who confided to his brother on June 23, 1823, that Chapin "is not fond of business except to oppose other physicians who speak ill of him" (Clark Papers, Clements Library, University of Michigan).

The preface to the manuscript, which appears on page 11 of the sixteen-page document held at the Buffalo and Erie County Historical Society, is as follows:

Held in Buffalo—Col. Chapin Erastus Granger U.S. Indian Agent & Cram were together—in a room—An audience had been procured with the Indians for Cram after some difficulty, by Col. C.[hapin]

—R.J. before they commenced approached the door and surveyed Cram with a rapid scrutiny truly penetrative but as truly decisive—R.J. had satisfied himself whether it was a great man like Connesaughty[2] with whom he was to draw the bow of Achilles or wield the Shield of Ajax—for with a mingled & indescribable erection of countenance he turned with a smiling but scornful composure, and joined the Indians who had assembled for the occasion

Sagoyewatha:

I arise to return you the thanks of this nation and to return them back to our ancient friends if any such we have—for their good wishes toward us in attempting to teach us your religion[.] Inform them we will look well into this matter[.] We have well weighed your exertions and find your success not to answer our expectations—But instead of producing that happy effect which you

---

he became a regional grand marshal for the Jackson campaign in late 1827, ranting against President Adams's "wayward dough-faces, all sided non-descripts or non-committals, the vote peddling blubbers, the political blacklegs, the renegado pimps, the treacherous bladders of the Kremlin . . . this vanguard of rats" (*Buffalo Emporium*, November 29, 1827).

2. Timothy Pickering. He was given this name at the council of Tioga, 1790.

so long promised us, its introduction so far has rendered us uncomfortable &
miserable—You have taken a number of our young men to your schools[.] You
have educated them and taught them your religion, They have returned to
their kindred & color, neither white men nor Indians. The arts they have
learned are incompatible with the chase & ill adapted to our customs[.] They
have been taught that which is useless to us. They have been made to feel ar-
tificial wants, which never entered the minds of their brothers—They have
imbibed in your great towns the Seeds of vices which are unknown in the Forest. They have become discouraged & dissipated—despised by the Indians,
neglected by the whites, and without value to either—less honest than the
former, and perhaps more knavish than the latter—

We were told that the failure of these first attempts were attributable to
miscalculation—and we were invited to try again by sending others of our
young men to different Schools to be taught by different instructors. Brother
The result has been invariably the same. We believe it wrong for you to
attempt further to promote your religion among us or to introduce your
arts, manners habits, & feelings[.] We believe that is wrong for us to encourage
you in so doing—We believe that the great Spirit made the whites & the Indians but for different purposes—(Here he went into a train of reasoning from
analogy)

[In] Our attempting to pattern your example the Great Spirit is angry—
for you see that he does not b[l]ess or crown your exertions[.] (Here Red Jacket
painted in the most glowing & descriptive colours the curse that seemed to
have descended upon all those Indians who had been made the objects of
pious but mistaken missions how imbecile, poor, effeminate, contemptible,
drunken lying, thievish cheating, malicious, meddlesome, backbiting, quarrelsome—degraded & despised, the poor vic[t]ims of civilized instruction had
become—having lost all the noble qualities of the Savage and acquired all of
the ignoble vices of the Whites—without one solitary exception—Where the
Indian had been bettered)—

But on the other hand we know that the great Spirit is pleased that we follow the traditions & customs of our forefathers for in so doing we receive his
blessing—We have rece[ive]ᵈ strength & vigor for the chase. The great Spirit
has provided abundance—When we are hungry we find the forest filled with
[game?] When thirsty we slake our thirst at the pure streams and springs that
spread around us—When weary the leaves of the trees are our bed—We retire
with contentment to rest—We rise with gratitude to the great preserver,—
renovated strength in our limbs and bounding joy in our hearts[.] We
feel blessed & happy—No luxuries no vices no disputed titles, no avari-

cious desires, shake the foundations of our Society—and disturb our peace & happiness—

We know that the great Spirit is better pleased with his red children than with his Whites—When he bestows upon us a hundred fold blessings more than upon you—Perhaps you are right in your religion—it may be peculiarly adapted to your condition—You say that you destroyed the son of the Great Spirit—perhaps this is the merited cause of all your troubles and misfortunes[.] But Brother bear in mind that we had no participation in this murder—We disclaim it—We love the great Spirit—and as we never had any agency in so unjust so merciless and so abominable an outrage, he therefore continues to smile upon us, and to give us peace joy & plenty. We pity you—We wish you to bear to our good friends our best wishes—Inform them that in compassion towards them, we are willing to send them missionaries to teach them our religion habits & customs—We would be willing they should be as happy as we are and assure them that if they should follow our example they would be more far more happy than they are now—We cannot embrace your religion—it renders us divided and unhappy—but by your embracing ours we believe that you would be more happy & more acceptable to the great Spirit—

Here (pointing his finger to several whites present, who had been captured when Children & brought up among them[3]) here, Br.[other] (with an animation & exulting triumph which cannot be described) here is the living evidence before you—Those young men have been brought up with us—They are contented & happy—Nothing would be an inducement with them to abandon their enjoyments & adopt yours—For they are too well aware of the blessings of our society & the evils of yours—But as you have our good will, we would gladly know that you have relinquished your religion productive of so much disagreement & inquietude among yourselves, & instead ther[e]of that you should follow ours—

Accept of this advice, Br.[other] & take it back to y[ou]r friends—as the best pledge of our wishes for your welfare (see page after next)[4] Perhaps you think we are ignorant & uninformed—Go then and teach the whites—select for example, the people of Buffalo—We will be Spectators and remain Silent. Improve their morals and refine their habits—Make them less disposed to cheat Indians—Make the whites generally less inclined to make indians drunk & to take from them their lands. Let us know the tree by the blossoms,

---

3. One of the people referred to was likely Jasper Parrish, the subagent.

4. On that page in the manuscript is the following addendum, prefaced with the words, "Add to R.J. Speech. Perhaps you think."

and the blossoms by the fruit.—When this shall be made clear to our minds we may be more willing to listen to you. But until then we must be allowed to follow the religion of our ancestors. Farewell, Brother.

Red Jacket

Sau-goo-ya-waught-ha

[Source: "Indian Collection," box 1, folder 1, BECHS B00-2; it is the likely copy text for Stone 1841, 206–9]

In Washington on Seneca Neutrality

FEBRUARY 13, 1810

SENSING THAT THE WESTERN INDIANS were intent upon war in alliance with the British, the Six Nations sent a delegation to Washington, D.C., accompanied by Erastus Granger to inform them of the situation. On February 13, 1810, Sagoyewatha addressed the following declaration of neutrality to the secretary of war, William Eustis. Jasper Parrish interpreted. The following document is taken from War Department records.

Red Jacket, in behalf of himself, and the other deputies of the six nations.,
To the Secretary of War
Brother,
As you have been appointed the Great War Chief of your nation, we are told, that to you all the communications from the different tribes of Indians residing in the United States must be made. Therefore, we the delegates from the Six nations of Indians have come forward to your great Council fire to make known our wishes, and we hope, you will listen with attention to our voice, and hear what we have to say.—
Brother,
There have been from time to time Treaties made between the United States and six nations of Indians; but, the principal treaty which now governs, and which binds us together, was made at Canandaigua, about fifteen years since—To this treaty we now call your attention.
At the time it was formed all the disputes between us were settled. It, also, pointed out the way in which any difficulties, or disputes, which afterwards might happen, should be adjusted.—
After this treaty was formed your Government appointed an agent to keep bright this Chain of friendship.—We were also told by your Commissioner, Colonel Pickering, that if the Chain became rusty and your agent could not make it bright, we should have liberty to send some of our Chiefs to the Seat of your Government, and there make known our complaints to our Great Father, the President of the United States.

Brother,

We were told by your Commissioner, that in time, difficulties might arise and disturb the peace and friendship then to be established. He said "We have some bad men amongst our people: there are also, some amongst the Indians, who, perhaps, will commit unfriendly acts on both sides; such as Stealing property from each other.["] In order, therefore, to preserve our peace, it was agreed in the treaty, that no private revenge, or retaliation should take place, but if either party were injured, complaint should be made to the offenders, of the injury done, and that compensation should be made to the Suffering party, and their minds made easy.—For some years this great Chain was kept bright; compensation was made on both sides for damages done by individuals. On our part we have to this day complied with the treaty, and still wish to hold fast to it; but Brother, let us remind you that your part has become *rusty*.

For three years past we have received injuries from the white people. Our Cattle and horses have been stolen and carried off; and altho' we have made complaint to your agent yet we have not received any compensation for our losses.

Brother,

We have thus far made known to you our minds, and in behalf of the six Nations whom we represent, we now call on your Government to fulfill this part of the Treaty, and make good the Damages done us by your bad people.

Brother,

Why should you hesitate to comply with a treaty you have made? With *you* it is but a small thing; to us it is of consequence: and will you suffer us to return with heavy hearts?—Shall it be said that the Government of the United States are the first to violate their Treaties?—

We acknowledge that the treaty has been faithfully fulfilled on your part, excepting that part of which we now complain, and as we believe there has been some mistake about it, we have no doubt, but, when you come to understand the thing, you will not be slow in doing us justice.

Brother,

We have often made our Complaints to the agents whom you have appointed. They have told us they had not the means in their hands to make satisfaction. We want to know whether the fault is in them. If it is not, we wish you now to instruct them that whenever we make satisfactory proof of losses, sustained by the bad conduct of your people, they should immediately satisfy our minds, by a reasonable compensation; thereby forever maintaining that peace & friendship so necessary to both nations.

Brother,

We ask your attention to what we further say—We often meet with our agents to do business, but have no proper place to hold Councils; sometimes they are held in a Blacksmith's shop; at other times in a Kitchen, or Bar-room.—You must be sensible how inconvenient it is to do business in such places.

As we are poor, we hope you will consider our Case, and feel willing to build us a suitable house to do business in.

Brother,

At the time we were making bright the Chain of friendship at Can-andaigua, the Commissioner on your part told us, that the time might come when your enemies would endeavour to disturb our minds, and do away the friendship we had then formed with you. That time Brother, has already arrived.

Since you have had some disputes with the British Government their agents in Canada have not only endeavoured to make the Indians at the Westward your enemies, but they have sent a war belt amongst our Warriors to poison their minds, and make them break their faith with you.

This Belt we exhibited to your agents in Council, and then sent it to the place from whence it came, never more to be seen amongst us.

At the same time, we had information that the British had circulated War Belts among the Western Indians, and within your territory. We rested not, but called a General Council of the Six nations, and resolved to let our voice be heard among our Western brethren and destroy the effects of the poison, scattered amongst them.—We have twice sent large deputations to their Council fire, for the purpose of making their minds strong in their friendship with your nation; and in the event of a war between the white people, to set still on their seats, and take no part on either side; so far as our voice has been heard they have agreed to hearken to our Counsel, and remain at peace with your nation.

In affecting this great object we have expended six hundred & twenty Dollars of our own money—this fact is known to your agents.

Brother,

If war should take place we hope you will inform us of it thro' your agents, and we will continue to use our influence, with all the Indians with whom we are acquainted, that they will set still upon their seats, and cultivate friendship with your people.

Brother,

We have now made known to you the business we came upon; if it is agreeable to your customs, we should be glad to have it laid before our father, the President, and we will wait till he thinks proper to give us an answer—

Washington City, Feb. 13, 1810

Sa-goo-ya-wat-haw

or Red   his   **X**   mark   Jacket

Pollard   his   **X**   mark

Capt. John   his   **X**   mark   Kill Buck

Edward   his   **X**   mark   French

Taken from the interpretation of Mr. Jasper

Parrish in presence of Erastus Granger, United States agent to the Six Nations. [Source:"Letters Received by the Secretary of War Pertaining to Indian Affairs, 1800–1823," M-271, reel 1, frames 529–36, DNA. Also in the Erastus Granger Papers, folder 14-18; shorter versions in Ketchum 1864–65, 2:419–21; Snyder 1978, 40–43; paragraph-length versions in Stone 1841, 218–19, and *ASPIA*, 1:804]

To Quakers in Philadelphia on the Education
of Two Seneca Boys

FEBRUARY 28, 1810

ON THEIR WAY TO WASHINGTON, the Senecas sent word to the Quakers in Philadelphia that they would like to have several of their children educated by the Friends. On their way home, the Seneca chiefs met with representatives of the Philadelphia Yearly Meeting's Indian Committee (PYMIC). The Quakers began the council and agreed to educating two Seneca boys, provided that they learn some mechanic arts (see Barton 1990; Jackson 1830).[1] They also agreed to the Senecas' request for farm tools for the Cayugas living at Cattaraugus. The PYMIC papers at Haverford College contain two similar versions of this speech, with nearly identical content. The following is the longer of the two. Jasper Parrish translated. Erastus Granger and three other Seneca chiefs were present: Capt. John Kill Buck, Neddy (Edward French), and Captain Pollard.

The Chief called Red Jacket in reply said that they felt thankful to the great Spirit, for favouring the Company present with health to meet, and the opportunity of hearing the voices of each other; he returned his acknowledgement of the kindness of friends in undertaking to seek for suitable places for the young men to be instructed, observing that the Genius of Men were different, and requesting to be informed what branches of knowledge friends were willing the young men should be instructed in, mentioning that one of them a nephew of his would be desirous of learning the art of Speaking on paper or making paper speak, and suggested the propriety of their learning several things & not being confined to one particular branch of business—Upon the views of friends being explained that reading, writing, and some handicraft would be advised—and that when suitable places were procured, they would

1. The boys' journey to the Quakers was delayed until the summer of 1816 because of the war ("Indian Records 1801–20," AB 25, p. 207, PYMIC; Jackson 1830, 66).

be informed thereof, and some way adopted for bringing them down he appeared satisfied, and proceeded to say he well remembered being in this City several years ago,[2] at a time when there were deputations from 16 nations of Indians here, and that they were informed by Government, that their manner of life had reduced them to great poverty & insignificance, and that unless they altered their mode of living and adopted that of the white people, particularly in tilling the ground they would in time dwindle to nothing and strongly advised them to make the alteration, That the Indians communicated this advice to a very large Council of Friends, and asked their opinion respecting it, that friends informed them, they approved of the advice, and told them that altho their means were small, they would be willing to encourage them to make the trial, by affording them some small assistance therein—Since that time however several of the Black Coated people have come amongst us and offered their services to preach to us, but on Considering the subject we were not able to discover any benefit to be derived from that mode of Instruction[3]—but in preference we highly approve of the measures adopted by you in the art of Cultivating the lands &c, in which I am happy to inform you many of our people have made a considerable improvement both in Cultivating the land and some of the mechanic arts—I am unable to express the thankfulness I feel for the many acts of kindness Your society have shewn to us, particularly when that old Gentleman pointing to John Elliot[4] and many others now no more, attended at our Treaties and I am happy in observing your disposition to pursue the same Track of Conduct your Fathers observed towards Indians, now they are removed to the world to the world [*sic*] of Spirits—

I now return you on behalf of myself and the three other chiefs present our thanks for the presents you mention you make us in order to brighten the Chain made by your Fathers & ours—

One of the friends expressing a wish that the Buffalo Indians would frequent the Town of New Amsterdam[5] less than they did, and avoid the intercourse with disorderly white people and abstain more than was the case from

2. Meeting President Washington in the spring of 1792.

3. The alternative manuscript reads, "Since that time several men have come amongst them and offered their services to Preach to them but no knowledge can be acquired in the Arts or in agriculture from words like that" ("Conferences with Indians, 1792–1865," item 185, AA43, PYMIC, Haverford College).

4. John Elliot was treasurer of the Indian Committee of the Philadelphia Yearly Meeting from 1803 to 1809.

5. Buffalo.

the use of Ardent Spirits it appeared to be well received by the Indians, and Red Jacket in reply said it was a subject that they had been considering of and two of the Chiefs then present were specially charged to exercise care in this respect—

He also said upon being questioned on the subject that it was their desire if the two young men came [to?] these parts that they should be innoculated with the Kine Pock [cowpox], having heard it was effectual in preventing the Small Pock [smallpox].

[Source: "Conferences with Indians, 1792–1865," item 77, AA43, PYMIC, Haverford College. A shorter version appears in Jackson 1830, 56]

Councils for Neutrality at Brownstown

September 1810

AS TENSIONS DEVELOPED between the United States and Britain leading up to the War of 1812, the western Indians saw an opportunity to side with the British to reclaim lost lands. A Shawnee delegation, possibly with Tecumseh, visited Buffalo Creek as early as August 1807, trying to convince Handsome Lake to come west (Sugden 1997, 159). In 1808 and in September 1810, the Six Nations attended pan-Indian councils at the mouth of the Detroit River in the Wyandot town of Brownstown (map 1). William Leete Stone lamented that there were no actual transcripts of Sagoyewatha's speeches at these councils, but several witnesses reported that Sagoyewatha counseled for neutrality and argued that the British were not reliable allies. John Norton recalled that Red Jacket pushed his point by dwelling on the Indians' humiliating loss to General Wayne near Fallen Timbers in 1794 when British closed the gates of their fort as the Indians retreated toward them (Densmore 1999, 77–79; J. Norton 1970, 285).

In a letter held in the Erastus Granger papers, William Hull wrote the following summary of one of Sagoyewatha's speeches in 1810 at Brownstown. Brief newspaper summaries of Hull's reports appear in the *American Watchman*, December 15, 1810, and *New Hampshire Gazette*, December 18, 1810.

Detroit 30th Sept 1810—

Sir,

The Chiefs and a large number of the young warriors of the Six Nations have been four or five weeks in this country, attending a general Council at Browns town—Inclosed are two speeches, one to the Prophet and the Shawnees residing on the Wabash—The other to the several Nations represented in the Council—They have likewise sent a very friendly speech to the President of the U.S.—Before the Council commenced, they invited me to attend—I was with them ten days, and witnessed all their proceedings—Near two thousand were present—I never have seen a more orderly assembly of men—In, and about the council house, were generally attending about

six hundred—During the ten days, I neither saw or heard of one being intoxi-
cated—The Mohawks and Cayugas from Upper Canada were present—they
made some difficulty, and endeavoured to produce a very different result—
They were entirely borne down by all the other nations—Red Jacket chief of
the Six Nations spoke the principal part of a day—He was listened to by at
least six hundred with the most profound attention—His discourse, and the
manner in which it was delivered, would have done honor to the celebrated
orators of ancient or modern times—After addressing each Nation separately,
and congratulating them on so general a meeting—he produced a number of
belts of old wampum which had been exchanged at former Councils, explained the proceedings of those councils, and the figurative signification of
the belts—He then entered into a consideration of the savage state before
they were connected with the white people—Explained the time and manner
the French people came among them—The consequences of it on their habits
and customs—Their connections with the British government. The events of
the revolutionary war—and their present connection with the American government & people. After giving their general histories he described their present situation, and considered the advantages and the disadvantages of the
savage and civilized state.—He then in a very impressive manner on the han-
dle of his Tomahawk, pointed out the manner in which they had retired from
the ocean towards the setting sun—laid his finger on their present position,
which was more than half the distance, then grasping the end of the Tomahawk, observed, if they proceeded on, they would drop off, and that would be
the end of them—He then observed to them that their situation was changed,
and it became necessary to change their mode of living—That the game had
left the country, where they now lived, & they must not depend on hunting
entirely for a support—That it was true they had received disadvantages from
their connection with civilized people—That such indeed was their destiny,
and they must make the best of it. Their interest now was to imitate the improvements made by their white Brethren—That they must retain the lands
they had reserved, and permanently settle on them—Build themselves comfortable houses, inclose & cultivate their farms, and attend to the domestic
arts in the same manner as they see their white brethren—In doing this their
great father of the seventeen fires had offered them his assistance.—He then
considered their connections with the white people in a political point of
view—Observed that wars among themselves and wars with the white people
had been their greatest calamities—That their Great Father of the seventeen
fires, had informed them, that he did not desire them to take a part in his wars
if he should have any—That they had no interest in them & ought not to

waste their blood in fighting for others—That all he asked of them was to re-main quiet at their villages, and take care of their corn fields, and their women and children—That he had likewise told them the consequences of taking any part against him—He concluded by recommending to them, all to agree to follow his advice.

This, Sir, is only a very general sketch of his speech. It was interpreted through several different languages, and the spirit and beauties of it, must have been in a great measure lost—I will endeavour to send you a more correct account of it hereafter . . . [Source: Erastus Granger Papers, folder 14-14; *IIDH*, reel 45]

Insulting the Wyandots and Delawares
at Brownstown

CA. 1808 OR 1810

THE FOLLOWING SPEECH, first appearing in Henry Schoolcraft's 1846 *Notes on the Iroquois*, appears to be of dubious authenticity. The speech may have come from Brownstown in 1808 or 1810. Schoolcraft, who went west to study the geology of the Mississippi river valley in 1818, gives no information about his sources. According to the Moravian missionary John Heckewelder, Sagoyewatha's remark about making the Delawares wear petticoats refers to a seventeenth-century event where the Six Nations requested that the Delawares "play the woman," or peacemaker, in a dispute between the Six Nations and the Dutch (Heckewelder 1819, 58–66; Jennings 1984, 161, 263, 301). As readers of Cooper's Leatherstocking tales know, Cooper thought it was a reproach when it actually may have been an expression of respect. It is likely that this fragment is the imaginative reconstruction of someone who had read Indian arcana in books, although it may have been based on an actual event. For example, the use of the French-derived term *Quatoghies* to refer to Hurons or Wyandots suggests someone comfortable with the language of Cadwallader Colden's *History of the Five Nations* (published in two parts in 1727 and 1747). The translation style does not seem characteristic of Sagoyewatha speeches of the 1800s.

"Have the Quatoghies forgotten themselves? Or do they suppose we have forgotten them? Who gave you the right in the west or east, to light the general council fire? You must have fallen asleep, and dreamt that the Six Nations were dead! Who permitted you to escape from the lower country? Had you any heart left to speak a word for yourselves? Remember how you hung on by the bushes. You had not even a place to land on. You have not yet done p[issin]g for fear of the Konoshioni. High claim, indeed, for a tribe who had to run away from the Kadarakwa.

"As for you my nephews," he continued, turning to the Lenapees, or

Delawares, "it is fit you should let another light your fire. Before Miquon came, we had put out your fire and poured water on it; it would not burn. Could you hunt or plant without our leave? Could you sell a foot of land? Did not the voice of the Long House cry, go, and you went? Had you any power at all? Fit act indeed for you to give in to our wandering brothers—you, from whom we took the war-club and put on petticoats." [Source: Schoolcraft 1846, 423–24]

Replies to Rev. John Alexander, and John Richardson, Esq.

MAY 1811

OTHER THAN THE 1805 REPLY TO CRAM, the two most popularly circulated Sagoyewatha speeches were published together by James D. Bemis in a pamphlet called *Native Eloquence*, which went on sale on September 6, 1811 (*Ontario Repository*, November 9, 1811). Both speeches were given at the same council at Buffalo Creek, and both likely translated by Jasper Parrish, whose attendance is pointed out in the speech text. The exact day of these May speeches is not known. The council was not discussed in extant area newspapers.

The first speech is the reply to Rev. John Alexander, appointed by the New York Missionary Society to serve as a missionary at Buffalo Creek. Alexander's job was to propose that the society be allowed to build a mission there. As is clear from Sagoyewatha's response, his offer was rejected. In their yearly report, the directors of the society gave two reasons why they thought Alexander's proposal failed. First, they blamed neighborhood whites for convincing the Indians that the religious mission was a ploy to get more lands from them. Second, although they defended Alexander's conduct as "honest and artless," they faulted him for not more explicitly stating to the citizens of Buffalo the nature of his "engagement" to the New York Missionary Society (New York Missionary Society 1812, 4). Apparently, Alexander did not make clear that the society paid him very little money (the account books show only one $100 payment to Alexander in 1811) and that he would need to be supported by the local population of Buffalo, a discovery that his opponents used to discredit him further. Alexander managed, however, to remain in Buffalo for a year. The society lamented that Alexander's reputation seemed to be permanently damaged by this misunderstanding and removed him as missionary as of June 1812. It would be a decade before the construction of a mission would again be discussed at Buffalo Creek. Although the Senecas rejected the mission, they did agree to a schoolhouse, run by the New York Missionary

Society's Jabez Hyde, which had twenty students by the end of the year (1812, 4–5, 14).

The second speech was a response to a land-sale offer made by a lawyer of the newly formed Ogden Land Company, John Richardson. On September 12, 1810, David A. Ogden, a lawyer for the Holland Land Company, bought from the Holland Company the preemptive rights to most of the Six Nations' reservations in New York state. The amount of land totaled 197,835 acres. Ogden agreed to pay $98,917 for the land, or roughly fifty cents an acre, payable in eight years with 6 percent interest accruing two years after the initial purchase date (Ogden Family Papers). Ogden needed to sell most of the land before the note became due in 1818, but he had to extinguish the native title first.

Five months later, on February 4, 1811, David Ogden created the Ogden Land Company. In addition to maintaining unqualified control of how the lands would be developed and sold, David owned half the shares of the company, and divided the remainder into one-twentieth shares among his business associates and brothers, most notably Thomas Ludlow Ogden, who was also a high-profile New York City attorney ("Articles of Agreement," Ogden Papers). David would take on other partners over the next years, offering them shares of his fifty-percent interest in the company but reserving for himself sole decision-making power over sale and management of the lands.

One of David Ogden's subsequent associates was John Richardson. Richardson had been involved in buying New York Indian lands since 1795, when he assisted in the purchase of the Cayuga reservation for a $1,000 annuity (Chapin Jr. to Pickering, July 31, 1795; ORWM, vol. 11, item 33). Richardson was working for Ogden in January 1811, but he was not a founding partner of the Ogden Company. There are very few records of Richardson's 1811 dealings with the company in the Ogden family papers, but later correspondence suggests that in 1811 Richardson offered to extinguish the Indian title for the Ogden Company within one year in exchange for the opportunity to buy Ogden Company land shares at fifty cents an acre (David Ogden to Richardson, May 1, 1812, Ogden Papers). There are no Ogden Company records pertaining to Richardson's visit to Buffalo Creek, but, as Sagoyewatha notes, Richardson made his offer without a U.S. commissioner present.

A year later, in 1812, even as war with Britain was imminent, Richardson was still working to promote the sale. His yearlong agreement with David Ogden had expired by mutual consent, but Richardson was planning on making one last attempt to convince the Indians to sell on May 20 or in mid-June. In a June 2, 1812, letter to Richardson, David Ogden voiced grave doubts about Richardson's prospects for success. He warned Richardson that failing to build an alliance with Horatio Jones and Jasper Parrish would doom the sale. Ogden did, however, offer Richardson the opportunity to buy almost 5,000 acres (a one-fortieth share in the company) at fifty cents per acre as a courtesy for the previous year's work for him (Ogden Papers). Whether Richardson accepted his offer is not known, but Richardson was unable to convince the Indians to sell before war broke out with England. Richardson does not figure prominently in later Ogden business, but he was apparently still working with the company in 1816 (Richardson to Parrish, February 13, 1816, Jasper Parrish Papers, not microfilmed, BECHS).

In addition to republication by Bemis, New York newspapers began circulating the Richardson and Alexander speeches in August 1811. For nationalist appropriations of Red Jacket's defenses of Indian rights in the context of the War of 1812, see the October 30, 1811, *New York Commercial Advertiser.*

Reply to the Rev. Alexander:

Brother; We listened to the talk you delivered to us from the Council of black coats[1] in New York. We have fully considered your talk, and the offers you have made us; we perfectly understand them, and we return an answer, which we wish you also to understand. In making up our minds we have looked back and remembered what has been done in our days, and what our fathers have told us was done in old times.

"*Brother;* Great numbers of black coats have been amongst the Indians, and with sweet voices, and smiling faces, have offered to teach them the religion of the white people. Our brethren in the East listened to the black coats—turned from the religion of their fathers, and took up the religion of the white people. What good has it done them? Are they more happy and more friendly one to another than we are? No, brother, they are a divided people—we are united—they quarrel about religion—we live in love and friendship—they drink strong water—have learnt how to cheat—and to practice all the vices of the white men, which disgrace Indians, without imitating the virtues of the white men. Brother, if you are our well wisher, keep away and do not disturb us.

"*Brother;* We do not worship the Great Spirit as the white men do, but we believe that forms of worship are indifferent to the Great Spirit—it is the offering of a sincere heart that pleases him, and we worship him in this manner.

1. Note in the original: "The appellation given to clergymen by the Indians."

According to your religion we must believe in a father and a son, or will not be happy hereafter. We have always believed in a father, and we worship him, as we were taught by our fathers. Your book says the son was sent on earth by the father—did all the people who saw the son believe in him? No, they did not, and the consequences must be known to you, if you have read the book.

"*Brother*; You wish us to change our religion for yours—we like our religion and do not want another. Our friends (pointing to Mr. Granger, Mr. Parish, and Mr Taylor)[2] do us great good—they counsel us in our troubles—and instruct us how to make ourselves comfortable. Our friends the quakers do more than this—they give us ploughs, and show us how to use them. They tell us we are accountable beings, but do not say we must change our religion. We are satisfied with what they do.

"*Brother*; For these reasons we cannot receive your offers—we have other things to do, and beg you to make your mind easy, and not trouble us, lest our heads should be too much loaded, and by and by burst.

Reply to John Richardson:

"*Brother*; We opened our ears to the talk you lately delivered to us, at our Council fire. In doing important business it is best not tell long stories, but to come to it in a few words. We therefore shall not repeat your talk, which is fresh in our minds. We have well considered it, and the advantages and disadvantages of your offers. We request your attention to our answer, which is not from the speaker alone, but from all the Sachems and Chiefs now around our Council fire.

"*Brother*; We know that great men as well as great nations, having different interests have different minds, and do not see the same subject in the same light—but we hope our answer will be agreeable to you and to your employers.

"*Brother*; Your application for the purchase of our lands, is to our minds very extraordinary. It has been made in a crooked manner—you have not walked in the straight path pointed out by the great Council of your nation. You have no writings from our great father the President.

"*Brother*; In making up our minds we have looked back, and remembered how the Yorkers purchased our lands in former times. They bought them piece after piece for a little money paid to a few men in our nation, and not to all our brethren; our planting and hunting grounds have become very small, and if we sell these we know not where to spread our blankets.

2. Erastus Granger, agent for Indian affairs; Jasper Parrish, subagent and interpreter; Jacob Taylor, a representative from the Quaker's Philadelphia Yearly Meeting Indian Committee.

"*Brother;* You tell us your employers have purchased of the Council of Yorkers a right to buy our lands—we do not understand how this can be—the lands do not belong to the Yorkers; they are ours, and were given to us by the Great Spirit[.]

"*Brother;* We think it strange that you should jump over the lands of our brethren in the East, to come to our Council fire so far off, to get our lands. When we sold our lands in the East to the white people we determined never to sell those we kept, which are as small as we can comfortably live on.

"*Brother;* You want us to travel with you, and look for other lands. If we should sell our lands and move off into a distant country, towards the setting sun—we should be looked upon in the country to which we go as foreigners, and strangers, and be despised by the red as well as the white men, and we should soon be surrounded by the white men, who will there also kill our game, come upon our lands, and try to get them from us.

"*Brother;* We are determined not to sell our lands, but to continue on them—we like them—they are fruitful and produce us corn in abundance, for the support of our women and children, and grass and herbs for our cattle.

"*Brother;* At the treaties held for the purchase of our lands, the white men with sweet voices and smiling faces told us they loved us, and that they would not cheat us, but that the king's children on the other side [of] the lake would cheat us. When we go on the other side [of] the lake the king's children tell us your people will cheat us, but with sweet voices and smiling faces assure us of their love and that they will not cheat us. These things puzzle our heads, and we believe that the Indians must take care of themselves, and not trust either in your people or in the king's children.

"*Brother;* At a late Council we requested our agents to tell you that we would not sell our lands, and we think you have not spoken to our agents, or they would have informed you so, and we should not have met you at our Council fire at this time.

"*Brother;* The white people buy and sell false rights to our lands; your employers have you say paid a great price for their right—they must have plenty of money, to spend it in buying false rights to lands belonging to Indians—the loss of it will not hurt them, but our lands are of great value to us, and we wish you to go back with your talk to your employers, and to tell them and the Yorkers, that they have no right to buy and sell false rights to our lands.

"*Brother;* We hope you clearly understand the words we have spoken. This is all we have to say. [Source: *Native Eloquence* 1811, 12–17; *New York Evening Post,* August 10, 1811; Stone 1841, 199–204; version in Densmore (1999) taken from the 1816 edition of *American Speaker,* 142–43]

Promises Neutrality to Agent for Indian Affairs

MAY 25, 1812

ALTHOUGH THE NEW YORK SIX NATIONS had agreed to stay neutral in the upcoming war, the decision split the confederacy geographically. The Six Nations' settlement in Canada on the Grand River leaned toward the British. In April 1812, the War Department heard that young Haudenosaunee warriors were planning to join the western Indians. At the following council on May 25, 1812, Superintendent Erastus Granger sought promises that the Six Nations would stay neutral and convince their Canadian relations to do the same. The Six Nations organized a delegation to go to the Grand River settlement, but it was unsuccessful (Densmore 1999, 81).

Several speeches from the War of 1812 are in the Erastus Granger Papers held at the Oswego campus of the State University of New York. In 1978, most of these documents pertaining to Red Jacket were published by Charles Snyder in *Red and White on the New York Frontier*. He regularized spelling and added capitalization and punctuation to make these very rough copies more readable. William Leete Stone's versions, transcribed from the same manuscripts, are retouched even more. As should be clear from the following transcript, the original documents were written in haste, probably scribbled in Granger's lap as Parrish translated. All spelling peculiarities are as they appear in the original documents.

After a mutual exchange of compliments, Granger writes that Red Jacket:

thanks me for advising our young warrears to listen to the councils of the old chiefs.—says not to listen to y.[oung] men.—

wishes the Interpreter to be very particular & make no mistakes the appearances now are the same as at the begining of the last war.—we are told that the Great King would punish his children—we were invited to assist & were promised many good things.—Clothing—money Liquor as long as waters run &c—

a Council was held.—an ox was roasted, Sir Guy Johnson, took the head and threw it into the fire—this is the way we shall punish the Rebels—a belt was then produced representing the British & Indians—a Heart in the middle. The Mohawks first took it & [advised? abused?] the rest, at length they all took it & danced the War dance. The Senecas were invited to go with the British for amusement. and were at length drawn into the War.—

we have related what took place last war.—you spoke then as you do now—the british speak as they did before we are now determined to listen to your words—there sits the deputation who are to go to Canada to speak to our Brothers on that side.—this is not private we wish the British to know it—the better for us—the British have tried to persuade us to cross—shew us a map of the Country—offered us great Seats if we would come over & take an active part—we have refused—we like our seats &c—

we have selected Men of sense to go to Grand river & perswade them to agree with us—it will not end here, our voice will be heard to the westward—they will listen to us.—

we have re[ceive]^d. a message—the Mowhawks have agreed to take up the hatchet but we hope they will hear to us.—

The deputation have rec^d. instructions—they have connections on that side—some may come here to live if they can get over.—

If war takes place we hope you will be candid and let us know what regulations you adopt.—we want to know at this time

Granger then gave the delegation a speech to take with them to Grand River. Red Jacket replied:

place our money from Phelps where it will bring us Interest take Land as security & enough. [Source: Erastus Granger Papers, folder 14-20; *IIDH*, reel 45; Ketchum 1864–65, 2:421–22]

To Grand River Indians Urging Neutrality

JUNE 7, 1812

JEAN BAPTISTE ROUSSEAU was a store owner, investor, and occasional agent and interpreter for the British Indian department. On June 7, 1812, he wrote to William Claus that several messengers had arrived at Grand River from Buffalo Creek.

"Red Jacket has sent a message by them to the Indians living on the Grand River, particularly the Wolf Tribe, whom he called Brothers, and says, 'I hope you will not go and make your Children poor by joining with the British Government in case of a dispute between them and the Americans. If you do, the Americans say, You will lose all your Land, and that it will be taken from you,—that it is wisest for you to remain Neutral because the promises the King may make to you, he will never perform. You may remember he did not fulfill his engagements to Captain Brant last War and I hope you will harken to what I now tell you, as a Token I send Eight strings of White Wampum.' " [Source: C. Johnson 1964, 193; also *Upper Canada State Papers* 1974, 79:28–32]

Rousseau's letter also includes a short speech by Young King, sent with Red Jacket's message, that encourages the Grand River Indians to take Red Jacket's advice.

To Erastus Granger on War with Britain

JULY 6–8, 1812

THE UNITED STATES declared war on Britain on June 18, 1812, and on July 6, Erastus Granger met with the Six Nations to formally explain the causes of the war to the Indians and to hear their concerns. The principal speeches of that council appeared in the first book published at Buffalo: *Public Speeches Delivered at the Village of Buffalo, on the 6th and 8th days of July, 1812 . . .* (see also Stone 1841, 224–34). Jasper Parrish translates:

SPEECHES.

    (This council was convened at the request of the Hon. E. Granger, Esq. Indian Agent. The Sachems, Chiefs, and Warriors of the Six Nations of Indians, residing in the United States, were present.)

Monday, July 6, 1812.
    RED JACKET
    Addressing himself to the Agent, spoke as follows.
    BROTHER,
    WE are glad of having an opportunity once more of meeting you in council. We thank the Great Spirit that has again brought us together. This is a full meeting. All our head men are present. Every village is represented in this council. We are pleased to find Mr. Parrish, our interpreter, is present. He has attended all our councils since the last war, and is well acquainted with all the treaties we have made with the United Sates.
    The voice of war has reached our ears, and made our minds gloomy. We now wish you to communicate to us every thing which your government has charged you to tell us concerning this war. We shall listen with attention to what you have to say.

Granger's speech announced that war had broken out between the United States and Britain over the impressment of over six thousand American sailors. He said that the president asked that the Six Nations take no part in the "quarrels" of white people and remain neutral, despite the request from Britain that they join them as allies. Although the president did not seek assistance from the Indians, Granger admitted that if a few of their young men really wished to go to war alongside the United States, possibly 150 or 200 might be allowed to join the army if they followed military discipline. He said he would wait until the next day for their answer.

RED JACKET'S ANSWER
TO
Mr. GRANGER'S SPEECH
Wednesday, July 8, 1812.

BROTHER,

WE are now prepared to give an answer to the speech you delivered to us in council the other day. We are happy to find so many of the *white* people present. We are not accustomed to transact important business in the DARK!. . . . we are willing that *the light* should shine upon whatever we do. When we speak, we do it with sincerity, and in a manner that cannot be misunderstood.

You have been appointed by the United States an Agent for the Six Nations. We have been requested to make you acquainted with the sentiments of those nations we represent. None of the Mohawks, Oneidas, or Cayugas, it is well known, are present. The number of treaties that have passed between the Six Nations and the United States, appears to be fresh in your memory. We shall only mention to you some things that were agreed upon in the treaty made at Canandaigua.

We were a long time in forming that treaty, but we at length made up our minds and spoke freely. Mr. PICKERING, who was then agent for the United States, declared to us that no breach should ever be made in that treaty. We replied to him, If it should ever be broken, you will be the first to do it. We are weak. . . . You are strong. You are a great people. You can, if you are so disposed, place yourselves under it and overturn it—or, by getting upon it, you can crush it with your weight! Mr. PICKERING again declared, that this treaty would ever remain firm and unshaken, that it would be as durable as the largest rock to be found in our country.

This treaty was afterwards shown to Gen. WASHINGTON. He said that he was satisfied and pleased with what the agent had done. He told us that no treaty could be formed that would be more binding. He then presented us with a chain which he assured us would never rust, but always remain bright. Upon this belt of wampum, (*holding up a belt of wampum, curiously wrought*) he placed a silver seal (upon which an eagle was engraved, representing the United States.) This belt we always have and always wish to look upon as sacred.

In the treaty, it was agreed that the Six Nations should receive a small annuity, to show the intention of the United States to continue friendly with them. This has been complied with. It was also agreed that, if any injury or damage should be done on either side, satisfaction should be made to the party injured. We were a long time in conference before we could make up our minds upon one article of the treaty—What punishment should be inflicted for the crime of murder? Mr. PICKERING said it should be *hanging*. We told him that would never do: that if a white man killed an Indian, the Indians would not be permitted to hang the white man. . . . the sacrifice would be considered too great for killing an Indian! We at length agreed, that conciliatory measures should be resorted to, such as would give satisfaction to all parties.

In cases of theft, as in stealing horses, cattle, &c. it was agreed that restitution should be made. In this article, the whites have transgressed twice, where the Indians have once. . . . As often as you will mention one instance in which we have wronged you, we will tell you of two in which you have defrauded us!

I have related these articles of the treaty to show you that it still remains clear in our recollection, and we now declare to you, in presence of all here assembled, that we will continue to hold fast the chain which connects us together. Some who first took hold of it, are gone! but others will supply their place.

We regret, extremely, that any disturbance should have taken place among the white people. Mischief has commenced. We are now told that war has been declared against Great Britain . . . the reasons for it are unknown to us. The Six Nations are placed in an unpleasant situation. A part of them are in Canada, and the remainder in the United States.

Whilst we were endeavoring to persuade those who live in Canada to remain peaceable and quiet, the noise of war suddenly sounded in our ears. We were told that all communication, between us and them would be prevented. We have since heard that they have taken up arms. We are very sorry to hear of this. They are our brothers and relations, and we do not wish that their blood should be spilt, when there is so little occasion for it. We hope that the passage is not so closely stopped, but that a small door may still be open by which we may again have an opportunity of seeing our brothers, and of convincing them to take no part in a war in which they have nothing to gain.

We know the feelings of the greater portion of them. We therefore believe, that if we have another opportunity, we can persuade them to have nothing to do with this war.—Our minds are fully made up on this subject, and we repeat, that it is our wish to see them once more, and to give them our advice about the path they ought to travel.

You (Mr. Parrish), are going to the eastward, you will visit the Oneidas and Cayugas—Relate to them faithfully what has taken place in this council; tell them all we have said, and request that a deputation of their chiefs may be sent to attend our council here. We wish that you would return with them.

(He then brought forward the belt which he had before held up in his hand, and requested Mr. Granger, and the others present, to look at it and observe whether it was not the one that had been presented to the Six Nations by Gen. Washington.

Red Jacket then held up another belt, much larger, of different colors, which appeared to be very ancient. He continued.)

Brother—I will now state to you the meaning of this belt. A long time ago the Six Nations had formed an union. They had no means of writing their treaties on paper, and of preserving them in the manner the white people do. We therefore made this belt, which shows, that the Six Nations have bound themselves firmly together; that it is their determination to remain united; that they will never do any thing, contrary to the interests of the whole; but that they will always act towards each other like brothers.

Whenever for the future, you see a small number of our people meeting together to consult about any matter of trifling account, we desire that you would pay no attention to it. It may give you uneasiness, when we have no intention to injure you. This happened but a few days ago: It seems that a white man and two or three Indians, living on the same creek, had a small conversation, which the mischievous talked about until the whole country was in an uproar, and many families left their country and homes in consequence!

The council held some time since at Batavia, was unauthorized by us, and we now declare to you, that none have a right to hold council any where except at this place, around the great council fire of the Six Nations.

We hope that you will not accept of any of our warriors, unless they are permitted by our great council to offer themselves to you. And we should be sorry indeed, if any of the whites should entice our young warriors to take up arms. We mention these things to show you that we wish to guard against everything that may interrupt our good understanding.

Brother—We hope that what has been said will be generally known to the white people. Let every one recollect and give a faithful account of it. We wish them to know that we are peaceably disposed towards the United States, and that we are determined to keep bright the chain of friendship that we formed with them at Canandaigua.

Brother—We have one thing more to which we would wish to call your attention. We present you the papers, (handing to the agent a small bundle of papers) which secure to us our annuities from the U. States. We would be glad to know if this war would affect our interests in that quarter. We also desire that you would inform us, whether the moneys we have deposited in the (late) bank of the United States, will be less secure, than if this war had not taken place. [Source: *Public Speeches* 1812, 5–31; Stone 1841, 224–34]

In his reply, Granger acknowledged their presentation of the belt of Canandaigua, and assured them that treaty would "hold fast," and the payment of their annuities would be unchanged by the war. He said that he thought little would come of sending more peace envoys to Grand River, and warned again of the dangers of assisting the British. After this exchange, several Buffalo Creek chiefs were permitted by British general Brock go to Grand River for a several-minute interview with the Six Nations there. They were unable to convince the British-allied Indians to stay neutral, but they were allowed to return to Buffalo Creek without harm.

On Taking Grand Isle

JULY 1812

UPON HEARING that the British had taken possession of Grand Isle, the Six Nations requested that they be allowed to join the war because their property was at stake. Shortly afterward, they formally declared war on the British (Stone 1841, 235). This text is taken from a Buffalo July 24 byline appearing in the *Otsego Republican*, a short-lived paper founded to circulate intelligence about the war.

Sagoyewatha to Granger:

BROTHER—

You have told us that we had nothing to do with the war that has taken place between you and the British: but we find that the war has come to our doors. Our property is taken possession of by the British and their Indian friends. It is necessary now for us to take up the business, defend our property, and drive the enemy from it. If we sit still upon our seats, and take no measures of redress, the British (according to the custom of you white people) will hold it by conquest—and should you conquer the Canadas, you will claim it upon the same principles, as conquered from the British. We, therefore, request permission to go with our warriors and drive off those bad people, and take possession of our lands. [Source: *Otsego Republican Press*, August 21, 1812; Stone 1841, 235–36]

Reply to Granger's Request for Troops

JULY 25, 1813

THE UNITED STATES was slow to ask the Six Nations for military assistance because they were not sure how the Indians would work in concert with American soldiers. Although General Peter B. Porter had not been officially asked by his superiors to recruit the Indians until September 1813, he began to do so in the summer (Fairbank n.d., 129–32; on the slow recruitment of Indians, see also Stone 1841, 238; Ketchum 1864–65, 2:428–29). On July 11, 1813, a group of Indian warriors and U.S. soldiers under the command of Porter skirmished with the British at Black Rock. Several principal Seneca chiefs also participated in an ambush on July 17 at Fort George, including Red Jacket (Stone 1841, 240–50). Upon Porter's request for aid at a council on July 25, 1813, Farmer's Brother notified Granger that each village would speak for its own volunteers. The texts are taken from Erastus Granger's papers. Jasper Parrish probably interpreted.

Red Jacket for the Senecas:

We are once more met in Council to give an answer to the Speeches made by you & Genl. Porter—It has taken time being of importance.—

We have heard your speeches—you wanted us to assist and watch to the edge of the water. We the Indians of Buffalo have agreed to what you requested.—You will now hear the decission of the old men.—

I speak for the Indians at Buffalo a part will be here for a time, others will then take thier places—we count the whole at Buffalo Village. We count all Who are to be on their guard.—We can not designate Numbers—Those who live in the Village will be on the ground on an allarm. The pay will be distributed among the whole, and be regulated by the number employed we the old men who have seen war will from time to time instruct, and regulate the young warriors.—We the chiefs of Buffalo turn out 162 Warriors to be under arms

This is all we have to say. the next who speak, are the Catturagus.—

Other chiefs, including Captain Shongo, Sharp Shins, and John Sky, volunteered thirty-nine men total. Cornplanter told the agent their warriors should be paid well, and not supplied with alcohol. See Snyder (1978) for complete text. Red Jacket then spoke:

You are now writing what has taken place this day.—the part we take in this war is not voluntary on our part[.] you have persuaded us into it—we hope you will say so to the President.—

You must not be displeased with what we say—Your voice was for us to sit still when the war begun, but you have beat us, you have got us into the War.—

If any of our friends the Six Nations, except the Mowhawks, should fall into your hands we hope you will treat them well—deliver them up to us—we will do the same by white persons we take—write to the Commander in chief, and let him know this [Source: Erastus Granger Papers, folder 14-25; *IIDH*, reel 45; Ketchum 1864–65, 2:429–31 (regularized spelling and clarifying phrases); Snyder 1978, 65–67 (regularized spelling and punctuation)]

To Granger on Payments to Seneca Warriors

OCTOBER 21, 1813

ALTHOUGH THE SIX NATIONS had formally declared war on the British in the summer of 1813, they were concerned that they were not getting proper treatment as soldiers. On October 21, 1813, Sagoyewatha addressed their complaints to Erastus Granger. Jasper Parrish likely interpreted.

Red Jacket spoke &—

Porter & my self said they [the Indian soldiers] should have pay for one month for guarding the lines[.] Genl. Wilkinson promised them pay for services.—Genl. W[ilkinson] went away but told them that Genl. McClure would fulfil.—we have not rec[eive]$^{d.}$ pay according to promise—we think you were not authorized to promise us—we think we are trifled with.—

We were promised that all horses & Cattle we should be free plunder[.] we took horses we had to give them up. We have been deceived.—

We the Senecas & Onondagas gave up the property we took—the Oneidas whom you have educated and taught your habits gave up nothing—We want you to state this to the President[.] we want permission to go to Washington[.] we are an Independent Nation—We have taken up arms in your favor—We want to know on what footing we stand.—We know not how long the war will last.—

It was agreed by all at fort George that we should send. we want a small deputation from the friendly Ind[ia].^{ns} at the Westward to meet us at Washington.—

Let us unite and in one season more we will drive the Red Coat from this Island—they are foreigners.—this Country belongs to us and the U States—

We do not fight for conquest, but we fight for our rights. for the land on Grand River.—

We hope our request will be Granted.

We trust you will make known our request to the P_t [President], we trust you will no deceive us.— [Source: Erastus Granger Papers, folder 14-25; *IIDH* reel 45; Ketchum 1864–65, 2:433–34 (with an additional introductory paragraph, and a patriotic addition at the end: "fight for our rights, for our country"); Snyder 1978, 71–72 (regularized spelling and punctuation)]

Farewell to Col. William Snelling

CA. 1815

THESE ARE SAGOYEWATHA'S PARTING WORDS to Col. William J. Snelling, with whom he served during the War of 1812, first published in 1833 in Snelling's paper, the *New England Galaxy*.

Brother: I hear you are going to a place called Governor's island. I hope you will be a governor yourself. I understand that you white people think children a blessing. I hope you may have a thousand. And above all, I hope, wherever you go, you may never find whiskey above two shillings a quart. [Source: *New England Galaxy*, July 13, 1833; also in Stone 1841, 280]

Peace Council at Niagara

SEPTEMBER 1, 1815

FOLLOWING AN AGREEMENT at a British-Indian council held at Burlington on April 24–27, 1815, the British convened a council to heal the differences between the Grand River Indians, who fought with the British, and the
Six Nations who fought on the side of the United States. Apparently held at
Fort George (the records say Niagara), the large council opened on August 31,
attended by both Grand River chiefs and New York Haudenosaunees. British
attendees included Lieutenant Colonel Robertson, commanding officer at
Fort George, and Deputy Superintendent of Indian Affairs William Claus, as
well as men of the garrison and surrounding towns. The interpreter is not
known, but transcripts are from William Claus's official correspondence.

Henry Tekarihoga, one of the leading chiefs at Grand River, welcomed
the Six Nations living in the United States to the council fire. He said, "We
are the same people with you, we are relations and of the same colour notwithstanding our having opposed each other in the Field during the late difference
between our Great Father the King of England and the Americans." He declared that the river was now open, and all obstructions removed that people
might pass freely in friendly intercourse once again. Echo, an Onondaga chief,
affirmed his words and "put the Tomahawk the depth of a pine tree under
ground." Old Eel, an Onondaga chief, concluded the ceremonies of the day by
thanking Claus for the opportunity to come together as one.

The following day, September 1, Tekarihoga asked to hear the New York
Indians' reply and Sagoyewatha responded:

Brothers In the name of the Indians from the other side of the River, I now
address myself to the King, the Commanding Officer and Colonel Claus our
head, and to the Six Nations, Wyandots and Shawanoes

Strings of Wampum

Brothers I am happy now to meet you in the usual friendly manner, and
you may be assured that what has happened was not from any animosity to-

wards our ancient Father and Friends—We are a poor people—We cannot do as we would—We are as Prisoners,—but the fetters are now off, and we are at liberty to communicate with our friends freely—We are not only of the same Nations but of the same families also—We therefore ought to be united and become one body.

Strings of Wampum.

Brothers You have informed us that the Kings Council Fire is again uncovered—We are also informed that the United States have done the same.— We seriously recommend that your people will now attend to your usual occupations of Hunting and agriculture, and that you pay due attention, to your women, who by our ancient customs have a voice in bringing up our Young people to the [practice?] of Truth and industry.

Strings of Wampum.

Brothers We have now to communicate to you a message which we received [from] the Delawares at the White River,[1] who say that they have fine Lands, and Game of every kind in great abundance—This message is directed to all the Six Nations, and we wish you to consider it.—

/2/ Strings of Wampum.[2]

Brothers The Road is now open, and we will be glad to have a visit from you at Buffaloe Creek.—Eating and drinking together may as well be omitted at present, our time being very short—rising and Shaking hands will do as well

Strings of Wampum.

They then mixed with each other, and Spoke to the Deputy Superintendent General as follows

Tekarihoga, Speaker,

Brother You have witnessed our proceedings, which it has pleased the Ruler of the World to assist us in—It has finished as we would wish, and we desire that you will immediately acquaint our Western Bretheren of the work we have been doing, and that we shall soon proceed to the west to meet them and perform the same Ceremony there, as was agreed upon last Spring in Council.[3] We now speak to you in One body, and we hope that we will be allowed to travel along the Road peacably and without being insulted by the Inhabitants—We request Provisions to enable us to Travel homewards.

1. Marginal note: "on the Waubash."
2. A second marginal note, referring to the "/2/" states, "2, returned by Tekarihoga saying that they did not understand the message."
3. Council at Burlington, April 24–27.

[Source: William Claus Papers, vol. 40 (MG 19, F1), microfilm reel C-1480, CNA]

Afterward, Claus expressed his satisfaction at the council, granted travel provisions, and warned Tekarihoga that it was the behavior of their young men that provoked the insults they had experienced (presumably, on their way from Grand River to the council). He said if they behaved peaceably, there should be no more insults.

Protesting Delayed Annuities

NOVEMBER 27, 1815

AT A COUNCIL with Erastus Granger at Buffalo Creek on November 27, 1815, the Six Nations proposed two items for discussion. The first issue was a delay in the annuity payments caused by the war. They had not been paid since 1814 and the Six Nations wanted Granger to go to Washington and get their money. The second item was an inquiry about whether they could petition Congress to grant them a tract of land in the west. Granger's response to the land question does not appear (see next entry for the Council at Sandusky). The translator is not stated, but it is probably Jasper Parrish.

Red Jacket addresses Granger:

Brother,

You must rise from you seat and go to the Council fire of your nation.— We have a message to send to our Great Father the president, and to the great War Chief of the United States.—

Brother,

You say if you go, we Must not lay too heavy a burden on you.—We have concluded to send our friend & interpreter Capt. [Horatio] Jones to help carry the pack.

We trust the United States will furnish you with provisions to go and return.—We are poor and cannot do it.—

Brother,

We were told that we ought to rise from our Seats, and take a part in the late War.—the quarrel was between White people.—We were determined to keep bright the Chain of Friendship.—When there was danger, our Warriors were by the side of yours.—Not one of our people joined the British.

Your Government made us promises.—as yet they have not been complied with.—You must speak bold.—

Our annuities, agreeable to the treaty, have not been paid punctually.—

The Tuscaroras were given to understand that compensation should be made for their losses.—

the Senecas sold a part of thier Country, and the Money was put into a bank.—the Bank is gone.—their Money formerly produced them from seven to eight Thousand Dollars—they will want next year, about the time of corn planting, two years' Interest.

the Senecas have been plundered by your Warriors.—they have stated their losses—you Must take on the account and present it.

The Onondagas, & Cayugas receive their annuities punctually from the State of New York.—The Senecas want their Father the President to plant their money in some bank in New York.— [Source: Erastus Granger Papers, folder 14-32; Snyder 1978, 82–83 (with regularized spelling and punctuation)]

To the Western Nations at Upper Sandusky on Land Sales and Indian Government

November 7, 1816

AS EARLY AS 1810, the Six Nations began to consider obtaining some of the western U.S. lands acquired in the Louisiana Purchase to insulate themselves from white encroachment (Hauptman 1999, 101–42; Houghton 1920, 163; O'Reilly 1838, 105–38). As Red Jacket notes in speeches on September 1, 1815, and January 4, 1818, the Indiana Delawares offered the Six Nations land prior to the War of 1812. After the war, the Six Nations decided to pursue the Delawares' offer and see if they could procure additional land in the west for their dependents. On November 27, 1815, they asked Erastus Granger if the government would be willing to grant them lands in the west. In August 1816, Sagoyewatha requested funding from the $500 Phelps-Gorham annuity to fund a trip to a pan-Indian council that the Six Nations had called for the rapids of the upper Sandusky (Fairbank n.d., 160–61; Granger to Parrish, August 29, 1816; Stone 1841, 283; map 1).

The Ogden Land Company was also a strong supporter of the Sandusky mission, paying George Hosmer (1781–1861), a Canandaigua lawyer greatly trusted by the Indians, and Jasper Parrish to accompany them on the delegation. Upon their return, Hosmer gave Robert Troup, an Ogden Company partner, a file of the speeches from the trip, but they do not presently exist in the Ogden Company papers. Hosmer was still alive when William Leete Stone wrote his biography and gave Stone his own copies of the speeches. The phrasing of Troup's correspondence suggests that he was looking at copies of the same speeches that Stone later published (Robert Troup to David Ogden, December 7, 1816, Ogden Papers). In his notes to the speech, Stone remarks that Red Jacket's "course of thinking and language" had begun to show traces of Euro-American assimilation. Hosmer may be responsible for embellishment although he claimed to have written it down as Parrish translated it.

Sagoyewatha speaks:

"BROTHERS OF THE COUNCIL,—LISTEN! You must recollect that a few years since some delegates from your elder brethren, the Six Nations, came to you. That council fire was kindled at Brownstown, by the mutual consent of the Six Nations; but we then requested that all important business should thereafter be transacted at this place. A few years after this, another delegation came to this council fire from your elder brethren, the Six Nations. We then thought appearances looked squally. We thought the United States and Great Britain were looking with jealous eyes at each other. It appeared to us a tremendous and destructive storm was approaching, bearing blood and carnage upon its wings. We then told you that if we were not on our guard we should feel that storm. We also told you that it was the policy of the red coats [1] to request at such times the aid of the Indians. We admonished you to take warning from the past, and told you to recollect that calamities which have befallen our nations in the wars of the pale faces. We then therefore solemnly requested you would be neutral in that contest. We advised you not to listen to their requests, but to sit still on your seats.

"At length the tremendous storm burst, and first in this quarter you were disturbed by the Virginians. Others of our brothers who listened to the voice from the other side of the water, and some of your warriors, united with the Virginians. Those warriors you took without consulting your elder brethren, the Six Nations. The consequence was, your whole land, and the place of your council fire, was smeared with blood. Our ancient records were dispersed, and many were wholly lost. Thus are we situated. There is now a delegation present from the Indians at large. A great council fire is kindled, whose smoke shall ascend to the heavens; and we now appoint this the place for kindling a great council fire, where all important business shall be transacted. In token we give you a large belt of wampum, brown and white, intermixed with strings.

"BROTHERS:—When we received your message to attend at this time and place, you requested a full representation should arise from their seats, for the purpose of making some general arrangement for the benefit of the Indians. We have attended agreeably to your request,—and shall now make some communications to remind you of former transactions. Whenever the two white nations are about falling into difficulties, we discover different languages are held out by the British that we must adhere to them, and when the storm is near by, they will present you with a sharp iron. This has always been the course of the red-coats.

1. Stone's note: "The English."

"BROTHERS:—You must be sensible that this continent was the gift of the Great Spirit. But in consequence of the wars that have taken place, we have been the perpetual sufferers. In all wars within my memory, we have lost territory by taking up the hatchet. The British have sold our country to buy peace. By the experience of the past let us learn wisdom, and close our ears to British counsel. War may again happen; and when it does you will be invited to mate with the British. If we continue to listen to their counsel, we shall soon be exterminated. Let us guard against this by forming a permanent union which shall protect us in future. To decoy you into their measures, the British allure you with many fanciful trinkets. But these are trifles when compared with our general and individual happiness. We now earnestly request you will exert yourselves to extend the sound of our voices to our brethren who are absent from this council.

"WARRIORS, LISTEN!—You recollect that we have now established at this place a council fire, to be under the care of the Wyandots. I request you to submit to the direction of the sachems, and not through pride to attempt to control them. It is planted in the centre of your country. Do not be flattered away by any white people who may wish to purchase your land. To command respect you must possess extensive territory. Keep your seats sufficiently large that you may not be crowded on any side by the whites. And do not ever attempt to transact any business except at this place, and then in the presence of the sachems. I hope that you will aid and assist the sachems in bringing back from the other side of the water [2] those of our brothers who have gone astray to the British. Take them by the hand in friendship, and forget their errors. They will add to your strength.

"MY YOUNGER BRETHREN OF THE SHAWANESE:—I now address myself to you. When we were created by the Great Spirit, we were all of one color. But it was his pleasure that we should speak different languages, and be placed in different countries. You must be sensible that you are foreigners. A number of years since you came to this country, and were taken under the protection of our brethren the Wyandots, who gave you a pleasant seat, where you enjoyed a delightful country, and shared in common with them the game of the forest. These proceedings came to the knowledge of the Six Nations. You had not resided here long before you became uneasy, and you have been first to produce disturbances, and been forward to effect the sale of lands which did not belong to your nation. You have been the authors of other difficulties between the red and white people. You have been forward in the late

2. Stone's note: "The Great Lakes."

difficulties, by listening to the voice from across the waters.[3] Where is now your head sachem? Where a part of your people? They lent an ear to the red-coats, and are now in exile beyond the waters. We admonish you to recall them,—unite them with their brethren,—form a band of union with the Wyandots. Settled on the seats of the Wyandots, your friends, listen to their counsel. It will be good. Listen also to the counsels of the Six Nations, your elder brethren. Do not attempt to transact important business, involving the rights of others, unless at the great council fire, and with the approbation of the Wyandots.

"SACHEMS OF THE MUNSEE AND DELAWARE INDIANS:—You are sensible that you are not the original proprietors of the country you now enjoy. You came from the east. We know the country you came from. You wasted away your inheritance and became wanderers. We gave you a seat on [the] White River,[4] where is plenty of game and pure water. And nothwith-standing this, your nation is dispersed. Some of your people have taken up the hatchet, united with the red-coats, and are now across the water. We request you will collect yourselves in one body, and settle yourselves on your lands at White River. Do this, and we will then unite ourselves together under one confederacy. We shall then have strength and be respected as well by the whites as by the more western nations."

(The speaker next proceeded to address the dispersed members of the Six Nations, residing on the lands of the Wyandots, admonishing them as he had admonished others, and counselling them to act in union and harmony, and to follow the advice of the Wyandots. He then addressed himself to Mr. Parish, and another officer in the Indian department, named Johnston:[5]—)

"BROTHERS:—We are happy to meet you both at our council. We of the Six Nations transact all our business openly, and not under the curtain. I have observed with what attention you have listened to me. I hope you will be will-ing to unite with us in bringing back our friends from beyond the water, and making us one band. Then we shall become one great family of children, under our great Father, the President. We ask your assistance. Let the commu-nication with the other side of the water be opened, and then we shall be able to bring back our friends from across the water. Our great Father we hope will not forget his red children; and as he now possesses much of our finest land, we

3. That is, Tecumseh and the British.
4. A tributary of the Wabash River in Indiana.
5. Col. John Johnson, a U.S. Indian agent greatly admired by the Ohio Indians. He was a close friend of Little Turtle.

hope he will be more liberal of presents than he has been. You must now be sensible that we are well pleased with presents. You may know this by the influence of British presents. They have won to the British cause many brave warriors. I hope that you will take much pains, now that we are at peace, in uniting all. Treat us well. We in common with you possess this soil. We have frequently heard your voice, when it was for our interest and happiness to listen to it. It would conduce much to our happiness to listen to the voice of the United States, and not be poisoned by the language of the red-coats. To make us happy do not crowd our seats. When you purchase lands still leave us some to move upon. This you will make known to our Father the President, and solicit his aid in opening our passage across the water to our friends.

"BROTHERS OF THE DELAWARES:—We received a message f[r]om you a number of years since, offering us a seat of land in your country. You said you had not forgot the favors heretofore received from the Six Nations, who took you under their care, until at length you travelled west to the country of White River. As you say you have not forgot past favors, are you now willing to offer the Six Nations, or any part of them, a seat in your country? This invitation has been often repeated. We now come forward to accept the offer. We request you will designate its extent, situation and boundary. We have applied to our Father the President for leave to move into that country, and to be assured that he will confirm your grant. We find it is necessary by his answer, that when you shall make such a grant, it must be done on paper, so that such conveyance may be confirmed. We should be unwilling to leave our present seats without a secure and permanent grant, securing a seat for us, our children, and children's children to the remotest generation. We request that if you are not authorized of yourselves to make such location, you will communicate our wishes to the neighboring nations, proprietors of the land, that they may make such location. This seat we shall expect to receive not as our exclusive property, but to be held in common for the benefit, as well of such of the Six Nations who may wish to settle upon it, as of any other Indians who may choose to take their seats there with us." [Source: Stone 1841, 284–93]

In the remainder of the council record, which is reprinted in Stone (1841, 290–93), Tear-unk-to-yor-on ("Between-the-Logs," Wyandot) and Cutte-we-ga-saw ("Black Hoof," Shawnee) both replied, acknowledging Red Jacket's speech. They said they would do their best to unite the dispersed Indians. Black Hoof admitted they had gone astray by following the Prophet, but the Prophet's power was now broken. He advised the Six Nations to look after themselves, noting that they too had become fragmented. He also accused them of being the first to sell their lands. He added that the Delawares on the White River were only permitted to live and hunt there. They were not the proper owners of the land they offered to the Senecas, but they had been there so long that they pretended to own the land. The council records then end without the Senecas' reply.

To the President and Secretary of War, Refusal to Move and Request for an Agent

JANUARY 4, 1818

THE FOLLOWING PETITION to the president was drafted during a council of December 29 and 30, 1817, at Buffalo Creek to protest the lack of a federal superintendent for the Six Nations. Erastus Granger retired without replacement in 1818 because of a new federal law that provided no agent to the Six Nations (Calhoun 1969–74, 2:286). Jasper Parrish continued to do the superintendent's work, but he was technically a subagent.

The original manuscript copy sent to the president, and signed by Red Jacket and Cornplanter, no longer exists in the letters received by War Department. This version was published about ten months later in the *Niagara Patriot* at the behest of Rev. Jabez Hyde, the schoolteacher at Buffalo Creek. Hyde's publication of the speech was motivated by his feeling that the Six Nations were being unfairly bullied by an Ogden-sponsored push to move them to Arkansas in early 1818 (Calhoun 1969–74, 2:286, 293, 368). Following a September 1818 Six Nations' council declaring their desire not to move to Arkansas, Hyde published four columns in the Buffalo newspaper to advertise the dishonesty of the land company's conduct (*Niagara Patriot*, October 13, 20, 27, and November 3, 1818. See also Calhoun 1969–74, 3:188, 255). The Six Nations did not get a response to the petition until June 1818, when Parrish met them in council to distribute the annuities. According to Hyde's account, Parrish held up a copy of the speech with two large black seals and said the president was very unhappy they had not written to him through their subagent (that is, Parrish). Parrish told them that the president had ordered it sent back to them and buried because they had sent it through improper channels and because the president did not know if it represented the united voice of the Six Nations. In his letter publicizing the affair, Hyde said the subagent's claims were patently false because Red Jacket and Cornplanter were both known to be leading chiefs of the nation (*Niagara Patriot*, October 27, 1818).

The interpreter of the speech is not known, but the biblical references, such as "sepulchres of the fathers," are similar to the petition of February 14, 1818, translated by Harry York.

Hyde's preface reads as follows:

The responsibility of publishing this document and other facts that I may communicate in relation to these Indians, I take on myself; the Indians have not been consulted, and are wholly ignorant of my purpose. I trust a sense of imperious duty moves me to bring before the public, a poor, miserable people, who have no helper; ready to perish.

Yours, &c.

JABEZ B. HYDE.

SENECA INDIANS.

NO. 1.

Extract of a talk of the Six Nations, to the President of the United States, sent by mail January 4, 1818, to the Secretary of War, for him to communicate to the President.

TO THE SECRETARY OF WAR,

Brother:

It is the desire of the Six Nations assembled at their great Council Fire, in their village near Buffalo, that you would please to lay the following Talk before our Father, the President of the United States:

Father:

From the fatherly care the Presidents of the United States have exercised towards their Red Children, we speak to our father in confidence, believing he will not turn away his ears from his Red Children. Having no agent through whom we might speak, we are persuaded that our father will not be displeased that we speak directly to him, as it were, face to face.

Father:

We need not tell you that we are a poor, ignorant people; unacquainted with the great affairs and wise management of our enlightened white brothers. We are distressed & alarmed—we have no where to look but to our father, whom we trust will bear with his children, should their fears appear to him to be groundless.

Father:

We are alarmed lest we lose our seats. Those men that say they have a right to purchase our lands, have been distressing us for a number of years with their plans to possess our lands; offering us in exchange lands to the westward. We decidedly told them we did not wish to part with our lands, desiring they would be at no more expense in visiting us on this errand, if we should alter our minds we would send them word. Some months after, a deputation of our brothers to the west visited us, offering us a large tract of their land a free gift, if we would accept it. We thanked our brothers for their generous offer, and promised at some future time, to send men to view the land. The war took place the next year—nothing more was done or heard of by us of this land, until the spring after the peace, when our brothers again visited us, making the same offer. It never entered into our hearts of leaving our present seats and going to the westward ourselves; but as there were many of the Six Nations in the Western Country who had no seat to set on, but what was liable to be sold from under them any day the owners chose, we rose up to consider the offer of our brothers, that we might provide for our scattered children. Through the assistance of our brothers Jones and Parrish and another great friend, who advised and assisted us,[1] we laid our circumstances and views before our father, the President of the United States, acquainting him with our offer—that with his approbation we would accept this land, provided the U. States would make it sure to us. Our father, the President, was pleased to certify his approbation, and that the land should be made sure to us agreeable to our request. On receiving this information from our father, the President, we sent on 8 men to view the land and take its dimensions.—Our brother, Capt. Parrish, went with them to do the writing, that it might be made sure to us, according to the word of our father, the President. *Our men found no land.* Col. Ogden (who is said to hold the right of purchasing our land) recommended us to send to Detroit, and Gov. Cass would put us in a way to find our land. We sent six men to Detroit, Gov. Cass informed our men that in September there would be a large Council of Indians of different nations meet at Fort Meigs; the Six Nations would do well to have a deputation there, they would then doubtless find their land. We send 12 men to Fort Meigs; instead of our western brothers having lands to give the Six Nations, they sold the seats from under those that were among them.

Father:

We are distressed. Capt Parrish has informed us that we could now exchange our lands for lands to the westward; he advised us to do it, or we should certainly lose them; for it was the determination of the government of the U. States, that the Indians should leave their present seats; those that did not exchange them would lose them.

1. Probably referring to Col. John Johnson or George Hosmer.

Father:

We are astonished and amazed! Our old friend, Col. Ogden, has altered his address to us; he has for years talked to us as a man that wished to purchase our lands, if we were pleased to sell: He now writes to us how we shall conduct [ourselves] on his lands which we occupy.

Father:

To whom shall we go, but unto you? We doubt not but many of our white brothers fear God, and ought to be trusted, but how shall we find them?

Father:

We fear that we have been deceived, & your predecessor imposed on. Strange things have come to our ears—that our message to your predecessor which we signed, was very different from what was read to us—that it said we were desirous of leaving our seats here and going to the west—provided we obtained lands to the westward, we relinquished our reservations here. If any thing like this was in our message we were basely deceived—We had but these objects in view, to inform our father, the President, of this offer of our western brothers; the opportunity that it offered for providing for our scattered children—to obtain his approbation and assurance that the land should be confirmed to us by the United States; any thing more, except providing provisions for our men while transacting business, was as base an imposition as ever was practiced.

Father:

We declare to you, we desire you to publish to all our white brothers, that it is our fixed and determined purpose to live and die on our present seats. It is sealed to us by the bones of our fathers. They obtained it by their blood. Our bones shall be beside theirs. It is the heritage of the Almighty. He gave it us. He it is must take it from us.

Father:

We mean no threat by this. We know we are in the hands of our white brothers, they can destroy us with ease. But they need not think to persuade us to part with our lands. As free men, we claim the right to choose between being killed outright, or a lingering execution, by being driven a thousand miles into the wilderness. Where, father, where would our white brothers have us go? The Indian claim to land is put out for more than a thousand miles to the west, except little plots for particular nations.

Father:

We have confidence in you; you cannot see your red children with their little ones driven off their land by stealth and fraud, leaving the sepulchres of their fathers, their farms, their farming tools and cattle, dying by families on the road, thro' hardship and privation. Exchanging all their advances to civilization, and all its comforts, for the hardships of the chase, without house or friend.

Father:

We have confidence in you; that if you see any device formed against us, you will frustrate it, and succor your red children. We have deceived no man: we have wronged no man. Our language has been one; we choose not to part with our land. If we have been needlessly alarmed, you will pity our ignorance, and forgive our childish fears.

Father:

We have many things to say. The character of our agent is of great importance to us. If any come to you for the office, having our request to recommend them, we wish to withdraw that request. We see so little into white men, that we feel incapable of choosing for ourselves.—We desire our father to choose a man that he can trust, and we will confide in him.

Father:

We trust that you will pardon the multitude of our words, and let none deceive you, that this is the voice of a few individuals, and not the voice of the Six Nations. It is the united voice of the Six Nations in the state of New York. The Chiefs of Buffalo, Cattaraugus, Genessee and Onondaga are now in council; we have the message of Allegany and Oneida with us, desiring we should speak to our father, the President, entreating him to consider and help us.

Our Father:

Will not be deceived; our words will find his heart. He will receive them.—They are the words of truth and soberness. We ask nothing but wherein we have been mistaken, we may be better informed—wherein we may have been wronged, we may be righted—wherein we may be in danger we may be protected, and that our white brothers may know our fixed purpose of living and dying on our present seats.

Father:

You will pity us; you will forgive us; your wisdom and goodness will succor us. Speak, father, speak to your children, that their minds may be at rest. Speak to their Council Fire at this place. Let us hear your own words; send them by safe hands; for we fear liers in wait are watching to devour your words, that they may not reach us.

May the Great Spirit preserve you many years a blessing to all your children. [Source: *Niagara Patriot*, October 13, 1818; reprinted in the *Cherry Valley Gazette*, November 19, 1818]

Petition for Protection to Governor Clinton

FEBRUARY 14, 1818

THE FOLLOWING SPEECH is the Senecas' response to the governor's yearly address to the legislature of January 27. In his paragraph-long summary of the state of Indian affairs in New York, Clinton said that it was likely that the Indians would "entirely disappear" within a half century if they continued to decline at their present rate. He felt it was in the Indians' best interest to remove to the west but only if they chose to go there voluntarily. He said that he was aware that they had been frequently injured and defrauded by their white neighbors, and he called for vigorous enforcement of the law to protect them (Lincoln 1909, 2:915–16).

This is one of the few speeches of the following decade where Red Jacket and his Christian peers signed a joint petition to the government. The interpreter was "Harry" York.[1]

To his Excellency De Witt Clinton, Esq. Governor of the State of New-York.
February 14th, 1818.
FATHER,
We learn from your talk delivered at the great council fire in Albany, your opinion of the condition and prospects of your red children.
FATHER,
We feel that the hand of our God has long been heavy on his red children. For our sins he has brought us low, and caused us to melt away before our white brothers, as snow before the fire. His ways are perfect; he regardeth not the complexion of man. God is terrible in judgement.—All men ought to fear before him. He putteth down and buildeth up and none can resist him.
FATHER,
The Lord of the whole earth is strong; this is our confidence. He hath power to build up as well as pull down. Will he keep his anger forever? Will he pursue

1. The name probably refers to Henry York. Snyderman reports he was frequently an interpreter employed at Cattaraugus, about whom little is known (Jackson 1957, 584).

to destruction the workmanship of his own hand, and strike off a race of men from the earth, whom his care hath so long preserved through so many perils?

FATHER,

We thank you that you fell [feel] anxious to do all you can to the perishing ruins of your red children. We hope, father, you will make a fence strong and high around us, that wicked white men may not devour us at once, but let us live as long as we can. We are persuaded you will do this for us, because our field is laid waste and trodden down by every beast; we are feeble and cannot resist them.

FATHER,

We are persuaded you will do this for the sake of our white brothers, lest God who has appeared so strong in building up white men, and pulling down Indians, should turn his hand and visit our white brothers for their sins, and call them to an account for all the wrongs they have done them, and all the wrongs they have not prevented that was in their power to prevent, to their poor red brothers who have no helper.

FATHER,

Would you be the father of your people, and make them good and blessed of God, and happy, let not the cries of your injured red children ascend into his ears against you.

FATHER,

We desire to let you know that wrong information hath reached your ears. Our western brothers have given us no land. You will learn all our mind on this subject, by a talk which we sent to our great Father, the President of the United States. We send it to you, that you may see it and learn our mind.

> [All names followed by "X his mark"] Red Jacket, Young King, Captain Billey [*sic*], Captain Pollard, Twenty Canoes, James Stephenson, Chief Warrior, Stride Town [Destroy Town], Wheel Barrow, Captain Cole, Big Kettle.

Done at the great council fire, Seneca Village, near Buffalo, 14th Feb. 1818.

HARRY YORK, *Interpreter*, his X mark

P.S. The above Chiefs request your Excellency to publish, or cause to be published, that article of the treaty between the state of New York and the Indians, that relates to their fishing and hunting privileges, which their white brethren seem to have forgotten. [Source:*Buffalo Gazette*, March 24, 1818; *Ontario Repository*, March 24, 1818; Lincoln 1909, 2:941–43]

Reply to David Ogden at Buffalo Creek

JULY 7–9, 1819

IN THE SUMMER OF 1819, the Ogden Company sought to convince the Buffalo Creek and Tonawanda Senecas to move south to the Allegany reservation on the New York–Pennsylvania border. They secured Judge Morris S. Miller as U.S. commissioner and Nathaniel Gorham Jr. as commissioner from Massachusetts to oversee the council (since the Hartford agreement of 1785, Massachusetts sent agents to oversee councils concerning their former holdings). Major Joseph Delafield, an agent working for the United States on the adjustment of international boundaries following the Treaty of Ghent, agreed to serve as Miller's secretary (Stone 1841, 295). Jasper Parrish and Horatio Jones were council interpreters; Parrish was the interpreter for Red Jacket's July 9 speech.

According to Delafield's journal, Miller and his deputation arrived at Buffalo Creek on July 1, but the Indians remained in council among themselves for several days more. Finally, on the afternoon of July 5, they met in council at Pollard's village, about five or six miles from Buffalo. It was heralded to be a very important council: a large party of "ladies" and spectators from Buffalo were in attendance with influential men such as Peter Porter and Judge John Greig (Delafield 1943, 230).

Miller convened the council on July 5 and explained that the president thought it was a good idea that the Indians consolidate at the Allegany reservation. Two days later, David Ogden gave a long speech rehearsing the history of preemption sales, and he complained that the Indians were frequently violating his rights. In his summary report to Secretary Calhoun, Miller said that he realized after Ogden's speech that the Indians did not want to consolidate at Allegany. The following day, July 8, Miller and Ogden revised their previous statements, saying that the consolidation plan could include the Allegany reservation and part of Cattaraugus as well. Ogden offered in the neighborhood of a $4,000 annuity for the removal plan, and he said he was willing to compromise more ("Letters Received by the Secretary of War Relating to Indian Affairs, 1800–1823," M-271, reel 2, frame 1460, DNA).

On July 9, in a speech that spectators said took about an hour, Sagoyewatha gave the reply of the chiefs. They rejected the Ogden proposal and demanded also that the preacher and the schoolmaster withdraw from the Seneca reservations. In a note to William Leete Stone, Secretary Delafield claimed that Jasper Parrish said it was difficult to keep up with Red Jacket's metaphors, but Delafield tried to copy everything Red Jacket said as literally as the interpreter spoke them (1943, 306–7). Internal evidence suggests this speech was interpreted paragraph by paragraph, or a few sentences at a time (after setting up a joke, Sagoyewatha responds to the audience's reaction, saying "some here laugh").

The transcripts below comprise a documentary history of federal records augmented by the journal accounts of Joseph Delafield.

July 3, 1819. From Delafield's journal:

Capt. Parish, the interpreter, dines with us & relates some good anecdotes of Red Jacket the Buffalo Chief. When holding a Treaty with Col. Timothy Pickering who was a favorite Com[ission]r. with Gen'l Washington, an obstinate debate ensued between him & Red Jacket, which lasted two days, without coming to any conviction. The Chief, uneasy and tired of debate says, "Had I but your language, Col. Pickering, or had you my language, so that we might meet on even ground, I would wind you around my finger in a moment!" [Source: Delafield 1943, 230–31]

On July 5, the council opened. Captain Pollard welcomed the commissioners. Afterwards, Judge Miller spoke. The text of his speech is from the National Archives.

Sachems, Chiefs, Warriors of the Seneca Nation,
Red and White Brothers assembled around this Council Fire,
By the Commission which has just been read to you, you will perceive that your great Father the President, has sent me here, to represent the United States, at this Council fire.

Brothers, I am instructed to declare in the name of your great Father, to all who are now sitting around this Council fire, his mind and his wishes, on matters of great importance to you all. I am not in any way instructed, pledged, or interested to promote the views of the white men, where these views are prejudicial to the rights of the red men; nor to promote the views of the red men, where they are prejudicial to the rights of the white men. The President of the United States is the common Father of both. He sends me to you with directions to explain his views; to speak his mind to both his red and white children; and to see that all proceedings here are just and fair.

Brothers, Listen to the words of your great Father. Listen to them attentively, and let them sink deep into your hearts; and may the Great Spirit who made and regards both red and white men, preside over your deliberations, and cause this Council to be productive of great good to both.

Brothers, After the unnatural war, which the King of England made on some of his white children on this side of the great water in the year 1776— and after the great Spirit had given Victory to the people of the United States, they and the red people of the Seneca nation again became Brothers, under their great Father, the President, who looks with an equal eye on all his children, whilst they remain under his care, and follow his advice.

Sachems, Chiefs, Warriors, of the Seneca Nation

Brothers Your great Father has cast his paternal eye over your nation. He sees you scattered here and there, in small parcels, every where surrounded by white people. He sees that you are fast losing your national character; and are daily more and more exposed to the bad examples of your white Brothers; without the restraint of their laws or religion. He sees that this frequent and uncontrolled intercourse, instead of doing good is doing injury to you and to them. Your Great Father sees all these things with grief and concern. He lays them much to heart; and thinks it impossible for you, under such circumstances, to retain the character of an independent nation.

Brothers, Your great Father has also understood that his white children in your neighborhood are dissatisfied at seeing the lands in your occupation remain wild and uncultivated; neither paying taxes, nor assisting to make roads and other improvements; nor in any way contributing to the public burthens as white peoples' lands do. Your great Father has been further informed, that you occupy more land than you can advantageously till, or use for any valuable purpose; whilst at the same time the scarcity of game prevents your engaging in those pursuits, to which your Fathers were accustomed.

Brothers, It is the wish of your great Father, that your scattered tribes should be brought more together. You are now weak and insecure. Should you contract your limits and come nearer together, it would add to your strength and security. So collected, the watchful eye of your great Father can embrace each of your settlements in one view. As white people shall become more strong, and you more weak, his powerful arm can then more effectually protect you. Then he can more conveniently administer to your comforts and instruction, and afford you more ready aid, in time of need.

Your great Father is also desirous that you should live at a greater distance from white people, so that you may be more secure in the enjoyment of your property. And that he can with greater convenience, and less expense, cause you to be instructed in agriculture, and the useful arts; and your children to be taught to read and write; and that your Nation may be thus rendered an industrious and happy people.

Brothers, Your great Father, taking all circumstances into consideration, thinks it would be proper and advisable for you, to sell to the proprietors the land you may not want, after condensing your settlements upon one or more of your Reservations. For his opinion is, that as the earth was given to mankind, to support the greatest number of which it is capable, it is not right for any tribe or people, to withhold from the wants of others, more than is necessary for their own support and comfort.

Brothers, Your great Father looking forward to your future and lasting good, is desirous that you should obtain from the proprietors, a release of their title in the Reservation you hold on the Alleghany river. This tract being remote from white settlements, and least exposed to intrusions from white neighbors, your great Father considers most suitable for a permanent seat, whenever you shall be disposed to concentrate there. Your great Father therefore does not recommend that you should at present, sell any part of that Tract; but on the contrary has instructed me to give my decided support to some arrangement with the proprietors if it can be effected at this time, upon just and fair terms, by which their right in that Tract, shall be conveyed to the use of the Seneca Nation, and their posterity forever. So that your title may be complete and perfect, like that which white men have in their lands.

Brothers, Should any of you wish to join that portion of your nation, who reside at Lower Sandusky,[1] or should you, or any of you, rather choose to form new seats of your own, and can obtain the consent of your red Brethren, your great Father sees no objection to your removal, either to Sandusky, or to any of the territories of the United States.

You will understand, and I beg your white Brethren to notice what I say, that this offer of a seat, is not intended in any way to diminish the price, which you ought to receive for the lands here. It is a voluntary offer of your great Father, and intended for your sole and exclusive benefit.

Brothers, The Congress of the United States, actuated by the same views as your great Father, have lately passed an act, placing an annual sum, at his disposition, to be expended for the purpose of improving the condition of the red men, residing in the vicinity of the white settlements.[2] I am not particularly in-

1. Wyandot country in central, northwest Ohio.

2. On March 3, 1819, President Monroe signed a bill providing for $10,000 annually for Native "civilization." The bill's regulations appear in Calhoun (1969–74, 4:295–96, 575–77, 697–98).

structed on this point; and therefore cannot speak the mind of your great Father as to the use he intends to make of the money, thus placed at his disposal. But it certainly is not reasonable to suppose, that your great Father, will give any aid contemplated by this law, to those who do not conform to his plans.

Red and white Brothers around this Council fire,

I hope you have listened to what I have said. Your mutual co-operation is necessary to accomplish the objects which your great Father has in view. You both have rights in these lands. You white Brothers, who in the Commission which has just been read, are called by your great Father "the Proprietors" have title by purchase under the State of Massachusetts. You red Brothers, who occupy these lands, have the promise of your great Father, in the Treaty of 1794, that you should remain on them, until you should think proper to sell, to those of his white children, who might have the right to purchase.

Brothers, These different rights over the same property, render it unprofitable to both of you. You who have the right of possession, cannot sell except to those, who have the right to purchase.

And you, who have the title, cannot cultivate or enjoy the lands, until the right to the possession is extinguished. Strangers in the mean time are committing trespasses and encroachments, to the injury and annoyance of both of you, and white people are getting on your lands, in violation of the Laws of the Country.

Brothers, These are serious evils; and they will increase with the increase of the white settlements. Your great Father foresees that they will press more and more severely on his red children, dispersed as they now are, until they will be finally overwhelmed by the mighty torrent of the white population.

Brothers of the Seneca Nation,

The question of acceding to the views of your great Father, is one of much interest and importance. Various opinions are entertained by good and benevolent men, on the question of altering your condition. Any plan having for its object a *change* will no doubt meet with opposition. And here I would admonish you to guard against the arts and designs of *bad men*, who may wish to deceive you. And I would also caution you against listening too readily to the hasty opinions of *good men*, who give you their advice, no doubt with friendly intentions, but whose views are short sighted and erroneous, and will be found in the end prejudicial to your best interests.

Brothers, The exertions of good men have been directed to your improvement for a long series of years; and the expectations which were indulged have not been realized. If you have not stood still, there is reason to fear, you have not advanced.

The benevolent objects of the pious and the good have not been effected. There has been no want of zeal or exertion; and it is reasonable to conclude, that the failure has proceeded from some radical defect in their plans. And unless another and a better plan is adopted, it is the opinion of wise men, who have thought much on this subject, that your Nation will dwindle, and finally become extinct.

Brothers, Your safe and correct course is, to rely on the advice of your great Father, the President. Does the advice to remain as you now are, come to you from men of talents, integrity, virtue and wisdom? Remember, that it was the talents, the integrity, the virtue, and the wisdom of your great Father, which raised him to the elevated station he now holds. And you certainly would be wanting in prudence and discretion to neglect his advice, and take that of any other individual. It is possible that the advice you receive from others, may proceed from personal and interested motives. But your great Father cannot be operated upon by such motives. He cannot be moved by ambition, for his power and authority are not increased by the arrangement he proposes. He already rules from the Saint Lawrence beyond the Mississipi; from the Ocean to the Lakes. His advice then is pure and disinterested, and ought to be taken in preference to all others.

Brothers, Your great Father the President, whose happiness it is, to promote the welfare of all his children, has not been inattentive to you. He knows your condition and would wish to make it more comfortable and secure. The History of your Nation is not unknown to him. He knows the lofty sentiments it has cherished. He knows the gallant actions by which it has been distinguished. He remembers that the tree of your glory and your strength flourished upon the mountain; that its branches extended in every direction; that its root struck deep into the earth, and its top reached to the clouds. He observes with regret, that while some of its branches have fallen in the lapse of time, others have been lopped off by your own improvidence; that some have been taken away by artifice; and others have been rent by the hand of violence; that what remains shews manifest symptoms of disease and decay; that the trunk itself, once so vigorous and healthful, is now covered with moss; that its top is bending with weakness; and that a destructive canker has fastened on its roots.

Brothers, The opinion of your great Father is not made up in haste. It is the result of much reflection. He is firmly persuaded, that an alteration in your present condition is indispensable. He has seen with regret that your present scattered and unprotected situation exposes you to acts of violence and injustice; while at the same time it presents serious obstacles in the way of all attempts to better your condition. And is on many other accounts unfriendly to your interests. He therefore recommends the course I have suggested.

Red and White Brothers around this Council fire,

You have heard the views and advice of your great Father. He does not wish to enforce his recommendation beyond the exercise of his paternal advice. But he hopes you will agree among yourselves. Consult then together in friendship, and see what can be done; and let harmony and good will prevail in all your deliberations.

You hold your conversation in languages unknown to each other; unless some caution is observed, mistakes may occur. I shall therefore take care, that all proceedings here, are fully explained, and distinctly understood.

I shall endeavor to perform the trust reposed in me, in obedience to the instructions I have received from your great Father, the President: and in such manner as will promote the best interests of all concerned.

It would give me pleasure to be enabled to report to your great Father the President that by the light of this Council fire, a path has been discovered, which promises to lead to a satisfactory arrangement for your gradual improvement; and a permanent provision for your safety and comfort. [Source: "Letters Received by the Secretary of War Relating to Indian Affairs, 1800–1823," M-271, reel 2, frames 1431–44, DNA]

After Miller had finished, David Ogden stood up and proposed that the council adjourn for a day for proper reflection. The Six Nations responded with a brief speech by Captain Pollard, the text of which appears only in Major Delafield's journal. Pollard thanked Miller for his speech, then assured him that the Indians had listened carefully to it. He acknowledged Miller's claims that the president's propositions were not made in haste, and that the president took a "full view" of the interests of the Indians and the whites. Pollard noted, however, that both Miller and the president seemed to be addressing themselves primarily to the Senecas, when in actuality they were addressing the Six Nations. Miller replied that he spoke primarily to the Senecas because his federal commission specified it, but he admitted that he also spoke to the Six Nations. The next day, Tuesday, Nathaniel Gorham Jr. arrived, the commissioner from Massachusetts. On Wednesday, July 7, the council fire was kindled by Red Jacket. Delafield's journal gives the following account of his speech:

"Brothers: you will recollect that the day before yesterday, we were preserved in health strength and spirits to meet you at our Council fire.

"The Great Spirit has protected us to the present time, and we are thankful again to meet you. You will recollect, Brothers, at that time we listened with attention to what we heard from the Com[missione]r. and from our Great

Father (the President) thro' his Comr. As this Council was called by the voice of our Great Father, you barely told us at that time of his views, and made known to us what care he had for his red children. You further promised us however that the Yorkers (meaning the proprietors) had communications for us. We now welcome you to this Council, and are ready to hear your communications.

"We see here our brother from Massachusetts (Judge Gorham). He is welcome to our Council. We are ready to hear him. Brothers, we wish you to open your minds to us. Let us hear frankly all that you have to say, that we may be ready to answer in reply."

Mr. Gorham took his seat. His Commission was read, when he address'd the Council, approving of the propositions made by the President. Mr. D.[avid] A. Ogden then spoke, and offered on the part of the proprietors to agree to the President's plans, having closed an able speech, explanatory of his title & the history of the Reservations. [Source: Delafield 1943, 233–34]

Ogden's speech from the National Archives:

Brothers of the Seneca Nation,

I rejoice to meet you at this time in the presence of the Commissioner whom our great Father has sent to attend this Council Fire. I join with him in praying that the great Spirit may preside over our deliberations, and lead us to adopt such measures, as may advance our mutual welfare and happiness.

Brothers, My principal object in asking our great Father to send a Commissioner to attend this Council, was to bring under his notice the situation of the Reservations you occupy, in order that your Rights and the rights of the Proprietors may be clearly understood, and that future trouble and disputes between us might be avoided.

Brothers, The Talk which was delivered at the opening of this Council, in the name of our great Father, and the prospect it opens, of drawing a plain and well marked line between us, will induce me to omit many things, that I had intended to say to you, but as it is possible, notwithstanding the advice of our great Father, that we may not come to any final agreement, it is necessary that these matters should not be entirely overlooked.

Brothers, Our great Father by the mouth of his Commissioner has told us, that we have both rights in these lands. But what these rights are, I am afraid we do not fully understand.

Brothers, More than thirty years ago, and soon after the treaty of peace between the United States and Great Britain a Convention was made under the authority of Congress, between the States of New York and and [sic] Massachusetts, both claiming these lands, by which convention the Pre-emptive or Proprietory Right, became vested in the State of Massachusetts, and the Right of Sovereignty and Jurisdiction in the State of New York.—

Twenty eight years ago, the State of Massachusetts, sold all the Pre-emptive or Proprietory Right in these lands to Samuel Ogden of New Jersey acting for Robert Morris then of the State of Pennsylvania.

Three years afterwards Robert Morris by the Treaty held at Big Tree, purchased the Indian Right to all the lands of the Seneca Nation, excepting those which were specially reserved, and which you now occupy.

Robert Morris about the same period sold nearly the whole of these lands, and among them the Allegany, Cattaraugus, Buffaloe Creek, Tonewanta, Tuscarora and Canadea Reservations to the Holland Land Company who afterwards sold the same to myself and my associates. The Gardiner [Gardeau] and other Reservations upon the Genessee River, by sales under Robert Morris are vested in Mr. [John] Greig and other proprietors most of whom are here present, or are represented. By these sales all the Right which Great Britain before the Treaty of Peace, and which New York and Massachusetts, by virtue of that Treaty and ancient charters had in those lands, became fully and completely vested in those proprietors, and their heirs and assigns forever;—and are now held by them in the same manner as the State of Pennsylvania, was formerly held by William Penn, under the crown of England.

Brothers, At the period of these transactions it was and still is unlawful, for any Indian Tribe in this State, to sell or lease the lands they occupy, except to the owner of the Proprietory Right or to permit White People to settle or reside upon such lands—or to sell the wood or timber growing on them.

Brothers—These Laws were well known to you all. Nevertheless White People are settled every where among you. Large quantities of timber are continually sold to, and carried off by white people, without any restraint, from the Seneca Nation, and in prejudice to my legal Rights.

Brothers, The Proprietors altho' well informed of these proceedings have hitherto forborne to complain to the President. But it may be well to remind you, that if you have the right to put white people upon these lands, the Proprietors have the same right. Many white people have applied to me to purchase the proprietory right, in small parts, of your Reservations, and if I had sold to these people, you would before this, have been overrun by them. And so, if I should encourage white people to cut timber on your lands, all that is good and valuable would be soon destroyed.

Brothers—I have always acted towards you with friendship and justice, and have been careful, not only to keep within the limits of the laws, but have also forborne, to exercise my legal rights, when I had reason to suppose that they might be abused to your injury or annoyance.—

Brothers—I have been sorry to find that you have not observed a correspondent conduct towards me. You seem to have thought little of my rights and as little of the laws. I do not say this in anger or resentment; I only wish to remind you that I have rights as well as you. If there should be any doubts as to the nature or extent of my rights, I should wish to have them fully explained, in the presence of the Commissioner of our common Father, so that if either of us are treading in a wrong path we may now be set right, and that we may hereafter keep in the Right Path.

Brother. At a former council some of you enquired of me whether the sale you had made of a part of the Buffaloe Reservation, to the Cayuga Indians, was good and valid.—I told you it was not in my opinion. But that I would enquire into the matter—I have done so, and the Law-officer of the United States, residing at Washington, has given me an opinion, stating that you are not authorized to sell any of your lands to Indians, who were not united with your Nation, at the date of Pickering's Treaty.[3]

Brothers, Do you complain of all these Restrictions upon the Rights of the native Indians—They are not of my creating—They have existed ever since the first settlement of this Country by the White People. But Brothers you ought not to complain of them; for these laws have often been to the red people, a most necessary protection.

32 years ago you sold all this tract of country for 999. years to Livingston and his associates,[4] who had not the Pre-emptive Right, and these laws then restored you to the Lands of your Fathers, and have since been the strong Fence by which you have been sheltered and defended in the enjoyment of them.—

3. The Treaty of Canandaigua, 1794.

4. On November 13, 1787, just prior to Phelps and Gorham's purchase of the preemptive right from Massachusetts (in April 1788), a brazen group of New York investors (headed by John Livingston, Caleb Benton, and Jared Coffin) managed to convince the Six Nations to lease the Phelps-Gorham lands for $2,000 a year for 999 years (see Maier 1984; Osgood 1892; Turner 1851). They also made a similar lease with the Oneidas on January 8, 1788 (Wandell 1942, 279–80). Livingston's associates argued that since they were not buying land, they were not infringing on Phelps and Gorham's preemptive right purchased from Massachusetts. However, the New York State legislature invalidated the lease in March 1788, an act that angered the Indians. Livingston was remarkably persistent in his attempts to get Indian land, circulating fliers for the citizens of western New York counties to secede from the United States in the early 1790s. He also unsuccessfully tried to sue the Ogden Company just prior to the War of 1812 with the claim the company owed him money on the basis of his earlier land transactions with the Indians.

Brothers—I bought the Pre-emptive Right to your lands many years ago. I can look back on those years and assert with truth, that I have never attempted to deceive or injure you in any way. When I first understood that you were desirous to obtain a Seat to the West, where preserving the Laws and customs of your Fathers you might build up the ruins of your nation—I then endeavored at your request, and with great expense and trouble to myself, to obtain a Seat for you, and I succeeded in getting a promise of one, from your Great Father as a *Gratuity*. You have now that promise *in writing,* in clear and explicit Terms.

Brothers. Some evil minded white men then told you that I wished you to accept that seat, by way of *exchange* for your lands here and you were displeased at me. These men told you what was not true. I always expected to pay you a fair price for your lands here, whenever you determined to sell them, expecting only (as I then told you) that you would treat with me upon more liberal terms, if you should conclude to accept the seat which I might obtain for you

Brothers. I afterwards understood that many of your white friends, were opposed to Your removal to the West, and that they were desirous to keep you here, and to make you farmers: to educate your children, and gradually to change your ancient customs and government.

Brothers, If such be your wishes, I am not opposed to them.—I have never opposed them. On the contrary I have told your white friends that I would co-operate with you and with them, in carrying your wishes into effect, in any way that might be thought most to your advantage

Brothers, I well know that the eyes of your great Father, and of his council the Congress, have been directed towards the *Red People,* placed as most of you are, in the midst of the white settlements, for two years past; and that a new system has been thought necessary in order not only to facilitate your improvement, but also to throw open your superfluous lands to cultivation, and thereby to add to the general wealth and resources of the State.

During the last session of Congress the Secretary of War made a report to them upon the subject of Indian affairs, which was followed up by a law authorizing the President to take measures for the improvement of the Indian Tribes, residing in the vicinity of white settlements, and placing a large sum of money annually at his disposition for that purpose.—

Brothers, We have all heard what our great Father has now said to us. I have slept upon his words, and they have made a deep impression upon my mind. I am willing to conform to the views of our great Father. It is my duty to do so and it will be my pleasure also, if I can at the same time gratify the wishes of the Seneca Nation, and contribute to their happiness and welfare.—

Brother, If I understand the advice of your great Father, it is, that you should draw nearer together, that you should retain as much land on any of your Reservations as you want, and sell the remainder upon fair terms. That the whole of the Allegany Reservation should be among the Lands to be retained, and that the Pre-emptive Right to that Reservation, should on fair terms, be released for the benefit of your nation as a permanent seat (if you should hereafter think fit to occupy it as such); and that those of you who choose to join your brothers at Lower Sandusky might, with their consent, be permitted to do so, and that such of you as may not incline to go there, might choose a seat elsewhere among your Red Brethren, and that these seats being offered as a gift from your great Father, are in no way to lessen the compensation you may be entitled to receive, on any sale of your Right to the Proprietors of the Pre-emption.

Brothers, It is the nature of all Bargains that they should be for the benefit of both parties, and on this basis, and in conformity with the views of our great Father, we are willing to treat with you. If any of you prefer to remain upon your present Seats, we shall be ready also with the approbation of the Commissioner of your great Father (if it can be obtained) to enter into satisfactory arrangements for that purpose, and as to those of you whose habitations may be within the limits of any tracts you may incline to sell, we are perfectly willing that you continue to occupy your present farms as long as you please to do so.

Brothers. The title we have in your reservations has cost a great deal of money, and much more has been spent in endeavoring to lay the foundation of some satisfactory arrangement, between you and the Proprietors. If no such arrangements can now be made the Rights of the present Proprietors must soon pass to other Hands, and to a much larger number. I hope you will always have to deal with honest men, but it is not likely, that you will ever again find all the Proprietors so well inclined, as we now all are, to promote your happiness and to conform to your wishes.—I would therefore urge you, to profit by their good dispositions; to sell what lands you do not want, and cannot possibly use.—To encrease your annuities, so as to make further provision against distress and want, when your crops fail; and above all, to avail yourselves of the offer of your great Father; of securing to yourselves a permanent Seat.

Brothers, I repeat that the Proprietors are willing to meet any reasonable propositions you may offer them. But if the Seneca Nation will come to no agreement, I have reason to fear that the Proprietors will be led to sell out their rights, and in small parcels, for a great number of people now stand ready to purchase, and you must expect that they will naturally endeavor to make the most of their rights, without consulting your wishes, as we have done.

Brothers, I have reduced this talk to writing. I shall now hand it to the Commissioner of our great Father, that he may see, how far his white children are willing to conform to his advice.

Brothers, I thank you for your friendly attention to what I have now said, and I sincerely pray that the chain of friendship may ever be kept bright between us. [Source: "Letters Received by the Secretary of War Relating to Indian Affairs, 1800–1823," M-271, reel 2, frames 1446–58, DNA]

Delafield's journal continues:

"Red Jacket speaks to his tribe, tells them they must deliberate in Council before they reply, and addressing the council said:

"We have now heard our Great Father, and we have heard Mr. Ogden. We must now take time to reflect upon the whole. When we are ready to meet again at the Council fire: we will send you word. We are slow, and the subjects are important; we have nothing further to kindle [at] this council fire." Adjourned. [Source: Delafield 1943, 234]

On July 8, 1819, Miller gave a short speech that stated that Ogden was willing to pay a $4,000 annuity for the Indians to consolidate at Allegany. He let them borrow a map of Allegany and noted that because some Indians were afraid there were not enough farm lands there for all the Senecas, he proposed that they could negotiate for additional holdings at Cattaraugus or at their other reservations [frames 1460–63]. The next day, on July 9, Delafield's journal notes:

The Council met at the Buffalo upper village, opened by Henry Abeel,[5] a Seneca, by the usual welcome, when Red Jacket, a chief of the Seneca nation, rose & delivered the following speech, first addressing the Commissioner Judge Miller. [Delafield 1943, 234]

Red Jacket's speech from the National Archives:

Brother,

We understand that you have been appointed by our great Father (the President) to make these communications to us. We thank the Great Spirit for the pleasant day that is given us, to reply, and we beg you to listen.

Brother, Previous to your arrival at this Council-fire, we understood that our Great Father had appointed a Commissioner to meet us. On your arrival you produced your Commission, and related, after the Commission was explained, the object of your appointment, and the wish of the President, in

5. Cornplanter's son.

sending you to the Council-fire of the Six Nations. We do not doubt that the sealed document you exhibited, contained the words of our Great Father. When first informed of your appointment, we expected that you was coming forward to meet us on a different subject. Since the war of the Revolution, we have held various treaties with our white brothers, and in this same manner We have entered into various compacts and agreements; we have made various speeches, and these things are all known to our great Father, and are lodged with him. We perfectly understand them all. The same interpreters were then present.

In consequence of what has taken place during the late war, we made known to our great Father, that we wished to have a Talk. Application was made by our interpreter, but it was not complied with. We sent a messenger to brighten the chain of friendship with our great Father; but he would not meet around the Council-fire, and we were disappointed. We now expected that the Commissioner he has sent, came forward to brighten the chain of friendship, and to renew former engagements.

When we made a Treaty at Canandaigua,[6] we thought it was to be permanent, and to stand between us and the United States forever. After several treaties had been entered into under our great Father Gen. Washington, large delegations of the Six Nations were invited to meet him. We went and met Gen. Washington in Philadelphia. We kindled a council fire. A treaty was then made; and Gen. Washington declared that it should be permanent, between the red and the white brothers; that this treaty should be laid on the greatest rocks; upon rocks that nothing could undermine; that it should be spread upon the largest rocks, exposed to the view of all. Brother, We shall now see what has been done by the United States. After this treaty of friendship had been formed and declared to be as lasting as the rocks, I then said that I did not doubt but what the United States would faithfully perform their contract. But I told our white brothers at that time that I had a fear, that, eventually they would feel a wish to disturb these contracts. You white brothers, have a faculty to disturb the stoutest rocks. On our part, we would not have disturbed those treaties.

A short time after our interview at Philadelphia, with our great Father Gen. Washington, a treaty was made at Canandaigua. By this treaty we widened our former engagements with our white brothers, and added some new ones. The Commissioner (Col. Pickering) then told us that this treaty should last and be binding, and without alteration for two lives. We wished to

6. 1794.

extend the term of this treaty much further and I then told the Commissioner, that the Six Nations would wish to make the treaty permanent, and establish a lasting chain of friendship; that on our part, we wished the treaty to last, as long as the trees should grow, and the waters run. Our brother then told us he would agree to it.

Brother, I commenced reminding you what had taken place between the United States and the Confederates of the Six Nations, and have last spoken of the treaty of Canandaigua (1794).—At the close of that treaty it was agreed (that treaty being as strong and lasting as by former comparisons I have ex-plained) that if any difficulties should occur; if any monster should come across the chain of friendship, that we should unite as one to remove those dif-ficulties; to drive away this Monster. We will in such case go hand in hand, and continue the chain already established. So it was agreed.

Brother, We discovered many years ago a difficulty arising in the way of peace and friendship. We heard such things from different quarters, from dif-ferent persons, and at different times; and thought that the time was not far distant, when the present difficulty would burst upon us.[7]

Brother, During the late war we intended to take no part. Yet residing within the limits of the United States, and with the advice of Gen. Porter, we agreed around our Council-fire, that it was right, and we took a part. We thought it would tend to promote friendship with our white brothers; to aid the arms of the United States; and to make our present seats still stronger. We took a part in the war for these purposes. What were the effects? We lost many of our Warriors. we spilt our blood in a cause between you and a people not of our own color.

Brother, These transactions are not new to your government. Records of these transactions are with the great Father, the President. You have come, brother, for a different purpose, than the one we expected. Your coming is to tell us of our situation; to tell us about our reservations; to tell us the opinion of the President that we must change our old customs for new ones; that we must concentrate ourselves, in order to derive the fair means you offer of civi-lization, and improvement in the arts of agriculture.

Brother, At the treaty of Canandaigua, we were promised on the part of your Government, that different kinds of mechanics, blacksmiths and Car-penters should be sent among us to improve us in these arts. And we were

7. Stone's version of this paragraph is slightly different: "BROTHER: Many years ago we discovered a cloud rising that darkened the prospect of our peace and happiness. We heard eventful things from different quarters, from different persons, and at different times, and foresaw that the period not very distant, when this threatening cloud would burst upon us" (1841, 301).

promised that farmers with their families should be sent, that our women might learn to spin. We agreed to accept them. We even made application for these benefits. We were told that the age of our children was not suitable; and none of our young men were taught. Other treaties have promised us these things. Neither farmers or mechanics have been sent among us.

Brother, We had thought that all the promises made by one President, were handed down to the next. We do not change our Chiefs as you do. Since these treaties were made with us, you have had several changes of your President—And we do not understand why the treaty made by one President, is not binding upon the other. On our parts we expect to comply with our engagements.

Brother, We are improving in our situation. See those large flocks of cattle. Look at those fences. These things were not seen formerly. We are surrounded by the whites; from them we can readily obtain cattle; and by what we procure from them we enlarge our improvements.

Brother, You told us, where the country was surrounded by whites, and in possession of Indians; when it was unproductive, not liable to taxes, nor to make roads, and other improvements, it was time to change.

As for the taxing of Indians, it is extraordinary. This was never heard of before since the first settlement of America. The land is ours by the gift of the Great Spirit. How can you tax it?—We can make such roads as we want, and we did so, when this soil was all ours. Now that we are confined to small reservations, we can easily make the roads we want; and assist in making public improvements.

Brother; Look back to the first settlement of this Country: And after that look at our present condition under the United States. Under the British Government we continued our growth in numbers and in strength. What has now become of the Indians, who extended themselves in large numbers to the Salt waters? They are become few and are driven back; while you have been growing rich and powerful. This land is ours from the God of heaven. It was given us. We cannot make land. Driven back and reduced as we now are, you still wish to cramp us more and more. These lands are ours given by the Heavenly Father. You tell us of a pre-emptive right. Such men you say own one reservation; such men another. But they are all ours: Ours, from the top to the very bottom. If Mr. Ogden should tell us, that he had come from heaven with the flesh on his bones, as he now is, and that the Heavenly Father had given him a title, we might believe him. The President has sent us word, you say, that it is our interest to dispose of our reservations. You tell us, there is a fine tract of land at Alleghany. This to[o] is very extraordinary. Our feet have covered every inch of that reservation. Such a communication as this has never before been made to us in any of our treaties. The President must have been disordered in mind,[8] or he would not offer to lead us off by the arms to the Alleghany Reservation.

You have heard of our treaty with the United States, and our understanding with them. Here is the belt of wampum that confirmed the treaty. This holds our hands together. Here too is the parchment. You know its contents. I will not open it. Now the tree of friendship is decaying; its limbs are fast falling off, and you are at fault.

Formerly we addressed the British as brothers. Now we call the President our Father. Probably among you are gentlemen with families of children. We consider ourselves the children of the President. What then would be your feelings, were you told, your children were to be cast on a naked rock, there to protect themselves?

The different claims you tell us of I cannot understand. We were placed here by the great Spirit, for purposes known to him. You can have no right to interfere. You told us, that we had large and many unproductive tracts of land. We do not view it so. Our seats we consider small; and if left here long by the great Spirit, we shall stand in need of them. We shall want timber. Land after the improvements of many years wears out. We shall want to renew our fields: and we do not think that there is any land, in any of our reservations, but what is useful.

Look at the white people around us and back. You are not cramped for seats; they are large. Look at that man (pointing to Mr. [Joseph] Ellicott) he has plenty of land: if you want to buy, apply to him. We have none to part with. Some here laugh. But do not think I trifle: I am sincere. Do not think we are hasty in making up our minds. We have had many councils, and thought for a long time upon this subject, and we will not part with any, not one of our reservations. We recollect that Mr. Ogden handed his speech to you, therefore I have spoken to you. Now I shall address Mr. Ogden.

Brother: You recollect when you first came to this ground, you told us you had bought the pre-emptive right: A right to purchase given you by the government. Recollect my reply. I told you you was unfortunate in buying. You said you would not disturb us. And I told you then, as long as I lived, you must not come forward to explain that right. You have come, but I am living. See me before you. You have heard our reply to the Commissioner sent by the

8. According to Captain Pollard's testimony at Livingston's Council of 1828, the phrase "disordered in his mind" should have been translated as "drunk or crazy."

President. And I again tell you that one and all, Chiefs & Warriors are of the same mind. We will not part with any of our reservations. Do not make your application anew in any other shape. Let us hear no more of it—And let us part as we met, in friendship. You discover white people on our reservation. It is my wish, and the wish of all of us, to remove every white man. We can educate our children. Our reservation is small. The white people are near us: we can send our children to their schools. Such as wish, can do so. The Schoolmaster and the Preacher must withdraw. The distance is short, for those who wish to go to them. We wish to get rid of all the whites. Those who are now among us make disturbances. We wish our reservation clear of them. [Source: "Letters Received by the Secretary of War Relating to Indian Affairs, 1800–1823," M-271, reel 2, frames 1465–76, DNA]

From Delafield's journal:

Govr. Ogden,[9] of N.[ew] Jersey, replied to Red Jacket, to the following effect: "Sachems Chiefs and Warriors of the Seneca Nation. We understand from the message of our Great Father that he wish'd you to get more together, that he might protect you; that you are not what you were, and that a different course of conduct must be adopted in regard to the red people or they would soon be extinguished.

"These things were meant in friendship, not enmity, in love not hatred. Brothers, we knew these things before. Here they are contained in these documents, set down for your good, not for your hurt. You knew them before the Comr. [commissioner] told them to you. We came to hear you speak freely upon these subjects. Your minds are as free as the winds. We meant not to control them. We are sorry if we have given you trouble or raised unpleasant feelings. We came to speak freely and in friendship. We have not wished to hurry you. When a proposition is made for the good of a party, we think the more it is thought of it, the better it will be liked; and so we think of this. We make fair & honorable offers, not a rocky Alleghany, but to buy what you do not want. We say nothing of Alleghany or Cattaraugus, but there is more land than you want—Money at interest is better than lands uncultivated. We said you might all remain if you wished. We will give you 4000 dlls. a year; and your women and children will then be made comfortable & free from want. This was friendship not hate. Stay or go; we say here is a free election for you.

"Brother, I am known to be the friend of red men, among your white Brothers. I came here in that character. To my judgement, I believed, where

9. Governeur Ogden was David Ogden's brother, one of the Ogden Company investors.

the whites are settled, and the game is all gone, the bow & arrow should give way to the plow and the spade. At Sandusky, I was informed, there was good hunt, bears, beavers, raccoons. At Cattaraugus good corn fields, and at other places good hunt. Now you are told to choose of these good things—is there any harm in that? I thought this reasonable. If those who come after us make propositions, I hope they may be more reasonable, but I doubt it—

"Brothers. This plan I thought most just. From past time, til now, we know the whites were made for toil and labor, the red people to delight in the chase and hunt. These lands would be cultivated by the whites, and you would live upon the fruits of their toil. This is right.

"Brothers. I hope you see that this is meant in friendship, [and] would be sorry if your feelings were hurt. Brothers, let this turn as it may, I shall be your friend. I always was, and always shall be the friend of red people. It is probable I shall never see you again. I am old. I must sell my right—I hope you will meet a better friend, but I don't believe it. Brothers, I hope we will part in love & friendship. Whenever I can do you good I will—but never hurt.

"Much has been said about Mr. Pickering's Treaty. To speak of that belongs to the Agent of the U.S. I am no Comr. I only say I do remember that in that Treaty it is said the Senecas may enjoy the Reservations until they chose to sell—It was plain then, that it was expected you would be ask'd to sell.

"You say Mr. Ellicott has land to sell. If he (the Commissioner) went to treat with him, he would not be affronted, as you seem to be. Brothers. Your Father the President never meant but to brighten the chain of friendship. You did him injustice, when you said his mind was disordered. Brothers, but one word more: in my opinion you have not understood the Agent's communication from your Great Father. It belongs to him to explain. You had better go and see the President. You have misapprehended him. He will set you right, and remove from you and your children false impressions."

The Comr. Miller then explained to the Nation that they had misunderstood him when they said they were to be taxed. Of Mr. Pickering's Treaty he said he knew it well. Of any promises made at that time, not contained in the treaty, he knew nothing. He then ask'd if anything further had been misunderstood, that it be explained. Upon which Red Jacket replied that he knew of nothing that wanted explanation—he hopes that Mr. Ogden understands that they will not sell a single foot of land. If he does not, it wants explanation.

There being no further business before the Council, the Comr. brightened the chain of friendship by a valedictory and covered the Council fire. [Source: Delafield 1943, 237–39]

Delafield's journal describes an interesting event that occurred after the day's council was over: With the Senecas at attention, Young King asked Judge Miller whether he would advise that they work on the Sabbath or not. Young King said that they had been discussing the issue among themselves for some time and it had caused great disturbance. Miller said that the answer he would give was purely his own and not representative of the government's views. He said that the president does not interfere among his white children on matters of conscience: "Standing as I do here, I cannot give a preference to any one description of Indians. The President gives protection to all. He will protect the Pagan & the Christian Party. The plan of improvement suggested by Joeny King [Young King] I consider efficacious" (Delafield 1943, 240).

July 10, 1819. From the National Archives:

A messenger was sent this 10th day of July 1819 to Mr. Com.ʳ Miller from a Deputation of Chiefs, of the Seneca Nation, stating that they were now in Council upon a subject connected with their Talk at the Council of yesterday, and were desirous of holding a Talk with the Commissioner of the United States

Mr. Com.ʳ Miller appointed 4 o'clock in the afternoon of this day for an interview; when the following chiefs appeared in behalf of the Nation:— Young King, Pollard, Destroy-Town, Jim Robertson, White Seneca [Seneca White], Capt. William Prentiss and Capt. Johnson.

Present Capt. Parrish & Capt. Jones, Interpreters.

Pollard made the following communication:

You recollect what took place in the council yesterday. The answer was in the first place a reply to you, and then to the Proprietors. You must have discovered something in that reply which was not correct—which was improper. You must also have discovered at our different meetings, that we are divided among ourselves.—This is true—It has been so, a long time.—We altho' a minority, have been reflecting how we could adopt the advice of good white men. And we have been reflecting, how it was possible that you should represent any thing in Council, but what came from our Great Father the President—Altho' you must have perceived that such insinuations were made yesterday by the Speaker. You might have plainly seen yesterday that the Speaker acknowledged your authority, your commission; but he did not admit that all the subsequent matter was derived from the President. One Sentence of the Speaker's hurt us very much. He intimated that the President was disordered in mind. It makes us very unhappy that he should have used this expression. Another very extraordinary idea was given by the Speaker. He said, that if the Yorker [Ogden] should tell us "he had come from Heaven and say that the Great Spirit had told him he had the title, we might believe him." was an expression that we as Christians think very wrong, and it hurt us very much.

After the Council dispersed, the followers of the Speaker collected and took him to task, for making these expressions. They were not agreed to among ourselves. He was not authorized to say these things; and it was proposed, that an apology should be made. The Speaker said, No—It has gone forth—let it stand. All the Chiefs of both parties excepting Red Jacket and Henry Abeel proposed making an apology. We have now an opportunity to come forward and make apology. In another thing he behaved improperly. He told you of many treaties down to Pickering's: coming to that, he held it up did not show it to you, saying you had a Copy at Washington. This we consider rude and indecent. He addressed our Great Father the President, as President. We consider the President our Great Father, and view him as a father, friend and protector; and call him so. He is the source of our life and of our enjoyment. The Speaker's explanation of his expression "that the mind of the President must have been disordered," makes the matter still worse, because he casts an imputation upon the Preachers, and others who have long been praying for our good. We view the Commission coming from the President, the same as coming from a Father to his children. The advice to concentrate and improve in agriculture we approve of. We see that the time has come for us to change our condition, to attend to husbandry. The negotiation about the land we all agreed to, and we likewise all agree, both parties, that the Speaker's language was harsh and improper. The President wishes we should concentrate, so as best to receive instruction. We took a view of this and concluded that the Speaker's answer was right. We all thought it was not right to part with the lands.

Our motive for calling on you now is to let you know our minds and feelings. We are divided among ourselves. The Senecas of which I am are divided. The Tuscaroras are all united, and wish to receive instruction and civilization. The Alleghanys are divided but principally receive instruction from the Preachers, and are with our party.

When I look back upon our ancestors, I see nothing to admire—nothing I should follow—nothing that induces me to live as they did. On the contrary, to enjoy life I find we must change our situations. We who are present have families and children and we have a respect for our children. We wish them to be enlightened and instructed, if we have not been. By this means their eyes will be opened. They will see the light, if we have not. We are getting old and cannot receive the instruction we want our children to receive: our children will know how to do business after we are dead and gone, and are under the dust; and they will bless us for giving them instruction, which their Fathers had been deprived of.—

The Tuscaroras have long time been receiving civilization. They are going on. They see the advantages their children are enjoying. It is but a few years that we have thought upon this subject, but we intend to persevere in spite of opposition, and teach our children to cultivate the land.

These communications we wish our Father the President should know. And hereafter when the President makes communications to the Senecas, we wish to have them made to us, the Christian party; and we will at all times be happy to hear from him in this way. This we think will have a good effect, and be a good lesson to our children. We are willing to receive instruction from such persons as our Father will send among us, and will adopt his advice, because we see, that, following Indian habits, we must inevitably decay and sink to nothing. You said we could not remain independent: we are sensible of this, and would undergo a gradual change: for instance, in case of crime now, we are not independent—we are punished. We foresee that we cannot remain independent.

One cause of this division among us, is because one party will school their children, the other will not. Another cause is placing white men as tenants on our farms—I did so, because advised by a white friend, and to show our people how white men farmed. This was my reason.

Pollard's speech ends here but Miller continues:

It was also communicated at this meeting thro' the Interpreter, that Red Jacket and Henry Abeel, were the only persons who declined making an apology for the rude expressions used by Red Jacket yesterday in his Speech; and that Abeel, it is supposed, instigated Jacket to say what he did.— [Source: M-271, reel 2, frames 1478–84, DNA; slightly retouched versions appear in Delafield 1943, 240–42; Stone states that his source texts were supplied to him by Delafield, and the only editorial changes he made were to delete repetitive passages (1841, 302–6)]

Variant Texts of the Reply to Ogden

1819

THE FOLLOWING SPEECH FRAGMENTS were given to William Leete Stone by Albert H. Tracy. Tracy was an ambitious and talented western New York lawyer and politician. He helped defend chief Tommy-Jemmy in 1821. Although the text is significantly different than the Delafield manuscripts of July 9, 1819, it covers the same points. Here, Red Jacket responds to "Ogden and the commissioner." Stone presents these as unconnected paragraphs, notable for their "literary" figures. The first paragraph, often circulated, is quoted by Robert Bingham in his 1930 essay on the "Trial of Red Jacket."

"We first knew you," said he, "a feeble plant which wanted a little earth whereon to grow. We gave it you,—and afterward, when we could have trod you under our feet, we watered and protected you;—and now you have grown to be a mighty tree, whose top reaches the clouds, and whose branches overspread the whole land; whilst we, who were then the tall pine of the forest, have become the feeble plant, and need your protection."

"When you first came here, you clung around our knee, and called us *father*. We took you by the hand and called you BROTHERS. You have grown greater than we, so that we no longer can reach up to your hand. But we wish to cling round your knee and be called YOUR CHILDREN."

"Not long ago you raised the war-club against him who was once our great Father over the waters. You asked us to go with you to the war. It was not our quarrel. We knew not that you were right. We asked not: we cared not: it was enough for us that you were our brothers. We went with you to the battle. We fought and bled for you:—and now," said he with great feeling, pointing to some Indians who had been wounded in the contest, "dare you pretend to us that our Father the President, while he sees our blood running yet fresh from the wounds received while fighting his battles, has sent you with a message to persuade us to relinquish the poor remains of our once boundless possessions,—to sell the birth-place of our children, and the graves of our fathers. No! Sooner than believe that he gave you this message, we will believe that you have stolen your commission, and are a cheat and a liar."

"You tell us," said he, "of your claim to our land, and that you have purchased it from your State. We know nothing of your claim, and we care nothing for it. Even the whites have a law, by which they cannot sell what they do not own. How, then, has your state, which never owned our land, sold it to you? We have a title to it, and we know that our title is good; for it came direct from the Great Spirit, who gave it to us, his red children. When you can ascend to where He is,"—pointing toward the skies,—"and will get His deed, and show it to us, then, and never til then, will we acknowledge your title. You say that you came not to cheat us of our lands, but to buy them. Who told you that we have lands to sell? You never heard it from us."

"Did I not tell you, the last time we met, that whilst Red-Jacket lived you would get no more lands of the Indians? How, then, while you see him alive and strong," (striking his hand violently on his breast,) "do you think to make him a liar?" [Source: Stone 1841, 311–13]

Petition to Secretary Calhoun for a New Agent

FEBRUARY 5, 1820

THE OSTENSIBLE COMPLAINT of this letter is that the Six Nations still lacked an agent (see January 4, 1818). The petitioners, writing from Tonawanda, were also growing distrustful of Jasper Parrish's conduct. The annuities were slightly smaller than in previous years, due perhaps to the recent decision on the part of the legislature to distribute part of the annuity money at Onondaga (Denniston to Parrish, May 27, 1818, Parrish Papers, BECHS, not microfilmed). Calhoun responded in writing to them on March 28, 1820, and forwarded a copy of the treaty they requested, but his letter was not saved (Calhoun 1969–74, 4:738; treaty in Maris Pierce Papers, BECHS). Two months later, Pollard and Young King were furious to find out that Red Jacket had implied to the secretary of war that the petition carried the assent of main council fire at Buffalo Creek (Calhoun 1969–74, 5:198–99).

Jack Berry, a chief, was one of the interpreters. Like Red Jacket, Berry was in disfavor with white authorities. In 1815, Erastus Granger wrote, "Jack Berry cannot be depended on—he is drunk at every council" (Fairbank n.d., 149, 190). Granger's manuscript papers, however, indicate he paid Berry fifty dollars a year for his services as an interpreter during the same period. "P. P. Pratt," the other interpreter, is Pascal Pratt, a trader and local friend of the Senecas who tried to ease tensions during the Tommy-Jemmy trial the following year (Densmore 1999, 96).

At the same time this petition was drafted, the Senecas also sent a memorial to Governor Clinton, protesting the pressure put upon them to sell their lands. The original petition has been lost. Clinton's response, which affirmed the Indians's right to hold their lands, can be read in Stone 1841, 309–10.

To the Honorable John C. Calhoun, Secretary of War of the United States
Brother. It is now thirty eight years since the Treaty was concluded at

Philadelphia, between the United States and the Six Nations of Indians, the terms of which as well as the treaty subsequently concluded at Canandaigua, we have the most perfect recollection of, and have on our part fulfilled them with equal punctuality.

It has since been found necessary sometimes to hold communications with our Father, the President of the U. States on the subject of the stipulations in the said treaties, the better to continue the relating of friendship which ought to exist between the parties, and these communications have heretofore been made by our agent appointed by the United States. We now have no such agent, and are obliged to state our grievances to you, hoping you will lay them before the President, who we are confident will cause them to be redressed.

(For about two years we have failed in receiving the usual amount of articles of Clothing, farming utensils, and other articles due us annually by the terms of the treaties, and we are unable to find out the cause of this deficiency.)

We who sign this address, are the same chiefs who signed the treaties; we are neither changed in our friendship towards the United States, nor in the religious principles of our forefathers, and in which we were born and educated.

You are doubtless aware, that there have been introduced among us persons, who have scattered the seeds of discord, and that we are divided into two parties—and that it has caused so much unhappiness and produced so many grievances, that we find it necessary to appeal to our father, the President, to apply a remedy—We hope and ask of him to appoint a commissioner to come and hold a treaty or conference, when we will state them particularly, and when, it is hoped, thro his mediation, our grievances may be healed.—

(We have been informed, that our annuity has been deposited in the Bank of Philadelphia, and we have also been informed by persons equally entitled to credit, that there are monies in the Bank for the four nations whom we represent. Should it please the President to send an agent or commissioner to treat with us, we wish that he may be prepared to inform us the truth on that point, in order to satisfy our minds.)

We have nothing further to say at present, except to request that we may be informed, as soon as convenient, and that the reply be directed under cover to Red Jacket, and Capt. Cole, or to either of them.

Done in Council at Buffalo, the fifth day of February, 1820.

Witness the signatures of the undersigned chiefs.

(Signed)

The following names appear in a column with the customary "X his mark" between first and last names: Red Jacket, Captain Cole, Twenty Canoes, Adjutant, Jack Berry, Twenty Canoes, jun., Big Kettle, Tommy Jemmy, Capt. MaGee, Cayuga George, Dennis Cayuga, Sam Harris, Robert Bob, John Smith.

In presence of P.P. Pratt, interpreter. Major [Jack] Berry, do. [Source: Jasper Parrish Papers, folder 1 of 2, BECHS, not microfilmed]

Dedication of the Merchant Schooner Red Jacket

SUMMER 1820

THE SCHOONER *Red Jacket* was launched at Black Rock just prior to July 1820. It was the first cargo sloop to have closing bulwarks, earlier sloops having open rails and stanchions (Walker 1902). Its maiden voyage was at the service of the British and American boundary commission on the Detroit River and Lake Huron from July to October 1820. The dedication was made at the port of Black Rock, but there are no extant newspaper accounts of the ceremony. William Leete Stone prints the following speech, which was given to him by Albert Tracy.

You have had a great name given to you,—strive to deserve it. Be brave and daring. Go boldly into the great lakes, and fear neither the swift winds nor the strong waves. Be not frightened nor overcome by them, for it is by resisting storms and tempests that I, whose name you bear, obtained my renown. Let my great example inspire you to courage and lead you to glory. [Source: Stone 1841, 364]

Request for a Quaker Schoolteacher at Tonawanda

SUMMER–FALL 1820

IN A LETTER written to the Indian Committee of the New York Yearly Meeting of Friends, Abraham Lapham gave the following extract of a speech given the previous summer or fall. The interpreter is not known.

To the Committee on Indian Affairs at New York

Dear Friends,

In compliance with the request of Red Jacket one of the chiefs of the six nations of Indians, I have undertaken to represent to you the wishes of the Indians residing at Tontewanda, communicated to me and several other Friends at Farmington at a conference with us in the past summer or fall—He stated that for a long time he had been strongly opposed to their becoming civilized or christianized, but that of late he had become convinced, as both fishing and hunting, in that part of the country, was nearly at an end, that unless they went to work and adopted the habits of civilized life, they must starve.

He stated also that some feint attempts had been made both by the indians and friends towards their civilization, but without much effect, and that now it was necessary for both friends & indians to be in earnest. As a necessary step towards the accomplishment of it he conceived it would be proper to establish a school, for the education of their children, at or near Tontewanda village—

He further stated that from long experience they had become convinced that full confidence might be placed in the society of friends, that in speaking to us he spoke to the whole society, and enjoined it on us to make their sentiments known—

Abraham Lapham Farmington 4th mo. 18th 1821.

[Source: Item 55a, Scrapbook of Miscellaneous Papers, 1807–1848, New York Committee on Indian Concerns, Friends Historical Library, Swarthmore College]

Petition to the Governor to Evict White Settlers and Black Coats

JANUARY 18, 1821

THE FOLLOWING MEMORIAL, written to Jasper Parrish to be conveyed to Governor Clinton, was submitted by Clinton to the legislature on February 7 (Lincoln 1909, 2:1076–77). This petition motivated the passage of New York State legislation two months later on March 31, 1821, prohibiting non-Indians from residing on Indian lands, a law that stood until 1825 (Densmore 1999, 93; T. Harris 1903, 348–49; Howland 1903, 149–50). The interpreter was Henry O'Beal, Cornplanter's son. The following appears as it does in the *Journal of the Assembly of the State of New York, 1821*.

Copy of a letter from Red Jacket, to Capt. Parish.

Canandaigua, 18 Jan'y. 1821

BROTHER PARISH,

I address myself to you, and through you to the Governor.

The chiefs of Onondaga have accompanied you to Albany, to do business with the Governor. I also was to have been with you, but I am sorry to say, that bad health has put it out of my power. For this you must not think hard of me. I am not to blame for it. It is the will of the Great Spirit that it should be so.

The object of the Onondagas is to purchase our lands at Tonnewanta. This and all other business that they may have to do at Albany, must be transacted in the presence of the Governor. He will see that the bargain is fairly made, so that all parties may have reason to be satisfied with what shall be done; and when our sanction shall be wanted to the transaction, it will be freely given.

I much regret, that at this time, the state of my health should have prevented me from accompanying you to Albany, as it was the wish of the nation, that I should state to the Governor, some circumstances which shew that the chain of friendship between us and the white people, is wearing out, and wants brightening.

I proceed now, however, to lay them before you, by letter, that you may mention them to the Governor, and solicit redress. He is appointed to do justice to all, and the Indians fully confide, that he will not suffer them to be wronged with impunity.

The first subject to which we would call the attention of the Governor, is the depredations that are daily committed by the white people, upon the most valuable timber on our reservations. This has been a subject of complaint with us for many years; but now, and particularly at this season of the year, it has become an alarming evil, and calls for the immediate interposition of the Governor, in our behalf.

Our next subject of complaint is, the frequent thefts of our horses and cattle by the white people, and their habit of taking and using them, whenever they please, and without our leave. These are evils which seem to increase upon us, with the increase of our white neighbors, and they call loudly for redress.

Another evil arising from the pressure of the whites upon us, and our unavoidable communication with them, is, the frequency with which our chiefs and warriors, and Indians, are thrown into jail, and that too for the most trifling causes. This is very galling to our feelings, and ought not to be permitted, to the extent to which, to gratify their bad passions, our white neighbors now carry this practice.

In our hunting and fishing too, we are greatly interrupted by the whites: our venison is stolen from the trees, where we have hung it, to be reclaimed after the chase; our hunting camps have been fired into, and we have been warned that we shall no longer be permitted to pursue the deer in those forests, which were so lately all our own. The fish, which, in the Buffalo and Tonnewanto Creeks, used to supply us with food, are now, by the dams and other obstructions of the white people, prevented from multiplying, and we are almost entirely deprived of that accustomed sustenance.

Our great father, the President, has recommended to our young men, to be industrious, to plow, and to sow. This we have done, and we are thankful for the advice, and for the means he has afforded us, of carrying it into effect. We are happier in consequence of it. But another thing, recommended to us, has created great confusion among us, and is making us a quarrelsome and divided people; and that is the introduction of preachers into our nation. These Black Coats contrive to get the consent of some of the Indians, to preach among us: And wherever this is the case, confusion and disorder are sure to follow; and the encroachments of the whites upon our lands, are the invariable consequence. The Governor must not think hard of me for speaking thus of the preachers. I have observed their progress, and when I look back to see what has taken place of old, I perceive that whenever they came among the Indians, they were the forerunners of their dispersion; that they always excited enmities and quarrels among them; that they introduced the white people on their lands, by whom they were robbed and plundered of their property; and that the Indians were sure to dwindle and decrease, and be driven back, in proportion to the number of preachers that came among them.

It is true, these preachers have got the consent of some of the chiefs, to stay and preach among us; but I and my friends know this to be wrong, and that they ought to be removed. Besides, we have been threatened by Mr. Hyde, who came among us as a school-master, and a teacher of our children, but has now become a black coat, and refuses to teach them anymore, that unless we listen to his preaching, and become Christians, we will be turned off our lands, and not allowed to plague us any more; we shall never be at peace while he is among us.

We are afraid too, that these preachers, by and by, will become poor, and force us to pay them for living among us, and disturbing us.

Some of our chiefs have got lazy, and instead of cultivating their lands, themselves, employ white people to do so. There are now, eleven white families, living on our reservation at Buffalo; this is wrong, and ought not to be permitted. The great source of all our grievances is, that the white men are among us. Let them be removed, and we will be happy and contented among ourselves.

We now cry to the Governor for help, and hope that he will attend to our complaints, and speedily give us redress.

RED-JACKET.

This letter was dictated by Red Jacket, and interpreted by Henry OBeal, in the presence of the following Indians, viz. [in a column] Red Jacket's son [apparently an error; probably refers to Cornplanter's son Henry], Corn Planter, John Fobb [Fopp], Peter Young, King's Brother [Peter, Young King's brother], Tone [Tom?] the Infant, Blue Sky, John Sky, Jemmy Johnson, Marcus, Big Fire, Captain [Tommy] Jemmey [Source: *Journal of the Assembly of the State of New York*, 44th Session, 1821, 392–94; also in *Ontario Repository*, March 27, 1821. A variant that lacks the final two paragraphs (about the future financial burdens of preachers and the eleven white families at Buffalo) appears in Drake 1841, 102–3; a version that begins with the middle paragraph, "our great father," appears in the *Niles Weekly Register*, April 14, 1821]

Defense of Chief Tommy-Jemmy

JULY 1821

ON MAY 5, 1821, a Seneca woman named Kau-qua-tau was killed at Buffalo Creek by Tommy-Jemmy (Soo-non-gize, or "Long Horns") for witchcraft. One of Jemmy's relatives had fallen ill and died, and Jemmy went to his fellow chiefs for counsel. The chiefs decided that the woman be killed as a witch. The woman was lured back from Canada where she was visiting, and a young warrior was charged with killing her. The young man's courage failed him, however, and Tommy-Jemmy led her into a field, plied her with whiskey, and cut her throat (*Albany Argus*, August 17, 1821; *Ontario Repository*, May 15 and July 24, 1821). Jemmy was reputed to be uncommonly intelligent, and his activity as a chief is indicated by his signatures on several political petitions prior to his arrest. He was the senior representative on a visit to England with five other Senecas in 1818, a yearlong trip financed by a combination of New York businessmen to display their customs as an attraction (*Buffalo Journal*, May 8, 1821; *Niagara Patriot*, September 1 and October 27, 1818; May 8, 1821; Bigelow 1896b, 415–16). Newspapers sympathetically characterized the arguments of the Indians and their defense lawyers, who argued that the state of New York had no jurisdiction to prosecute the case. Although convicted of murder in February 1822, Jemmy was pardoned (see Densmore 1999, 97; *Ontario Repository*, May 28, 1822).

The trial was well attended. Because the New York authorities were aware of the Senecas' anger, they allowed space for a large Native contingent in the courtroom. According to one of the attendees, Orlando Allen, Red Jacket participated in jury selection, in one instance asking a potential juror to remove his "goggles" so he could better read his expression (Bryant 1879, 352). In a widely reprinted comment, the *Albany Argus* noted the appearance of Red Jacket at this occasion: "There is not perhaps, in nature, a more expressive eye than that of Red Jacket; when fired by indignation or revenge, it is terrible; and when he chooses to display his unrivalled talent for irony, its keen sarcastic glance is irresistible." Before Red Jacket was admitted to give evidence in the case, he was asked if he believed in future rewards and punishments, and the existence of God. He replied, "Yes! much more than the white men, if we are to judge by their actions" (*Albany Argus*, July 27, 1821). William Leete Stone tells the story that on cross-examination, Red Jacket was asked his rank. He answered with a "contemptuous sneer and said, 'Look at the papers which the white people keep the most carefully [the treaties]. They will tell you what I am' " (Stone 1841, 320).

Although Horatio Jones served as court interpreter and gave testimony about his knowledge of Indian law, Red Jacket chose Pascal Pratt as his interpreter (Bryant 1879, 371). Pratt, a local trader fluent in Seneca, was a friend of both Red Jacket and the accused.

Responding to allegations of Indian superstition, Red Jacket replied:

What! do you denounce us as fools and bigots, because we still continue to believe, that which you, yourselves, sedulously inculcated two centuries ago? Your divines have thundered this doctrine from the pulpit—your judges have pronounced it from the bench—your courts of justice have sanctioned it with the formalities of law—and you would now punish our unfortunate brother for adherence to the superstitions of his fathers! Go to Salem! Look at the records of your government, and you will find hundreds executed for the very crime which has called forth the sentence of condemnation upon this woman, and drawn down the arm of vengeance upon her. What have our brothers done more than the rulers of your people have done? And what crime has this man committed by executing in a summary way, the laws of his country and the injunctions of his God? [Source: *Albany Argus*, July 27, 1821; *Niles Weekly Register*, August 4, 1821, 358–59; Stone 1841, 320–21; Drake 1841, 103–4]

Petition to Remove Parrish and Jones, and Refusal to Move to Green Bay

MAY 3, 1823

THE FOLLOWING PETITION was written at a council at Tonawanda to request Jasper Parrish's removal as subagent to the Six Nations, as well as the removal of Horatio Jones from Indian business. Sagoyewatha had just returned with Cornplanter and Jack Berry from a March 1823 visit to Washington to demand Parrish's removal (Parrish to Calhoun, March 28, 1823). As is clear from the text, the Tonawanda chiefs saw this memorial as part of a yearlong attempt to depose Parrish. The Tonawanda chiefs had met the year earlier on August 8, 1822, to list their complaints about Parrish. They printed a handbill of their proceedings. Although the handbill does not seem to have survived, a December 12, 1822, statement from Capt. Pollard declared that the pagans alleged that Parrish took a bolt of "the most valuable cloth" from the annuities for his own use, and that he routinely subtracted money from Indian annuities (Peter Porter Papers, microfilm, reel 4, item B-40, BECHS). Parrish responded by declaring that Red Jacket was drunk for two days during the August council. Parrish's statement, signed by the leading Christian chiefs, was published in several local newspapers in the autumn of 1822, but it does not seem to be extant. Red Jacket replied to their allegations in a lengthy speech in the November 15, 1822, *Republican Advocate*, which was recently located (see p. xx). The 1822 Tonawanda council handbill was sent to Secretary Calhoun, who had Peter Porter investigate the charges. Porter's January 6, 1823, report exonerated Parrish (Calhoun 1969–74, 7:403) and damaged the chiefs' allegations, as had a lengthy January 8, 1823, letter to Calhoun from the Christian Indians declaring their satisfaction with Parrish ("Letters Sent by the Secretary of War, Registered Series, 1801–1870," M-221, reel 98, DNA). For a background on the proposed move to Green Bay, which had been proposed for several years, see Horsman (1999; map 1).

The spelling and grammar of the following manuscript is poor enough that one might suspect it was a first draft, but it appears to have been received as is by the Secretary of War's office. The deposition at the end of the letter declares it was written by Samuel B. James as it was translated to him in council, but it does not state who the interpreter was. James also states that he was the author of the Tonawanda council proceedings published in August 1822. Because the manuscript is erratically punctuated with very few commas or periods, bracketed punctuation has been added to ease readability. The name of the person that the Tonawanda chiefs wanted to replace Parrish is illegible: "Gensare" or "Genson," probably James Ganson (*Republican Advocate*, November 15, 1822). In an April 4, 1823, letter from David Ogden to Porter, Ogden, who also had inscrutable penmanship, apparently spelled the man's name as "Gavion." He was the son of a local tavern keeper (Peter Porter Papers, microfilm, reel 4, BECHS).

Our Great father and friend the president and the Secretary Mr Calhoun we take the liberty once more to send you our talk[.] a Great number of the Chiefs of the different tribes of Indians which Compose the six nations have once more assembled at the Counsil house in the Village of Tontawanda and we send you the result and the long talk we have had.

Three of our Chiefs have we sent down to see you this winter past to represent and tell you our grievances with a great expense and trouble as the expense has to be bourne equally amongst the different tribes of Indians, and we thank the great good spirit they have returned to us once more safe and sound and we received them with open arms to smoke the pipe of peace once more[.] for that we were Glad[.] Yesterday we kindled the great Counsil fire at this place and the Counsil is now opened and the three Chiefs have laid all papers & every thing before us which has been done and we are well satisfied with every thing but one which we will now tell you what[.] We are dissatisfied that Parish is not put one side[.] we must have him out[.] we will have him removed[.] he shall not be our agent any longer[.] it was the main object of our visit and expense to you last winter[.] he has imposed upon us long enough[.] you say we must prove his evil deeds or you will not put him one side, this we are about to do and we pray you to hear your red breathren when they appeal to you for help.

The writing are now before you what was done at the great Counsil at Tontawanda last August[.] our determinations and intentions are the same now and it must be done[.] we all as one say it shall be done[.] we mean to hang to untill he and Jones is put one side. We are now agoing to tell you in addition to what we told you last summer (and the papers are before you) what he has done[.] the bad deeds he has committed and the evils he has brought upon us[.] we have caught him in a great many lies[.] Last war Parish came to us with letters and papers which he told us Came from head quarters the City Washington[,] which we have since found out was all false[,] that he either lied or the letters and papers were forged[.] Parish was to work at us in this way with his false papers for sometime[.] But when the orders did in reality come from head quarters we seized our arms with cheerfulness and flew to the field of battle to fight the enemy and protect our property. He has [taken?] to work with us another way[.] he has joined in with the black coats and sent them amongst us in order to cause a division amongst us and make two parties which he has affected[.] there is already a division amongst us Caused by the black Coats which makes us unhappy[.] [he?] say, it is your orders that the priests shall settle amongst and teach our children[.] we want nothing to do with black coats but threads[.] we want nothing but our own fashioned way of living[,] but he Say we must have them[,] the President and Secretary say so[.] but we believe he lies or you would have told us last winter when we Came to see you. he tells us that you tell him he must do thus and so[,] his orders are so and so and they shall be obeyed but we have found out that you never told him so and that he has no such orders as he tells us of[.] now will you keep a man in office who tells lies[,] and even tells lies about you[?] there is lying some where between you or him for he tells us one thing and you another[.] if he has lied he ought to be put one side[.] you appointed him and will you suffer him to abuse the trust [reposed?] in him and make you appear ridiculous[?] He has told us there was a great country of land for us at green bay [Green Bay] that we must leave this place and go there[.] he said his orders were from you that we must take our annity [annuity] and pay for land. There now who lies[?] did you ever tell him so. if you did we want to know[.] we have never sent any person to Green bay to look for land for us[.] if any other nation wants to go to Green bay let them[.] as for us we intend to stay where we be or do as we please and not be drove there by Parish & Jones[.] now here is another thing we will tell you about Parish and Jones

We told them sometime ago if they would be our friends and always take our part when we got into any difficulty with the white people or should be imposed upon by any one which they both agreed to do we would give them each a mile square of Land below black rock which we did and now they have sold that land and let what will happen[.] they turn upon their heel and do not trouble themselves in the least about it[.] we can never Get them or either of them [to our?] Counsils[.] And another thing about Jones we gave him a large tract of land on Genesee river to always be our friend and take our part but he has turned against us[.] we have always been Good to Jones and made him rich but he has turned traitor to us[.] Little Beard when we sold our lands on Gene-see river saved a tract of land at that place for himself and family[.] now Jones has got possession of it and built a small town on it and when any thing is said by us to him about it Oh put me to Jail is all the answer can be got[.] we are now telling you what Jones has done what a rogue and villain he is[.] will you keep such a man as that in office[?] when he will lie cheat and every thing else that is bad[.] you say we must prove their villany[.] we have now proved it[.] Look at this and look at what we told you Last August and then say will you put them one side[.] we say both shall be put out[.] we are determined they shall be cut off from any help from us.

We are very sorry you have paid any attention to General Porters letter who is a very Great friend to Parish & Jones[.] we never knew any thing about it and he consulted but a few Indians and those of the other party[.][1] the gen-eral opinion of the Chiefs was not consulted[.] there are but very few who are friendly to them but we tell you we are the majority and where there is any dispute the majority always [becomes rule?] and we are the most by far ten to one who are determined they shall be removed[.] we have nothing to do with Porter[.] he was last war all the time telling and urging us before we had any orders from head quarters to rise and fight[.] and he is now the one employed by those who have the right to buy our lands to get it surveyed[.] we have found out what Porter means[.] he is a great friend to Parish & Jones and Ogden who wants to get us divided and a quarreling among ourselves so they can have our lands[.] they dont care any thing about us[.] they would be glad if we were away beyond the big waters[.] if they could get our land Porter would be glad to keep Parish and Jones in for it makes a good living for them[.] they are Great friends[.] you thought by Porters letter you could not put them one side[.] but we will have nothing to do with Porter[.] it is to you our father your red breathren appeal for Justice[.] We think you like Porter better than what we do[.] he has not always done right by us[.] We have told you and we now tell you we have had our eye on a person by the name of [James?] [Ganson?] for our agent and it is our request that our goods be purchased in New York and sent to [Ganson?], for him to take Charge of also the money[.] it must be sent to him this Season for we think he will do us Jus-tice[.] we will have nothing to do with Parish[.] he had better keep away from us[.] he promised us when we were dissatisfied to give up or resign[.] Our good have been growing less & less every year since Granger has been put one

1. That is, the Christian party: Captain Pollard, Young King, and Little Billy.

side[.][2] the hoes axes chains & plows we are satisfied with but the rest such as money Cloathing Powder Lead Kittles &c &c we have never [drawn?] since Parish was in[.] all the rest of the agents we have ever had we were satisfied with so you cant think all this disturbance is for nothing[.] Sometime ago you told us we must do better[.] must cultivate our lands build better houses fences &c that we have done and we are very thankful to you for your advice[.] we have minded you[.] our young men work on our land raise grain hogs horses Cattle &c build good houses fences &c[.] we have [so much?] Good houses and fences you would think [so?] if you should Come and see them.

At this time there is not so many Chiefs assembled at the Counsil as there was at August last about three four or five from each town and from [some?] [here?] but they are the first Chiefs of the nation[.] we have removed our Counsil fire from Buffalo to this place the Counsil fire will [hereafter?] be kindled at the Village of Tontawanda and all Communications on papers sent to us must be sent to Batavia[.] we want you to send us an answer to this immediately[.] what will be done and send the same to the Post office in the Village of Batavia[.] Tontawanda May 3rd 1823

The petition is signed by customary "X" marks in two columns. Column one: Red Jacket, Black Chip [Black Chief?], Captain Strong, John Fop, William Johnson, Hot Bread, Onandago Peter, Jimmy Johnson, Black Face, Black Chip [sic], Elk Hunter, Big Line, Stiff Knee, Captain Cos [Cole?], Chief Warrior, Jack Berry. Column two: Cornplanter, Twenty Canoes Junior, Halftown, Big Knife, Peter King, John Sky, Jimmy Hudson, Bare Foot, Jack Snow, John Dennis, Snow, Blue Sky, Major [Burney?], Henry Obail, Captain Crow, Captain Jimmy, Charles Obail, Long Board.

Attest SB James[;] John Johnson. Greene County I Samuel B James being duly sworn do depose and say that I was present at the Indian Counsil on the [8th?] of August last That I did the writing which was done at the special instance and request of the Chiefs that Printed Copy I enclosed and sent to the President at the special instance and request of the Chiefs that the same was substantially the result of the proceeding at the Counsil except that it ought to been two thousand and [one?] Indians in the [lieu?] of three at the Counsil this was a mistake in the Printer that I saw every Chief affix his name or mark to the petition and that I wrote it as the intentions on result of the Council as it

2. At the expiration of federal law, Erastus Granger lost his post as agent to the Six Nations in 1818. Parrish stayed on a subagent, however.

was interpreted to me as near as I could I also say I was present as the Counsil on the 3rd inst and drew the writing for the Chiefs at their request that the above is a true Copy of the proceeding in substance as interpreted to me as near as the same could be known that I saw every Chief affix his name or mark the above [instrument?] and also I saw John Johnson witness the same.

SB James

Subscribed and sworn to this 8th day of May 1823 before me,

Jus. Peace

[name illegible]

[Source: "Letters Received by Secretary of War, Registered Series 1801–70," February 1823-March 1824, M-W, M-221, microfilm reel 98, DNA]

Request to Sell the Gardeau Reservation

JUNE 10, 1823

THE GARDEAU RESERVATION was sold without much controversy. It was relatively small by Six Nations standards (18,000 acres) and had few Senecas on it, mostly Mary Jemison's family relations (Hauptman 1999, 149–51). According to Laurence Hauptman's concise account of the history of the sale, in 1817 New York State passed a law making Jemison a private citizen, which allowed her to begin to sign away the lands she possessed to Micah Brooks and Jellis Clute (7,000 acres). Judge John Greig and Henry B. Gibson, both associates of the Ogden Company, had bought the preemptive rights of most of the remaining acres in 1818. At Greig's request, Secretary Calhoun appointed Major Charles Carroll U.S. commissioner for the sale (Calhoun 1969–74, 8:185–86). Greig and Gibson concluded the sale on September 3, 1823, for $4,286. There are no records of the council negotiations. The land sale was never ratified by the U.S. Senate (Hauptman 1999, 152).

Red Jacket may have been the speaker of this message, or he may have signed this letter simply out of national protocol for unanimity. Horatio Jones, a signing witness, probably translated.

Buffalo June 10th 1823

Jasper Parrish Esq. Agent to the Six Nations

Brother,

We the chiefs of the Seneca Nation understand that a small part of our Tribe Twenty three in number, residing on one of our small Reservations which is remote from any other on the Genesee river have expressed a wish to sell that reservation to the person or persons having the Lawful right to purchase the same.

We therefore request you and in our name to make application to our Father the President of the United States to appoint a Commissioner to attend the sale of our Gardeau reservation above alluded too or such part of it as may

be agreed to be sold at a Council for that purpose in the usual way of selling Indian lands.

Your friends and brothers,

*Signed as customary in a column by mark: Red Jacket, Capt. Strong, Capt. Pollard,
Young King, Little Billy. The witnesses signed in a column: Lucius Storrs, Jellis
Clute, Horatio Jones*

[Source: "Letters Received by the Secretary of War, Registered Series,
1801–1870," February 1823–March 1824, M-W, M-221, microfilm reel 98,
DNA]

On Separate Races and Religions

CA. 1822–25

THE FOLLOWING FRAGMENTS come from William Leete Stone, who obtained the manuscript from lawyer Joseph W. Moulton, a New York historian who lived in Buffalo during the 1820s. Both its high-flown language and quasi-biblical content suggest embellishment, although Sagoyewatha frequently remarked on the differences between races. Nothing is known about the translator or circumstances.

Red Jacket speaks:

"As to civilization, among white people, I believe it is a good thing, and that it was so ordered that they should get their living in that manner. I believe in a God, and that it was ordered by him that we, the red people, should get our living in a different way, viz: from the wild game of the woods and the fishes of the waters. I believe in the Great Spirit who created the heavens and the earth. He peopled the forests, and the air and the waters. He then created man, and placed him as the superior animal of this creation, and designed him as governor over all other created beings on earth. He created man differing from all other animals. He created the red man, the white, the black, and yellow. All these he created for wise, but inscrutable purposes," &c.

Stone then adds summary: "To prove this he reasoned from analogy, from the varieties in the same species, and from the different species under a common genus in all other animals, whether quadruped, fowl, or fish,—pointed out their different modes of living, and showed that they each had a distinct designation assigned to them in the grand arrangement of the animal economy by the Great Spirit. He proceeded:—"

"This being so, what proof have we that he did not make a similar arrangement with the human species, when we find so vast, so various, and so irreconcileable a variety among them, causing them to live differently, and to pursue different occupations. As to religion, we all ought to have it. We should adore and worship our Creator for his great favors in placing us over all his works. If we cannot with the same fluency of speech, and in the same flowing language, worship as you do, we have our mode of adoring, which we do with a sincere heart,—then can you say that our prayers and thanksgivings, proceeding from grateful hearts and sincere minds, are less acceptable to the Great God of the heavens and the earth, though manifested either by speaking, dancing, or feasting, than your's, uttered in your own manner and style?" [Source: Stone 1841, 351–52]

Petition to the Secretary of War for a New Agent, Complaints about Christians, and the Green Bay Purchase

MARCH 9, 1824

BECAUSE OF HIS UNABASHED SUPPORT of Oliver Forward and the Ogden Land Company, Jasper Parrish was distrusted by the pagan Senecas of Tonawanda. The following letter was signed by members of the pagan party and pagan-sympathetic Alleganys. The letter was dictated in the presence of J. W. Clark and interpreted by Jacob Jimeson, who was actively seeking favor as an interpreter for both the pagan party and the Ogden Company. Although the letter does not specify Sagoyewatha as its primary author, its content seems highly characteristic of him and is rendered elegantly by the Dartmouth-educated Jimeson. Although the chiefs were concerned about Parrish's corruption, their ostensible complaint here is that he lived too far away in Canandaigua to be of assistance.

The chiefs of the Seneca Indians to the Secretary at War

We the chiefs and warriors of the Seneca tribe of Indians through you, ask our feelings to be expressed to our great father the President of the United States. We want him to know that his friends the Senecas as well as the six nations are in trouble. We have no agent within an hundred miles of the place, where our great councils are held, though we were told that one should reside near us in whom we had confidence—The white people keep us in trouble by [settling?] on our lands, which they have no right to do—What is worse than this, some of them pretend to be teaching of the will of the great Spirit—They tell us what his words are, which they say are written in a book—The book we cannot understand—The people who teach it, look more to our lands, than they do to the good or bad world where they say we must all go—If they care about getting us to the good world after death, why do they lye & cheat so much to get the things in this life, which they tell us are of no consequence—

243

They tell us we shall be all alike before the great Spirit. If we do as they say, why then do they put themselves so much above us here and try to get our property, when their great master will make them like the Indians hereafter— Their words are smooth, but the red children of our father the President, believe their hearts are very rotten.—We wish to inform our father the President, that we have religion as well as the white people, we believe there is a great and good Spirit who governs and rules over the whole world, we have also ceremony to worship *him* which we are well-pleased, and *that* have been handed down to us by our forefathers, and we retain it in its primitive state; this we think is agreeable to your government and to the treaty made between us and the United States, and in which treaty [encourages?] us to improve our lands, houses, raising cattle, building mills, and all kinds of husbandry, in which we should [always?] endeavor to imitate our white brethren.—Also we would inform our father the President, particularly, that we do not disapprove of educating our children at the expense of their parents, not be dependent on foreign aid, or on people who wear black coats whose characters we have described above—And when our young men return to our places we want them to do business for us, and not say as the black coats "we cannot employ them because we do not know that they are men of the good Spirit," but we believe we are all of the good spirit, we think he made us all, takes care & protects our bodies; we do not disagree and split our religion into hundred parts, we do not prosecute, slander, degrade, and debase each other on account of religion, expect those whose ceremonies have been adulter[ated] with the white people's religion, or rather imbibed the notion of despising the people who do not perform the same rites though they can not read the book, nor understand the English tongue; what is worse than this? They think (and treat accordingly) they are not so good as they, say they "you must go to the bad spirit, & I am going to the good spirit you are not good enough to be with me;" this we do not like, because we think the great Spirit never made partitions or different places for his children to live in after death.—We also believe there is a bad spirit who troubles all bad people in this world, whether it is the same spirit the black coats call devil who they say has a big pond of fire that cannot be put out by water where he puts all bad people. Few words more then we shall close our talk,[.] at present, There are some of our tribe displeased with the Green Bay purchase, think it is a cheat, and the privileges we now have from the government to be taken away from them, but we hope that will never be the case, we look to our father for justice and protection.—Again we say we must have an agent here who must have a cane (a salary) from the government to walk with, at any distance and velocity to [punish?] the people who often steal our property—when this [is done?] we shall consider the chain of friendship brightened to its former luster.—

> Done in the presence
> of JW Clark
> Jacob Jimeson
> Buffalo March 9th 1824

Two columns of names appear, all followed with "his mark": Red Jacket, Peter King, Green Blanket, Blacksnake, Big Kettle, Twenty Canoes (Sr & Jr), Charles Obail, Tagwanica, Snow, Four Head [Big Forehead], Chief Warrior, John Snow, [Gononlohha?], Old Johnson, Isaac Mohawk, Delaware Chief, Barefoot, Blue Sky, Capt. Cole, Peter, Sam Harris, Two Guns, [Genon?].

[Source: "Letters Received by the Office of Indian Affairs," Seneca Agency 1824–34, M-234, microfilm reel 808, frames 17–19, DNA]

Petition to Legislature to Keep
Missionaries Off Indian Land

FEBRUARY 15–16, 1825

USING THE CHRISTIAN SENECAS FOR SUPPORT, missionaries began to petition the New York State legislature for modification of the 1821 law forbidding their dwelling on Indian lands. In 1824, Judge Samuel Wilkeson, an influential Buffalo politician, spoke in favor of changing the law and of the benefits of a missionary presence (Stone 1841, 394; Lord 1896; Bigelow 1896a; Wilkeson 1902). Wilkeson spoke in favor of a bill, sponsored also by the United Foreign Missionary Society, that made it partially through the legislature only to be withdrawn after vehement opposition by legislators who cited Red Jacket's recent speeches against the missionaries (*Ontario Repository*, June 23, 1824).

As he had become accustomed, Red Jacket addressed the following letter to Governor Clinton while the state legislature was in session. According to the *New York Statesman*, it was submitted to the legislature by state representative Calvin Fillmore on February 16, and it was subsequently forwarded to the Committee on Indian Affairs. The interpreter is unknown, but it shows greater literacy than some of the early 1820 texts, indicating possibly Jacob Jimeson or Jack Berry. Berry had accompanied Sagoyewatha as his interpreter in March 1823 on a trip to Washington to speak to Secretary of War John Calhoun (Fairbank n.d., 190).

To the Governor of the Council Fire at Albany.

BROTHER—About three years ago, our friends of the great Council Fire at Albany, wrote down in their book, that the priests of the white people should no longer reside on our lands, and told their officers to move them off whenever we complained. This was to us good news, and made our hearts glad; these priests had a long time troubled us and made us bad friends and bad neighbours. After much difficulty, we removed them from our lands, and for a short time have been quiet, and our minds easy. But we are now told that the priests have asked liberty to return; and that our friends of the great Council Fire are about to blot from their book the law which they made, and leave their poor red brethren once more a prey to hungry priests. Brother, listen to what we say! These men do us no good. They deceive every body; they deny the Great Spirit, which we and our fathers before us have looked upon as our Creator. They disturb us in our worship; tell our children they must not believe like our fathers and mothers, and that if they do, they will be burned for ever in a great lake. They tell us many things which we do not understand and cannot believe. They tell us we must be like the white people; but they are lazy and won't work, nor do they teach our young men to do so. The habits of our women are worse than they were before these men came among us, and our young men drink more whisky. We are willing to be taught to read and write, and work, but not by people who have done us so much injury. Brother, we wish you to lay before the Council Fire, the wishes of your red brethren. We ask our brothers not to blot out the law which has made us peaceable and happy, and not to force a strange religion upon us. We ask to be let alone, and like the white people, to worship the Great Spirit as we think it best. We shall then be happy in filling the little space in life which is left us, and shall go down to our fathers in peace.

Signed by Red Jacket, Green Blanket, Big Kettle, Robert Bob, Twenty Canoes 1st [Sr.], Twenty Canoes 2d [Jr.], Capt. Snow, Two Guns, Doxtator, Bare Foot, Broad Head [Big Forehead], Chief Warrior, Black Chief, Corn Planter, Elk Hunter, Bear Hunter, Fish Hook, John Sky, Blue Sky, Hot Bread, Black Snake, and several others. [Source: *New York Statesman*, February 22, 1825; *Black Rock Gazette*, March 15, 1824; Stone misdates the speech as having occurred in 1822 (1841, 394–95)]

Reply to McKenney about Missionaries on the Reservations

CA. 1825–28

THOMAS L. MCKENNEY was a commissioner of Indian affairs during the late 1810s, and later the first director of the Office of Indian Affairs under the Adams and Jackson administrations. From 1836 to 1844, McKenney published a three-volume ethnographic work, *The Indian Tribes of North America*, containing many Indian biographies. In it, he records a short speech Sagoyewatha once gave in response to a question asked of him about why he disliked missionaries. Although McKenney's political hostility to Sagoyewatha over land sales makes him an untrustworthy source (Manley 1950), McKenney reports that a former agent to the Six Nations was also present, Israel Chapin Jr., whose role as a still living witness may contribute somewhat to the speech's authenticity. William Leete Stone, who pointed out suspicious Sagoyewatha speeches when he saw them (such as a story of Red Jacket's eloquence in a speech with Farmer's Brother; see Stone 1841, 126–27), reprinted McKenney's account without caveat.

McKenney narrates:

I asked him [Sagoyewatha] why he was so much opposed to the establishment of missionaries among his people. The question seemed to awaken in the sage old chief feelings of surprise, and after a moment's reflection he replied, with a sarcastic smile, and an emphasis peculiar to himself, "Because they do us no good. If they are not useful to the white people, why do they send them among the Indians; if they are useful to the white people, and do them good, why do they not keep them at home? They are surely bad enough to need the labour of every one who can make them better. These men know we do not understand their religion. We cannot read their book; they tell us different stories about what it contains, and we believe they make the book talk to suit themselves. If we had no money, no land, and no country, to be cheated out of, these black coats would not trouble themselves about our good hereafter. The Great Spirit will not punish us for what we do not know. He will do justice to his red children. These black coats talk to the Great Spirit, and ask for light, that we may see as they do, when they are blind themselves, and quarrel about the light which guides them. These things we do not understand, and the light they give us makes the straight and plain path trod by our fathers dark and dreary. The black coats tell us to work and raise corn: they do nothing themselves and would starve to death if somebody did not feed them. All they do is to pray to the Great Spirit; but that will not make corn or potatoes grow; if it will, why do they beg from us, and from the white people? The red men knew nothing of trouble until it came from the white man; as soon as they crossed the great waters they wanted our country, and in return have always been ready to learn us how to quarrel about their religion. Red Jacket can never be the friend of such men. The Indians can never be civilised; they are not like white men. If they were raised among the white people, and learned to work, and to read, as they do, it would only make their situation worse. They would be treated no better than negroes. We are few and weak, but may for a long time be happy, if we hold fast to our country and the religion of our fathers." [Source: McKenney and Hall 1836, 1:6–7; Stone 1841, 333–34]

Petition to Governor Clinton for Inquiry
into 1826 Land Sale

MARCH 15, 1827

ON MARCH 10, 1826, while the federal legislature was still in session, Erie County representative Daniel G. Garnsey asked the Committee on Indian Affairs to appoint a commissioner for a treaty with the Senecas to consolidate at Allegany. He claimed Red Jacket supported the proposal (*Buffalo Emporium*, March 25, 1826). Suspicious of this unusual claim, the committee tabled Garnsey's resolution but they eventually succumbed to political pressure and recommended the appointment of a commissioner upon the "possibility" that the Senecas may want to sell some of their lands. Oliver Forward, who was a business associate of the Ogden Company employees, was appointed commissioner by Secretary of War Barbour to superintend the council.

The ten-day council concluded on August 31, 1826, when the Ogden Land Company bought outright four of the smaller Seneca reservations (Big Tree, Canawaugus, Squawkie Hill, and Canadea) as well as sizable portions of the Buffalo Creek, Tonawanda, and Cattaraugus reservations for $2,583 (Oliver Forward to President Adams, January 30, 1827). Although Sagoyewatha signed the treaty, he violently opposed the sale. Afterwards he immediately began a campaign to invalidate the treaty by charging bribery and coercive behavior by the commissioner. His allegations were easily proven during a government investigation over the following year. Many of the agents admitted bribing the chiefs (this was, in their view, standard treaty protocol), but they protected Forward by denying that he knew what they were doing. Horatio Jones testified in May 1828 that "Judge Forward in council urged the Indians to sell the land—Red Jacket pressed his hands upon him & told him to set down for that he was transcending his powers or duty & that he ought to shut his mouth & open his ears. Red Jacket & Judge Forward indulged in personal abuse toward each other—it arose from Jacket's calling his powers into question" ("Letters Received by the Department of Indian Affairs," Seneca Agency in New York, 1824–32, M-234, microfilm reel 808, frame 95, DNA). Jabez Hyde, the missionary to the Senecas, testified that Forward asked all whites to leave the room but Hyde listened at the door. Forward denounced Red Jacket, saying the Treaty of Big Tree would have been signed without him. Hyde said that Forward threatened the Indians that the government would be displeased if they did not sell (suggesting that they would be driven from their lands by force with no financial compensation at all). He said that Parrish addressed the Indians in Seneca and told them to sell as well (reel 808, frame 98).

Forward's unscrupulous conduct on behalf of the Ogden Company is indicated by his destruction of any records of the council proceedings. His brief letter to the president on January 30, 1827, simply informed him that the sale was made and that Red Jacket's complaints were spurious.

Although part of this remonstrance is obviously a collaboration with other pagan chiefs, the letter itself was attributed to Sagoyewatha during the following year's controversy. This remonstrance and another sent to Washington on May 19 were part of the Christian Indians' grievances against Red Jacket when they convened to depose him in September 1827. Because the official Six Nations council house was at Buffalo Creek since the early 1800s, the Christian Indians felt that the Tonawanda council had no right to petition the government on behalf of the Senecas. In the days leading up to this petition, Red Jacket's wife declared her intention to convert to Christianity. It was commonly rumored at Buffalo Creek that he threatened to leave her if she converted, which he shortly did (Howland 1903, 152).

The petition was signed by John Sky, Clear Sky, Red Jacket, Jimmy Johnson, Capt. Jimmy, Squire Brook, Big Fire, John Look, Big Kettle, and sixteen others. It was sworn before Dan Dana, justice of the peace, and interpreted by Henry Johnson. Jellis Clute, a copurchaser of Mary Jemison's lands in the Gardeau reservation, was an interpreter and business associate of the Ogden Company (Hauptman 1999, 150).

To His Excellency the Governor of the State of New York

The undersigned Chiefs and Warriors of the Senaca Nation in council convened at Tonnawanda, beg leave to lay before his Excellency their grievances together with a statement of facts relative to the late Treaty held at Buffalo with the United States Commissioner appointed for that purpose, and the Agent of the Company holding the preemption right.

We would inform his Excellency that [duplicity?] was used to bring the Indians to a compliance with the terms proposed.

After the Indians had been in council thirteen days, an interpreter was sent by the United States Commissioner, and asked the principal Chiefs if they had made up their minds to sell, saying at the same time it was a matter of indifference whether they sold or not. If they did not sell he should write to the President and Secretary at War, and they would show us the way to the Cherokee country.—When these expressions were made, it struck the minds of the Indians that they had better sell even for a small compensation, than to be driven from their lands.—And many other strategems were resorted too— Among them we would mention the following.—Mr. [Jellis] Clute & Mr. [Horatio] Jones living at Genesee river went among the Indians, and put money in the pockets of the most influential chiefs, as bribes—Red Jacket also states in Council that Messrs Jones and Clute offered him the sum of two hundred dollars down & sixty dollars when ever he should call for it, and would settle on him for life one hundred dollars annually in addition to the salary which he [was to?] receive if he would use his influence. Which offers he rejected. He also states that when at Canandaigua on his way to Albany the winter past, Judge Grigg [Greig] met him, and said to him Red Jacket, you had better [keep?] of the two hundred and sixty dollars offered you and return home. It will be useless for you to go to Albany.—Chief warrior of the Cataragus also states, that Mr. Parrish offered him the sum of two hundred dollars [down?], and one hundred dollars annually during life, if he would give his influence in assisting the sale of the whole reservation. Which offers he rejected, saying it is not a compensation for a small piece of their land at Cataragus—After the Treaty was concluded, Mr. Jones gave him fifty dollars, saying at the time, what a fool you was that you did not aid us in this purchase. He is now able and willing to refund it. At the conclusion of the Treaty the United States Commissioner stated to the Indians that a letter had been received from Washington stating that Red Jacket was opposed to the whites having the benefit of their lands, and that they had better devise some means to put him out of office.—

Colonel Pollard a principal chief expressed a wish to Big Kettle that the Governor would do all in his power to get their lands back, and did not doubt that he might effect it. That the monies which had been paid to the chiefs should be paid back by them. That he for one was willing to refund the money which had been paid him at any time.—

We have ascertained that the number in the Senaca nation in favor of the Treaty is two hundred and thirty six—And the number against the Treaty is one thousand seven hundred and sixty six—Leaving a majority against the sale of one thousand five hundred and thirty—From the forgoing statement of facts respecting the sale of the lands, we think fraud and deception in the pur-

chase is manifest, and we look with confidence to the rulers of the State & Nation to do us justice, and request the assistance of Your Excellency to reinstate
us in our lands. Which we shall ever hold in grateful remembrance.

Done at Tonnewanda in council this 15th day of March in the year of our
Lord 1827.

*The letter is concluded with three columns of names, all described as Tonawanda
chiefs and signed "his X mark": Col. 1: John Sky, John Fopp, [Big?] Sky, Red
Jacket; Col. 2: Jimmy Johnson, Capt. Jimmy, Squire Brooks; Col. 3: Big Fire, John
Look.*

[Source: "Letters Received by the Office of Indian Affairs," Seneca Agency
1824–34, M-234, microfilm reel 808, frames 59–60, DNA]

On Coercion and Bribery at the Ogden Council of 1826

MAY 18, 1827

IN A JULY 1, 1827, LETTER exchanged among Quakers monitoring Indian affairs, the authors quote Sagoyewatha making the following declaration on May 18, 1827. The letter was written by Samuel Parsons, clerk of the New York Yearly Meeting, and Willet Hicks, and addressed to Philip Thomas, clerk of the Indian Committee of the Baltimore Yearly Meeting, and Thomas Ellicott. The interpreter is not mentioned.

The letter quotes Red Jacket:

Last season a council was called for purchasing our lands. Our Great Father's name was used. Those who wanted to buy our lands, continued by putting money into the pockets of the religionists, and offering bribes to the religious chiefs, to persuade them it was best to sell. But the Pagan Party (as they call them) always refused to sell. So one party was set up against the other, which made great difficulty and trouble amongst us. When we were considering the subject whether to sell our lands or not, Oliver Forward (who says our Great Father sent him) got up, went to the Table, and drew the articles before we agreed to sell the land. He said, "take so much from Buffalo, so much from Tonewanta, so much from Cattaraugus, and swept all from Genesee.["] Then he said " 'Tis all one, whether you sign it or not; if you don't, your great Father the President will drive you off, and you will not get a cent for your lands; he will only show you the way to the Cherokee Country."

He (Red Jacket,) stated in addition that threats had been used, and bribes offered to effect the sale: that he himself had been offered $260, and an annuity of $100 during life. [Source: "Letters Received by the Office of Indian Affairs," Six Nations Agency 1824–34, M-234, microfilm reel 832, frame 229, DNA]

Petition to the President for Inquiry into 1826 Land Sale

MAY 19, 1827

AS THEY HAD DONE TO CLINTON, Red Jacket and the pagan chiefs also petitioned the president to look into the 1826 sale. The interpreter was Henry Johnson, who occasionally translated for Red Jacket in the late 1820s, but the manuscript also contains the voice of someone familiar with legal terminology. Writing to Secretary of War Barbour on July 20, Oliver Forward denied virtually every allegation contained in the petition, but he did notice that the memorial was written with more grammatical skill than some of Red Jacket's other petitions. Forward suspected that someone in the village of Batavia helped write it, but he doubted that the witness, Mr. Parmenio Adams, had the skills to do it (Oliver Forward Papers, microfilm M82-1, BECHS). Adams had also witnessed Sagoyewatha's initial protest of the 1826 sale (now apparently lost) from Batavia in the fall of 1826.

The only extant records of this petition are held in the Oliver Forward papers at the Buffalo and Erie County Historical Society. There are two versions with only superficial differences. The text presented here shows a more accurate knowledge of the names of the Indians who signed, but it is otherwise poorly spelled. Although the petition is not entirely Sagoyewatha's (among other things, he is referred to in the third person), much of it is told from his point of view and it shows evidence of his characteristic mannerisms—from the history lesson at the beginning to the remarks about Jones and Parrish's fat stomachs at the end. Although Red Jacket was unable to depose Parrish as subagent, his request that the government withhold ratification of the treaty was successful despite the fact that the terms of the 1826 sale were confirmed in later ratified treaties.

To our Father the President of the United States

We the chiefs and principal men of the Senaca Tribes or Nation beg leave to represent to our father the President, that it was some years after the white poeple first discovered us, before there was any name mentioned, then there was a name mentioned by the name of General Washington, his name sounded through the United States, and that he was the one to regulate the Government of the United States; that long time since a great council fire was kindled, by which our father Washington and Red Jacket the Great chief of the six nations with many others set down and smoaked the pipe of *peace;* at which time our father Washington entered into a treaty with the above named chiefs and others and bound themselves together in the bonds of Friendship and there agreed that both parties should use thier best endeavours that the same might be kept from *rust.* Yet if by unforseen accidents the same should be tarnished by either party or should appear so to be, neither party should hastily turn to the right or left, but should make known his greivances to the other party, that wrongs might be righted and greivances adjusted. Under the smiles of the Great Spirit we have until lately enjoyed the priviledges granted by that treaty except that of hunting. Under these circumstances our father the President will not be surprised that we are willing to let him know the pain that is in our hearts in consequence of the misconduct of some of the white poeple in attempting to get from us our lands and homes. And your red children further beg you leave to state to our father the President the following facts.

That Oliver Forward Esqr of the village of Buffalo on or about the first of September last reported himself to the chiefs of the said Senaca nation as being an agent appointed on the part of the United States to superintend in behalf of said chiefs and red children of the Senaca nation a Treaty to which they had been called with a view to ask them to sell a part or all of thier reserved lands. That he informed the said chiefs that the reason why he had been so appointed was to save expenses of travel, he being at Buffalo and could attend to it without much trouble, whereas great expenses would be incurred by sending a man all the way from the City of Washington. That Esquire Forward then requested to be informed by the said chiefs whether they would not sell thier reserved lands to the Ogdens & Company who were the persons who called them into a treaty or council and he (Forward) further stated that it was the request of our father the President to be informed whether they would or would not sell thier lands. (and red Jacket says) he told me to take the subject into consideration and said "Come to me with your answer in two days."

Jacob Jamieson was at the time my interpreter and according to his request I called on Esqr Forward on the second day subsequent to that request & I mistrusted that they at the time were trying to lead me away, and for that reason I took with me another interpreter and he Forward would then have nothing to say to me on the subject. At this time our poeple began to mistrust me and asked me what Esqr Forward wanted of me or why he sent for me. To which I replied that Forward wanted to know whether we were willing to sell our lands. After which the chiefs came to the conclusion to send to the several reservations and call the poeple together with a view to determine on an answer to Forwards request, and they answered we are all stingy of our lands. After which the young King [Young King] went to Canandaigua and informed John Greigg Esqr [Greig] of a time when a Treaty was to be held at Buffalo— When Greigg arrived at Buffalo, Red Jacket informed the Chiefs that they had no business to do with him of any kind, but they were anxious to have his business, Red Jacket still told the Chiefs to let Mr Greigg alone and not enquire any thing about his business, that if he does tell us his business he may crowd us very hard, and also informed Forward and Greigg that we would not let them have any of our lands, On which Mr Greigg with some warmth of feeling, arose from his seat and walked the room and told Red Jacket that he *would* have the land and Forward also arose and informed the chiefs that it would be a very sorry thing to them if they did not sell their lands and continued saying the company will like it all the better for you refuse to sell, and in that case you will not get one cent for your lands as you will be driven off them by the President of the United States. The chiefs then retired into the woods for the purpose of consultation, viewing the President as a father to his red children to think that he would drive them off, the small piece of land which remains to your red children from the large territory given them by the Great Spirit above & which your red children peaceably occupied until driven back by the white poeple upon the small scraps of land which they now occupy was grievous and hard to think of. and our only hope was Mr Forward had no authority from our father to make such a statement. Upon consultation the chiefs still concluded not to sell thier lands—On which Jasper Parish told them that if they did not sell it would be a serious thing for them as there was a set of commissioners appointed by the President to go to the west and look out a tract of land for them. Mr Greigg then took down the names of the Chiefs and their places of residence and also all the reservations Viz. all those along the Genesee river Cattaraugus, Buffalo and Tonnawanda Creeks.

By this time some of the Chiefs after having been told by Horatio Jones, Gillis Clute [Jellis Clute], Jacob Jamieson & Jasper Parrish not to mind what Red Jacket said, that he was always against selling thier lands came to the conclusion that the Government was against them, that they could not help themselves, and accordingly gave thier consent to sell a portion of thier lands—

Your red children would further state in addition to the aforesaid means made use of to compel us to sell our lands, that we have positive proof that bribes were offered to and received by certain men of our nation to induce them to consent to a sale to the amount of one hundred dollars each—also that the sum of 260 dollz was offered to Red Jacket and refused, and to the chief warrior of Cattaraugus tribe, as stated by himself. Parrish and Jones did offer to become bound to pay him the sum of one hundred dollars annually during his life by his first consenting to a sale of thier lands, which offer was also refused and spurned at; with the reply that he did not want the gentleman's (Jones & Parrish's) money but wished to keep his land—To John Fopp one of the principal chiefs at Tonnawanda was offered by Horatio Jones one hundred dollars which was refused by said Fopp saying that he wished to keep his land & did not want his money.

By these unfair means your red children have been constrained and coerced into a sale of thier lands and it is the opinion of the chiefs that it was done very much at the instance and influence of Jones & Parrish to which two men the chiefs have been a very good poeple so much so that they have fattened them up until their bellies hang over thier knees—very fat men indeed—Our hearts felt and still feel sad to think our agents should be with them and against us.

Permit us further to state that of our poeple it has been ascertained that there are 2606 who are opposed to the sale of thier lands, while on the other hand it has been ascertained that the number in favor are 430.

Your red children feel determined not to release thier lands & possessions unless compelled to do so by our fathers power which we are unable to resist. but we have every assurance that the hand of our father will not be raised against a handful of his suffering children—

Your red children feel determined not to release thier lands & [possessions?] unless compelled to do so by our fathers power which we are unable to resist. but we have every assurance that the hand of our father will not be raised against a handful of his suffering children—

Your red children most humbly pray, and indulge the hope that our father will appoint commissioners living out of our immediate vicinity, whose duty it shall be to make due inquiry amongst our nation and of our neighbors respecting the Treaty made the season past and the conduct of our agents; for we do feel that we have good ground of complaint against them, therefore we would humbly request our Father not ratify the said treaty till the cause shall be thoroughly investigated and facts known respecting its being brought into being, and the conduct of those who acted in the same and our poeple are fully and firmly determined to receive no part of the money engaged to be paid for the said lands—

We also humbly request our father to appoint for us other men in the place of Parrish and Jones as our agents whose conduct in the treaty has been that of an enemy rather than protectors and supporters of the rights and interest of your red children—

Your red children cannot close this communication to thier father with out expressing thier feelings of gratitude towards him for all favors heretofore received at his hands, with a full belief that thier prayers will be heard and justice done in the premises; they are weak and poor but with their last might of strength will ever be obedient to justice—and at all times send forth thier prayers for long life and choicest blessing of the Great Spirit to rest on our fathers head. Dated at the Council House of the Senaca Nation May 19th AD 1827 and signed as follows viz.

Column 1, all names separated by an "X" signifying "his mark": Tomey James, Robert Stevens, Jack Snow, Captain Crowe, David Bigfire, Sanforth Chief, General Washington [Destroy Town], Skintaugh Squatter, Tekeh Quagh, Chyan Dugaugh, Captain James, Blue Sky, John Hook, Black Chief, Captain David, James Clumpfoot

Column 2: Red Jacket, William Shanks, John Fopp, James Johnson, Chief Warrior, Captain Snowe, Joseph Tuhawanga, Isaac Davis, Levi Halftown, Munsey Chief, Squire Brooks, Henry Obail, Black Fan [?], Henry Johnson interpreter, Black Smith, John Blackchief, Joe Cathaws, Jugoona Jebechah

All the above names chiefs did at the time make thier marks in my presence Henry Obail excepted who wrote his own

attest P[armenio] Adams— [Source: Oliver Forward Papers, microfilm M82-1, BECHS; reprinted with corrected spellings in Bingham 1931, 458–64]

Council to Depose Sagoyewatha as Chief, and His Response

SEPTEMBER 15 AND OCTOBER 16, 1827

THE GOVERNMENT BEGAN an investigation of the 1826 land sale in early 1827. On May 19, 1827, Sagoyewatha and other members of the pagan party wrote an affidavit of protest to President Adams to have the sale overturned on the grounds of improper procedure and corruption (Hauptman 1999, 156–57; Oliver Forward Papers, BECHS). The Christian Senecas (in concert with Ogden representatives) countered with their own statement to Adams on September 13, 1827. Although the findings of the government investigation were delayed until December 28, 1828, it did not approve of the transaction. The Senate never ratified the sale, but it did not oppose it either. As a result, the purchase was never revoked.

The controversy over the sale angered Thomas McKenney, who informed the Buffalo Creek Christian leaders that the president would be pleased with them if they removed Red Jacket as chief ("Letters Received by the Office of Indian Affairs, 1824–1881," M-234, reel 808, frames 71–73, DNA). They deposed Sagoyewatha as chief two days after sending their petition to Adams. The transcript of their council's decision was translated by Jacob Jimison (BECHS, MSS C00-1, box 14, folder 2). The following text is from the first published edition appearing in the *Buffalo Emporium*, which was subsequently sent to the secretary of war.

"We, the Chiefs of the Seneca tribe, of the Six Nations say to you, Yau go ya wat haw (or Red Jacket,) that you have a long time disturbed our councils; that you have procured some white men, to assist you in sending a great number of false stories, to our father the President of the United States, and induced our people to sign those falsehoods at Tonnawanta as Chiefs of our tribe, when you knew they were not Chiefs; that you have opposed the improvement of our nation, and made divisions and disturbances among our people; that you have abused and insulted our great father, the President; that

260

you have not regarded the rules, which make the Great Spirit love us; and which make his red children do good to each other; that you have a bad heart, because in a time of great distress, when our people were starving, you took and hid, the body of a deer you had killed, when your starving brothers should have shared their proportions of it with you; that the last time our father, the President, was fighting against the king, across the great waters, you divided us, you acted against our father, the President, and his officers, and advised with those who were not friends; that you have prevented, and always discouraged our children from going to school, where they could learn, and abused and lied about our people, who were willing to learn, and about those, who were offering to instruct them how to worship the Great Spirit in the manner christians do; that you have always placed yourself before them, who would be instructed, and have done all you could to prevent their going to schools; that you have taken goods to your own use, which were received as annuities, and which belonged to orphan children, and to old people; that for the last ten years you have often said the communications of our great father to his red children, were forgeries made up at New-York by those who wanted to buy our lands; that you left your wife, because she joined the christians, and worshipped the Great Spirit as they do, knowing she was a good woman; that we have waited nearly ten years for you to reform, and do better; but are now discouraged, as you declare you never will receive instructions from those who wish to do us good, as our great father advises, and induce others to hold the same language.

"We might say a great many other things, which make you an enemy to the Great Spirit, and also to your own brothers, but we have said enough, and now renounce you as a Chief, and from this time you are forbid to act as such—All of our nation will hereafter regard you as a private man, and we say to them all, that every one, who shall do as you have done, if a Chief, will in like manner, be disowned, and set back where he started from, by his brethren.

Declared at the council house of the Seneca Nation, Sept, 15, 1827. [Source: *Buffalo Emporium*, September 24, 1827]

All the following names are listed in one column, followed by "X his mark": Ga-yan-quia-ton, or Young King; Ha-lon-to-wa-nen, Captain Pollard; Jish-ja-ga, or Little Billy; Ta-on-yau-go, or Seneca White; Jo-nish-har-de, or Jas. [James] Stevenson; Go-non-da-gie, or Destroy Town; Ho-no-ja-cya, or Tall Peter; Tat-wau-nou-ha, or Little Johnson; White Chief; Ha-sen-nia-wass, or White Seneca; Ten-nau-qua, or Doxtaten; Ha-ja-on-quist, or Henry Two Guns; Ska-nie-da-a-yo, or John Snow; Sa-ta-ga-onyes, or Twenty Canoes; Ha-squi-sau-on, or Jas. Stevenson, jun.; O-qui-ye son, or Capt. Strong; Ta-yout-ga-ah, or Capt. Thompson; Geo.[rge] Silverheels; Wm Jones; Jas. Robinson; Blue Eyes; John Pierce; Sa-he-o-qui-au-don-qui, or Little Beard; Barefoot; Lewis Rainy; Capt. Jones.

The account of Sagoyewatha's reaction was first printed in the October 20, 1827, Black Rock Gazette (no longer extant) and reprinted in the October 27 Albany Argus.

A few days after this council was held, Red Jacket sent to the several tribes, composing the Seneca Nation, and informed them of what had been done. Several of the tribes sent deputations to Red Jacket, who called a council; to be held at the upper Council House, Seneca Village Reservation; and which was convened on the 16th inst.

The following are the names of the principal chiefs and warriors who were present:—Red Jacket, Big Kettle, Fish Hook, John Fop, Green Blanket, Jimeson, John Look, Jack Berry, John Hemlock, Tommy Jimmy, Jimmy Johnson, Captain Jimmy, Levi Halftown, Young Green Blanket, David Stevens.

Jack Berry acted as interpreter, assisted by a gentleman of Buffalo, who is well versed in the Seneca language.

The document of the Christian party, disowning Red Jacket, was then read to them, by a gentleman present, and which was explained to the council by the chief Jack Berry, who rendered it in the Seneca tongue. While this was doing, a smile occasionally moved the features of the venerable relic of a past age; but his demeanor in general was dignified and imposing.

A long consultation now took place; during which the chief Levi Halftown addressed the council, giving them the views of the Cattaraugus tribe: he said that but one voice was heard in his tribe, and that was the voice of indignation against the persecutors of so great a chief as Red Jacket.

Information was stated to have been received from the tribe at Allegany; that a large majority was for respecting and continuing Red Jacket as chief.

The chief Big Kettle, then rose; and stated that his brothers of the council, had chosen him to deliver their sentiments[.] He took up the complaints against Red Jacket, and said they knew what was the cause of the council of the Christian party, denouncing Red Jacket on the 15th of Sept. It was something about a letter written to the president by Red Jacket, by direction of a council held at Tonnawanta, last spring. That the government sent the letter back to the agent, who came out and told the Senecas that the chief Red Jacket was old, and ought to set down, &c.

He said, that the present council was convened to do justice to Red Jacket. That the charges against him were all quite groundless and frivolous.

That he had got the minds of the chiefs present, who represented the opinions of the several tribes, and they now proclaim emphatically to the nation, that they never will consent that the chief Red Jacket set down—no, they want him to rise up—they believe that he can perceive the true path—that he is now in the true path—where they wish him to continue until the Great Spirit takes him away. Long has he, said the chief, presided among us. He was always the friend of his nation—the friend of Indians. He has always given his voice against selling their lands. He has attended all the councils where treaties were made. He was the companion of the Great Washington—when Washington first took him by the hand; he was governour of all the states—and the chief Red Jacket was one of the principal chiefs of the Six Nations, &c. &c. &c.

The chief Red Jacket, after an impressive pause, rose, and addressing himself to the gentleman present, stated, that this day our chiefs in council, have first been correctly informed of an attempt to make me sit down, and throw off the authority of a chief, by twenty-five misguided chiefs of our nation. You have heard, he said, what my associates in council have said and explained, in regard to the foolish charges against me. This is the legal and proper manner to meet these charges—and the only way in which I could notice them. Charges which I despise; and was it not for the concern which the respected chiefs of my nation feel for the character of their aged chief, now before you, I could fold my arms and sit quietly under these slanders.

The Christian party have not proceeded legally, according to our usages, said the chief Red Jacket, to put me down. It grieves my heart when I look around and see the situation of my people; once united and powerful; now, weak and divided. I feel sorry for my nation—when I am gone to the other world—when the Great Spirit calls me away—who among my people can take my place? Many long years have I guided the nation[.]

In respect to the long string of complaints against me, said Red Jacket,—I look upon them as biting me,—as arrows aimed against my reputation, and against my life. These things are ridiculous[.]

Red Jacket here alluded to the fact stated by Big Kettle, respecting the origin of this attempt to oppose him, from which it was gathered that he and the agent differed in opinion about some communications.

The Lord gave his red children their lands—General Washington said they were sure—the Great Spirit has marked out a clear path for his children—the Christian party, by advice of the white people, have left this plain path and gone among weeds—they have abandoned the path and religion of our fathers. We worship as we always have done.

He said that when himself and Major Berry were at Washington city, four years ago, the secretary at war, Mr Calhoun, told them, that when *black coated men* wanted permission to go on Indian land, they were told to go, if the Indians did not object; but the government gave no orders.

He said, in conclusion, that he should not silently consent to be put down. As long as I can raise my voice, I shall oppose such measures; as long as I can stand in my moccasins, I will do all I can for my nation! [Source: *Albany Argus*, October 27, 1827]

The Christian chiefs responded to the news of this council by denying that it was a valid Seneca council of sachems. A month later they published the following statement:

We the Chiefs of the Senecas have been told by the white people, that it had been printed in some papers, that the former Chief, RED JACKET, had been restored to favour by a great Council of the Six Nations. No such Council has been held, nor have the other tribes any thing to do with us. We have told him in Council to sit down, and he cannot get up again, until we take him by the hand, and that we shall do, when he becomes a good man, and not before.

There must be very bad men among the white people or such stories would not go abroad, because they are not true." [Source: *Buffalo Emporium*, November, 26, 1827]

Signed with the marks of Young King, Pollard, Destroy Town, Seneca White, James Stevenson, John Snow, Little Johnson, Tall Peter, James Stephenson, Henry Two Guns, Capt. Strong, Capt. Thompson, George Silverheels, William Jones

Livingston's Council and Sagoyewatha's Reinstatement as Chief

JUNE 25–JULY 4, 1828

THE U.S. GOVERNMENT was aware that the land sale of 1826 was not a valid treaty. Although Oliver Forward and Jacob Jimeson strenuously denied any wrongdoing, Judge John Greig, an Ogden Company associate who helped bribe the chiefs, wrote to Barbour on September 17, 1827, that bribes had been used ("Letters Received by the Office of Indian Affairs, 1824–1881," M-234, reel 832, 236, DNA). Coupled with Red Jacket's strident public denunciations of the affair, Secretary of War Barbour and McKenney were obliged to send a commissioner to investigate. Depositions were taken in early May from the translators and employees of the Ogden Company, many of whom freely admitted their acts of intimidation and bribery. Several white and Indian sources claimed that it was the president or his officers who recommended that the Christian Senecas remove Red Jacket as chief, an embarrassment that the government hoped a conciliatory inquiry might remedy. In late June, Judge Richard Montgomery Livingston of Saratoga met for the three-day council, taking statements from the Senecas and attempting to heal the religious and political strife that divided them.

Livingston's fifty-five-page report was a scathing indictment of the sale. He wrote that the chiefs expressed a unanimous desire to retain their lands until the last day of the negotiations, when they were convinced to sell only after being threatened in private by Forward that they would get pushed off their land in any event. In a vivid explanation of what happened on the final day of the council, Livingston wrote, "the terrors of a removal enchained their minds in duress, and becoming petitioners in turn they submitted to the terms dictated—to sell a part to preserve the residue. A panic pervaded the mass . . . many if not all signed reluctantly, and some while in the act of signing protested against the procedure as oppressive & fraudulent" ("Letters Received by the Office of Indian Affairs, 1824–1881," Six Nations Agency 1824–34, M-234, reel 808, frame 72, DNA). Livingston indignantly noted that the Ogden Company subtracted treaty expenses and bribes from the total sale price, and he stated that Young King supported the removal of Red Jacket as chief only because of the recommendation of the president of the United States. Livingston's report begins with a seven-page summary abstract, and its appendix contains copies of supporting affidavits and copies of the council proceedings of June 25–28. The following text is taken from Livingston's report and appendix. The council notes do not list all attendees or interpreters, but both Oliver Forward and Jacob Jimeson were present.

On June 25, 1828, Red Jacket welcomed Livingston to the council with these words:

Brothers, a Commissioner from our Great Father the President is now before us—In conformity to ancient usage among our people it is proper that we should welcome him to our council fire. Brothers, with your permission I will discharge that duty—(Then addressing Mr. Livingston, he said) "Brother, our hearts are filled with gratitude, that our Great Father the President has been so mindful of us as to appoint a Commissioner to inquire into our troubles— Some of us who felt agrieved presented our petitions to him, that this might be done, and in the spirit of our first Treaty, he has been prompt to comply with our request—which to us is a subject of rejoicing & thankfulness. Brother, We receive you as the Representative and Commissioner, appointed by our Great Father the President—and we welcome you to our council fire. We are happy to perceive that the Great Spirit has protected you through the fatigues of a long journey, and brought you in health to visit us. Brother, we will now attend to whatever you may have to communicate. [Source: "Letters Received by the Office of Indian Affairs," Six Nations Agency 1824–34, M-234, microfilm reel 808, frame 111, DNA]

The next day, on June 26, Livingston began the council by declaring that he came to heal a divided nation. He said that he used to play with Indians as a boy and was a good friend. He said that if any white men were guilty of wrongdoing, they should "point them out" and that he was asking for help to "make the chain bright." Red Jacket rose in response, and Livingston gave the following account of his talk.

Red Jacket: He would concisely state some of their grievances & allude to the fountain from whence they flowed. At the first Treaty the whites stipulated to afford protection and comfort to his nation; such as would be desirable & productive of great good to the Indians—They were not suffered long to anticipate the promised good, ere the missionaries came among them—They came with much deportment and fair professions—and he with others were beguiled to consent to receive them upon trial. Experience soon taught his people, that they had committed an error—his offense of *his* glory consists in his having struggled without ceasing to correct that error—When we wander from that straight path We should strive to return to it. The promised good first came in the shape of a schoolmaster. But the coat of the schoolmaster like that of the deer, soon changed and became a *Preacher.* He was stricken in years—he had traveled much and been observant of the evil effects of missionary efforts among other nations. Some of his brothers have yielded to its influence—He & his associates will wait for a natural appetite ere they embrace the proffered good, and until its benign effects upon their brethren shall have recommended it. Missionary efforts produced unseemly things. The young were emboldened to usurp the place and to assume the province of the Reverend in years & in rank. He has attended meeting when the Stripling Priest has represented him as not knowing whether a cat or a Dog was his God. He was taught without the instruction of others and believed in *One God.* It was his lot to be surrounded with those who entertained different religious opinions, and he was resolved to refrain from all broils or misunderstanding with his White brethren—He will specify the causes of their troubles—The whiteman's settling on their lands. The Syren voice of Priests, the Black Coat & the Agent (pointing to them) are the causes. The Agent by permission to such as choose. The preacher dressed & fed by Whitemen & who labors not, except on the Sabbath. He says he drops that subject, but refers it to the Commissioner. The path of the Whiteman's worship would be crooked to them—their own is straight to their view. He will now call attention of the Commissioner to the *Late Treaty* [of 1826]. He went at the instance of his nephew (pointing to Dr Jimeson) to see Forward from whom he received the information that Forward was appointed Commissioner to preside in Council & superintending the negotiations relative to the purchase of Indian Lands. Forward suggested to him that it might be proper as a preliminary step to consult some of the chiefs, to which he made no reply: but came again with two Interpreters. Forward objected to more than one Interpreter, & wished to consult but few of the Chiefs—Such as he consulted were averse to selling and resolved to call a Genl. Council and express the disapprobation of the Nation.—His nephew, (Dr Jimeson) cautioned him against calling such a council. But [asserting?] in their firmness he did not doubt but they would adhere to their resolution not to sell—After Mr. Greig arrived at the opening of the council, Forward, evinced a deep interest in promoting the sale—rose and advocated it. He made Forward sit down. Forward was more strenuous in his exertions to subserve the interests of the Company than any other person—

He and his associates would not yield to the pressing solicitations. They were neither won by the temptations of a Bribe nor terrified by the threats of a removal—He & his associates were always adverse to selling—Gibson & Parish took him on a former occasion a year before into a dark & private room and endeavoured to win him to their purpose—Gibson offered him $360, reminding him of his poverty, and urged in the most pressing manner his acceptance of the stipend—He was poor—they tempted him with wealth—but he rose above the temptation. He rejected their offers, because it would have been criminal to have received them & betrayed the Interests of the Nation—His friends all stood up, & would not hearken to Gibson, nor would they closet or Caucus with him.—At the late treaty when by an irresistible influence a majority had been brought to yield; obsequiously or out of complaisance & from a delusive notion of honour, he proposed delay to extricate them from their difficulty—But the Treaty was hastened to a conclusion—While Forward, Greig & others laboured within doors to promote the sale, Clute & others, he believed were privately filling the pockets without—Money prevailing with some over love of Family & Lands. But it was not money alone—much was said to alarm them—Forward advised the Nation to cast Red Jacket off that he was authorized by the Government to request them to do it. The Nation have not done it—but somebody has injured him at Washington—When there lately the Secretary of War showed him a paper by which he was put down as a Chief—and would not recognise him as one. His nephews (Jas. Johnson &)[1] who were with him at Washington, at his instance held an interview with the president, and he finally met a friend who kindly offered to introduce him, & did procure him an interview in person—The President received him kindly, & heard him patiently and gave him assurances that the subject of the Remonstrance should be inquired into—When there, a duplicate of a paper from Greig was handed in—The President did not recollect having appointed Forward—The Secy at War observed that the government did not covet the Lands, belonging to the Seneca Nation. Col. McKinney the head man in the Indian Office suggested the propriety of a division according to their numbers of the Residue of their Lands—His business at Washington was to procure the appointment of a commissioner to investigate the subject of complaint, in which he has succeeded. As he was ever a chief and assisted in every Treaty between our Govt. & his nation, from the date of this medal, pre-

1. An empty space for a name was left here in the manuscript. Jas. Johnson is possibly an error: Manley reports it was Henry Johnson who went to Washington with Red Jacket. The man who accompanied them was Stephen Fitch of Batavia (Manley 1950, 157, 166). James Johnson was the son of Jimmy Johnson, an important traditionalist chief from Tonawanda.

sented to him by Washington (*holding it up*), he was ever mindful of their provisions, & hoped that they might never be infringed—If the United States do not know that they are powerful & happy, deal justly with the dependent & enfeebled nation to which he belongs, it will be a stain upon their fair fame which time cannot obliterate, and the more especially, as they who were once Brothers, have assumed the appelation and Guardian care of Fathers. Strong, a Cattarageras chief was the first of his associates to consent to the sale, Black Snake of Allegany, then signified his approbation, a very few except those of the Christian party, consented until they were all *dragged* into it—Yesterday the money was offered to them, but preferring their Land, they would not touch the money. The opposition think themselves endowed with more wisdom than their Forefathers. He does not concur in that opinion. He entertains a confident hope, that the influence of the Great Spirit will inspire the mind of the President with wisdom to decide the most efficacious means to adjust their difficulties, and to restore their nation to Harmony—In conclusion he would observe, that he acts from no other motives than to benefit the Nation.—those who now live & their posterity; and he offers up an aspiration that the evils of the past may yet be remedied.—

After this speech, Big Kettle, Capt. Pollard, Capt. Strong, Chief Warrior (from Cattaraugus), John Fopp, and Blacksnake all spoke, either testifying to bribes offered, or explaining why they signed. Capt. Pollard, of the Christian party, took time to complain that Red Jacket never had council authority to call President Monroe "drunk or crazy" in 1819 ("Letters Received by the Office of Indian Affairs," frame 124). Capt. Strong disputed Pollard's charge, saying it had been previously "decided in council." As Blacksnake was explaining that Old Cornplanter had asked Red Jacket to give up his "fruitless" attempt to resist the land companies, Sagoyewatha interrupted him and pointed at Oliver Forward:

You see what trouble you have made—if you had held your tongue in Council, this would not have happened. (to the Commissioner) Reference has been made to Miller's Council[2]—Miller compared me to a Wolf—But I may yet catch the Wolf. At that council I was invited through [Jellis] Clute to dine with Mr. Ogden—I accepted the *gentleman's* invitation—When I sat down by him, he slapped me on the thigh and said he had come too early to purchase I being alive—and laughingly said, he would set a trap to catch a Wolf (meaning him, being of the Wolf tribe). Ogden said he would not in person have condescended to deal with so trafficking a people as the Christian Party—But

2. July 1819.

when I was dead, he would come with speed. There has been deep Policy used by the Ogden's to bring about the appointment of Mr. Forward. That he understood the President and the Sec.ʸ of War (Mr. Barbour) to say that they knew nothing about it—and that they did not want our Lands. Col. McKinney [McKenney] had acted officiously in the business. There was much conversation between President & Sec.ʸ & Col. McKinney—they cornered him and he admitted that he had done it—McKinney's excuse was that he supposed Forward was a proper man for the business—one who would open his ears, without opening his mouth to aid the Company.

James [Henry?] Johnson corroborated the details of his trip to Washington with Red Jacket. Young King, the leading Christian chief at Buffalo Creek, said that Red Jacket was always the first to want to sell land, and complained that Red Jacket says "we support the devil" when we support civilization. He said that they deposed Sagoyewatha because he was troublesome, and even abandoned his wife for her Christianity. He concluded the council for the day by submitting a copy of the September 15, 1827 council resolution that was printed in Buffalo. The council resumed the next day on June 27. Livingston's summary of Red Jacket is as follows:

He alludes to the paper submitted last night by Young King. It was a foul and malignant attack upon his private character—reflecting disgrace upon its authors and ought not to have been introduced into this, As I did not come here to inquire into Domestic quarrels between him and his wife[.] as to the subject of his killing the deer alluded to in the paper, it was not calculated to enlighten the President's mind on the subject of his liberality. His people who had often partaken in the fruits of the chase, with him well knew what character he sustained for Generosity. As to the scandalous charges made against him, his friends knew how to appreciate them and it did not become him to speak & defend himself, against such vile charges.

Big Kettle continued with a passionate defense of Sagoyewatha, and he reiterated that the 1826 sale was so corrupt that even Nathaniel Gorham, the son of one of the men at the Phelps-Gorham Purchase, did not want his name on the treaty ("Letters Received by the Office of Indian Affairs," frame 142). Oliver Forward responded by denying the statistics in Red Jacket's March 18 and May 19, 1827, remonstrances. In a long speech railing against Sagoyewatha, he said, "An evil dispised man could do more injury than 6 well inclined men could rectify." He concluded that proof of Red Jacket's lies were contained in a letter that shows Barbour appointed Forward as commissioner, not McKenney (frame 144). James [Henry?] Johnson spoke again of the details of his Washington trip with Red Jacket. He affirmed that in their meeting with the president, McKenney admitted that he told the president that he appointed Forward as commissioner. Several Indians then spoke, the pagans requesting that their names be removed from the treaty, and the Christian Indians requesting that money be paid to them (for what is not clear).

On June 28, Livingston gave a long summary speech that encouraged the Christians and pagans to heal their wounds. He advised them to stay away from the spirit of religious persecution. He promised that they would not be forced to emigrate. He blamed both sides for ill-advised fighting and encouraged them to pursue agriculture, not hunting.

The Indians counseled for several days in private, and on July 4, Livingston again met them in council. Red Jacket said in substance:

he looked mildly on the past,—acknowledged his liability to error—promised reformation—apologized for the past and alluding to the determination of the majority of the nation to sustain him, laid down near Pollard the deposing decree for the other side to display their magnanimity &c by its destruction ("Letters Received by the Office of Indian Affairs," frames 167–68). [Source: "Letters Received by the Office of Indian Affairs," Seneca Agency, 1824–34, microfilm reel 808, frames 111–68, DNA]

Pollard rose and said their difficulties were serious and not completely buried. He listed ten points of contention, insisting that proper channels of communication be followed (that is, no more councils in Tonawanda) and that the pagans conform to the president's desires. He also said that Red Jacket's promise was too general. A dispute in etiquette arose and Livingston jumped in and said he thought both sides had come to terms. Red Jacket and Pollard shook hands. Big Kettle promised the Tonawanda Indians would live up to their end of the bargain. Pollard then "rent the decree" of Red Jacket's deposition and "cast it on the floor" (frame 168).

Request for a Teacher from the New York Quakers

JANUARY 20, 1829

IN A LETTER to the New York Yearly Meeting appearing in Halliday Jackson's 1830 *Civilization of the Indian Natives*, Red Jacket made the following request. The interpreter is unknown. Jackson mistakenly dated the letter January 20, 1830, when it was actually written in 1829, a year before Sagoyewatha died.

To the Society of Friends of the City of New York.

"At the treaty of Philadelphia with William Penn and the Six Nations, we considered William Penn as a friend to us, not wishing to cheat us out of our lands, but to pay us a full value for them. Since that time, the society of Friends have treated us very kindly—they have never shown a disposition to wrong us out of our lands, but seemed to wish to cultivate friendship with us, and to let us have our rights and privileges—and to enjoy our own religion. But there are certain persons residing among us, at present, who we believe have a different object. They say they have been sent by the Great Spirit, but we do not think the Great Spirit would send people among us, to cheat us out of our lands, and to cause disturbance to rise amongst us, which has made a division in our nation. No, we do not think the Great Spirit sent the blackcoat's among us for any such purpose. There is at present five thousand of our people and upwards, who wish the society of Friends to send a suitable person among us, to teach our young men how to till the ground, and our young women the art of domestic manufactures, and our children to read and write. If our friends feel disposed to comply with our wishes, we shall be happy to receive them, and will cause all necessary buildings to be erected for their use—we think by having this plan carried into effect, the nation once more would be united, and become a happy people.

Your friend,

his

signed Red   **X**   Jacket

mark

[Source: Jackson 1830, 96–97]

Sagoyewatha's Death

JANUARY 1830

SAGOYEWATHA DIED on January 20, 1830. Red Jacket's last recorded speech was first published six years after his death in 1836. It is unfortunate that the source for his last testament was his political opponent, Thomas McKenney, but William Leete Stone, who often pointed out his doubts about suspicious texts, reprinted the speech without comment. According to the testimony of Sagoyewatha's descendants several decades later, the account is true. In March 1852, there was an attempt to move Red Jacket's grave because successive visitors had stolen most of the marble stones for keepsakes. At a Buffalo meeting convened to decide whether to move the grave, a Cayuga who had apparently married into Sagoyewatha's family, Dr. Peter Wilson, said Red Jacket did not want any whites disturbing his bones. Clearly echoing the repeated "let not" clauses appearing in McKenney's biography, Wilson said, "He forbid, in his last moments, the pale face to follow his remains when his spirit should leave them to unite with the Great Spirit. So let the white man not touch them. We the few broken remnants of the Senecas, will bear them away with us" (*The Friend*, June 26, 1852: 327; Densmore 1999, 121). His bones were finally obtained by his stepdaughter, Ruth Stevenson, who eventually donated them to the Buffalo Historical Society with the approval of the Seneca Council in 1884. Red Jacket's remains were then interred at Forest Lawn cemetery and reburied alongside several Christian peers from the 1820s: Young King, Little Billy, Pollard, Destroy-Town, and Tall Peter (*Red Jacket* 1885, 63–64, 81–86).

In the last days of his life, Sagoyewatha said:

"I am about to leave you," said he, "and when I am gone, and my warnings shall be no longer heard, or regarded, the craft and avarice of the white man will prevail. Many winters have I breasted the storm, but I am an aged tree, and can stand no longer. My leaves are fallen, my branches are withered, and I am shaken by every breeze. Soon my aged trunk will be prostrate, and the foot of the exulting foe of the Indian may be placed upon it in safety; for I leave none who will be able to avenge such an indignity. Think not I mourn for my-self. I go to join the spirits of my fathers, where age cannot come; but my heart fails, when I think of my people, who are soon to be scattered and forgotten."

Just before he died, he is reported to have added:

"Bury me," said he, "by the side of my former wife; and let my funeral be ac-cording to the customs of our nation. Let me be dressed and equipped as my fathers were, that their spirits may rejoice in my coming. Be sure that my grave be not made by a white man; let them not pursue me there!" [Source: McKenney and Hall 1836, 1:12]

Anna C. Johnson Miller, who adopted one of Sagoyewatha's step-grandchildren for two years and who also knew one of his step-daughters, gives the following account of Red Jacket's last words. It was first published nearly twenty-five years after his death but merits attention on the basis of Miller's relationship with Red Jacket's de-scendants and associates. According to Miller's narrative, the "cross" Red Jacket mentions in this speech was made of stones set in gold, but there are no other histori-cal accounts of Red Jacket wearing such Christian jewelry. In her preface to the speech, Miller reports that when cholera forced Red Jacket from council, he knew that he was dying. With his wife and daughter by his side, he said:

"I am going to die," he said, "I shall never leave the house again alive. I wish to thank you for your kindness to me. *You* have *loved* me. You have always prepared my food, and taken care of my clothes, and been patient with me. I am sorry I ever treated you unkindly. I am sorry I left you, because of your new religion, and am convinced that it is a good religion and has made you a better woman, and wish you to persevere in it. I should like to have lived a little longer for your sake. I meant to build you a new house and make you more comfortable, but it is now too late. But I hope my daughter will remember what I have so often told her—not to go in the streets with strangers, or asso-ciate with improper persons. She must stay with her mother, and grow up a re-spectable woman.

"When I am dead, it will be noised abroad through all the world—they will hear of it across the great waters, and say, 'Red Jacket, the great orator, is dead.' And white men will come and ask you for my body. They will wish to bury me. But do not let them take me. Clothe me in my simplest dress—put on my leggins and my moccasins, and hang the cross which I have worn so long, around my neck, and let it lie upon my bosom. Then bury me among my peo-ple. Neither do I wish to be buried with Pagan rites. I wish the ceremonies to be as you like, according to the customs of your new religion if you choose. Your minister says the dead will rise. Perhaps they will. If they do, I wish to rise with my old comrades. I do not wish to rise among pale faces. I wish to be surrounded by red men. Do not make a feast according to the customs of the Indians. Whenever my friends chose, they could come and feast with me when I was well, and I do not wish those who have never eaten with me in my cabin, to surfeit at my funeral feast." [Source: Miller 1855, 195–96; shorter version in Conover 1884, 13]

Red Jacket's funeral, held at the Mission House on January 21, was attended by both pagan and Christian Indians. A Christian service followed statements in Seneca made by the pagan chiefs present (Buffalo Republican, January 23, 1830; also Albany Argus, February 8, 1830).

Biographical Glossary

References

Index

Biographical Glossary

Allan [Allen], Ebenezer: One of the founding personalities of Rochester, New York, Allan had been a British Ranger during the Revolution who eventually settled as a trader in the Genesee valley. He built the first sawmill at the Genesee Falls, and he was constantly involved in questionable economic deals, political intrigues, and (quite likely) murder (Seaver 1992, 115). At one point, he kept several wives, Lucy Chapman (white), and Sally (Seneca; Mary and Chloe's mother), and, for a short time, even took in a third, Morilla Gregory (116). Unable to secure any land for himself, he moved to Canada in 1793–94, where he died. The improvements he made on his daughters' property, which he sold to Robert Morris, would become an issue at the Treaty of Big Tree in 1797 (Turpin 1932, 331).

Aupaumut, Hendrick: A Stockbridge warrior who had fought for the Americans during the Revolution. (See Ronda and Ronda 1979.)

Berry, Jack (Do-eh-saw, or Donnegoesha, "One Who Pushes Hard"): Chief Berry was the son of an Indian woman and a white trader. He lived several miles north of Buffalo Creek at Jack Berry's Town. He was one of the Senecas who captured Horatio Jones at the behest of a Seneca woman who lost her son during the Revolutionary War and who wanted to adopt another. Berry befriended Jones and helped him run the gauntlet after his capture (G. Harris 1903, 391–416). Pickering wrote in 1790 that Berry was reputed to be a "very excellent translator" (PP, 60:59). During the pagan-Christian controversies, he was a traditionalist and ally of Red Jacket.

Brant, Joseph (ca. 1743–1807) (Thayendanegea, "He Places Two Bets"): Brant was an influential Mohawk chief whose lasting achievement was the establishment of the Six Nations Grand River reservation in Upper Canada. His sister Molly married Sir William Johnson. An active ally of the British during and after the Revolution, he was known for conducting military raids against the New York State colonists. After the war, his allegiance to the British was rewarded in 1784 by a several-hundred-square-mile reservation along the Grand River, held in trust by the British crown. He was often at odds with Red Jacket, and the two were distrustful of each other. The final ten years of his life were marked by frustration with British authorities, however, who often blocked his attempts to sell portions of the land to raise sorely needed money for his people. Educated for several years at Eleazar Wheelock's Indian School in

Lebanon, Connecticut, Brant helped to translate a bilingual Mohawk-English prayer book and kept up an extensive political correspondence for much of his life. (See Kelsay 1984; Stone 1838.)

Butler, John (1728–1896): Born in Connecticut, Butler served as an officer during the Seven Years' War and became a lieutenant colonel during the Revolution. A friend of Sir William Johnson, Butler became famous for working with the Indians. Butler's Rangers carried out many successful raids against the colonial forces in upstate New York and Pennsylvania, the most famous being the Wyoming Massacre. After the war, Butler settled at Niagara as deputy superintendent of Indian affairs for the British, where he was greatly liked and trusted by the Senecas. Butler was a partner in the Niagara Genesee Land company that helped promote the Phelps-Gorham Purchase of 1788. He died in 1796. (See Kelsay 1984; Maier 1984; O. Turner 1851; Graymont 1972.)

Chapin, Cyrenus: See introduction to "A Variant Text of the Reply to Cram."

Chapin, General Israel, Sr., & Captain Israel, Jr.: Born in Hatfield, Massachusetts, Chapin Sr. rose from captain to brigadier general during the Revolution and also worked part time as a procurer of supplies for U.S. troops, subcontracting orders from Oliver Phelps. His family moved to Canandaigua in 1790, and there he was appointed agent for Indian affairs until his death in 1795. The Senecas liked Chapin—he was said to be an unpretentious farmer at heart, and upon his death, they asked that his son take his place as agent (see O. Turner 1851, 291). His son, Captain Israel Chapin Jr., was federal agent to the Six Nations from 1795 to 1802. He was appointed just after his father died, and he lost his post with the incoming Jefferson administration to Callender Irvine, who in turn was replaced by Erastus Granger in 1803.

Claus, William: Claus was appointed deputy superintendent of the Six Nations at Fort George in October 1796, just after the death of Colonel John Butler in May (Kelsay 1984, 157–59). William Claus was Sir William Johnson's grandson through his father, Daniel Claus, who married Johnson's daughter in 1762. On September 30, 1800, William Claus became deputy superintendent of Indian affairs for Upper Canada, a position he held for twenty-six years until his death. According to Kelsay, William was wary of how his father lost his commission through political intrigue and became a circumspect professional administrator.

Cleaveland, Moses: Born in Canterbury, Connecticut, in 1754, Cleaveland was the founder of Cleveland, Ohio, where he headed the first surveying expedition of the Connecticut Land Company, of which he was a coproprietor. Cleaveland was Revolutionary War veteran and graduate of Yale. He died in Connecticut in 1806.

Cornplanter (Ki-en-twa-ke; ca. 1732–1836): A distinguished Seneca warrior chief from Allegany, Cornplanter was the son of a Seneca woman and a Dutch trader named John Abeel, or O'Bail, born at Canawaugus (Avon), New York (Philips 1956, 606n). Cornplanter had the same mother as Handsome Lake. He fought in the Seven Years' War (with the French) and the Revolution (with the British) and owned extensive lands at Allegany. Among his many noteworthy activities, he is remembered for several moving speeches he gave in Philadelphia in 1790 (see *ASPIA*, 1:141) and his friendly relations with the Quakers. By 1800, Cornplanter's presence at several embarrassing treaties (Fort Stanwix in 1784 and Harmar/Muskingum in 1789), coupled with his acceptance of money from land companies, made the Buffalo Creek Senecas wary of his motives (Stone 1841, 129; Savery 1837). Cornplanter was a strong advocate for the sale of Big Tree in 1797. In 1809, he fought with Handsome Lake over execution for witchcraft, which he no longer supported, and obliged Handsome Lake to move away from Allegany. Cornplanter died at Allegany in 1836, over 100 years of age. (See Abler 2005; Jackson 1830, 1952, 1957; Stone 1841, 423–56; Symes 1995; Wallace 1972.)

Cusick, Nicholas: Cusick, a Tuscarora warrior from a well-regarded family, worked as an interpreter and died in Lewiston, New York, in 1840. Cusick's son was an historian of the Tuscaroras. (See Bacon 1903, 182; McKenney & Hall 1933, 30.)

Ellicott, Joseph: Trained by his elder brother as a surveyor in Pennsylvania, Ellicott rose from being a surveyor for the Holland Land Company to its resident agent, charged with selling 3.3 million acres of land to new settlers. All his life, Ellicott had a reputation for being brusque and rude, but by the late 1810s he had become overweight and subject to deep fits of melancholy. He was dismissed from the company's employ in the early 1820s for being unable to block road taxes against the company, as well as for enraging influential Clintonians. After his firing, Ellicott's depression worsened and he eventually hung himself in 1826. (See Chazanof 1970; Ellicott 1937.)

Farmer's Brother (Honayawas): A highly respected Buffalo Creek sachem, Farmer's Brother fought with distinction in the Seven Years' War (with the French), the Revolution (with the British), and the War of 1812 (with the Americans). He was probably born in the 1730s. He was among the leading chiefs at Buffalo Creek and a close friend of Red Jacket's. He was proud of his military conduct, and there were several anecdotes of his career circulated in newspapers in the 1820s (see his biography in the *Ontario Repository*, August 14, 1821, the basis of Thatcher's and McKenney and Hall's biographical entries). He was widely thought to have led the fight at Devil's Hole in the 1760s, where he drove an entire party of English soldiers into the Niagara gorge, leaving only two survivors. In council, he was reputed to be sober and sensible, and his opinions carried great weight. He was a traditionalist, and when he died of natural causes in 1814, the senior sachems became Captain Pollard and Young King, who both converted to Christianity. (See Stone 1841, 409–19.)

Forward, Oliver (1780–1833): Forward was a Niagara County judge and state assemblyman. Born in Connecticut in 1780, Forward came to Buffalo in 1809 after living for about six years in Aurora, Ohio. A brother-in-law of Erastus Granger, he soon took over Granger's duties as postmaster and port collector, and he became a trustee of the city. Among his many activities, he ran a stage coach business and was director of the Bank of Niagara. He was an effective sponsor of Buffalo's bid to get the Erie Canal from 1819 to 1823. A leading Buffalo citizen, Forward was a friend and associate of the Ogden Company directors. (See Sheldon 1879.)

Good Peter (Agwelondongwas, "Breaking of Twigs"): Good Peter was a well-liked Christian Oneida war captain and orator. He fought against the Americans during the Revolution. Young Peter was his son. (See Drake 1841, 106–7; Hauptman 1999, 40–42.)

Gorham, Nathaniel, Jr. and Sr.: Born in Charlestown, Massachusetts, Gorham Sr. (1738–1796) was a successful merchant who rose to a number of political positions. He was a delegate to the Massachusetts Constitutional Convention, elected to Congress in 1784, and a delegate to the federal Constitutional Convention as well. In 1788, he purchased the preemptive right to most of western New York State from Massachusetts with Oliver Phelps. Unfortunately, Phelps and Gorham were unable to make their payments to Massachusetts, and they were forced to forfeit most of their property back to the state, a business humiliation from which Gorham never recovered. He died in 1796. His son, Nathaniel Jr., moved to Canandaigua in the early 1790s to look after his father's land investments, where he became town supervisor and president of the Ontario Bank. Nathaniel Jr. died in Canandaigua in 1826. (See Humphrey 1927.)

Granger, Erastus (1765–1826): A politically ambitious Jeffersonian (his cousin was Gideon Granger, Jefferson's postmaster), he was appointed federal agent to the Six Nations from 1803 to 1818. He simultaneously held the positions of postmaster at Buffalo Creek, county judge (1807–1817), and town supervisor of Buffalo (1816–1817). (See Snyder 1978; "Documents and Miscellany" 1896, 385–86.)

Greig, John (1779–1858): His name is spelled a variety of ways in the historical literature: Grigg, Greigg, Grieg. Greig was born and educated as a lawyer in Scotland, and he moved to Canandaigua in 1800 where he married a daughter of General Israel Chapin Sr., Clarissa Chapin. Greig became a prosperous lawyer, landowner, and citizen and was appointed regent to the state university in 1825 and chancellor in 1845.

Because of his marriage and business contacts, Greig was one of Stone's informants about Sagoyewatha's life. (See Hauptman 1999.)

Handsome Lake (Ganio'dai'io or Con-ne-di-yea; d. 1815): Considerably overshadowed in his youth by his powerful half-brother, Cornplanter, Handsome Lake awoke after a great sickness in 1799 and claimed that he had experienced a religious vision (the *Gaiwiio* or "Good Message"). He prophesied the regeneration of the Seneca people if they returned to native traditions, resisted land sales and intermarriage with whites, and abstained from alcohol and gambling (Parker 1968; Wallace 1972, 239–321). Although Handsome Lake invigorated and modernized Haudenosaunee traditions, he attempted to suppress opposition to him by villainizing his personal and political enemies, often women (Wallace 1972, 263–91; for the changing understanding of women's roles in Haudenosaunee life, see Allen 1986; Bilharz 1995; Mann 2000; Richards 1957; Rothenberg 1980; Tooker 1984). The tension between Red Jacket and Handsome Lake is evident in one version of the *Gaiwiio* which features Red Jacket, like Sisyphus, forever carrying wheelbarrows full of dirt as punishment for being the first to sell Indian land (Parker 1968, 68). In another version, however, Farmer's Brother is the one punished (Morgan 1990, 254–55). Handsome Lake sometimes quarreled with his brother Cornplanter over land use, and after Handsome Lake had a woman put to death for witchcraft in 1809, he moved from his reservation at Oil Spring to Tonawanda where his political reputation waned steadily until his death in 1815. (See Wallace 1972, 239–302.)

Hyde, Jabez: A missionary schoolteacher appointed by the New York Missionary Society in 1811, Hyde is known for translating hymns into Seneca, and for his sympathy for the Indians. In 1819, Oliver Forward wrote to Jasper Parrish that Hyde was a "poor, ignorant, lying dirty, Idle, infamous hypocrite, and will no doubt do much mischief to the Indians" (Oliver Forward Papers, BECHS). Although Hyde was not liked by many, he worked hard to protect the Senecas and remained living with them even after he was removed by the society after 1825. Despite Hyde's work for the Senecas, Sagoyewatha opposed Hyde's missionary activities, and two were antagonists until 1826. By that point Red Jacket seems to have realized Hyde was a friend. (See Houghton 1920; Howland 1903; Hyde 1903; New York Missionary Society 1812.)

Jacquette, Peter: Sometimes called Peter Otsaquette, he was an Oneida sachem only twenty-six years old when he died in Philadelphia in 1792. When Jaquette was twelve years old he was taken to France by Lafayette at the close of the revolution, and well educated. Upon his return, he became unhappy and dissolute. He apparently died of pleurisy. (See Drake 1841.)

Jimeson, Jacob (T'we-wa-nate): Jimeson (or as his name is also spelled, Jemison, Jameson, or Jamieson) was the grandson of Mary Jemison, and Red Jacket's nephew (although the term "nephew" can sometimes refer simply to being of the same tribe or clan). Jimeson was sent to Dartmouth from 1816 to 1818. By 1823 Jimeson was studying medicine with Dr. Cyrenus Chapin, and he also apparently agreed to serve as a teacher of Seneca youth in league with Sagoyewatha's plan to permanently expel the missionaries "neck and heels" from the reservation (T. Harris 1903, 344–45; *Albany Argus*, December 19, 1827). By 1826, however, Jimeson was working as an interpreter for the Ogden Land Company on behalf of the Christian party (Hauptman 1999, 154). He became a surgeon's mate in the U.S. Navy in 1828, and died of fever aboard ship in 1836. (See Fenton 1969.)

Johnson, Henry or Hank: Henry Johnson was Red Jacket's primary interpreter from 1827 to 1829. He was a white captive, adopted by the Seneca. He was taken so young from his parents that he could not remember them. He was known for being sober, lived in Cattaraugus, and had a Delaware wife. (See Manley 1950, 163–64.)

Johnson, William: Apparently no relation to the family of Sir William Johnson, he was an early settler of Buffalo in 1780–81, where he ran a tavern and an Indian store, and often served as an interpreter (Hill 1923, 1:51–52, 61, 76; Fairbank n.d., 86). His wife was Indian, and he was an important Indian liaison and interpreter at the Livingston lease and the Phelps-Gorham Purchase of 1788. He was an associate of Joseph Brant's and was appointed British Indian Department interpreter in 1788 (Maier 1984, 17). For this reason, Timothy Pickering had him barred from attendance at the Treaty of Canandaigua in 1794. Johnson's manuscript narrative while at the Glaize in 1792 records his astonishment at Red Jacket's persuasive abilities (Johnson 1792).

Jones, Horatio (Hoc-Sa-Go-Wah, "Handsome Boy"): Jones was born in 1763 in Dowington, Pennsylvania, to the son of a gunsmith who believed in physical training. He joined the Bedford Rangers in 1777 and was captured during Sullivan's march in 1779 (Stone 1841, 415); G. Harris writes he was captured in 1781, which seems to be an error (1903, 389). In addition to Jones's ease learning Seneca, he earned the Senecas' respect by often besting his captors in fights and races while held captive as a teenager. After successfully running the gauntlet, he was adopted from Captain Shongo's possession by a Seneca woman. He was freed in 1784 and settled with his wife, Sara Whitmore (who had also been a captive), on Seneca Lake. He served as an interpreter at Livingston's lease in 1788 and at a variety of major councils afterward, including the case of Stiff-Armed George. By the 1800s, he had become a significant landowner, having been given a mile-square tract by the Senecas (initially gifted in council in 1798, confirmed at the sale of the Mile-Wide Strip, 1802; see map 5), as well as purchasing 1,280 acres of Little Beard's Town in 1802. Eventually he became a paid interpreter for the Ogden Land Company in the 1810s and an opponent of Red Jacket. He died in 1836. For a vivid biography of Jones's early life, see G. Harris (1903).

Little Beard (Sequi-dong-quee): Little Beard is remembered in the *Narrative of Mary Jemison* as a fierce warrior (Seaver 1992, 103). He participated in the 1778 raid on Cherry Valley (Kelsay 1984, 232). He was also thought to have helped torture Lieutenant Thomas Boyd during the same period Horatio Jones was captured in 1779.

Little Billy (Jish-kaa-ga, "Green Grasshopper"): A war chief, Billy was frequently a spokesman for the warriors as well as the women in the 1790s. He was reputed to have been Washington's guide prior to Braddock's defeat in the Seven Years' War, but it seems unlikely, given most of Billy's Seneca peers served with the French. He died in 1834 and his bones were reinterred along Red Jacket's in 1884 at Forest Lawn cemetery. (See Bryant 1885, 84.)

Morris, Robert: Morris, a signer of the Declaration of Independence, was well-connected Philadelphia investor who had used his own collateral to borrow money to help subsidize the Revolution. Like George Washington and many other leading Americans of the 1790s, he became heavily indebted through speculation in land (see Taylor 1995; Royster 1999). After Phelps and Gorham defaulted on two-thirds of their payments to Massachusetts, Morris and his designee, Samuel Ogden, bought the balance of the preemptive rights from Massachusetts in 1791. Although he secured title to nearly four million acres of New York State from the Senecas at the 1797 Treaty of Big Tree, he was still unable to meet his financial promises and went to debtor's prison from 1798–1801. He died five year later. (See Chernow 1977.)

Obail, Henry: Son of the Allegany chief Cornplanter, Henry was sent to be educated by the Quakers in Philadelphia but only stayed several months before returning to Allegany. He eventually became a member of the pagan party during the controversies of the 1810s and 1820s and moved to Tonawanda. He was a close ally of Red Jacket's in the final decade of his life. (See Abler 2005; Stone 1841, 456–58.)

Ogden, David A.: Born in 1770, David was one of the many children of Abraham Ogden of Morristown, New Jersey. David became a lawyer for the Holland Land Company and was charged with suing Robert Morris for funds owed to the company. For David's later role as founder of the Ogden Land Company, see the prefaces to speeches "Replies to Rev. John Alexander and John Richardson, Esq. May 1811," "Reply to David Ogden, July 1819," and "Petition to Governor Clinton for Inquiry over 1826 Land Sale, March 15, 1827." In concert with Oliver Forward, who acted as sale commissioner, David Ogden's land company finally succeeded in buying the majority of Seneca reservation land through bribery and intimidation in August 1826. David's brothers and business partners included Thomas Ludlow Ogden, a lawyer for Alexander Hamilton, and Governeur Ogden. David died in 1829. (See Ogden Papers.)

Parrish, Jasper (1767–1836): In July 1778, eleven-year-old Parrish was captured with his father by Delawares in Pennsylvania and, as was customary, forced to run through a gauntlet of clubs as part of his initiation. After learning Delaware for two years, he was sold to the Mohawk warrior David Hill for five years, learning Mohawk also (Manley 1932, 105). Freed at Fort Stanwix in 1784, he had almost forgotten how to speak English. After his captivity, he received only a year's formal education in reading and writing. His translating skills, however, eventually earned him a position as an official government interpreter in 1790, which paid $200 a year. In 1803, he was appointed subagent for Indian affairs of the Six Nations, a position he held until 1829. He was reputed to know six Indian languages. Although he and Sagoyewatha fell out of friendship during the Christian-pagan controversies of the early 1820s, the high estimate the Indians had of him and Horatio Jones is reflected in Seneca gifts to them of one-mile-square tracts of land in 1798, confirmed at the Mile-Wide-Strip Treaty of 1802. (See Parrish 1903; G. Harris 1903; map 5.)

Phelps, Oliver: Born into a large farmer's family in Connecticut in 1746, Phelps became a trader, moving to Massachusetts by 1770. He was a supply superintendent during the Revolution and built a small political career in Massachusetts, becoming friends with Nathaniel Gorham. Together they bought from Massachusetts the preemptive right to sell western New York Indian lands, payable in depreciated state notes. They convinced the Indians to sell in 1788, but they defaulted on their payments to Massachusetts by 1790. Phelps settled in Canandaigua and became a judge and federal representative to Congress. He was a leading stockholder of the Connecticut Land Company, which surveyed the Ohio Western Reserve for settlement, but he died in debt in 1809. (See Maier 1984; Rose 1950; O. Turner 1851; Wandell 1942.)

Pickering, Timothy: Born in Salem, Massachusetts, in 1745, and graduated from Harvard in 1763, he became a quartermaster in the Revolution. Politically ambitious, he moved to Pennsylvania in 1785, seeking preferment with the new government. After performing well as federal commissioner at Indian councils in 1790 and 1791, he was awarded the job of postmaster general by Washington. He was very well liked by the Six Nations, who felt he was a good listener who kept his promises. The second half of Pickering's career was less successful. He was accused of pro-British sympathies. Although elected to Congress as a Federalist in the age of Jefferson, he was censured in 1811 for disclosure of secret documents. He retired to Massachusetts in 1820 and died in 1829. (See Phillips 1966.)

Pollard, Captain (Ka-o-un-do-wand, Kaoundowana): Highly respected for his military valor in the Revolution and the War of 1812, Pollard was chosen a sachem in 1812. He was the son of an English trader and a Seneca mother. Several of his speeches appear in Stone's biography of Red Jacket. He was an early convert to Christianity, as his speeches at the Ogden Council of 1819 show. He and Red Jacket were bitter antagonists on the issue of missionary presence until 1828. He died in 1841. His bones were reinterred alongside Red Jacket's at Forest Lawn in 1884. (See Bryant 1885, 83–84.)

Porter, Peter B.: Porter began his career as a Black Rock salt dealer and became a general during the War of 1812, a congressional representative, and agent of the Ogden Land Company. By 1822, he was among the wealthiest men in the state and a strong advocate for Indian removal (Hauptman 1999, 121–43).

Sheehan, Walter Butler (W. B.): Nephew of Colonel John Butler, Sheehan was a British Indian department interpreter, as well as secretary to John Butler's Niagara Genesee Company in 1788. (See Maier 1984.)

Smith, Joseph: Smith was a white man captured by the Indians during the Revolution at Cherry Valley. In 1780, he met Horatio Jones, also a captive, and the two became lifelong friends and business associates (G. Harris 1903, 423). They served as translators at Livingston's lease in 1787 and later acted as business partners with Livingston's associates (485–81). Pickering confesses in his journal that Horatio Jones was reputed to be a better interpreter than Smith. Pickering preferred Smith, however, because he feared that Jones was an "unprincipled fellow" who possessed great influence over the Indians (Jones, at this time, was often in the company of the British).

Street, Samuel: Born in Wilton, Connecticut, he moved to Niagara in 1777. He was a partner in the sutler firm of Goring, Street, and Bennett in the lucrative business of selling food and other supplies to the military garrison of Fort Niagara. He later took Thomas Butler, son of John Butler, as a business partner. He attended the Phelps and Gorham Purchase of 1788 as both an interpreter and a business associate of Colonel Butler's Niagara Genesee Land Company, which had promised to assist Phelps and Gorham for a small share of their lands. (See Maier 1984; O. Turner 1851.)

Young King (Ga-yan-quia-ton, Gui-en-gwah-toh): Born near Canandaigua in 1760, Young King was the nephew of Old Smoke, who was one of the first settlers of Buffalo Creek. Because of this relationship, he was respected as a leading chief, even though he was not thought to be as wise as his uncle. He was believed to have participated in the Wyoming massacre. When he was younger, he liked to drink and lost part of his arm in a brawl. He converted to Christianity in the 1810s and became known as a sober and serious chief. Bryant tells an anecdote of him chopping wood for the church with his one good arm (1885, 81–82). He and Red Jacket were political opponents during the 1820s. Young King died in 1835.

References

Abler, Thomas S., ed. 2005. *Chainbreaker: The Revolutionary War Memoirs of Governor Blacksnake as Told to Benjamin Williams*. 1989. Reprint; Lincoln: Univ. of Nebraska Press.

Alden, Timothy. 1827. *An Account of Sundry Missions Among the Senecas and Munsees*. New York: J. Seymour.

Allen, Orlando. 1903. "Personal Recollections of Captain Jones and Parrish, and the Payment of Indian Annuities in Buffalo." *Publications of the Buffalo Historical Society* 6: 539–46.

Allen, Paula Gunn. 1986. *The Sacred Hoop: Recovering the Feminine in American Indian Tradition*. Boston: Beacon.

American State Papers, Indian Affairs. 1998. 2 vols. 1832. Reprint; Buffalo: William S. Hein.

Axtell, James. 1985. *The Invasion Within: The Contest of Cultures in Colonial North America*. New York: Oxford Univ. Press.

Babcock, Louis L. 1927. *The War of 1812 on the Niagara Frontier*. Buffalo: Buffalo Historical Society.

Bacon, David. 1903. "Rev. David Bacon's Visits to Buffalo in 1800 and 1801." *Publications of the Buffalo Historical Society* 6: 183–86.

Barton, Lois. 1990. *A Quaker Promise Kept: Philadelphia Friends' Work with the Allegany Senecas, 1795–1960*. Eugene, OR: Spencer Butte Press.

Beauchamp, William Martin. 1978. *Wampum and Shell Articles Used by the New York Indians*. 1901. Reprint; New York: AMS.

Benn, Carl. 1998. *The Iroquois in the War of 1812*. Syracuse: Syracuse Univ. Press.

Bigelow, Albert. 1896a. "The Harbor-Maker of Buffalo." *Publications of the Buffalo Historical Society* 4: 85–91.

———. 1896b. "The Indian Show of Storrs & Co." *Publications of the Buffalo Historical Society* 4: 415–16.

Bilharz, Joy. 1995. "First among Equals? The Changing Status of Seneca Women." In *Women and Power in Native North America*. Edited by Laura Klein and Lillian Ackerman, 101–12. Norman: Univ. of Oklahoma Press.

Bingham, Robert W. 1930. "The Trial of Red Jacket." *Buffalo Historical Society Museum Notes* 1, no. 4 (November–December): 1–12.

———. 1931. *The Cradle of the Queen City: A History of Buffalo to the Incorporation of the City*. Buffalo: Buffalo Historical Society.

Blacksnake. n.d. "Narrative." In "Notes of Border History." Draper Manuscript Collection. Microfilm. Reel 47, vol 4: 13–82.

Blanchard, Rufus. 1880. *Discovery and Conquests of the Northwest*. Chicago: Cushing, Thomas & Co.

Bryant, William C. 1879. "Orlando Allen: Glimpses of Life in the Village of Buffalo." *Publications of the Buffalo Historical Society* 1: 329–71.

———. 1885. "Sketches of the Five Indian Chiefs Re-Intombed with Red Jacket: The Young King, Captain Pollard, Little Billy, Destroy Town, Tall Peter—The Unknown Braves." In *Red Jacket: Publications of the Buffalo Historical Society* 3: 81–87.

Calhoun, John C. 1969–74. *The Papers of John C. Calhoun*. Edited by Robert L. Meriwether and W. Edwin Hemphill. 27 vols. Columbia: Univ. of South Carolina Press.

Calloway, Colin G. 1987. *Crown and Calumet: British-Indian Relations, 1783–1815*. Norman: Univ. of Oklahoma Press.

Campisi, Jack. 1988. "From Stanwix to Canandaigua: National Policy, States' Rights, and Indian Land." In *Iroquois Land Claims*. Edited by Christopher Vecsey and William A. Starna, 49–65. Syracuse: Syracuse Univ. Press.

Campisi, Jack, and William A. Starna. 1995. "On the Road to Canandaigua: The Treaty of 1794." *American Indian Quarterly* 19, no. 4 (Fall): 467–90.

Catlin, George. 1989. *North American Indians*. Edited by Peter Matthiessen. 1841. Reprint; New York: Viking.

Chafe, Wallace L. 1963. *Handbook of the Seneca Language*. Bulletin 388. Albany: New York State Museum and Science Service.

———. 1967. *Seneca Morphology and Dictionary*. Smithsonian Contributions to Anthropology 4.

Chanzanof, William. 1970. *Joseph Ellicott and the Holland Land Company*. Syracuse: Syracuse Univ. Press.

Chernow, Barbara A. 1977. "Robert Morris: Genesee Land Speculator." *New York History* 58: 195–220.

Cheyfitz, Eric. 1991. *Poetics of Imperialism: Translation and Colonization from the Tempest to Tarzan*. New York: Oxford UP.

Clark, John W. Papers. Clement Library. University of Michigan. Ann Arbor, Michigan.

Cleaveland, Moses. Papers. Western Reserve Historical Society. Cleveland, Ohio.

Clinton, De Witt. 1849. "The Iroquois: An Address Delivered Before the New York Historical Society Dec 6, 1811." In *The Life and Writings of De Witt Clinton*. Edited by William Campbell, 205–66. New York: Baker and Scribner.

Colden, Cadwallader. 1994. *The History of the Five Indian Nations Depending on the Province of New York in America*. 1727, 1747. Reprint; Ithaca: Cornell UP.

Conover, George S. 1884. *The Birthplace of Sa-Go-Ye-Wat-Ha, or the Indian Red Jacket*. Waterloo: Seneca Country News Book.

Covell, Lemuel. 1804. *A Narrative of a Missionary Tour Through the Western Settlements of the State of New-York and into the Southwestern Parts of the Province of Upper Canada . . . in the Year of 1803*. Troy: Moffity & Lyon.

Cumming, John, ed. and intro. 1979. "A Missionary among the Senecas: The Journal of Abel Bingham, 1822–1828." *New York History* 60, no. 2 (April): 1 57–93.

Da Costa Nunes, Jadviga. 1980. "Red Jacket: The Man and His Portraits." *American Art Journal* 12, no. 3 (Summer): 4–20.

Delafield, Major Joseph. 1943. *The Unfortified Boundary: A Diary of the First Survey of the Canadian Boundary Line from St. Regis to the Lake of the Woods*. Edited by Robert McElroy and Thomas Riggs. New York: Privately printed.

Densmore, Christopher. 1987. "More on Red Jacket's Reply." *New York Folklore* 13, no. 3–4: 121–22.

———. 1999. *Red Jacket: Iroquois Diplomat and Orator*. Syracuse: Syracuse Univ. Press.

Dippie, Brian. 1984. *The Vanishing American: White Attitudes and U.S. Indian Policy*. Lawrence: Univ. of Kansas Press.

"Documents and Miscellany." 1896. *Publications of the Buffalo Historical Society* 4: 385–86.

Downes, Randolph C. 1940. *Council Fires on the Upper Ohio*. Pittsburgh: Univ. of Pittsburgh Press.

Drake, Samuel G., ed. 1841. *The Book of the Indians*. 1832. Reprint; Boston: Antiquarian Books.

Draper, Lyman. 1980. *The Draper Manuscript Collection*. State Historical Society of Wisconsin. Microfilm, 123 reels. Teaneck, NJ: Chadwyck-Healy.

Ellicott, Joseph. 1937. *Reports of Joseph Ellicott*, vol. 1. Edited by Robert Warwick Bingham. Buffalo: Buffalo Historical Society.

Emlen, James. 1965. "The Journal of James Emlen, Kept on a Trip to Canandaigua, New York, September 15 to October 30, 1794, to Attend a Treaty Between the United States and the Six Nations," edited by William N. Fenton. *Ethnohistory* 12, no. 4 (Autumn): 279–432.

Evans, Paul Demond. 1924. *The Holland Land Company*. Buffalo: Buffalo Historical Society.

Fairbank, Dorothy May, ed. n.d. Annotated typescript of the Jasper Parrish Papers, Letters and Documents Relating to the Government Service of Jasper Parrish among the Indians of New York State. Lucy Maynard Salmon Collection. Box 3. Vassar College, Special Collections. Poughkeepsie, N.Y.

Fenton, William N., ed. 1969. "Answers to Governor Cass's Questions by Jacob Jameson, a Seneca (ca. 1821–1825)." *Ethnohistory* 16, no. 2 (Spring): 113–39.

Furtwangler, Albert. 1997. *Answering Chief Seattle*. Seattle: Univ. of Washington Press.

Ganter, Granville. 2000. " 'You Are a Cunning People Without Sincerity': Sagoyewatha and the Trials of Community Representation." In *Speakers of the Northeastern Woodlands*. Edited by Barbara Mann, 165–95. Westport: Greenwood.

Gallagher, Gary W., and Alan T. Nolan, eds. 2000. *The Myth of the Lost Cause and Civil War History.* Bloomington: Indiana Univ. Press.

Granger, Erastus. Papers. Marshall Family Papers. Special Collections of the Penfield Library. SUNY Oswego. Oswego, N.Y.

Graymont, Barbara. 1972. *The Iroquois in the American Revolution.* Syracuse: Syracuse Univ. Press.

Haas, Marilyn L. 1994. *The Seneca and Tuscarora Indians: An Annotated Bibliography.* Native American Bibliography Series, no. 17. Metuchen: Scarecrow.

Harris, George H. 1903. "The Life of Horatio Jones." *Publications of the Buffalo Historical Society* 6: 383–514.

Harris, Thompson S. 1903. "Journal of the Rev. Thompson S. Harris . . . 1821–1828." *Publications of the Buffalo Historical Society* 6: 281–378.

Hauptman, Lawrence, M. 1999. *Conspiracy of Interests: Iroquois Dispossession and the Rise of New York State.* Syracuse: Syracuse Univ. Press.

Heckewelder, John. 1819. *An Account of the History, Manners, and Customs, of the Indian Nations Who Once Inhabited Pennsylvania and the Neighboring States.* Philadelphia: Abraham Small.

Hill, Henry Wayland, ed. 1923. *Municipality of Buffalo, New York: A History, 1720–1923.* 4 vols. New York: Lewis Historical Publishing.

Holland Land Company. 1982. Papers. Fredonia: State University of New York at Fredonia. Microfilm, 202 reels.

Holley, John Milton. 1796. "Journal, April 28–Nov. 5, 1796." Manuscripts Relating to the Early History of the Western Reserve. Container 4, folder 86 (microfilm reel 4 of 6). Western Reserve Historical Society. Cleveland, Ohio.

Holmes, Elkanah. 1801. "Letter from the Rev. Mr. Holmes, Employed by the New-York Missionary Society, as a Missionary to the Seneca and Tuscarora Tribes of Indians, in the State of New-York." *New York Missionary Magazine,* 58–75.

Horsman, Reginald. 1999. "The Origins of Oneida Removal to Wisconsin, 1815–1822." *The Oneida Indian Journey from New York to Wisconsin, 1784–1860.* Edited by Laurence M. Hauptman and L. Gordon McLester III, 53–69. Madison: Univ. of Wisconsin Press.

Houghton, Frederick. 1920. "History of the Buffalo Creek Reservation." *Publications of the Buffalo Historical Society.* 24: 3–168.

Howland, Henry H. 1903. "The Seneca Mission at Buffalo Creek." *Publications of the Buffalo Historical Society* 6: 125–61.

Hubbard, Niles, J. 1886. *An Account of Sa-Go-Ye-Wat-Ha, or Red Jacket and His People.* Albany: Joel Munsell's Sons.

Humphrey, George H. 1927. "Nathaniel Gorham." *Publications of the Rochester Historical Society* 6: 297–99.

Hyde, Jabez B. 1903. "A Teacher Among the Senecas: Historical and Personal Narrative of Jabez B. Hyde, Written in 1820." *Publications of the Buffalo Historical Society* 6: 239–74.

Indian Speeches; Delivered by Farmer's Brother and Red Jacket. Two Seneca Chiefs. 1809. Canandaigua: Printed by James D. Bemis.

Iroquois Indians: A Documentary History of the Diplomacy of the Six Nations and their League. 1984. Edited by Francis Jennings and William N. Fenton. Woodbridge, CT: Published for the D'Arcy McNickle Center for the History of the American Indian at the Newberry Library.

Jackson, Halliday. 1830. *Civilization of the Indian Natives; or, a Brief View of the Friendly Conduct of William Penn Towards Them in the Early Settlement of Pennsylvania. . . .* Philadelphia: Marcus T. C. Gould.

———. 1952. "Halliday Jackson's Journal to the Seneca Indians, 1798–1800," edited by Anthony F. C. Wallace. *Pennsylvania History* 19, no. 2 (April): 117–47; part 2 (July): 325–49.

———. 1957. "Halliday Jackson's Journal of a Visit Paid to the Indians of New York, 1806," edited by George S. Snyderman. *Proceedings of the American Philosophical Society* 101, no. 6 (December): 565–88.

Jemison, Peter G., and Anna M. Schein, eds. 2000. *Treaty of Canandaigua 1794: Two Hundred Years of Treaty Relations between the Iroquois Confederacy and the United States.* Santa Fe: Clear Light Press.

Jennings, Francis. 1984. *The Ambiguous Iroquois Empire: The Covenant Chain Confederation of Indian Tribes with English Colonies from Its Beginnings to the Lancaster Treaty of 1744.* New York: Norton.

Jennings, Francis, and William N. Fenton, eds. 1985. *The History and Culture of Iroquois Diplomacy.* Syracuse: Syracuse Univ. Press.

Johnson, Charles M., ed. and intro. 1964. *The Valley of the Six Nations: A Collection of Documents on the Indians of the Grand River.* Toronto: Champlain Society.

Johnson, William. 1792. "Journal of William Johnson's Proceedings from Niagara to Westward." Simcoe Family Papers. Microfilm. F 47 1-2-4. Archives of Ontario. Toronto, Canada.

Kelsay, Isabel. 1984. *Joseph Brant, 1743–1807: Man of Two Worlds.* Syracuse: Syracuse Univ. Press.

Ketchum, William. 1864–65. *An Authentic and Comprehensive History of Buffalo.* 2 vols. Buffalo: Rockwell, Baker, and Hill.

Klinck, Carl Frederick. 1961. *Tecumseh: Fact and Fiction in Early Records, a Book of Primary Source Materials.* Englewood Cliffs: Prentiss-Hall.

Knox, Henry. 1792. Broadside. *Causes of the Existing Hostilities Between the United States and Certain Tribes of Indians Northwest of the Ohio . . . Published in Obedience to the Orders of the President of the United States.* Philadelphia: D. C. Claypoole.

Konkle, Maureen. 2004. *Writing Native History: Native Intellectuals and the Politics of Historiography, 1827–1863.* Chapel Hill: Univ. of North Carolina Press.

Krupat, Arnold. 1992. *Ethnocriticism: Ethnography, History, Literature.* Berkeley: Univ. of California Press.

Lincklaen, John [Jan]. 1897. *Travels in the Years 1791 and 1792 in Pennsylvania, New York, and Vermont. Journals of John Lincklaen.* New York: G. P. Putnam's Sons.

Lincoln, Charles Z., ed. 1909. *Messages from the Governors.* 10 vols. Albany: J. B. Lyon.

Lindley, Jacob. 1832. "Account of a Journey to Attend the Indian Treaty . . . in the Year 1793." *Friends Miscellany* 2 (January–February): 49–156.

Lord, John C. 1896. "Samuel Wilkeson." *Publications of the Buffalo Historical Society* 4: 71–85.

Maier, William L. 1984. *Samuel Street of Niagara, the New York and Niagara Genesee Companies, Who Is Who at the July 1788 Buffalo Creek Treaty—and Why, and the Phelps & Gorham Purchase.* Webster, N.Y.: W. L. Maier.

Manley, Henry S. 1932. *The Treaty of Fort Stanwix, 1784.* Rome, N.Y.: Rome Sentinel.

———. 1950. "Red Jacket's Last Campaign, and an Extended Bibliographical and Biographical Note." *New York History* 31, no. 2: 149–68.

Mann, Barbara Alice. 2000. *Iroquoian Women: The Gantowisas.* New York: Peter Lang.

McKenney, Thomas L., and James Hall. 1836. "Red Jacket." *The Indian Tribes of North America*, vol. 1: 1–13. Philadelphia: E. C. Biddle.

Miller, Anna C. Johnson. 1855. *The Iroquois; or, The Bright Side of Indian Character.* By Minnie Myrtle [pseud.] New York: D. Appleton.

Mohawk, John C. 2000. "The Canandaigua Treaty in Historical Perspective." In *Treaty of Canandaigua 1794: Two Hundred Years of Treaty Relations between the Iroquois Confederacy and the United States.* Edited by Peter G. Jemison and Anna M. Schein, 43–64. Santa Fe: Clear Light Press.

Moore, Joseph. 1835. "Joseph Moore's Journal of a Tour to Detroit, In Order to Attend a Treaty . . ." *Friends Miscellany* 6 (February): 289–343.

Morgan, Henry Lewis. 1990. *League of the Iroquois.* 1851. Reprint; Secaucus, NJ: Carol Publishing.

Morris, Thomas. 1797a. "Diary of the Proceedings of a Treaty Held with the Seneca Nation. . . ." Holland Land Company Papers. Fredonia: State University of New York at Fredonia, 1982. Microfilm, reel 28 of 202.

———. 1797b. Letter to Robert Morris, May 29, 1797. Henry O'Reilly Collection of Western Mementos. Indian Affairs, vol. 15. New York Historical Society. New York City.

———. 1797c. "Rough Memoranda of the Treaty of Big Tree." Henry O'Reilly Collection of Western Mementos. Indian Affairs, vol. 15. New York Historical Society. New York City.

———. 1844. "Personal Memoir of Thomas Morris Concerning the Settlement of the Genesee Country, Oct. 1844." Henry O'Reilly Collection of Western Mementos, vol 15. New York Historical Society. New York City.

Murray, David. 1991. *Forked Tongues: Speech, Writing, and Representation in North American Indian Texts.* Bloomington: Indiana Univ. Press.

Native Eloquence, Being Two Public Speeches Delivered by Two Distinguished Chiefs of the

Seneca Tribe of Indians, Known Among the White People By the Names of Red Jacket and Farmer's Brother. 1811. Canandaigua: J. D. Bemis.

New York Missionary Society. 1812. *Report of the Directors of the New-York Missionary Society Presented at Their Annual Meeting Held on Tuesday April 7, 1812.* New York: J. Seymour and John Street.

Norton, Charles D. 1879. "The Old Black Rock Ferry." *Publications of the Buffalo Historical Society* 1: 91–112.

Norton, John. 1970. *Journal of Major John Norton.* Edited by Carl F. Klinck and James J. Talman. Toronto: Champlain Society.

Ogden Family Papers. William L. Clement Library. University of Michigan. Ann Arbor, Michigan.

Ong, Walter. 1982. *Orality and Literacy: The Technologizing of the Word.* New York: Routledge.

O'Reilly, Henry. Collection of Western Mementos. Indian Affairs. New-York Historical Society, New York City.

———. 1838. *Settlement in the West. With Sketches of Rochester.* Rochester: William Alling.

Osgood, Howard L. 1892. "History of the Title of the Phelps and Gorham Purchase." *Publications of the Rochester Historical Society* 1: 21–31.

Parker, Arthur C. 1916. *The Constitution of the Five Nations, or The Iroquois Book of the Great Law.* Albany: State Univ. of New York Press.

———. 1943. "The Unknown Mother of Red Jacket." *New York History* 24, no. 4 (October): 525–33.

———. 1968. *The Code of Handsome Lake, the Seneca Prophet.* In *Parker on the Iroquois.* Edited by William N. Fenton. 1913. Reprint; Syracuse: Syracuse Univ. Press.

———. 1998. *Red Jacket: Last of the Seneca.* 1952. Reprint; Lincoln: Univ. of Nebraska Press.

Parrish, Stephen. 1903. "The Story of Jasper Parrish, Captive, Interpreter, and United States Sub-Agent to the Six Nations." *Publications of the Buffalo Historical Society.* 6: 527–38.

Pease, Seth. 1796. "Journal, May 9–Nov. 1796." Manuscripts Relating to the Early History of the Western Reserve. Container 4, folder 88 (microfilm reel 4 of 6). Western Reserve Historical Society. Cleveland, Ohio.

Philips, John. 1956. "A Nineteenth-Century Journal of a Visit to the Indians of New York," edited by Merle H. Deardorff and George S. Snyderman. *Proceedings of the American Philosophical Association* 100, no. 6 (December): 582–612.

Phillips, Edward Hake. 1966. "Timothy Pickering at His Best: Indian Commissioner, 1790–1794." *Essex Institute Historical Collections* 102 (July): 185–92.

Pollard, Charlotte. 1903. "Red Jacket." *100th Anniversary of the Town of Junius: 1803–1903.* Buffalo.

Prucha, Francis Paul. 1994. *American Indian Treaties: The History of a Political Anomaly.* Berkeley: Univ. of California Press.

Public Speeches Delivered at the Village of Buffalo on the 6th and 8th days of July 1812 by the Hon. Erastus Granger, Indian Agent, and Red Jacket, One of the Principal Chiefs and Speakers of the Seneca Nation . . . Respecting War Against Great Britain. 1812. Buffalo: S. H. and H. A. Salisbury.

"Records of the Councils and Speeches to and by Indian Nations in Upper Canada, 1796–1803." BV Indians. Misc. Microfilm, reel 24. New York Historical Society. New York City.

Red Jacket. 1885. Buffalo: Buffalo Historical Society.

Reilly, Paul. Papers. E. H. Butler Library Archives. Buffalo State College. Buffalo, N.Y.

Richards, Cara. 1957. "Matriarchy or Mistake: The Role of Iroquois Women through Time." In *Cultural Stability and Cultural Change.* Edited by Verne F. Ray, 36–45. Seattle: Univ. of Washington Press.

Richter, Daniel K. 1992. *The Ordeal of the Longhouse.* Chapel Hill: Univ. of North Carolina Press.

Robie, Harry. 1986. "Red Jacket's Reply: Problems in the Verification of a Native American Speech Text." *New York Folklore* 12, no. 3–4: 99–117.

———. 1987. Response to Christopher Densmore. *New York Folklore* 13, no. 3–4: 123.

Ronda, Jeanne, and James P. Ronda. 1979. " 'As They Were Faithful': Chief Hendrick Aupaumut and the Struggle for Stockbridge Survival, 1757–1830." *American Indian Culture and Research Journal* 3, no. 3: 43–55.

Rose, William Ganson. 1950. *Cleveland: The Making of a City.* New York: World Publishing.

Rothenberg, Diane. 1980. "The Mothers of the Nation: Seneca Resistance to Quaker Intervention." In *Women and Colonization: Anthropological Perspectives.* Edited by Mona Etienne and Eleanor Leacock, 63–87. New York: Praeger.

Royster, Charles. 1999. *The Fabulous History of the Dismal Swamp Company: A Story of George Washington's Times.* New York: Knopf.

Savery, William. 1837. *A Journal of the Life, Travels, and Religious Labors of William Savery.* Edited by Jonathan Evans. Philadelphia: Friends Bookstore.

Schoolcraft, Henry R. 1846. *Notes on the Iroquois.* New York: Bartlett and Welford.

Seaver, James E, ed. 1992. *A Narrative of the Life of Mrs. Mary Jemison.* Introduction by June Namias. 1824. Reprint; Norman: Univ. of Oklahoma Press.

Seeber, E. D. 1947. "Critical Views of Logan's Speech." *Journal of American Folklore* 60: 130–46.

Seelye, Elizabeth Eggleston, with Edward Eggleston. 1879. *Brant and Red Jacket.* New York: Dodd, Mead.

Severance, Frank H. 1903. "Quakers Among the Senecas." *Publications of the Buffalo Historical Society* 6: 165–68.

Sheldon, James. 1879. "Life and Services of Oliver Forward: Read before the Society, January 25th, 1875." *Publications of the Buffalo Historical Society* 1: 373–90.

Shoemaker, Nancy. 1991. "The Rise or Fall of Iroquois Women." *Journal of Women's History* 2, no. 3 (Winter): 39–57.

Simcoe, John G. 1923. *The Correspondence of Lieut. Governor John Graves Simcoe*, vol. 1 and vol. 5. Edited by E. A. Cruikshank. Toronto: Toronto Historical Society.

Snyder, Charles M., ed. 1978. *Red and White on the New York Frontier: A Struggle for Survival*. Harrison, N.Y.: Harbor Hill.

Snyderman, George S. 1954. "The Functions of Wampum." *Proceedings of the American Philosophical Society* 98, no. 6 (Dec): 469–94.

Stone, William Leete. 1841. *The Life and Times of Sa-Go-Ye-Wat-Ha, or Red-Jacket*. New York: Wiley and Putnam.

———. 1845. *Life of Joseph Brant—Thayendanegea, Including the Indian Wars of the American Revolution*. 2 vols. 1838. Reprint; Cooperstown: H & E Phinney, 1845.

———. 1866. *The Life and Times of Sa-Go-Ye-Wat-Ha, or Red-Jacket*. Preface by William Leete Stone Jr. New York: J. Munsell.

Sugden, John. 1997. *Tecumseh: A Life*. New York: Henry Holt.

Symes, Martha. 1995. "Cornplanter." In *Notable Native Americans*. Edited by Sharon Malinowski, 92–95. Detroit: Gale.

Taylor, Alan. 1995. *William Cooper's Town*. New York: Knopf.

Thatcher, Benjamin Bussey. 1840. "Red Jacket." *Indian Biography*, vol. 2. 1832. Reprint; New York: J & J Harper.

Todorov, Tzvetan. 1984. *The Conquest of America: The Question of the Other*. Translated by Richard Howard. New York: Harper and Row.

Tooker, Elizabeth. 1984. "Women in Iroquois Society." *Extending the Rafters: Interdisciplinary Approaches to Iroquoian Studies*. Edited by Michael K. Foster, Jack Campisi, and Marianne Mithun, 109–23. Albany: State Univ. of New York Press.

Turner, Katherine C. 1951. *Red Men Calling on the Great White Father*. Norman: Univ. of Oklahoma Press.

Turner, Orasmus. 1850. *Pioneer History of the Holland Purchase of Western New York*. Buffalo: George H. Derby.

———. 1851. *History of Phelps and Gorham's Purchase*. Rochester: William Alling.

Turpin, Morley Bebee. 1932. "Ebenezer Allan in the Genesee Country." In *Centennial History of Rochester, New York*, vol. 2: *Homebuilders*. Edited by Edward R. Forman, 313–38. Rochester, N.Y.

Upper Canada State Papers. 1974. Ottawa: Public Archives of Canada. Microfilm.

Vanderwerth, W. C., comp. 1971. *Indian Oratory: Famous Speeches by Noted Indian Chieftains*. Norman: Univ. of Oklahoma Press.

Walker, Augustus. 1902. "Early Days on the Lakes: With an Account of the Cholera Visitation of 1832." *Publications of the Buffalo Historical Society* 5: 287–318.

Wallace, Anthony F. C. 1971. "Handsome Lake and the Decline of the Iroquois Matriarchate." In *Kinship and Culture*. Edited by Francis L. K. Hsu, 367–76. Chicago: Aldine.

———. 1972. *Death and Rebirth of the Seneca*. 1969. Reprint; New York: Vintage.

Wandell, Samuel H. 1942. "Oliver Phelps." *New York History* 23 (July): 275–82.

Washington, George. 2002. *The Papers of George Washington: Presidential Series*. Edited by Robert F. Haggard and Mark A. Mastromarino, vol. 10 edited by Philander D. Chase. Charlottesville: Univ. of Virginia Press.

White, Richard. 1991. *The Middle Ground: Indians, Empires, and Republics in the Great Lakes Region, 1650–1815*. Cambridge: Cambridge Univ. Press.

Wilkeson, Samuel, Jr. 1902. "Biographical Sketch of Samuel Wilkeson." *Publications of the Buffalo Historical Society* 5: 135–45.

Wilkinson, Norman B. 1979. "Robert Morris and the Treaty of Big Tree." In *The Rape of Indian Lands*. Edited by Paul Wallace Gates, 257–78. New York: Arno.

Index

Page numbers in *italic* indicate a map or photograph.

Norton, John, 135, 136, 156
Notes on the Iroquois (Schoolcraft), 159

Obail, Charles, 237, 245
Obail, Henry. *See* Obeil, Henry
O'Beel. *See* Cornplanter
Obeil. *See* Cornplanter
Obeil, Henry: biography of, 285; as
    interpreter, 227, 229; land sale of 1826
    and, 259; petition for removal of Parrish
    and Jones, 237
Ogden, David A.: 1819 attempt to buy
    Seneca land, xxi, 198–219; attempt to
    purchase reservation land in 1811,
    162–63; biography of, 285; claim to
    ownership of Seneca land, xxi, 198, 202,
    205–7; at council at Buffalo Creek (1819),
    204, 205–10; land sale of 1826 and,
    220–21, 269–70; on Red Jacket's
    opposition to missionaries, xxiv–xxv; on
    replacement for Parrish, 234
Ogden, Samuel, 18, 206, 285
Ogden, Thomas Ludlow, 162, 215–16
Ogden council, 250–53, 254, 255–59
Ogden Land Company: 1819 attempt to buy
    Seneca land, xxi, 198–219; 1826 land
    purchase, xxviii, 250–53, 254, 255–59,
    265–66; corruption of Jones and Parrish,
    xxiii; council at upper Sandusky and, 185;
    formation of, 162; founder of, 285;
    Jimeson as employee of, 284; land sale of
    1826 and, 250–53, 254, 255–59;
    Livingston's law suit against, 207n. 4;
    Parrish's support of, 243; push to move Six
    Nations, 191, 192–93; Red Jacket's
    opposition to, xxviii; request for Six
    Nations to move to Allegany reservation,
    198
Ohio, *xxxiv*
Oil Creek reservation, *xxxiv*
Old Johnson, 245
Old Smoke, 64, 287
Oliver Forward papers, 255
Oneidas: allegiance in War of 1812, 170; at
    council at Newtown Point, 26; at council
    of condolence for Chapin, 68; death of
    chief during Treaty of Canandaigua
    negotiations, 62; disposition of plunder,
    177; Holmes and, 103; lease of land to

Livingston, 207n. 4; loss of lands, 12, 104;
    missionaries to, 103, 104; presence
    requested at Buffalo Creek council, 172;
    results of land sales, 87–88, 89n. 1;
    welcome to white people, 13
Ong, Walter, xxii
Onondaga, *xxxvi*
Onondaga Peter, 237
Onondagas: annuities of, 184; at council in
    Geneseo, 115; at council of condolence
    for Chapin, 68; at council on church-
    school, 129, 130; disposition of plunder,
    177; Handsome Lake's effect on, 111;
    request for agent to sell reservation land,
    108; results of loss of land, 88; sale of
    Mile-Wide Strip and, 117; sale of
    Tonawanda reservation, 227; at Stiff-
    Armed George's trial, 119; welcome to
    white people, 13
Ontario Gazette, 119
oral language, xxii
Ordeal of the Longhouse (Richter), xxx
Osgood, Howard L., 2
Otetiani. *See* Red Jacket
Otsego Republican, 174
Ottawas, 112–14

pagan party: distrust of Parrish, 243; eviction
    of white people, 215, 227–30; at funeral of
    Red Jacket, 274; land sale of 1826 and,
    254, 270–71; petition for inquiry into
    1826 land sale, 250–53, 254, 255–59, 260;
    petition for removal of Parrish and Jones
    and, 233–38; petition to keep missionaries
    off Indian lands, 246–47; reconciliation
    with Christian Senecas, 271; response to
    deposition of Red Jacket, 262–64
Painted Pole (Shawnee chief), 46, 48, 49
Painted Post, *xxxiii*
pan-Indian council at Brownstown, 156–58
pan-Indian council at Sandusky, 56, 58
pan-Indian council at upper Sandusky,
    185–90
Parish, John, 22
Parker, Arthur C., xxv, xxx
Parrish, Jasper: as adviser to Indians, 164;
    assistance in westward movement, 193;
    biography of, 286; capture of, xxiii, 285; as
    carrier of message from Cleaveland,

(1819), 199, 204; deposition of Red Jacket and, 261, 264; interpreter for petition for inquiry into 1826 land sale, 252; land sale of 1826 and, 269; petition for protection to Governor Clinton, 197; petition for removal of Parrish and Jones and, 233; petition to Secretary Calhoun and, 222; at Quakers' yearly meeting, 153; reinstatement of Red Jacket, 271; sale of Gardeau and, 240; signing of declaration of neutrality, 152

Porter, Peter B.: career of, 287; at council at Buffalo Creek (1819), 198; investigation of Parrish, 233, 235–36; on pay for Indians, 177; recruitment of Indians for War of 1812, 175, 212

Potawatamies, 112–14

Powell (British captain), 19

Pratt, Pascal, 222, 224, 232

preemptive rights: Morris's purchase of, 17–18, 85–94; Ogden Land Company's purchase of, 162; Ogden's explanation of, 205–6, 209; Ogden's purchase of, 208; Red Jacket on, 213, 214, 221; Treaty of Big Tree and, 85–94

Prentiss, William, 217

presents: given at Newtown Point, 31, 32; given at Tioga Point council, 6, 14; given at Treaty of Big Trees, 86; given by Washington in Philadelphia, xxvii, 33; giving of at councils, 6–7; to influence Indians, 189; from Quakers, 154; for sale of Mile-Wide Strip, 126, 127

Presque Isle, *xxxii, xxxiv,* 67

presumptive rights, 85

Price, David, 82, 100, 112, 113, 135

prisoners of war, 25, 26, 49, 176

Proctor, Thomas, 16, 17, 19–20

property rights, 36. *See also* preemptive rights

Prophet. *See* Handsome Lake

provisions for council attendees: for council on western Indian alliances, 151; at peace council at Niagara, 181–82; price of land affected by, 117; request to Cleaveland for, 74–75; to Washington, D. C., 108, 109

Public Speeches Delivered at the Village of Buffalo, on the 6th and 8th days of July, 1812, 169

Quaker journals, 61–67

Quakers: advice on liquor and white people, 153–55; aid to Indians, 164; influence on Handsome Lake, xxviii; letter to on land sale of 1826, 254; offer to educate Indian boys, 153; request for teacher from, 226, 272; at Treaty of Canandaigua negotiations, 61, 62, 63–64, 65–66; visit at Buffalo Creek reservation, 134

race: differing customs of, 12; Great Spirit's treatment of, 37; religion and, 75–76, 103–5, 120, 130, 141–42, 163–64, 241–42, 249

Rainy, Lewis, 262

Randolph, Beverly, 59

Ransom (interpreter at Niagara), 77

Red and White on the New York Frontier (Snyder), 166

Red Jacket: at 1791 council on assisting Proctor, 16; at 1792 council on progress at Glaize, 51–55; at 1796 council on Western Reserve, 73–76; at 1798 council on dissatisfaction with Treaty of Big Tree, 95–96, 97–99; at 1805 council on removal of Brant, 135–37; at 1811 council on mission and Ogden Land Company offer, 161–65; at 1812 council on War of 1812, 169–73; at 1819 council in reply to Ogden Land Company, 198–219; address to Connecticut General Assembly, 72; agreement to go to Canandaigua land council, 81; biographies of, xxix–xxxi; birth and childhood of, xxv–xxvi; on Black Rock ferries, 100–101; on brokering peace with western Indians, 19, 20–21, 42–44; chest medal received from Washington, xxvii, 33; on church-school, 130–33; on coercion and bribery at Ogden council (1826), 254; comments about Morris, 79, 80–81, 86; context of speeches of, xxix–xxxi; at council at Fort Erie, 56–58; at council at Fort Niagara, 77–79; at council at Geneseo, 115–17; at council of Newtown Point, 22–32; at council of Tioga Point, 1, 3, 4–15; death of, xxix, 273–75; on death of General Chapin, 68–70; debate with Pickering, 199; declaration of neutrality, 151–52; on